WITHDRAWN

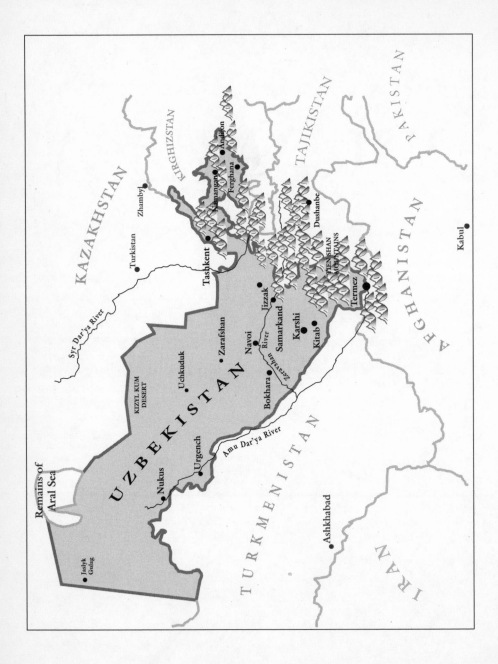

DIRTY DIPLOMACY

The Rough-and-Tumble Adventures of
a Scotch-Drinking, Skirt-Chasing,
Dictator-Busting and Thoroughly
Unrepentant Ambassador Stuck on the
Frontline of the War Against Terror

CRAIG MURRAY

SCRIBNER

NEW YORK   LONDON   TORONTO   SYDNEY

SCRIBNER
A Division of Simon & Schuster, Inc.
1230 Avenue of the Americas
New York, NY 10020

First Scribner hardcover edition October 2007

SCRIBNER and design are trademarks of
Macmillan Library Reference USA, Inc., used under license
by Simon & Schuster, the publisher of this work.

For information about special discounts for bulk purchases,
please contact Simon & Schuster Special Sales:
1-800-456-6798 or business@simonandschuster.com

Designed by Kyoko Watanabe
Text set in Adobe Garamond

Manufactured in the United States of America

1   3   5   7   9   10   8   6   4   2

Library of Congress Cataloging-in-Publication Data is available.

ISBN-13: 978-1-4165-4801-0
ISBN-10: 1-4165-4801-7

For Bryan Harris,
a friend in need

We travel not for trafficking alone:
By hotter winds our fiery hearts are fanned:
For lust of knowing what should not be known
We make the Golden Journey to Samarkand.

—JAMES ELROY FLECKER, 1884–1915

ENRON

Kenneth L. Lay
Chairman and
Chief Executive Officer

Enron Corp.
P. O. Box 1188
Houston, TX 77251-1188
(713) 853-6773
Fax (713) 853-5313

dup -taxed prev

April 3, 1997

Via Fax: 512/463-1849

The Honorable George W. Bush
Governor of the State of Texas
PO Box 12428
Austin, Texas

Dear ~~Governor~~ *George* Bush:

   You will be meeting with Ambassador Sadyq Safaev, Uzbekistan's Ambassador to the United States on April 8th. Ambassador Safaev has been Foreign Minister and the senior advisor to President Karimov before assuming his nation's most significant foreign responsibility.

   Enron has established an office in Tashkent and we are negotiating a $2 billion joint venture with Neftegas of Uzbekistan, and Gazprom of Russia to develop Uzbekistan's natural gas and transport it to markets in Europe, Kazakhstan, and Turkey. This project can bring significant economic opportunities to Texas, as well as Uzbekistan. The political benefits to the United States and to Uzbekistan are important to that entire region.

   Ambassador Safaev is one of the most effective of the Washington Corps of Ambassadors, a man who has the attention of his president, and a person who works daily to bring our countries together. For all these reasons, I am delighted that the two of you are meeting.

   I know you and Ambassador Safaev will have a productive meeting which will result in a friendship between Texas and Uzbekistan.

                    Sincerely,

                    Ken

bush-3.doc

Natural gas. Electricity. Endless possibilities

CONTENTS

DIRTY DIPLOMACY

PREFACE

THIS IS THE STORY OF MY MISSION AS BRITISH AMBASSADOR TO Tashkent in the years 2002 to 2004. To the best of my knowledge and ability, this is a true story, though largely from memory.

But most important, it is the truth as perceived by me. Our backgrounds, experience, emotional states, the acuity of our senses and the depth of our understanding all affect our perception. Different people can thus experience the same events and have a different take on what happened. I am not saying that mine is uniquely correct. This is what, it seemed to me, happened, and how it felt to be me experiencing it.

I also wanted to debunk the notion that I am a heroic figure. I am not. Standards of morality vary, and many would judge that in my private life I behaved pretty badly. In the small hours of the night I tend to agree. What I think I did right was to refuse to go along with some absolutely dreadful things the United States and the United Kingdom were at best overlooking, probably condoning and arguably encouraging in the name of the War on Terror.

When I was at school, I recall, we used to debate how we would have reacted had we been German in the 1940s, and been ordered to go along with some of the horrors of the Nazi regime. I don't think in my wildest dreams I imagined I might ever actually face that kind of dilemma. But my brilliant career, to ambassador at age forty-three, ended with me writing in an official telegram to Jack Straw, British foreign secretary: "I will not attempt to hide my contempt for such casuistry, nor my shame that I work in an organisation where colleagues would resort to it to justify torture."

Something happened on September 11, 2001, that caused the West to lose its moral bearings in a way that led government machines, and those who worked in them, to move a significant way down the path of contempt for individuals. The Nazis went down it a lot farther, but it is undeniably the same path the Nazis took. To me, the astonishing thing was that my U.S. and U.K. colleagues, ordinary, decent people, followed unquestioningly down that path. The scary thing is the eagerness of the authoritarian forces in government, grouped around George W. Bush, to grasp this opportunity to try to land a lethal blow on Western liberalism. I have a feeling that liberalism will yet prove too strong for them. It is both my hope and belief that we will one day look back on this period as we now look back on McCarthyism, with disbelief at our own aberration.

If we lose liberalism, al-Qaida has won.

I may have got the odd date wrong. A few names have been changed to protect the guilty, several to protect the innocent and a very few because I could not remember the real ones. I have not used any established system of rendering Russian or Uzbek names, opting for a personal choice of what is readable.

Several conversations are given in English that originally took place in Russian.

SHEPHERDS BUSH, LONDON
NOVEMBER 2006

CHAPTER 1

Awakening

CHRIS LOOKED SURPRISED.

"OK, let's go" was not a standard reaction from a British ambassador to the news that a dissident trial was about to start. The Land Rover drew up to the embassy door and out I went, still feeling pretty uncomfortable at people calling me "sir," opening doors and stopping their normal chatter as I passed.

We turned up outside the court, whose small wicket entrance led through an unprepossessing muddy wall into a dirty courtyard containing several squat white buildings. Like much Soviet construction, it looked unfinished and barely functional. To enter the courtyard we had to give passport details to two policemen sitting at a table outside the gate. They took an age to write down details with a chewed-up pencil in an old ledger. I was to find that the concealment of terrible viciousness behind a homely exterior was a recurring theme in Uzbekistan.

About a hundred people were hanging about the courtyard waiting for various trials to begin. I was introduced to a variety of scruffy-looking individuals who represented different human rights organizations. Their dress was eccentric even in the ethnic and social kaleidoscope of Tashkent, ranging from tweed, and sweaters apparently knitted poorly out of old socks, to garish Bermuda beachwear with fake designer specs. Oddly, the seven or eight I met seemed to belong to the same number of different organizations, and most of them would not talk to each other.

One short but distinguished-looking man, with a shock of white hair and big black specs, was so self-important he wouldn't talk to anyone at all. Chris, bustling round doing the introductions, pointed to him and said, "Mikhail Ardzinov—he says it is for you to call on him." I was puzzled, as the question of who called on whom involved taking about eight paces across the courtyard. Chris explained that Ardzinov was feeling very important, as his group was the only one that was *registered*, and thus legal. The others were all illegal. Peculiarly, Ardzinov's registered group was called the *Independent* Human Rights Organization of Uzbekistan. None of this meant much to me at the time, and I certainly hadn't been an ambassador long enough to feel my pride mortified by taking eight paces, so I went and shook the man's hand. I received a long, cool stare for my effort.

But even at first meeting, some of these people could not help but impress. One gentleman had been a schoolteacher until he was thrown out of his job for refusing to teach the president's books uncritically. He now spent time at trials of dissidents, normally the less reported ones in obscure places. He documented them painstakingly by hand, and sent details to international organizations. I asked how he lived, and he said largely on the kindness of others. Judging by his clothes, gaunt face and sparse frame, that kindness was a limited commodity. I asked if he was not in danger of arrest. He said he had spent "only" a total of four months in custody in the past three years. An unhealthy flush burned in his cheeks and his eyes alternated between a normal genial twinkle and flashes of real anger. They were unforgettable, yet they are not the eyes I saw that day which haunt me still.

Nor are Dilobar's. Lovely as she was, I am afraid I cannot recall her eyes. But mine had been drifting during the conversation to her full but graceful figure in blue as she stood under an old corrugated-iron canopy to my left, tall and striking amid a group of older local women in their flowered dresses, velvet jackets and *hijabs*—a colorful Muslim scarf that in Uzbekistan covers the hair but none of the face. Her fine black hair flowed long and free down her back. Her cotton dress was full, reaching right to the neck, wrists and sleeves, and of a light flowing blue, though close fitting around her slim waist.

Chris brought her over and introduced her as Dilobar Khuderbegain-ova. Something was hammering insistently at my dulled senses. What was wrong—Khuderbegainova—Oh! This was the sister of the victim of this show trial. Yes, her eyes were filling with tears. Her brother was going to be executed, and I was checking out her legs through her dress. I was filled with self-loathing.

She said with great dignity that her brother was a good man, and the whole family would remember me for coming. I thanked her and held out my hand. Another mistake. Muslim women don't shake hands with strange men. For a moment she was taken aback but then she held out her hand and clenched mine firmly, and a smile almost troubled her lips. I wanted to say, "Don't worry," and promise to help, but realistically, what could I do—and if I could do nothing, why was I there?

Chris was looking at me curiously.

"Bit hot," I said, and went and sat down under a tree to think. My momentary self-hate turned to real anger against a system that tortured thousands and executed hundreds, and against fellow diplomats for their complacent acquiescence.

We waited two hours in the heat for the trial to start. It was 111 degrees in the shade that day, and we didn't have much of that in the courtyard. There was a sudden bustle of activity, then we entered through a door that led straight onto stairs down to a basement. The atmosphere changed completely. The short staircase was lined with perhaps a dozen paramilitaries—Ministry of Interior forces—in gray camouflage, carrying machine guns. There was so little space left to pass that a tense scrum developed. I was only about three steps down when one of the militia, for no reason I could discern, pulled me back by the arm. I snapped. Wheeling round, I grabbed him by the throat and pushed him back against the wall (modesty requires me to point out that he was a very small militiaman). I raged uselessly in English, "Don't you touch me, do you hear? Do not touch me."

Silence fell, and everyone looked aghast. I don't think the militia knew who I was, but I was obviously foreign and therefore probably not shootable. These people pushed others about all their lives, and no one ever pushed back. My little militiaman gave a nervous laugh, and chatter started up again. We carried on down to the courtroom as though nothing had happened.

The atmosphere in the courtyard had been apprehensive but resigned. Now all was tension. The six prisoners were already in the "dock." This was a large cage, constructed roughly out of what looked like concrete reinforcing rods welded together, not straight but strongly, and lots of them. It had been painted white in situ, with lashings of paint so thick they had oozed down the spiraled grooves in the rods, and congealed there in pendulous blobs. The concrete floor around it was heavily spattered. The cage door was fastened with two enormous padlocks. Fourteen heavily armed militiamen stood shoulder to shoulder around the cage. The six accused squatted inside on what looked like two low school benches, with not quite enough room for the three men on each.

Loved ones tried to push between the guards to say a few words of encouragement. The accused barely turned their heads, though some managed wan smiles. All were gaunt, clean-shaven with shorn hair. Five looked middle-aged and, from the ripples of skin, as though they had once been better fleshed. Their hair was whitening. The sixth, Khuderbegainov himself, looked like a teenager (he was twenty-two). He coughed periodically and cast his eyes around quickly and furtively, in contrast to the languor of the others. He looked very skinny indeed.

Of the six, three had already been in jail for some two years. The charges were multiple, but different permutations of the six were charged with a number of different offenses. For example, three were charged with the armed robbery of a jeweler, four with the murder of two policemen. All were charged with attempting to overthrow the government and undermine the constitution.

This was one of a series of trials of Muslim activists in Uzbekistan. I knew some of the statistics already—Human Rights Watch alleged some seven thousand political or religious prisoners. I had heard allegations of torture, but not in detail. In three weeks of Foreign and Commonwealth Office (FCO) and other U.K. government briefings prior to my taking up post, there had been scarcely a mention of human rights, and none of torture. The briefing I had been given put the emphasis first on FCO internal management procedure, second on Uzbekistan's supportive role in the War on Terror and third, on Central Asia's economic and commercial potential in hydrocarbons, gold, cotton and agroindustry. I could have written a paper on hydrocarbon pipeline options for Central Asia, but nothing had prepared me for the reality of the "War on Terror" as I was about to encounter it.

In the courtyard I had met a helpful young man called Ole, from Human Rights Watch, who let me share his Uzbek interpreter in the court. He filled me in on some background that I later checked out. Two of the people charged with murder had actually been in jail at the time, serving their sentences for "religious extremism." And over a dozen other people had already been convicted of these murders. There was no suggestion that they were in conspiracy, or even knew each other, or that the murders had been carried out by a mob. The simple Uzbek government tactic was that a genuine crime (and two policemen had indeed been murdered) would be used to convict lots of opposition people. And they would, of course, not be listed as political prisoners but common murderers, rapists or whatever. In that year—2002—some 220 prisoners were officially executed in Uzbekistan, in addition to those murdered in police or security service custody, in prison, or who simply "disappeared."

The courtroom was chokingly hot. I felt beads of sweat running down my shirt. The judge looked like First Goon out of central casting: swarthy and thick-set, floppy hair swept back, dressed in black trousers and a white shirt that strained at his belly. He started out with a harangue at the prisoners for wasting the court's time.

The jeweler who had suffered the armed robbery said that three of the men, wearing balaclavas, had tied him up and held him, robbing him of an improbably large sum of money. They had shot at him with pistols but missed. A defense lawyer asked him why no bullets or bullet holes had been found in the room. The jeweler supposed rather weakly that the bullets had gone out the window. As he was allegedly tied up on the floor at the time, the defendants must have been very bad shots indeed. The defense lawyer was making hay with this.

The judge had been ostentatiously not listening whenever the defense spoke, whittling at his fingernails with his knife or chatting with the rapporteur, who equally stopped writing whenever the defense said anything. But somehow it must have penetrated the judge's thick skin that this prosecution witness was not going down well. He interrupted the defense lawyer with a sharp rebuke, and then instructed the defendants to stand.

He harangued them again, saying that they represented evil in society. They were thieves and murderers who sought to undermine Uzbekistan's independence and democracy. Their list of crimes was long and it would be better if they admitted it. He concluded that he was astonished that they had found the time to commit so many crimes, when they had to stop to pray five times a day. He evidently considered this a hilarious sally and guffawed loudly, as did the prosecutor, rapporteur and various other cronies. But I noticed a few narrowed eyes among the militiamen. Later he again amused himself hugely by interrupting a defendant: "I don't suppose anyone could hear you through your long Muslim beard," snapped the judge. "I see the prison service removed it for you!" He several times told the defense to shut up and stop wasting time.[1]

The jeweler was asked to identify which three of the six had robbed him. He peered uncertainly at the benches—plainly he had no idea. Pressed by the defense, he managed to identify—and the odds against this must be high—entirely the wrong three. This got the judge very angry.

"You are mistaken, you old fool!" he bellowed.

The judge then read out the names of the three who were charged with this particular crime, and asked them to stand.

"Are these the men?" he asked the terrified jeweler, who stammered his assent.

"Let the record show they were positively identified by the victim," said the judge.

This was pure farce, but I had to pull myself back to the terrible reality behind this bizarre charade. These six nervous men stood to be shot. The family would not be informed of the execution, so for months would not know if their loved one was dead, believing him perhaps dead while he still languished, and perhaps alive when he was well rotted. This was a deliberately refined cruelty as was the practice—inherited from the Soviets—that when the family was finally informed of the death, they would be charged for the bullets that killed him.

It was at this minute I was caught by those eyes I will never forget—they were Khuderbegainov's. He had spotted me in the crowd, a Westerner in a three-piece suit, out of place and time. Who was I? Maybe this strange apparition brought some kind of hope. Maybe the West would do something. *Maybe he wasn't going to die after all.* The drowning man had caught a fleeting glimpse of straw on the surface. His eyes bored into mine, small, dark, intense, filled with a desperate hope. He was urging me, with every mute fiber of his being, to do something. I looked back. I don't do telepathy, but stared at him, trying to say: "I will try, in God's name, I will try," with my own eyes. He smiled and nodded, a confidence shared, and then looked away again.

Again, I suffered a wave of self-loathing: *What am I doing here? What right have I to give false hope—is that not just one more cruelty?*

BUT THIS MOMENTARY doubt was replaced by an iron resolve—I would help; I would work tirelessly to stop this horror in Uzbekistan. I would not spend three years on the golf course and cocktail circuit. I would not go along with political lies or leave the truth unspoken. The next bit of the trial set that resolve, like catalyst added to epoxy resin.

An old man was assisted to the witness stand. He had a little white beard and sparse white hair, and wore a black lacquered skullcap and a dull brown quilted gown. He was shaking with fright. One of the accused was his nephew. His statement was read out to him, in which he confirmed that his nephew was a terrorist who stole money to send to Osama bin Laden, and had traveled to Afghanistan to meet Bin Laden.

"Is this your testimony?" asked the prosecutor.

"But it's not true," replied the old man. "They tortured me to say it."

The judge said that accusations of torture had been dismissed earlier in the case. They could not be reintroduced.

"But they tortured me!" said the old man. "They tortured my grandson before my eyes. They beat his testicles and put electrodes on his body. They put a mask on him to stop him breathing. They raped him with a bottle. Then they brought my granddaughter and said they would rape her. All the time they said, 'Osama bin Laden, Osama bin Laden.' We are poor farmers from Andijon. We are good Muslims, but what do we know of Osama bin Laden?"

His quavering voice had become stronger, but at this he physically collapsed and was helped out. The judge then stated that the prisoners' connection with Osama bin Laden was not in doubt. They had confessed to it.

I had seen enough and left. Those three hours in court had a profound effect on me. If these were our allies in the War on Terror, we were not on the clear moral ground that Blair and Bush claimed so braggingly.

I SENT A TELEGRAM back to London, explaining in detail what I had seen at the trial. Shortly thereafter, a sentence of death was passed on Khuderbegainov and long sentences given to his "accomplices." The

Human Rights Policy Department in the FCO agreed we should take up the case, and the wheels clunked into motion for the long process of agreeing to an EU démarche, or formal protest.

In the meantime, Dilobar and her father came to my office. I welcomed them, accepted their thanks for attending the trial and said that I had been shocked by what I saw. I asked the father what they could tell me by way of background to the trial.

This was the first time I had encountered a phenomenon that was to bedevil me for the next two years: the inability of Uzbeks in human rights cases to tell their story in a plain, concise manner. This is well recognized by those working in the field. Various reasons are given—sheer terror at saying anything against the government, the effect of social shaming and the cultural propensity for roundabout storytelling. But the phenomenon is very real, and frustrating.

The Khuderbegainovs, a well-established Tashkent family, were previously in favor with the regime. The father was a former head of a Tashkent state radio station. He told me the story of when he had been arrested for questioning. They came for him while he was attending a family wedding. He was in tears as he told this, and seemed unable to get past his despair at being arrested in such a humiliatingly public fashion, and his astonishment that a wedding should be violated.

Weddings hold an important position in most cultures, but Uzbek society takes this to extremes, with a family not infrequently spending three years' income on a daughter's wedding. So no doubt it is very bad form to violate one. But the poor man, holding back his tears, had spent thirty minutes telling me nothing but that he had been arrested at a wedding. With his son sentenced to death, this was hardly the most important point.

I therefore asked Dilobar to continue the story. I learned from her that her brother had received an education at one of the Saudi-funded Arabic schools opened in Tashkent in the 1990s. Following the bombings there in 1999,[2] these schools were closed down and many of their pupils and former pupils imprisoned. Eventually this well-connected family received warning that her brother was to be arrested, and he ran away to Tajikistan, where he made contact with rebel groups. From there he was sent to Afghanistan to fight with the Islamic Movement of Uzbekistan

(IMU) alongside the Taliban, but he didn't like what he saw and ran away from there too.

For a year he scratched out a living as a bazaar trader before eventually being arrested crossing the Tajik/Uzbek border. He was then imprisoned for some months in Uzbekistan and severely tortured, which had caused permanent liver damage. Under torture he had confessed to the range of crimes featured in the trial. The family had not known he was taken until the trial began. During the period of imprisonment, the father himself was imprisoned. His brutal interrogation ostensibly focused on the whereabouts of his son, who in fact was already in custody at the time.

I judged that Dilobar believed this story herself. I wondered whether this was the whole truth about Khuderbegainov's involvement with the IMU and the Taliban, but even if it wasn't, he plainly had not received a fair trial on the charges for which he had been sentenced to death. I thanked the impressively composed and articulate Dilobar and her father, and promised to do what I could. We had already decided to move for an EU démarche, but I was racking my brains for further action that might forestall the execution, and decided to contact the UN.

THE NEXT DAY Chris came into my office and tossed a brown envelope onto my desk.

"You may not want to look at these—they're pretty horrible," he said.

I was beginning to understand enough about the country to have an inkling what might be in the envelope, and I waited until the cook, Galina, had brought in my cappuccino and biscuits before opening it. It contained a number of photos of a naked corpse, a heavy, middle-aged man. His face was bruised and bloodied, and his torso and limbs were swollen and a livid purple. He was such a mess that it took a little while for me to work out what I was looking at. I said a short prayer, rather to my own surprise.

I then went back through to Chris's office.

"Where did we get these?"

"His mother. That's Mr. Avazov. He was a prisoner in Jaslyk gulag, right up in the desert. That's where they take the hard-line dissidents. Anyway, his body gets delivered back to his mum in a sealed metal casket. She's ordered not to open it and to bury it the next day. A local *militsiya* is left to guard it. Anyway, *militsiya* man falls asleep and Mum sneaks down, gets the casket open, body onto the kitchen table, and gets out the Kodak."

"Without waking up the *militsiya* man?"

"He was probably drunk."

"Look, Chris, I don't know what happened to this poor bugger, but I think we should go big on this one. I really want to get serious with this regime, and this could be the case we need. But we have to be certain of our ground."

Chris mused, "The photos are pretty good. I am sure Alistair in Human Rights Policy Department in London said that they could get pathology reports done, if they had good enough photos."

"Great. Try it."

MY APPEARANCE AT the Khuderbegainov trial had caused quite a stir. Ambassadors in Tashkent just did not attend dissident trials. It brought Matilda Bogner, head of the local office of Human Rights Watch, to the embassy to see me. Matilda was a pleasant Australian in her early thirties, with a broad open face, long brown hair swept back into a ponytail and a penchant for peasant dresses.

"They tell me that you're not like a normal ambassador," she opened.

"I certainly hope not," I replied. "I am struggling to work out what this embassy actually used to do all day."

"Not a lot," she said. "Chris is good, but I think he was pretty well frustrated."

She filled me in on the human rights situation, and it was grim. No opposition parties, no free media, no freedom of assembly, no freedom of religion, no freedom of movement. Not only were exit visas required to leave the country, you needed an internal visa or *propusk* in your passport just to leave the town where you lived. Matilda reckoned there were, at an absolute minimum, seven thousand people imprisoned for their religious or political beliefs. She filled me in on the cases of Elena Urlaeva and Larisa Vdovina, who had recently been committed to a lunatic asylum for demonstrating outside the parliament. Both were now strapped to their beds and receiving drug treatment that amounted to a chemical lobotomy.

I thanked Matilda, and said I hoped we would be able to work closely together. I asked her about the attitude of other embassies. She said the U.S. embassy was in denial. It viewed President Karimov as an essential partner in the War on Terror, and had convinced itself that he was a democrat. Of the other embassies, only the Swiss really gave a stuff about human rights. Unfortunately, the countries that genuinely cared about human rights—the Scandinavians, Dutch, Irish, Canadians and Australians—didn't have embassies in Uzbekistan.

A FORTNIGHT LATER, Chris received the report on the photos of the corpse of Mr. Avazov. The pathology department of the University of Glasgow had prepared a brief but detailed report of their findings. The victim had died of immersion in boiling liquid. It was immersion rather than splashing because there was a clear tidemark around the upper torso and upper arms, with 100 percent scalding underneath. Before he was boiled to death, his fingernails had been ripped out and he had been severely beaten around the face. Reading the dispassionate language of the pathology report, I was struck with a cold horror.

CHAPTER 2

Instructions

I HAD BEEN SELECTED OVER A YEAR PREVIOUSLY FOR THE POSITION of Ambassador to the Republic of Uzbekistan. After receiving this news, I still had a further six months to work as British deputy high commissioner in Accra, Ghana. Following that, I had six months in London urgently trying to learn Russian. I then had the chance to spend six weeks as a student in St. Petersburg, putting a gloss on those new language skills. I returned from there in June 2002.

My wife, Fiona, and the children were waiting for me at Heathrow airport.

I had bought Fiona a small Fabergé egg.[1] It was a beautiful little enameled and jeweled item, and Fiona seemed very happy with it, as did the children with their presents.

My son, Jamie, was fourteen, my daughter, Emily, eight. Jamie was at Glenalmond, a Scottish public (which in Britain means private) school. It was only mid-June, but already Jamie was on holiday. It is a general rule in Britain that the more expensive the school, the fewer weeks you get for your money. Emily was at the local state primary school in Gravesend, where we lived. Fiona now drove us home there around the M25, in our old Renault 21 station wagon.

There was a lot to do before setting out for Tashkent. I returned immediately to attending the Diplomatic Service Language Centre in the Old Admiralty Building on the Mall. There we worked hard to get me through the Russian-language functional-level examination. Normally you would take this after eleven months of study, but I had only six. The exam was tough, but I passed.

I also had to attend a series of individual briefings with government departments and others with an interest in Uzbekistan.

The most important contact I would have was with the Eastern Department of the FCO. This department would be my direct-line management, responsible for my instructions but also for my budget and management issues. As the geographical department, they had the direct responsibility for the embassy, although much of my reporting on a day-to-day basis would be aimed at Foreign Office functional departments, such as the Counterterrorism Department, the United Nations Department and the Human Rights Policy Department. That is not to mention the other London ministries, such as the Department for International Development (DFID) or the Ministry of Defense (MOD), to which we also reported. But the Eastern Department was the starting place.

The atmosphere in the department was unpleasant—heavy, pompous and serious. A pall of misery appeared to have settled. I don't think I ever saw people there joke and smile together. There was plainly something wrong, but I wasn't going to be working in the department—indeed, I was going to be several thousand miles away—so I wasn't too worried by my intuition.

The head of the department, Simon Butt, would be my line manager. He saw me briefly in his splendid office overlooking St. James's Park. He seemed a cold fish and said pretty quickly that he had largely delegated Uzbekistan to his deputy, Dominic Schroeder.

Dominic looks like an actor made up to play the mikado. He is tall, with a big belly and a round bald pate. He greeted me much more warmly, and talked chiefly about managerial questions. The embassy was expanding in the light of the new importance attached to Uzbekistan post–9/11. In particular, a defense section had been added, headed by an army colonel. This meant that the office accommodations were no longer sufficient.

The ambassadors had lived in a flat on the first floor of the embassy. Now the offices were being expanded to take over the whole building. They therefore needed to find a new residence for the ambassador. This had not been easy due to the lack of large houses in Tashkent, and when they had finally found one, it was still being built, and would need a lot of extra work to bring it up to U.K. standards. Dominic said that the new residence would not be ready for my arrival. This would mean an eventual extra move of house, and that the offices would be cramped in the meantime.

I was excited about the prospect of my first ambassadorship, and these did not strike me as major problems. Dominic went on to add that in Tashkent the ambassador's car was only a Land Rover Discovery. In next-door Kazakhstan, the ambassador had a Jaguar, and Dominic would be sympathetic if I wanted to upgrade. I said that if I did that, I would prefer a Range Rover to a Jaguar. Uzbekistan was a big country with a lot of desert and mountains.

Finally Dominic asked me if the ambassador, Christopher Ingham, had spoken to me about Chris Hirst. I said that he had.

I had attended an Eastern Department discussion on Central Asia. This had centered on oil and gas potential, and mostly focused on Kazakhstan. I had, however, had the chance to meet Christopher Ingham. This was the only time I ever saw my predecessor. He was a thin man with a slight stoop. He wore gold spectacles and his thinning hair was brushed over the top of his head. He wore a sharply cut, charcoal gray pinstriped suit, and a fawn-colored Burberry raincoat, which he seemed reluctant to take off.

In a tea break of the meeting, Christopher and I adjourned to a small room for a ten-minute private discussion. He wanted to brief me about the staff of the embassy.

It was an ominous conversation. Apart from myself, there were only four other members of the diplomatic service in the embassy. Jackie ran the registry—which meant archived the papers—and would do confidential typing for me at a pinch, though she was also an entry clearance officer—she did visa interviews and issued visas. Dave Muir was third secretary and management officer, responsible for logistics, and also an entry clearance officer. Chris Hirst was the third secretary responsible for political reporting and project work. Karen Moran was second secretary and my deputy head of mission, responsible for managing the office, looking after British commercial interests and for consular work—giving necessary support to British citizens in the country. And that was it.

That is an extraordinarily small team for a senior diplomat to have, both in number and in rank. In Ghana, I managed a whole chain of first secretaries, with second and third secretaries under them. In Tashkent, Christopher told me bluntly, he had no political support at all. Even Karen was not an actual second secretary, but an acting one. Chris as third secretary was the lowest of diplomatic ranks. No one in his mid-thirties would still be a third secretary unless there were problems with him. None of these staff was judged to be, to use the FCO management-speak of the time, "a policy-capable officer."

As Christopher said, I would be on my own.

He added that Karen was a very good administrator, but that she and Chris had an "FCO attitude." He meant that they had no interest in interacting with Uzbekistan, or learning anything about its culture. They did not have Uzbek friends, or any deep knowledge of the country. He went on to say that there had been some difficulties with Chris, and that the Uzbeks had complained about his behavior. However, he had defended Chris robustly, and had been congratulated by the FCO for doing so. He had left papers for me in the office in Tashkent on the subject.

This meeting left me feeling slightly mystified but not unduly worried. If the rest of the staff were as incapable as Christopher Ingham suggested, it would be difficult to provide London with a good volume of quality reporting on political, economic and other issues. On the other hand, I knew I was professionally very capable of a high volume of wide-ranging output. Plainly there was some wider problem with Chris and Karen, but I would take them as I found them.

Dominic now produced an official communication, dated February 4, 2002, that he had sent to Christopher Ingham about the Uzbek allegations against Chris Hirst. It strongly supported his defense of Hirst and included the line: "We are glad that you are offering Chris your full support at what is clearly a stressful time."

Dominic made plain that, in the event of any further complaints against Chris Hirst from the Uzbek authorities, they would expect me to follow my predecessor in offering Hirst full support. I told Dominic that I was much more worried about the lack of any capable political staff in the embassy. Would it be possible, for example, to replace Karen with a first secretary when she left in eighteen months?

"My dear Craig," said Dominic, "it is not many years ago that the

Tashkent embassy was one man with a suitcase in a hotel bedroom. We still expect our ambassadors in Central Asia to have a bit of pioneer spirit."

I assured him I had plenty of that, but said I would revert on staffing once I had bedded in.

I visited British American Tobacco, the largest U.K. investor in Uzbekistan. However, they plainly weren't that interested in meeting me and produced only their head of security for Central Asia, although he did give me a very good lunch at their headquarters at Temple, London. I did a bit better at Rothschilds Bank, where I had lunch with several directors. They handled the sales of Uzbekistan's gold production—the sixth largest in the world. Following my posting as deputy high commissioner to Ghana from 1998 to 2001, I knew a great deal about gold and the factors affecting its world price, and that was a valuable lunch.

Fiona and I were guests for dinner at the home of the Uzbek ambassador, Professor Faizullaev. He lived in a surprisingly modest home on a fenced and guarded estate in Hammersmith. He was a charming man with a kind wife and pleasant student-age children. They had cooked for us Uzbek *plov,* the national dish, consisting of pieces of lamb cooked in saffron rice and shredded carrot. The rice is plumped up with vast quantities of cooking oil. The food was delicious, although Mrs. Faizullaev complained that she had to use sunflower instead of cotton oil, and couldn't find white carrots. The ambassador explained to us that there were many regional variations of *plov,* with extra ingredients such as almond, sultana or chickpea. There were, he said, 220 different kinds of *plov.* He preferred Tashkent *plov* to Samarkand *plov.*

"What kind is this?" Fiona asked.

"London *plov,*" said the professor. "It's the two hundred and twenty-first."

It was a very pleasant evening, and Faizullaev wanted to make only one major political point. He said that he had been targeted by protestors, who had damaged his car and plastered posters on his house, as well as regularly demonstrated outside the embassy. The British government should do more to defend the embassy. Uzbekistan was an ally of the U.K. and greatly valued this partnership. The protestors were mostly from a "terrorist organization," Hizb-ut-Tehrir, which should be banned.

I replied that the right to demonstrate was an important liberty in the U.K., but of course his car and home must not be damaged. I promised to report his concerns to the FCO.

As British ambassador, you are the representative of Her Majesty the Queen. My official title was to be Her Majesty's Ambassador Extraordinary and Plenipotentiary. Before you go out to your post, you call on the queen to talk about your mission.

Only I wasn't going to. It was Jubilee year, and the Queen had too many public engagements to find time to talk to dull ambassadors. I would therefore be calling on Princess Anne and Prince Andrew instead. I was worried about this, because I was afraid Fiona would be bitterly disappointed. Fiona is a monarchist; I am not. But in fact she was quite pleased. I had organized state visits for the queen in Poland and in Ghana, so Fiona had already met and spoken with her. She had not met Princess Anne or Prince Andrew, and so was happy to add a couple more royals to her collection.

I had to wear morning dress, which consisted of striped trousers, a long gray frock coat with tails, a gray waistcoat and a top hat. These were hired at a substantial cost to the FCO. This seemed to me rather a waste of taxpayers' money. I owned a lot of high-quality suits, so why I had to be dressed like an extra from *My Fair Lady* was beyond me. I could have worn my kilt if they wanted me to look more impressive. In fact, the FCO was spending a great deal of taxpayers' money on fancy dress for various royal functions. Fiona naturally needed a new dress, hat, gloves, shoes and handbag for the event. The cost of those fell to me.

The unit of the FCO that looked after the needs of ambassadors in the U.K. was called heads of mission section. I asked Hazel, the very helpful lady who ran it, why we had to do this fancy dress bit rather than wearing an ordinary lounge suit.

"Buckingham Palace did relax the dress code a few years ago," she said, "but then an ambassador turned up in a linen suit. The queen was really shocked so we had to go back to morning dress again."

Good God! A linen suit? No wonder we lost the Empire.

AT THE FCO, we joined up with four other ambassadorial couples and then set off in a convoy down the Mall with motorcycle outriders. We swept through the palace gates and under the central arch of the facade to an inner courtyard, where a line of flunkies opened the doors as the vehicles drew up. We were quickly ushered through a variety of chambers into a large room.

Buckingham Palace is not the greatest palace in England, in terms of either size or quality of architecture. But it is probably the best maintained and most sumptuously furnished. The highly ornate cornices and pilasters were clean and crisp, while fresh gold leaf glittered everywhere. The scarlet, gold-bordered carpets also looked brand-new. Across these, long, broad runners of precisely the same carpet were laid in diagonal paths marking the routes for visiting tourists, but even these strips seemed as pristine and unmarked as the substantive carpets beneath, which they were supposed to protect.

The ambassadorial couples were spread out around the room. Princess Anne and Prince Andrew were brought in and each was escorted by a courtier around the groups, the princess clockwise and the prince counter. Fiona and I therefore had separate three-minute conversations with each. The prince joked that he was unlikely to come to Tashkent on a ship's visit, it being landlocked. As we were talking, you could see from his eyes that he wasn't really interested and was thinking of something else, probably how quickly he could get away from this boring meeting. By contrast Princess Anne looked shrewdly at me. She said she thought the government of Uzbekistan was a real problem. She had visited Uzbekistan with the Save the Children Fund, and was concerned about declining standards of health and education and increasing child poverty.

As I discovered, that was the most clued-up observation anyone made to me before I went out to Tashkent.

The last calls I had to make were on FCO ministers. Mike O'Brien was the junior minister with specific responsibility for Uzbekistan. My first appointment with him was canceled with half an hour's notice. It was rearranged for the following week, and this time I made it to his office, where I waited for half an hour while his private secretary desperately tried to locate him. He had been meeting another Labour MP in a bar at lunchtime, and afterward had said he was going for a walk in St. James's Park. He hadn't returned. After half an hour we gave up, and again rescheduled. The third time he was actually there for the meeting, and I found him particularly vacuous. He seemed a prime example of a New Labour politician: all haircut and presentation. If he had any insights on Central Asia, he didn't deign to impart them to his new ambassador. He read a few platitudes about the War on Terror from the briefing the Eastern Department had given him.

I then had to call on the British foreign minister. I was ushered through to the secretary of state's great room and sat in an ornate chair opposite Jack Straw, who lounged on a vermilion ormolu sofa. He had my CV in front of him, and observed I was not from the usual background of his ambassadors, being state school and Dundee University. He then asked me about my interest in Scottish folk music, and whether I sang. He asked what the main British commercial interests were in Uzbekistan, said I was going to a difficult part of the world and he wished me luck. The interview lasted under ten minutes. As I was walking out he called after me, "Oh, and Craig—whenever you get to . . . wherever it is you're going . . . tell them I'm thinking about them."

That was the extent of my instructions.

CHAPTER 3

London to Tashkent

WE LEFT FOR HEATHROW AIRPORT IN A CHAUFFEUR-DRIVEN GOV-
ernment Ford Galaxy, with my brother Stuart driving behind in the
Renault with all the extra luggage. At Heathrow we drove round airside to
the VIP lounge. The luggage was all set out in a long line against the wall,
and a man from Alitalia, Uzbek Air's Heathrow handling agent, was label-
ing it up while swearing volubly. Luckily the children don't understand Italian. We settled into the VIP lounge. Jamie was being very patient with
Emily and they were doing a quiz in a magazine. He was taking in everything around him as though memorizing every detail to tell his mates at
school. Emily, as always, was completely unfazed and seemed to find nothing remarkable, even when I told her that this was a private place where the
queen came before getting on a plane.

Quite shortly it was time to leave. We hugged Stuart good-bye. The
luggage had gone, and nobody had said anything about paying for excess
baggage, which was good news. We got back into the government car,
which drove us all of twenty yards to a flight of steps at the foot of the
Uzbek Air 747.[1]

Uzbek Air's first-class cabin fully met international standards of comfort, circa 1970. There were large gray leather seats, configured six across,
two at each side and two in the middle. These were comfortable but did
not recline far and did not have individual television monitors. The cabin
was clean, but the carpet worn right down with black, greasy-looking
patches at the entrances to the aisles.

There were three rows of first-class seats—eighteen seats in all—but
we were the only passengers in this cabin. We had a hostess and two bathrooms all to ourselves. The hostess wore a dark green uniform with a tight

knee-length skirt and a jacket over a white blouse. She was fairly pretty but heavily built, with solid hips and thighs. Just before the plane started to roll back, the Uzbek Air station manager came up the steps to shake my hand and give some flowers to Fiona, which was a pleasant touch. He offered any future assistance we needed and seemed genuinely jolly.

We chatted excitedly about what might lie before us in Tashkent. We had little idea of what to expect in terms of the sights, sounds and feel of the place.

After a while the hostess appeared with a bottle of Uzbek champagne. This was more than half empty, and had a paper serviette screwed into the neck to act as a stopper. With about three inches of tail sticking out, it looked like a Molotov cocktail. Fiona and I declined this treat, and while Jamie looked keen, he wasn't offered.

Next we were given a menu—one between four of us. This was a plush production with hard green leather covers and a knotted golden cord looped around the spine. There was a choice of about eight starters and main courses, divided into Uzbek and European dishes. Emily was disappointed at the lack of a children's menu but cheered when we found a hamburger on the main menu. Jamie, who even as a small child would happily eat whitebait, frogs' legs or African land snails, opted for the most outlandish-sounding Uzbek dishes. Fiona and I chose something sensible. The girl came back to ask what we wanted; I noted she had no notepad and inwardly congratulated her on her memory. I ordered for everyone, showing that I had a memory too. When I had finished she remained standing uneasily, hopping from leg to leg as though she needed to go to the bathroom.

"Er, we have the feesh," she said.

"I am sorry?" I replied.

"The feesh we have," she said, perhaps concerned about her word order.

"Do you mean you don't have the other things?"

Again, that look of relief that she had managed to communicate.

"But there is feesh."

I looked at the family, who were all grinning broadly, except Fiona, who looked a bit cross.

"OK, we'll have four fish."

"Three feesh," she replied.

"Sorry," I apologized as British people usually do when there is a problem that is not our fault, "that's four fish." I gestured to my left to show that we were four.

"We have three feesh," she said.

"There are four of us," I observed. "What else do you have?"

She looked around with darting eyes, as though seeking a way to escape. Then composure returned with a further smile of relief.

"Sand-wich," she said, pronouncing it distinctly as spelled.

This was better. Perhaps the children would prefer sandwiches to indeterminate fish.

"What kind of sandwich do you have?"

"Feesh," she replied, "feesh sandwich."

We settled for three fish and a fish sandwich. I looked at the menu—there was no fish on it except a starter of smoked mackerel on a bed of lettuce. We wondered what would come. Fiona squeezed my arm and smiled. "And this is first class! I wonder if there are just three fish to feed the whole plane?"

"Jesus managed it," Jamie observed.

THE FISH TURNED UP—it was indeed the smoked mackerel on a bed of lettuce, only what had been intended as a cold starter was now a hot main (indeed only) course. It had been microwaved, including the lettuce, which was now like watery spinach with an unpleasant metallic flavor. Fiona's meal was suspiciously lighter than the others, and when the sandwich appeared it was hot smoked mackerel and slimy hot lettuce between two bits of bread.

I think we all just picked at some of the fish; Emily ate the bread from the sandwich. The hostess picked up on the fact that we were less than thrilled with the service. She seemed crestfallen, so we were all especially nice to her for the rest of the journey. We had green tea, which was our first time, and found it very pleasant with sugar and lemon. Emily loved the tea bowls, though it is beyond me why people want to keep burning their fingers thousands of years after the invention of the handle.

A projector came down from under the central lockers and a film started to display on a screen on the central bulkhead immediately in front of me. Jamie moved from his window seat on the left, the better to see the central screen. However, he soon moved back. If we had been expecting entertainment we were disappointed. First there came a caption: "Uzbekistan's 10th Anniversary Independence Day Celebrations 2001." There followed a long stage show consisting of dancers, acrobats and singing soldiers. It reminded me of the style of Maoist China. This show continued on a loop for the rest of the journey, starting again whenever it finished.

A QUICK WORD on the history of Uzbek independence.[2] In 1991, when the hard-line communists launched a military coup against President Gorbachev, junior Politburo member President Karimov of the Uzbek Soviet Socialist Republic, and the other Central Asian leaders of SSRs within the USSR, supported them. They were bitterly opposed to reform and to the breakup of the Soviet Union, which threatened their harsh and corrupt control over their own fiefdoms.

When Yeltsin defeated the hard-liners after the siege of the Moscow White House, the Gorbachev/Yeltsin liberal era briefly triumphed and it became clear to Karimov and his like that remaining in the USSR would mean toying with democracy, capitalism, liberal reform and the loss of their own totalitarian power. They suddenly did an amazing U-turn and became converts to national independence. But they now left the USSR in order to keep the Soviet system, not to destroy it.

That simple fact escaped conservative politicians in the United States of America, and astonishingly still did. Even as I was in the air, U.S. Treasury Secretary O'Neill was in Tashkent hailing Karimov precisely as someone who had helped bring down the Soviet Union. These simpleminded U.S. Republicans were confusing Karimov with Walesa, Havel and others in Eastern Europe who were fighting communism in the name of liberty. Karimov was fighting liberty in the name of communism, until it became more convenient to use the name of nationalism instead. After all, the move from Soviet totalitarianism to fascist totalitarianism is not a difficult one. The mechanisms remain the same. It just requires a slight tweaking of symbols and rhetoric.

My struggles with these problems lay ahead of me as we landed smoothly at Tashkent airport sometime after 2 A.M. It was a six-and-a-half-hour flight and Tashkent is five hours ahead of the U.K. At the front of the plane we had our own flight of steps, and our own VIP bus was waiting for us. A lady with dyed orange hair and matching lipstick stood in the glare of the apron floodlighting, calling out for "Mr. Mooray" and asking us for our luggage tags. A quick rustle among rucksacks dug up the covers of the used tickets, to which they were stuck. I tore them off and handed them, with bits of torn ticket cover, to the lady. She looked Russian, I noted, as she handed them on to a small, Asian-, indeed Mongol-looking man who had materialized out of the darkness beside her. He scurried off.

The lady then conducted us onto the bus, which drove us some two hundred yards to the left-hand side of the airport terminal. Here a side door led us through into the VIP lounge, which was lit only by dim emergency lighting. A closer peer around revealed that the lighting was so dim in order not to wake the staff. We walked forward to a low metal barrier, guarded by a green Formica and glass booth, in which an immigration officer was sleeping, the peak of his gold-braided green hat resting in the tips of the fingers of the hand that cushioned his head resting on the counter. His mouth was open.

I had asked the embassy to let the Uzbek Ministry of Foreign Affairs (MFA) know that I didn't expect them to mount a formal reception at such an unholy hour. Plainly my fears were unfounded.

It proved pretty difficult to wake the immigration officer—I had to bang on the window, while Jamie gave several very loud hellos, charged with the full force of teenage sarcasm. Eventually the immigration officer came to, and with a somewhat resentful air got out of his booth and switched the lights on. He then returned and I passed our passports under the glass screen to him. He looked at his computer station, which in its turn appeared difficult to awaken, and tapped in our passport details at what seemed inordinate length. As he finished with each one, he stamped it and eventually handed me all four back, without a word or a smile. He pressed a pedal, the metal barrier opened and we went through.

Round to our right was a lounge projecting out onto the apron, with three glass walls obscured by long off-white vertical blinds. The fourth side, to our left as we entered, was open to the VIP customs area and the exit. A strikingly beautiful, multicolored Oriental carpet, featuring floral patterns on a dazzling white background, covered most of the floor, with square leather sofas arranged around the walls, facing in. A central table held water and juices but only dirty glasses. Two people, a man and a woman, were sitting on one of the sofas.

The woman was wearing a knitted pink cardigan. She wore gold wire spectacles with thick lenses, perched on a beaky nose, giving her a somewhat owlish appearance. She looked in her early forties. But her smile was wide and generous, which was quite a feat at that time in the morning. She had been deep in conversation with the man, but she leaped up when she saw us. I surmised, correctly, that this was Karen Moran.

"Good evening, Ambassador," she said in a deep, rather husky voice with a pronounced Midlands accent. "Or should I say good morning? Well, I am Karen, your deputy, and this is Chris, third secretary and, more importantly, my partner."

Chris stood up. About five feet eleven inches tall, he wore dark slacks and a T-shirt and looked notably strong and well muscled. He carried himself almost unnaturally well, his back rod straight and his head high. His hair was close-cropped, almost shaven, which overemphasized his jug ears. He had a broad face and forehead but rather small eyes. He broke into a grin. His accent was Yorkshire: "You did well to wake him up"— he gestured with his head toward the immigration officer, who was settling down to sleep again. "You'll have to wait about an hour for your luggage. You might as well sit down."

We were feeling pretty exhausted by now, and an hour waiting for the luggage didn't sound welcome.

"How many bags do you have?" asked Chris.

"Sixteen," I replied, trying to sound casual, as though this amount of luggage were perfectly normal.

"Maybe an hour and a half, then." Chris grinned again.

"Of course," said Karen, "*we* don't qualify for the VIP lounge. But in fact I think it's quicker to go through the normal channels. You have to queue for passport control, but you can pick your own luggage off the carousel. Otherwise there's a little man trying to identify bags from the microscopic serial numbers on the tags as they go round."

"'Course it's not possible," interjected Chris, "so they just wait until everyone else has collected their luggage, then what's left must be the VIP luggage. Except that by that time it's probably been nicked off the carousel. Good place, eh?"

It was about forty-five minutes before the luggage turned up, wheeled in by two short Asian men on what looked like very old luggage trolleys. The cases were piled up crazily and appeared bound to collapse as they were pushed along. Somehow they didn't.

Three customs officials had been waiting for us at a counter. As no one else had come through the VIP lounge, we were the only customers for this particular detachment. They were armed with one of the big luggage scanners that you can put suitcases through. As we moved past they asked the porters to put the luggage through the scanner, but Chris intervened, thrusting his diplomatic ID rather aggressively at the chief customs officer, to within about two inches of his nose. We then swept past at some speed.[3]

Two white Land Rovers were waiting for us, with diplomatic license plates, which were light blue in Uzbekistan, with white numbers. One was 16 CMD—the letters being the internationally recognized code for the ambassador's or flag car, standing for "Chef de Mission Diplomatique." The second was 16 CD 02. The *CD* stands for "Corps Diplomatique," and I gathered that "16" must be the designated number for the British embassy.

They were both Land Rover Discoveries, in which the luggage compartment is pretty small. The drivers had some difficulty fitting in all our luggage, themselves, the four of us and Chris and Karen, but eventually we managed it. Chris gave a tip each to the porters, who left happily. Karen introduced me to the drivers: Valeri, who was to be "my" driver, was a short, wiry Russian, rather girlishly handsome. He gave me a shy smile. The other, Gafur, was a large, strong-looking man with graying hair and Asian eyes set deep in a florid face. He had a large, roguish grin and a strong handshake, and carried himself with a swagger. Both looked genuinely cheerful and welcoming; neither spoke English. It was immediately apparent that neither Karen nor Chris spoke Russian. Communication in the embassy must be interesting.

I was a wee bit disappointed that the flag car was only a Discovery. Dominic Schroeder had mentioned to me that he felt this was insufficiently prestigious. Certainly a Range Rover would be better.[4] It didn't worry Emily, though, who was delighted with the Union flag flying from the chrome mast on the right side of the bonnet. This was not the first time I had flown a flag—I had regularly been chargé d'affaires in Accra, for example, and flown the flag when the high commissioner was abroad. But this was the first occasion I had flown my own flag as ambassador in my own right. I felt a surge of pride and something of a lump in my throat as I thought about how proud my father would have been had he lived to see this.

It was a dark night, and we couldn't see much of the town as we drove from the airport to the embassy. The roads were all metaled, and had tram lines up the middle. A series of colorful lighting displays, with snowflake and bird themes, were strung across the streets from lampposts. There were miles of them, which was rather surprising. The illuminations included giant signs made up of lightbulbs atop blocks of flats either side of the airport road. To the left was WELCOME TO UZBEKISTAN! and to the right GOOD LUCK! which caused some amusement.

It was about a twenty-minute drive to the embassy, a two-story building made of a warm and mellow brick, now bathed in orange sodium light. A couple of large guards in black suits and ties had opened the gates as we swung in, and came running to shake my hand, and then help with the luggage.

We entered the embassy through the front door, which led into a vestibule with a heavy oak door to our right. A magnificent red Bokhara carpet covered the floor. Karen led the way up a wide staircase, passing walls covered in lime-washed antique oak paneling. We arrived at a landing from which high French windows, again in light oak, led out onto a balcony, from which a large flagpole projected. There were huge double doors to our left, and a smaller but still substantial one to our right. Karen opened the way through the large doors on the left into the ballroom. This was a beautifully proportioned room some sixty feet in length, with a wide arch across about two-thirds of the way along. The right-hand wall was pierced with numerous high windows, hung with extremely heavy gold-brocaded curtains, tied with great tasseled scarlet cords. A rich gold fitted carpet had obviously been made to measure, with a magenta foliate border running eighteen inches in from the walls all round. It was evident from the sills that the external walls were at least three feet thick. There were two sets of double doors through the wall on the left into the dining room. These openings were again paneled in light oak. The light was from gold and crystal chandeliers, while the furnishings gleamed in mahogany and fine cloths. The overall effect was sumptuous.

The cases and bags were piling up on the landing. Karen and Chris said good night and took their leave as we went through to the dining room. There the cook was waiting. She had prepared a lamb casserole with roast potatoes. It was after four in the morning local time; after eleven in the evening U.K. time. I don't think any of us was really hungry, but she was obviously worried about how we would receive her food, so I did my best to eat.

Galina looked thin and strained. The old cleaner, Irina, was also there and had started unpacking clothes and putting them away into drawers. She had formed an immediate bond with Emily, despite the lack of a common language, and they were doing this together.

The flat was divided into two halves. The stairs, landing, storerooms and kitchens formed a band down the middle. Off to one side were the ballroom and dining room. To the other side, through the smaller door off the landing, was a separate wing with a long corridor off which opened four bedrooms. The bedrooms at either end were en suite, with beautifully appointed bathrooms featuring designer British tiling of the highest quality, and even tacky touches like gold-plated taps. The master bedroom was as sumptuous as the ballroom, with the same curtains and carpeting, and featuring two even larger crystal chandeliers of very good quality. It was about twenty-five feet square. The other bedrooms were well, though less spectacularly, furnished. The two bedrooms that were not en suite had the use of three full suite bathrooms across the corridor. Indeed, there were seven toilets in the residential part of the property. Like so much else, that seemed perhaps a little excessive. There was a beautiful range of fitted mahogany wardrobes in the main bedroom. On the side of this range, immediately to the left as you entered the bedroom, was posted an A4 sheet of paper containing, in large bold type, the emergency phone numbers of the international clinic and local hospitals. A slight chill went down my spine at this. It seemed an ill omen as we moved into our new, high-status life.[5] It was already getting light as we dispersed into our deep, comfortable beds and fell asleep.

* * *

AFTER A FEW hours' sleep I awoke. It was nine-thirty on a Thursday morning, and beneath me the embassy would be working away. I bathed, shaved, brushed my teeth, dressed in a three-piece suit and walked out into the dining room, where Galina was waiting to make me breakfast. I ate quickly, anxious to get downstairs and inspect my domain. As I left the dining room Galina asked me if I wanted my cappuccino at 11 A.M. She had always taken down cappuccino and biscuits for Christopher Ingham at eleven. As it seemed important to her, I agreed.

A keyboard with a dozen hooks hung outside the kitchen, and I took a bunch of keys from the hook marked OFFICE. I went down to the door off the vestibule, and one of the keys indeed unlocked it. I went through into my office.

This was disappointing. It was very small—about ten feet square. A large modern modular white wood workstation took up nearly half the space. It held a computer, a green-shaded desk light, a mahogany letter rack, an antique brass inkwell set, a huge green leather-bound blotting pad and a variety of china and brass ornaments.

The windows of the office looked out onto a narrow stretch of lawn and the high but elegant wrought iron railings that separated the embassy from the street. Half the width of the street was then further boxed off by huge concrete blocks, to provide a discreet parking area and to give adequate standoff for a level of protection against car bombs. The entrance to this outer area was protected by a lifting heavy metal bar, striped red and white as they always are. A further sliding gate then protected the embassy area proper inside the railings. The bar and gate were set at ninety degrees to each other, so a heavy vehicle that crashed the bar would have to turn right very sharply to attack the gate, something most unlikely to succeed with any momentum.[6]

Aside from the windowed wall, the other three walls of the small office each held a door. One, from the vestibule of the residence, I had just entered through. Above this was a window, through which I could be watched at work from the residence stairs. In the opposite wall a door led through into Karen's office—I walked through and said hello, and she inquired brightly how I was. I told her I just wanted to get my bearings for a bit, and then would talk things through with her. I returned to my office and this time opened the third door, in the left-hand wall as you came from the vestibule. This led into a short, narrow corridor. A wooden door at the end had a lock on it, which I recognized as functioning as a combination lock from the other side. To my left off this corridor was a heavy steel door painted a dull green, with a large iron lever to operate the lock, protected by a combination dial. This, I realized, must be the registry. I went back and got the combination from Karen, declining her offer to open it for me. I managed the lock, swung open the great heavy door, unlocked the less heavy but still substantial wooden inner door and went in.[7]

The registry is the heart of an embassy. Here is kept the sensitive communications equipment for transmitting back to London, and all the top-secret cipher material to program the equipment with. A leak from any of our registries could result in unfriendly intelligence services being able to decode all of our international government communications. Here also is stored bugging and counterbugging equipment and other sensitive stuff. This is where secret and top-secret documents are stored, and where an embassy's confidential files are indexed and held. The registry is the domain of the registry clerk, usually the most junior of the British staff, and the most indispensable.

Jackie was the registry clerk, though now, and indeed most of the time, she was in the consular section conducting visa interviews. The registry was tiny. I worked out it was located under the stairs of the residence. It consisted of two cupboard-sized rooms, one opening off the other. In the first was a narrow desk and computer workstation, a filing cabinet and a steel cupboard containing our "dips." These were trays on shelves on which incoming papers would be placed for the recipient by Jackie. All the documents in the registry were in steel cupboards and cabinets with their own combination locks, to give a further level of security. This first room of the registry was about four feet wide by eight feet long, and I had to squeeze my ample stomach against the filing cabinet to get through.

The second room was even more cramped, containing more filing cabinets and the communications equipment, plus the large air conditioner needed to keep this vital equipment at the right temperature. This room was the same size as the other, but limited still further by an extremely sloping ceiling (the stairs). The keyboard for the communications equipment had to be balanced on top of the screen, which, when you think about it, is extremely difficult to operate.

The equipment was some generations behind current FCO technology. It still operated through the ordinary Uzbek telephone lines. The encryption should render that still safe from interception, but it meant you were dependent on the Uzbek telephone system. Even without ill will, that could not always be relied upon, and very often when there was a line, it was not of sufficient quality to carry the signal. It could take hours or sometimes days to send a telegram.

Worse, the communications equipment stood alone. The computers on desks in our office were networked to each other but not to the comms, which had a completely different operating system. So if I wanted to send a telegram, I would have to draft it on my own computer, print it out, then give it to Jackie, who would type it up again into the comms equipment. Given that 90 percent of Jackie's time was taken up with visa work, getting this done was difficult.

I stood in the registry for a while, thinking over the unexpected problems that were starting to come home to me. I then went back to Karen, who took me round the rest of the embassy. There was not much of this.

We went through to the cramped visa and consular section. Jackie was wearing jeans and a brown T-shirt. She had brown curly hair, a husky voice with a West Country accent and a Celtic-knot tattoo on the top of her left arm. Dave Muir was also conducting interviews. About fifty, he had a ready smile and a world-weary air. He was ex-army and was the archetypal old lag. He always knew an easier way to do anything, and whenever confronted with an idea would immediately declare it impractical.

Two local assistants, Shahida, and Zhenya, worked in the section. Shahida was Uzbek and dark, Zhenya Russian and blond. They both had short, layered haircuts and a professional air.

Through a large bulletproof window a small room—perhaps twelve feet square—housed the customers. About twenty of them were packed in, but there was a large queue outside the railings of the embassy waiting for admission. Dave raised his eyebrows to the ceiling to indicate the hopelessness of the task. Zhenya was theoretically my part-time secretary also. She dealt with my diary, issued invitations and helped organize functions. But again she was too tied up with consular and visa work.

Her desk and computer were in the visa section, across the other side of the building from me, which was an impractical place to have your secretary.

Accounts and administration were handled by Nafisa and Shadia, who said hello shyly from behind a mound of papers. Asol, a severe-looking lady always dressed in black, was the receptionist on the main reception, an armored entrance in the right flank of the building, separate from both the residence entrance in the main facade and the visa entrance in the left flank.

Off reception a large office held the commercial section and the Department for International Development (DFID). Both had only one Uzbek member of staff. The commercial section was run by Lena Son, an ethnic Korean. There are some 400,000 ethnic Koreans in Uzbekistan.[8] Lena was short and slim with shiny bobbed hair. She greeted me with a wide grin. She turned out to be a real treasure—perhaps the most competent member of staff I have ever had, anywhere. Atabek represented DFID. He too was very impressive. Tall and slim, in a well-cut suit, he spoke with great assurance and a slight American accent.

Karen's office was in a corner and could only be entered through Lena and Atabek's office or through mine, as indeed the only internal route up to the residence was through my office. The registry corridor was the only area not accessible to the Uzbek staff. These arrangements were very cramped, and we had to get used to people traipsing through our offices while we were working.

One further wing of the embassy housed the information section, where Chris Hirst worked in a long room lined with beta videocassettes on various aspects of the U.K. The cassettes were to be given to TV stations for free transmission. This was surprisingly effective in countries that struggle to fund program making. They included travelogues on English gardens and a series on successful black entrepreneurs in Britain. As propaganda goes, it was not very harmful.

Chris sat at one desk, and the other desk in this cluttered room was empty. I asked Chris who worked there, and he said the position of information assistant was vacant at the moment. He was unpacking more bundles of material from the information department in London, and I was a bit worried by the impression that the bulk of it seemed to get no further than shelves in the embassy. On a counter sat an old stand-alone PC that was our only link to the Internet, and that pretty intermittent.

Finally I entered a room on the opposite side of the corridor from Chris. This was something of a broom cupboard, with no natural light. There my defense attaché, Nick Ridout, was seated opposite his assistant, Vakhida. Nick was a colonel in the Royal Military Police. He spoke good Russian and had an interest in exploring the history and geography of the country. He seemed genuinely glad to see me. I was pretty shocked at his office accommodations. All in all, there seemed a great deal to sort out at the embassy.

Having become acquainted with my notably small staff, I arranged to give them a pep talk at the start of the next morning. The main message I tried to get across was that I wanted the embassy to make a positive difference to Uzbekistan—to run projects, provide services and to influence the policy of the government of Uzbekistan, the policy back in London and the policy of international institutions, in such a way that the lives of the people in Uzbekistan would be discernibly better for our work.

Over the next few days it became plain that this would be an uphill struggle. The embassy had not been used to an active role. After the staff meeting I asked Zhenya to stay behind, and told her I wanted to pay introductory calls on all the British businesses in Uzbekistan. She seemed startled and asked if I would not prefer them to come to see me. I explained that I wanted to look round the operations, meet the staff, get a feel for what their problems were and whether I could help. I couldn't understand why this perfectly normal request was greeted with such surprise and skepticism by Zhenya. There were only about thirty British companies active in Uzbekistan.

THE FIRST COMPANY I visited was called 3C. It was a small developmental consultancy run by long-term expat James McGrory. As we neared in the car, Valeri was leaning out the window looking for it, and given how few British companies there were in Uzbekistan, I was surprised he didn't know. As the flag car eventually drew up outside his offices, just off Mustakillik Square, James stood outside on the pavement. He was a strong bear of a man, with a ruddy beard, massive shoulders and an even bigger paunch. He looked elegant in a white blazer over a lilac shirt. He had a red carnation in his lapel, which matched his florid complexion, and held a white panama in his hand as he rushed to open the door for me.

He led me up to his office, which was on the second floor and consisted of a couple of rooms leased from the Uzbek state institution that owned the building. He introduced me to the man and woman who comprised his staff, and made me a pleasant cup of green tea.

James seemed extremely happy that I had come, and said that it meant a huge amount to his staff, who indeed seemed terrified into silence when I spoke to them. James had been there more or less since independence in 1991, and had seen all three previous British ambassadors to Uzbekistan. But I was, he said, the first one to visit his offices.

I was incredulous. To me it was a basic requirement to visit the British companies.

James provided advice and assistance to foreign companies looking to invest in Uzbekistan, which was a nightmare of regulation. The laws were so restrictive that in order to be able to operate, every new venture needed a specific statute, issued as a presidential decree, stating what that venture was allowed to do. This needed to be incredibly detailed, because anything not specifically permitted by the decree would be deemed illicit by venal officials looking to be paid off. After some relaxation in the mid-nineties, the situation had deteriorated further and become such a nightmare that foreign investment had almost completely halted. So business was scarce for James. Uzbek economic policy was so hopeless that the International Monetary Fund (IMF) had closed their office and left. With this, much of the aid flow had dried up, which, as aid project consultancy was James's other main area, made the overall outlook pretty bleak for him.

James added that the business climate was so poor that the British community in Tashkent, which had been a couple of hundred in 1995, was now down to about forty. I was subsequently able to confirm this. The embassy had consular responsibility for not just Brits in Uzbekistan, but for several other nationalities who did not have embassies there, including Irish, Australians, New Zealanders, Finnish, Dutch and others. Our total list of consular residents in the whole country had declined from over 500 to 120 as economic opportunity dwindled. The French and German embassies confirmed the same picture. The Indian community had fallen from 5,000 to 500. The only community that was increasing was the American, which had a massive influx of military and intelligence personnel and other aid workers following the opening of the U.S. airbase in Uzbekistan at Karshi Khanabad in the aftermath of September 11.

James had given me a lot of food for thought, and my first real insight into the totalitarian nature of the Uzbek regime. I knew already that it had an appalling human rights record, practiced torture, did not tolerate political opposition and had an entirely state-controlled media. Just three days of reading Uzbek newspapers and watching Uzbek TV news had shown me that. Every single TV news item began, "Today the president of the Republic of Uzbekistan, His Excellency Mr. Islam Karimov . . ." There was an astonishingly heavy police presence in the city, with a knot of policemen on every street corner. There was also a palpable air of fear. Everyone was scared, and even the embassy Uzbek staff dropped their eyes and lowered their voices if you asked them about the political or economic situation. But in my briefings in London, the FCO had spoken as though this were a Southeast Asian model—a highly authoritarian state providing stability in which capitalism was flourishing and society developing. In fact, every day it became more and more plain to me that this was more like a North Korean model, with government stultifying not just political life, but all social, religious and commercial life as well.

Two of the more valuable of these commercial calls I made were on Wakefield Services, a cotton-grading company, and Case Tractors. The latter is a U.S. firm, but was supplying tractors to the Uzbek market from their factory in Basildon, Essex.

From them, I started to learn something of the Uzbek cotton industry. This is an astonishing story. Cotton plantation was introduced here by tsarist Russia to counter the fall in supplies caused by the American civil war. After 1945 there was a massive expansion, and Uzbekistan produced 70 percent of the cotton for the USSR and its satellites, feeding textile mills from Lodz to Vladivostok. Now it was the world's fifth-largest producer, and second-largest exporter, of cotton. The cotton fields were watered by an amazing forty thousand miles of main irrigation canal, with uncountable miles of branches. These open canals and furrows were extremely inefficient—over 90 percent of the water was lost to evaporation. This massive outtake of water for the Uzbek cotton system was responsible for over 80 percent of the loss of supply to the Aral Sea.

More simply put, the Uzbek cotton industry had caused the world's biggest single environmental disaster, as a whole sea had vanished. That was only the start of the environmental consequences. Cotton was a monoculture in Uzbekistan, and most of the land under cultivation had grown the same crop for over fifty consecutive years. Crop rotation was simply not practiced. The result was complete soil exhaustion, necessitating the use of millions of tons of fertilizer. Similarly, keeping the cotton healthy after years of providing the same cotton diet for pests and diseases required application of pesticides at many multiples of safe levels.

The residue of this vast chemical cocktail drained off into the Aral Sea, or as the rivers no longer reached it, into the beds of the remnants of the great Amu Dar'ya and Syr Dar'ya, known to the ancients as the Oxus and the Jaxartes. The shrinking Aral Sea was now an ever-more-concentrated chemical soup, wreathed in clouds of yellow, choking mist. Disease levels, and particularly the incidence of congenital diseases, had gone sky high in Karakalpakistan, Uzbekistan's northern province.

The cotton was grown on state farms by a tied labor force. Sixty percent of the Uzbek population worked on these farms. Not only did Uzbeks need an exit visa to leave the country, they needed a visa or *pro-pusk* to move from town to town or to leave their farm—and they wouldn't get one unless they could afford a hefty bribe. As the standard salary on an Uzbek state farm was 2,000 *sum*—that's two dollars—a month, they wouldn't ever be able to move away. In short, most of the workers in Uzbekistan were cotton slaves, just as surely as were African slaves in the nineteenth-century United States. At Case Tractors, I was told that in Soviet times, over 70 percent of Uzbek cotton was machine picked. Now that figure was under 10 percent.

The monopoly purchasers of cotton were two state trading companies. They bought from the state farm for virtually nothing—the farm got one-thirtieth of the farm gate price of cotton in neighboring Kazakhstan, where the industry had been privatized. As the state trading companies sold the cotton on the international market at world prices, they were massively profitable. Their offices in Tashkent were clad in shiny blue glass, and their executives drove luxury cars. They paid a percentage of their revenues to the state budget, but this was totally nontransparent. The state budget was a secret, as were the revenues of the trading companies. All this left massive scope for stealing, which the Karimov family and their adherents were exploiting to the full.

As I LEFT James McGrory, he again held the door open for me to enter the Land Rover and made some remark about it not being a terribly posh car for an ambassador. That reminded me, and as we drove away I broached the subject.

"How old is the Land Rover, Valeri?"

"Three and a half years, Ambassador."

"Time to get a new car, then?"

"No, Ambassador, I don't think so." He gestured toward the odometer. I squinted from the back at the kilometer reading.

"Ten and a half thousand kilometers! In three and a half years! That's about sixty kilometers a week! What do you do for a living?"

"It's not my fault, Ambassador. I can only go where the ambassador tells me."

Obviously these British companies hadn't been visited before. When I got back, I spoke with Karen.

"Karen, this is a big country. The flag car has hardly any miles on the clock. How do we get around?"

"Well, when the ambassador went on tour, he normally flew."

"Are the flights good?"

"No, but the MFA puts on flights for diplomats sometimes."

"But wouldn't he send the flag car ahead to use when he got there?"

"No, the MFA will provide a vehicle."

"Let me get this straight. You are telling me we only go around this country on Uzbek-government transport and with Uzbek-government escort. How the hell are we supposed to find out what's really happening?"

"Well, we don't travel that often."

Plainly Karen was getting uncomfortable with this line of questioning, and I sensed it would not be productive to pursue the question of how much of the country she and Chris had seen in the past. We had an office meeting every Monday, and I made plain at the next one that I expected we would do much more traveling in future, to build up contacts and gather information around the country. Nick Ridout looked particularly happy about this.

ON SEPTEMBER 1, Fiona and I had to attend the Independence Day celebrations. These cast a further lurid light on the nature of the regime. The massive illuminations I had seen on the way from the airport were in preparation for Independence Day. For two days before, the entire city center, covering several square miles, was sealed off as preparations were made for the celebratory show in Mustakillik Square.[9]

Our invitation to attend the Independence Day celebrations, cast in a formal note from the MFA as instructions rather than an invitation, said that ambassadors must be seated by five-thirty. We left the embassy around five-fifteen. I knew that the center had been sealed off, but I hadn't realized just what that meant. The city's entire transport system was suspended. A series of concentric rings of steel surrounded Mustakillik Square. They were formed of trams, trolleybuses, buses and trucks. Each security ring had a single entrance, at the opposite side to the entrance to the previous circle, so it was like threading your way through a maze.

The scale of the thing was enormous. We drove around many miles of trams, parked bumper to bumper. All the vehicles comprising these rings were jammed up against each other so they absolutely touched and there was no possibility of anyone squeezing through. The only way would be under, but there were several armed soldiers for each vehicle. The outer circles were mostly trams and trolleybuses, the inner circles mostly buses and army trucks. There were in total thousands of vehicles. I was staggered at the sheer dislocation involved in sealing off such a vast area of the city, the inconvenience to people and to businesses, and the crippling of ordinary transport, all for a regime showpiece. It said volumes about the relative importance of state and private sector. I should add that Tashkent is no small city. It has a population of two and a half million, and was the fourth-largest city in the USSR, the home of much Soviet heavy industry and especially a great concentration of armaments manufacture.

We eventually made it through, and were met at the car park by a smooth, English-speaking young man from the MFA. He escorted us to the temporary stadium built for the event, where ambassadors were seated in the order of their arrival in Tashkent. We were seated between the Israeli and the South Korean, who both grinned. The South Korean produced earplugs, which he said the Italian had warned him to bring.

I had presumed that, if we had to be seated at five-thirty, it would begin at six. But six came and went, and nothing happened. As did six-thirty. By seven my backside was getting sore on the plastic seat and I was getting really angry. By the time President Karimov arrived on the dot of seven-thirty, I was livid.

After some speeches the show came on. We had been forced on the plane to sit through a video of the event from the year before, several times. This was just the same: ranks of goose-stepping, singing soldiers and massed tiny tots with balloons, interspersed with Uzbek folk songs and pop singers. A peculiar note was struck by ranks of showgirls who wouldn't have looked out of place in the Moulin Rouge. That cheered me up a bit. The South Korean was lucky with his earplugs—the volume of the music was incredible. It was like being at a rock concert with your head stuck in the bass bin. The plastic seats vibrated like crazy. It went on and on and on. By the time it finished after 11 P.M. with a fireworks display, we had been seated for over five hours.

My mood was not improved by waking up the next morning, still with a loud ringing in my ears from the pounding they had taken. I went down to work and dictated a formal diplomatic note to the MFA, thanking them for inviting me to their interesting show, but saying that it was a gross discourtesy to ambassadors to ask them to be in their seats two hours before an event started. I suggested ambassadors did not constitute a security risk, and requested that future invitations indicate not only what time they wished us to attend, but also what time the event would actually start. I then copied this note to all other embassies.

This caused a sensation. I did not yet know it, but the Uzbek government routinely treated foreign ambassadors with a lack of courtesy bordering on contempt. None of my colleagues had ever raised a whimper before. I was viewed as fantastically daring, and backslapped by the entire diplomatic community. Speaking out for the privileges and dignity of ambassadors made me terrifically popular with the diplomatic corps.

I was to find speaking out on human rights a different matter.

*   *   *

WHEN I FIRST SPOKE to Chris about his job, he told me that he did a lot of human rights stuff, then he added rather resentfully that he didn't expect me to be very interested in that. Now he entered my office and told me that an important dissident trial was beginning that morning, featuring a terrorist suspect named Khuderbegainov.

CHAPTER 4

Diplomacy

Strictly speaking, you are not an ambassador until you have presented your letters of credence, or credentials. These are two letters from your own head of state. One recalls your predecessor as ambassador, and the second appoints you. You have to deliver these in person to the head of state of the country to which you have been appointed.

President Karimov was receiving me and the new Israeli, Japanese and South Korean ambassadors, one after the other. I went with Karen to support me and make sure I didn't lose the letters. I had decided to perform this ceremony in Scottish Highland dress.

I had asked London if I could say something on human rights, in addition to the script I had been given on standing shoulder to shoulder against terrorism and the value we placed on commercial and educational relationships. The FCO had surprised me by replying immediately with a couple of pretty strong sentences on the need for Uzbekistan to improve its human rights record.

The reception was held at the presidential offices in central Tashkent—the president lived in a palace outside the city at Durmen and drove in a huge convoy to work every morning, causing massive road closures and disruption. I was shown through to a vast marbled hall. In the glare of television lights I walked up to Karimov, Karen two paces behind me. We shook hands, Karen handed me the letters from the queen and I handed them to Karimov. He then led me through to a side room. There were five Louis XIV chairs for Karimov, his foreign minister Abdulaziz Komilov, an interpreter, Karen and me. The doors were closed, blotting out the TV cameras, and we sat down to talk.

Karimov was about five foot seven inches, but muscular with a short, broad neck and a thick, jowled face. His Asian eyes were deep set and his skin sallow. His nose was small and wide, his mouth narrow and thin. He moved easily and seemed very assured. His eyes were less dark than his skin color would suggest, and bright with a shrewd intelligence. He had played for twenty years at the top level of a power politics where if you lost, you died, and had ruthlessly eliminated large numbers of people who had crossed him. He wasn't going to be fazed simply by my putting on a kilt.

"I am delighted to see you, Mr. Ambassador," he said through his interpreter. Interestingly, he was speaking Russian rather than his official language, Uzbek. "I have always had the greatest admiration for the wisdom of the United Kingdom. You have had many generations to develop that wisdom."

Subtext: Don't expect any rapid change toward democracy here.

He continued, "One great example of the wisdom of your government, on which I must congratulate you, is that you have just made a derogation from the European Convention on Human Rights to enable terrorist suspects to be detained in the United Kingdom without trial."

Subtext: Don't you lecture me *on human rights; people who live in glass houses . . .*

"The greatest misfortune in the history of the Uzbek people is what happened in what you call the Great Game. Unfortunately, the British were never able to make any progress toward Central Asia, and their efforts to do so met with some very great historic defeats."

Subtext: Your country doesn't really cut that much ice around here.

"It would have been infinitely better for our people if they had been conquered by the British and not by the Russians. Our whole history of development, and especially economic development, would have been different. As it is, of course, we know only the central planning system. You must realize we are a hundred years behind."

Subtext: Don't expect any rapid changes toward capitalism.

"Of course, the danger of militant Islam is a threat to the very existence of Western civilization. For a decade we Uzbeks stood alone to defend the West against Islam. When the allies came to fight the Taliban, it was late. We are still the frontline against Islam. We were vital to the allied effort against the Taliban. We are a poor country and this cost us a lot of resources. It is natural that we should anticipate that, just as our geostrategic position was essential for operations against the Taliban, so it will be also essential for operations to reconstruct Afghanistan. Uzbek companies should be fully employed in this work. We are also the frontline of defense for the West against the flow of narcotics. This too is very expensive for us."

Subtext: Give us a lot of money.

THERE WAS A LOT more of it, but you get the idea. It was a masterly performance. In particular, his opening observation on detention without trial in the U.K. was very shrewd in preempting my own complaints. He was well-informed, as our derogation from the European Convention had only just happened.[1]

I had a number of business points to raise on which we wanted presidential assistance; these included the establishment of the Tashkent campus of Westminster University, the Oxus Mining joint-venture proposal and the Trinity Energy oil extraction contract. Karimov had a good mastery of the detail on each, which was very impressive as he had no notes. As things were going well, I threw in the need for the British Council to find larger premises, which Karimov told his foreign minister to look at sympathetically. Karimov positively beamed with pleasure when I delivered my message of gratitude for Uzbek support in the War on Terror, and ostensibly looked out the window when I delivered my couple of sentences on the need to improve Uzbekistan's human rights record.

He did, however, respond obliquely to this when he gave me what I came to dub his "paranoid speech"—I was to hear it several times, and it was the speech he gave to every Western visitor.

Karimov said Uzbekistan was surrounded by enemies. Afghanistan was still prey to Taliban supporters and their colleagues in the Islamic Movement of Uzbekistan. Following the Tajik civil war, extreme Islamic militants formed part of the government of that neighboring state. Furthermore, Uzbekistan had to combat a return of Russian influence. Russia had troops in Tajikistan and an airbase in Kirghizstan. Uzbekistan was the region's only reliable ally for the West.

Uzbekistan also faced destabilization from the flow of narcotics through Afghanistan and Tajikistan. A more insidious threat came from

China. Substandard goods would undermine Uzbek production. These goods did not comply with safety standards and might be deliberately poisoned. In the light of all these threats, Uzbekistan was obliged to protect itself by measures that were, regrettably, authoritarian.[2]

The first time you heard this litany it was actually quite impressive. It certainly swayed a number of prominent Western officials and politicians, including Donald Rumsfeld and German foreign minister Joschka Fischer. However, I knew enough to distrust Karimov's arguments. I now learned that, while he might be a thug, he was a complex and shrewd one with a profound grasp of detail. I learned two other things. Contrary to diplomatic corps opinion, he understood English. Even though he waited for the interpreter, plainly from his eyes he was following and understanding what I said. Finally, although he was widely rumored to have leukemia, he seemed pretty healthy to me.

As I left, Karimov presented me with a heavy Uzbek robe of the finest silk, striped in many colors.[3] For the next few weeks Uzbek television showed pictures of me in my kilt, being greeted by Karimov. They put it on between showings of the Independence Day celebrations.

I was still continuing my calls on British companies, but having presented my credentials now had further calls to make—on Uzbek ministers and on my fellow ambassadors. This is a protocol requirement, but also quite useful as an information-gathering exercise.

I decided to start with my EU colleagues. Three other EU countries—France, Germany and Italy—had embassies in Tashkent. I started with my French colleague, whose embassy and residence were in a much grander Russian colonial palace than ours, just a couple of hundred yards up the same street.

While we had local guards, at the French embassy I was saluted by smart French military guards in black uniforms and peaked caps. They escorted me through to the main entrance, where I was shown through a series of plush modern offices; the old palace had been substantially remodeled on the inside. Eventually I met my new French colleague, Jacques-Andre Costilhes. A short, black-haired, balding man in his early fifties, eyes sparkling with humor behind brown spectacles, Jacques-Andre looked on the world with wry detachment.

He described the economic situation as disastrous; commercial firms found it increasingly difficult to operate and poverty was increasing. But there were always niches where individual firms could make money. He announced proudly that a French company had made a breakthrough into the state-dominated cotton sector. As for political reform, that was not to be expected. For the development of democracy, realistically we should wait thirty years.

At this point I interjected that, having just been involved in the successful development of democracy in Ghana, I was not so convinced it was impossible in Uzbekistan, where there were such advantages as a high literacy rate. But to progress toward democracy, immediate changes were needed in areas of human rights such as media freedom, while I was concerned about the reports of thousands of political prisoners.

"Listen, my friend," said Jacques-Andre, "the human rights situation is terrible. Everyone knows it. But Uzbekistan is an important ally, nowadays, for the United States. They say that Karimov is a hero in the War on Terror. They have thousands of troops here, and an air force. This is their game. So, we do not mention human rights. If you do, it will achieve nothing, and only make trouble. This is a fabulous country. To see Samarkand, Bokhara, is wonderful. French archaeologists are working on the ancient civilizations of Afrosiyab and Khorezm. The history here is incredible. There is much to do, and the EU nations only require a very little reporting. None of us have major interests here. Me, I do not want to live with trouble in my life."

MY GERMAN COLLEAGUE, Martin Hecker, was ensconced in a large, purpose-built, concrete embassy. He prided himself on a career spent working in the communist bloc, and believed this gave him special insight into the Karimov government. He was tall and spare with a shock of gray hair and blue eyes in a strong face. He too spoke of the impossibility of change, and said the key skill was to understand the mentality of the Karimov regime, and work with them. He stood up and moved to a striking painting on his wall. It was a stable with blurred figures, perhaps indicating a nativity scene. It was painted cunningly so that what looked like the interior was the exterior next time you looked.

"This is an illusionist painting," he said. "It is very fine. It holds an important truth. What is real is not the specks of paint on the paper.

What is real is the impression implanted in your brain. In Uzbekistan we have an illusion that there is progress. The Americans wish to believe this illusion. But the existence of the illusion is itself the most pertinent fact.

"You know, the only thing we can do in practice from this terrible situation is to rescue individuals. This I have done—artists, musicians, writers. We have given many political asylum." He reeled off a few names, which at that time meant nothing to me. "You know," he concluded, "when you cannot affect the general, you must concentrate on the particular."

My ambition remained larger. If we couldn't affect the general, why were we all here?

THE FRENCH AND German embassies each had about thirty diplomatic staff, with counselors, first secretaries and the full range of a normal embassy. We had just six, all but me very junior. The Italians were on the same kind of scale as we were.

But my Italian colleague's office was about the size of my embassy, with beautiful thick carpets and expensive furniture. I was shown into his office by three absolutely gorgeous young women, one Italian and two Uzbek, who were a cliché of office sexiness; white low-buttoned blouses exposing a terrific amount of cleavage, hip-hugging short black skirts with stockings, shiny black high heels. I wondered if this was an Italian diplomatic uniform.

I was installed at one end of his cavernous office waiting for the ambassador, who was preceded into the room by a toy white dog that immediately jumped onto my lap and started slavering all over me, tiny paws on my chest, licking my face. The ambassador came hurrying over, attracting away "Mitzi" with a biscuit. He then sat down in the chair opposite me, and smiled.

Leopoldo Ferri de Lazara had the most beatific appearance imaginable. He had snowy white hair and wore a spotless white linen suit over a pale blue shirt with an open, wide collar. His smile was concerned and kindly, and he had a perpetual air of being slightly puzzled by where he was and what was going on around him. He looked like someone playing God in an old Jimmy Stewart film. He had previously been ambassador to Thailand, and had met his present wife there. Several of his ancestors had been doges of Venice—he had brought their portraits in oil, together with a selection of other contents of his Venetian palace, with him to Tashkent.[4]

Now, on first acquaintance, we sat there as we sipped tea from paper-thin antique china, and Leopoldo eyed me quizzically. He was refreshing to meet because he was much less mealymouthed than other ambassadors about the situation in the country. It was dreadful, and getting worse. The Americans, he declared, were stupid if they thought that supporting a dictator like Karimov was a recipe for long-term stability. The problem with the Americans was not that they failed to learn from history, but that they never understood the complexity of a situation, either at the time or in retrospect. He bemoaned the absence of an EU delegation in Tashkent. The EU Commission had very little understanding of what was happening in the country, and the influence of the EU was nil.

Leopoldo gave an attractive and civilized critique, but showed little sign of any spur to action. This was misleading—over the next year he was to become a most valuable and proactive ally.

The Uzbek government had, on the very day of my arrival, done something extremely baffling. It had physically sealed all its land borders, and closed down all the bazaars in Tashkent. The formal retail sector was very little developed, and the bazaars were simply large open-air markets where 95 percent of consumer needs, from food to clothes to televisions, were retailed. Tashkent had been a major trade center for thousands of years, and the bazaars were as old as that. Suddenly they were closed.

The government had cited health and safety reasons for the closure. The border closures they justified first on the basis of preventing the spread of disease, then as necessary to prevent an influx of substandard consumer goods.

After a couple of weeks it had become clear that this was no temporary measure. Word started to come in from the provinces of bazaars being closed down in other cities. The dislocation effects were extreme—about forty thousand people were directly employed in the bazaars, and probably a larger number in cross-border trade to stock them.

Eric Reynolds, a shrewd Scottish consultant who had been working on an EU project on market management, gave me some valuable insights.

The formal retail sector was dominated by Deputy Prime Minister Alisher Usmanov, a powerful figure whose family owned all the main supermarkets and the largest food-importing company, which had a monopoly on many major commodities, for example, sugar.[5] His competition came from the small traders who carried on the time-honored baggage trade within Central Asia. Wham! All competition had just vanished.

With shop prices at multiples of bazaar prices, and the lack of competition encouraging shopkeepers to jack up prices further, suddenly people in Tashkent couldn't afford to eat.

James McGrory and another excellent British consultant, Peter Reddish, who represented the EU Commission in Tashkent, filled me in further. The Uzbek government was under heavy pressure from the IMF and international community to float the currency, the *sum*. Previously it had been much overvalued, but conversion into dollars had been strictly controlled. In other words, you could get a ridiculously large amount of dollars for your *sum*, if you were a member of the regime and could get permission. Otherwise you couldn't get any.

While not opening up to free conversion, the Uzbek government had started to devalue the *sum*. This seriously struck at the perks of regime members, and a trade-and-retail monopoly was a good way of replacing these perks.

Equally, if free currency conversion did come so anyone could buy dollars for *sum*, the liberalizing effect could be negated by sealing the borders, thus not allowing anyone but the favored few to do anything with dollars if they got them.

It was at just this interesting time that an IMF mission came to town to assess Uzbekistan's economic progress. If progress was achieved, Uzbekistan would be eligible for a standby agreement and Karimov could get his mitts on hundreds of millions of dollars of IMF money. That seemed to me undesirable.

The IMF mission was blessed with an excellent Russian economist. We had lunch together and he shared the above analysis. The term used for *corruption* in the IMF is "economic rent." The antitrade measures were a means of transference of access to economic rent by the elite, from currency access monopoly to trade access monopoly, he declared.

All of which caused a problem for the United States. Having firmly adopted Karimov as a client, they were trying very hard to get the IMF to agree to a standby arrangement. The U.S. ambassador had arranged for a lunch with the ambassadors of the G8 to meet the IMF delegation over lunch. The Russian economist had said he expected some pressure at the lunch, and asked me to back him up.

I had not yet met my U.S. colleague, who had not attended the Independence Day celebrations. The United States residence was in a huge traditional Uzbek house, which fronted straight onto the pavement. Uzbek houses are square in design with a large internal courtyard garden. The U.S. ambassador, John Herbst, greeted me warmly at the door. He was a tall, gangling man with long arms and large hands. He had a fine face with a long thin nose, and wore thick black-rimmed spectacles. He had unruly black hair, which he would run his fingers through in thought, leaving it sticking up. There was something of the schoolboy about him.

We were about twenty around the lunch table, which had John Herbst at one end and the head of the visiting IMF mission, a Dutchman named Eric with an extremely bad wig, at the other. Herbst invited a rather nervous lady named Kathleen to make some opening remarks. She was from the U.S. Treasury, and worked as an adviser inside the Uzbek Ministry of Finance. She stressed the progress made in devaluing the *sum* and in building up foreign reserves, and praised Uzbekistan's debt repayment record.

Invited to give the mission's observations, Eric called on the Russian economist to comment. He agreed progress had been made in devaluation, but said that the Uzbeks were nonetheless behind schedule on current account convertibility. But the recent antitrade measures must be a matter of major concern, and raised fundamental questions about the Uzbek government's commitment to economic liberalization. He was immediately backed up by the resident World Bank representative. This was a grave, bearded Englishman named David Pearce, and he spoke scathingly about the lack of structural reform, particularly on privatization and utility pricing.

The U.S. ambassador then suggested the IMF had the choice of saying the glass was half full or half empty. He saw it as half full. If the progress the Uzbeks had made so far was not rewarded, it would be a slap in the face for the reformers in the Uzbek government, who would lose influence. The French ambassador supported this view, and said that a

French company had been given an important contract in cotton trading, which was a start to privatization.

I should explain why we were pontificating in this way. The IMF is
governed by a board composed of the member nations, rather like the UN
is governed by a Security Council. The United States and the other major
contributors from the G8 have the most weight on the board. The IMF
staff—as represented by Eric and his mission—would present a report
with recommendations, in this case on Uzbekistan and the prospects for
a standby agreement. But it would be the board members who made the
decision, which is why we were discussing it now. Our home governments
would decide on how the board would vote—in the case of the U.K., the
Treasury and the DFID would have the most say. But as Western governments are not full of experts on Uzbekistan, the report and recommendations sent back by their ambassadors in Tashkent, following this lunch,
would have a big influence on the decision.

Eric had a fine line to tread. He had to come up with something intellectually credible, and square this with the desire of the IMF's biggest
shareholder—the United States—for a positive report, at a time when
the Uzbek government was busily ruining its own economy. He also had
to produce a public statement agreed to by the government of Uzbekistan, which was a member of the IMF too.

As the new kid on the block, I had not yet said anything, which had
the advantage that I was able to do some justice to my excellent lunch.
Eric was now talking, and saying that the Uzbek government was claiming a current economic growth rate of 8 percent. This brought laughter
around the table. Eric then said that they were negotiating a figure with
the Uzbek government and thought that their report would say 3 percent
growth.

I was startled into interrupting.

"I'm sorry?"

"Three percent, Ambassador. I think the Uzbek government will
agree to a figure of three percent."

"Well, maybe they will, but it can't be true. I have been visiting a lot
of companies since I came, and talking to people active in various areas
of the economy, and I haven't met one person who doesn't think this
economy is shrinking, not growing."

"I agree," said Leopoldo. "If you wanted an example of how to ruin an economy, then the Uzbek government provides it."

Eric temporized, "Well, the difficulty is there are no independent institutions providing economic statistics, and I certainly agree that government statistics can be misleading. But if you are forced to rely on anecdotal evidence, that is not very reliable either. But consider this. This is largely an agricultural economy. Agriculture accounts for more than sixty percent of gross domestic product. Last year there was a very bad harvest, of both cotton and grains. This year there is a harvest—well, let's not say good, but fair. That already will give you a lot of economic growth."

John Herbst was eyeballing me in a less than friendly manner. "Well, I think that is a very logical explanation on economic growth. Let us look at devaluation now . . ."

I didn't listen to his next few words because I was perusing rapidly a table of statistics David had passed across to me. What were they? Judging by David's eyebrows, there was a killer fact in here somewhere. What the hell was it? Oh . . .

"I am sorry, John," I said, "I just want to clarify something that perhaps I didn't understand on the growth figures. Eric, you said that agriculture was sixty percent of the economy, so that there must be growth this year due to a good harvest, while last year was a bad harvest. Did I understand you?"

Eric, who was trying to eat his lunch, looked up and nodded.

"But," I continued, "by the same logic, last year there must have been a fall because of the very bad harvest. Yet I see the IMF posted a figure last year of four percent economic growth. Now, that just can't be true, can it?"

Eric looked at his papers. "Well, in logic it would be possible if there was also a very bad harvest in the preceding year."

"But there wasn't," said Leopoldo. "It was a good harvest."

The ensuing silence was broken by the German ambassador, Martin Hecker.

"Evidently our young British colleague is an economist. We should be grateful for our number to be augmented in such a fashion. But perhaps we should also remember that Uzbekistan is not Washington or London, or perhaps, I might even say, Berlin. The application of logic does not always apply. Indeed we may say," he gave a discreet sound between a laugh and a cough, "that in the situation we have here in Uzbekistan, logic cannot be a suitable diagnostic approach because the situation itself is not rational. What is required is a more holistic approach, based perhaps on a broader understanding and experience."

Which meant: Let's bend the facts. That is what the international community has done, consistently. The World Bank states that from 1993 to 2003, Uzbek GDP fell from 13.1 billion dollars to 9.9 billion dollars. Yet the IMF has accepted a positive growth figure for all but one of those years, and an average growth figure of 4.2 percent in this period. The best bit is that the World Bank still carries both figures in impossible combination in its Uzbekistan briefing paper.

The lunch established my reputation for being difficult and outspoken, while convincing me that the U.S. was willing to bend any fact in defense of its ally Karimov. It also made me very popular with the IMF staff, including Eric, who was used to being pressured by ambassadors to be soft rather than hard.

THE FOLLOWING DAY I made my courtesy call on John Herbst. There were about sixty diplomats at the U.S. embassy, in addition to all the nondiplomatic staff, the military, the advisers in Uzbek government ministries and a large number of U.S.-aid-funded American personnel.

The Uzbek Karshi Khanabad airbase, known as K2, used to be one of the largest in the Soviet Union. It now housed three squadrons of the U.S. Air Force, guarded by a couple thousand U.S. troops. Halliburton, Dick Cheney's former company, had contractors building the improved airbase facilities and extending the aprons to take more planes. Halliburton was assigned its own U.S. Marine guards. Herbst had a big job, an important part of which was keeping the Uzbek government sweet.

The K2 airbase had been useful for supporting U.S. operations in Afghanistan. Now that the Americans had Baghram airbase in Kabul and access to other Afghan airfields, K2 was no longer necessary for this purpose. But the U.S. had been cock-a-hoop at taking over a major Soviet airbase, and were now preparing for a permanent stay.

The Pentagon had formulated a new doctrine to ensure control of the "wider Middle East." By that, they meant the Middle East as we understand it, plus the Caucasus and Central Asia, which is, of course, a massive belt of oil and gas resources. This "wider Middle East" was to be surrounded by "lily pads." These were airbases that had a permanent garrison but the potential to "open out"—be rapidly expanded to take reinforcement for a massive projection of U.S. military force anywhere throughout the area. The giant airbase at K2 was the easternmost, and one of the most important, of these lily pads. So the U.S. relationship with Uzbekistan was essential to a much wider geostrategic plan.[6]

To house the vastly expanded U.S. operation, a gigantic new embassy was being constructed in Tashkent. This really was a magnificent project, designed to be the headquarters of a U.S. viceregal hegemony over Central Asia. Construction—by Halliburton, naturally—was to start on the great complex in 2004. The design resembled nothing so much as one of Saddam Hussein's great presidential compounds.

In the meantime they had crammed five times more people into the U.S. embassy building than it was designed for—it was initially an old Soviet office block, and so badly built that, shortly after my visit, a U.S. diplomat was almost brained by a huge lump of concrete falling out of the front wall. It was surrounded by a huge, ugly concrete and wire fence, and not even the British ambassador's car was allowed through the front gate. I had to dismount in the street, pass through gate security on foot, enter the building and then be escorted through numerous layers of security by U.S. Marines until I met John Herbst in the tiny attic office, overflowing with books, to which he had retreated in the face of a flood of new staff.

John Herbst was a career diplomat, unlike most U.S. ambassadors, who are party donors. But no one is going to give a million dollars to the Republican party to be made ambassador to Uzbekistan. John was a deeply intellectual man who was basically shy and lacked social skills. I was surprised by how disliked I found he was by almost all of his senior diplomatic staff. Much of that came down to policy—the majority of them were decent people, and up close the Karimov regime was so obnoxious that cooperating with it would make any decent person choke. John, though, was a true believer, whose heart was entirely in the Bush agenda, and was particularly keen on the fact that Karimov was such a strong supporter of Israel.[7]

Now John and I started by going over the economic arguments about the IMF again. He had a disconcerting habit of pausing to consider his reply when engaged in thought about the argument, and these pauses could be really long—about twenty seconds. Most of us cover these moments with empty phrases while we think, but he didn't bother. I had got used to this by the time we got on to human rights.

John argued that the human rights situation was improving. He said that the abolition of the office of censor, earlier that summer, had been a major advance.

"But what are you talking about?" I replied. "The media is completely censored. There is absolutely no real news at all—it's the most arrant propaganda."

"Well, Craig, I don't know how extensive your research has been. But we have a major media project, and there have been a couple of articles in the regional press which have been critical of the decisions of regional officials. And Ruslan Sharipov has published articles attacking government corruption."

"That hardly affects the general picture—they sound like exceptions that prove the rule, from the very fact that you can list the only articles that aren't government propaganda. But the human rights situation is desperate. Do you realize how many torture cases there are now documented?"

"If you are referring to the boiling case, I know you're making a big thing of it, and we are very concerned. But it is an isolated incident. I have never heard of a parallel case. And there has been a real advance on torture. In the Ferghana Valley, three policemen have been convicted of the murder of a detainee. That was after a case which I took up personally with Karimov. That is undoubtedly real progress. Previously officials have been completely immune from any fear of retribution. Nothing will do more to change the behavior of the police and security services."

"I still think that is a drop in the ocean. Human Rights Watch and other NGOs reckon there are some seven thousand prisoners of conscience, held for political and religious beliefs. I must say, from my own research I am starting to think that is an underestimate."

"Yes, but most of those are Muslims."

"I'm sorry?"

"I mean Muslim extremists. Most of those prisoners are Muslim extremists. You know, Karimov has a genuine problem that you can't ignore. He faced armed incursions from the Islamic Movement of Uzbekistan. These bad guys really exist. They are not imaginary. You know, we are all caught up in the War on Terror. We didn't want to be. Nobody in the United States asked for the Twin Towers to be attacked. But we find ourselves defending our very lifestyle. And Karimov is part of that defense."

"Yes, but all the evidence is that the vast majority of those in jail aren't terrorists at all. I don't think they are extremists. Even the ones convicted of membership of Hizb-ut-Tehrir mostly aren't really members. Those who are, aren't violent. The evidence is planted. Most of them are just in jail for following their religion. They aren't extremists."

"You don't think the Taliban were extreme?"

"Yes, I think the Taliban were extreme."

"Well, think about it. Most of these guys who are locked up, if they were in power, they would impose the same kind of society. Have you ever been to Broadway? That's what they call the kind of recreational area here. I like to sit on Broadway and have a quiet beer, watching the Uzbek girls go by in T-shirts and skirts. You know, this society is Western in some ways. If these guys in jail got their way, you would have none of it. No Broadway, no beer, no T-shirts, certainly no miniskirts."

"Look, accepting for a moment that those in jail do want that—and I think that's open to doubt—if that's what they want, they are entitled to their view, as long as they don't turn to violence to try to achieve it. I don't call them extremists."

"Well, that's where we differ. A fully Islamic society, with sharia law, is extremist. Extreme Islam is itself a kind of institutionalized violence. Do you realize how many women would be oppressed if the Islamists got into power? You know, I had six U.S. congressmen visiting here this week. They were given a briefing on human rights by Mikhail Ardzinov of the Independent Human Rights Organization of Uzbekistan. He told those congressmen, straight out, that most of these so-called prisoners of conscience—not just most, the large majority, he said, the large majority—ought to be in prison. Now here's another step forward: Ardzinov's organization has been registered and is fully legal."

"I'm beginning to see why."

"That's really not fair. Ardzinov has a very brave record over many years."

"I look at this another way. People are being locked up because they are Muslim. So are other political dissidents, but most prisoners are locked up for being Islamic. There are no fair trials, and there is a lot of torture in the prisons. We are being seen to support this regime, so we are making Muslims hate us. We are provoking terrorism, not fighting it."

John looked weary, as though he had heard this all before.

"Look," he said, "Karimov's got to keep a tight grip on the Muslims. He also wants to drive forward a reform agenda, but he's facing a lot of resistance from within the governing party. And his biggest problem is his own training. Karimov is a Soviet-trained economist. The problem is, he thinks he understands economics, but all he knows is a lot of false precepts. Karimov is the best Uzbek leader we'll get, and he's not personally corrupt."

That really did throw me. Herbst was understandably keen to put the best possible gloss on the regime, but this bit about Karimov not being corrupt was so far at variance with all received information, it made me wonder just how out of touch Herbst was.[8]

My NEXT CALL was on Rustam Azimov, the minister for economic affairs. I wanted to meet him before sending off my telegram about what to do at the IMF. He was touted by the Americans as a leading reformer, and certainly looked like an Italian banker, with his sharp silk suits and American accent. He stressed the progress made on devaluation and foreign currency reserves.

I pressed him on why there had been almost no progress on privatization, and particularly annoyed him by describing most of the privatization as false, involving shifting of assets between entities that were all ultimately state owned. He replied with a barrage of statistics that were patently untrue—I wondered how on earth he could trot them out with a straight face, but I suppose it was Soviet training.

He got pretty angry when I questioned why the borders were closed. He simply denied they were closed. I told him I had visited several border crossing points myself, as had other EU embassies, and they were indeed shut. He looked at me levelly.

"You are mistaken," he said. "They are not closed. They are controlled."

He *really* got angry when I asked him when there would be a move to privatization in the cotton industry. No country, he declared, would allow the privatization of its most important industry. I told him that statement was simply wrong, and further pointed out that Kazakhstan next door had privatized its cotton industry, resulting in a threefold increase of production very quickly. Azimov became quiet and intense.

"That is untrue. Any increase is due only to criminals smuggling Uzbek cotton."

"I don't think that's true. As you know, the cotton is mostly sold through the Liverpool Cotton Exchange. The figures on increasing Kazakh production come from the traders. Anyway, privatization is the answer to smuggling. Cotton sells for the market price in Kazakhstan, that's why it gets smuggled there. If you had a market price here, it wouldn't be smuggled."

"Ambassador, this is not Poland. Privatization here would lead to mass unemployment and social collapse. You know, I am a director of the European Bank for Reconstruction and Development. I am the longest-serving director. Let me tell you this. Poland only survived privatization because it received eighteen billion dollars of economic assistance from the West. We have received almost nothing."

It was very much Azimov's style to blind you with statistics and his air of great assurance, but yet again he was talking complete rubbish. Having run the economic section of the British embassy in Warsaw, I knew this stuff.

"I am sorry, Minister," I said, "but you're simply mistaken. Poland didn't receive one billion dollars, let alone eighteen. Besides I don't think it would have helped. East Germany did receive massive transfers, and Poland didn't. Yet Poland grew quicker than East Germany. Other factors are far more important, like labor costs and deregulation. In fact, I would argue too much subsidy can be harmful."

Azimov sat back, a satisfied look on his face: "There is no point in arguing with someone who simply follows the dogma of the economic liberal."

*   *   *

IT WAS SEPTEMBER 11, 2002—the first anniversary of the destruction of the Twin Towers. I had been invited to a commemoration held by the U.S. embassy in the ballroom of the Intercontinental Hotel in Tashkent. I was attending with mixed feelings. Of course I felt unalloyed sorrow and even despair at the heartlessness of this terrorist act. Yet the United States was using this horror to provide a screen for pushing its very material interests in oil and gas. In Uzbekistan this took the form of giving strong backing to an extremely unpleasant dictatorship. I had, in just one month, seen how that regime operated close up, in the Khuderbegainov trial and in the case of the dissidents who had been boiled to death. I had also seen Colin Powell, astonishingly, certify Uzbekistan's human rights record to Congress as acceptable, and seen the U.S. protect Uzbekistan from justified criticism in the IMF over its continued Soviet and increasingly kleptocratic economic policy.

Security was heavy, and after a long queue for the metal detectors I entered the ballroom and had a Coke and some cashew nuts, while saying a few polite but somber words to diplomatic colleagues. The ceremony was simple—John Herbst read out a text about the atrocity and the evils of terrorism, supported by Uzbek Foreign Minister Komilov. A tape was played of a mobile telephone call from the Twin Towers, suddenly cutting off.

For the next few days I struggled with my conviction that, in supporting Karimov, the U.S. had got its Central Asian policy thoroughly wrong, and that we in turn were wrong to follow the U.S. I knew that as ambassador it was my duty to inform Jack Straw and Whitehall of my view. But I was also aware that my view would be acutely unpopular, especially with my own immediate line manager, Simon Butt, and with 10 Downing Street. I knew that to say what I wanted to say was likely to damage my career pretty severely. I talked it over with Fiona, who said that I should remember my obligation to supporting my children, but she appreciated that my conscience must come first. She then rather sourly concluded that she did not know why I was consulting her, as I always did what I wanted anyway.

In this period I received in my office a young analyst named Duncan from the FCO's research analysts. He was researching regional security issues in the former Soviet Union and he was most concerned about the threat of increasing Islamic militarism in Uzbekistan feeding through into international terrorism.

I was relieved to find that Duncan shared my analysis. He felt that the Karimov regime had no intention of adopting real reform, was completely beyond the pale on human rights and was creating a tinderbox through harsh repression leading to resentment and reaction. He was the first to point out to me that the neoconservatives in the Bush camp, particularly the so-called intellectuals of the religious right, were talking of a United States–Israel–Uzbek axis driving a military wedge into the heart of Islam—thinking picked up by Donald Rumsfeld in his "lily pad" policy.

Duncan told me the research analysts despaired of our blind support for Bush in Central Asia, which had somehow been subsumed into the U.S. notion of the "wider Middle East." The Eastern Department held a radically different view from the research analysts and were, driven by Simon Butt and Dominic Schroeder, blindly "Atlanticist," or pro-American. The policy of backing nasty dictators would certainly rebound on us—it always does—but they just couldn't see it.

FCO research analysts have a key role in assimilating material from media, academic and other open sources, combining it with diplomatic reporting and intelligence material and then analyzing the result. To give an idea of their role, they lead in discussions between Whitehall and the U.S. National Security Council. They play an important role in the Joint Intelligence Committee and its subcommittees.

They would therefore have been central to the preparation of the dossier on weapons of mass destruction in Iraq. I had always found our research analysts to be very bright, with a strong reputation in the academic world and a lot of personal integrity. It was therefore beyond me how they had signed up, as they must have, to the dossier. I asked my visitor whether it was the rubbish it seemed, or whether there was knockdown evidence I was unaware of. He said the dossier was indeed the rubbish it seemed. There were no Iraqi WMD. History has proven him right.

I hadn't asked the next question, but it hung in the air between us.

"You're wondering why we signed up to it?" he asked. "Well, I can promise you it was awful. The pressure was unbelievable. People were threatened with the end of their careers. I saw analysts in tears. We felt, as a group, absolutely shafted. Actually, we still do. You know, I think we are all a bit ashamed that nobody had the guts to go public, resign and say that the WMD thing is a myth. But MI6 really hyped it. The DIS [Defence Intelligence Service] tried to block it, but they couldn't."

On September 16, I locked myself in my office and spent the first half of the morning writing a long telegram on the IMF and Uzbek economic policy, specifically stating that we should oppose, within the IMF and other international financial institutions, attempts by the United States to get an easy ride for Uzbekistan, particularly as they were based on false claims about progress in economic reform.

The telegram included these paragraphs:

> 13. In 20 years in power, 11 of it in charge of an independent country, Karimov has overseen extraordinarily little economic liberalisation and I see no reason to believe he has changed his views now. The only two people I have met in three weeks who profess to believe that Karimov really intends to introduce genuine market reforms are the US Ambassador and the MFA press spokesman. I do not see how, with even the slightest scrap of integrity, the IMF can approve this so-called reform programme. I have worked on economic affairs in post-communist transition countries and in developing countries. This country is not in transition and is not developing.

> 14. I have asked the views of my diplomatic colleagues as I paid my courtesy calls. Let me be very plain about the next point. I have been told separately by the World Bank and EBRD resident representatives, and individually by the French, German, Italian, Slovak, Czech, Polish, Indian, Pakistani and Russian Ambassadors, that a political deal has been reached in Washington, post September 11, that in return for American use of Uzbek air facilities the IMF would approve the Uzbek economic programme (after pulling out in disgust two years ago). The World Bank rep and the Russian Ambassador (both angrily), plus the French, Italian and Pakistani ambassadors (cynically) and the German and Czech Ambassadors (sadly), made explicit their view that this meant approval would be given whether the Uzbeks deserved it or not.

> 15. The German Ambassador pointed to a painting on his wall named "Illusion." He said that if you went to the theatre to see an illusionist you

all enjoyed the spectacle of seeing a man walk on air. You knew it was really impossible, but to remove the curtain would spoil the show. When the IMF came we would all be in the theatre marvelling at the reforms and agree not to look behind the curtain.

16. Which is a good analogy but a stupid idea. This is not an entertainment but affects real lives—especially the poor of Uzbekistan, who have African levels of poverty in this terribly unequal and appallingly governed society. Without real economic reform soon poverty will worsen still further. And that will breed more Islamic fundamentalism (see MIFT). You do not encourage real reform by applauding fake reform. The poor of Uzbekistan should not become more victims of September 11.

MIFT stands for "My Immediately Following Telegram." I then drank a cup of coffee, went to the bathroom, stared out the window and sucked on my pen. When I returned to my desk, once I started the telegram, it came fluently, and my fingers on the keyboard could not keep up with my thoughts. It contained in a few paragraphs the concentrated essence of a month's experience in Tashkent, a month's thinking and soul-searching. This is what I wrote:

FM Tashkent
TO FCO, Cabinet Office, DFID, MODUK, OSCE Posts, Security
  Council Posts
16 September 02
SUBJECT: US/Uzbekistan: Promoting Terrorism

SUMMARY
  1. US plays down human rights situation in Uzbekistan. A dangerous policy: Increasing repression combined with poverty will promote Islamic terrorism. Support to Karimov regime a bankrupt and cynical policy.

DETAIL
  2. The Economist *of 7 September states: "Uzbekistan, in particular, has jailed many thousands of moderate Islamists, an excellent way of converting their families and friends to extremism." The* Economist *also spoke of "the growing despotism of Mr. Karimov" and judged that "the past*

year has seen a further deterioration of an already grim human rights record." I agree.

3. Between 7,000 and 10,000 political and religious prisoners are currently detained, many after trials before kangaroo courts with no representation. Terrible torture is commonplace: the EU is currently considering a démarche over the terrible case of two Muslims tortured to death in jail apparently with boiling water. Two leading dissidents, Elena Urlaeva and Larisa Vdovina, were two weeks ago committed to a lunatic asylum, where they are being drugged, for demonstrating on human rights. Opposition political parties remain banned. There is no doubt that September 11 gave the pretext to crack down still harder on dissent under the guise of counter-terrorism.

4. Yet on 8 September the US State Department certified that Uzbekistan was improving in both human rights and democracy, thus fulfilling a constitutional requirement and allowing the continuing disbursement of $140 million of US aid to Uzbekistan this year. Human Rights Watch immediately published a commendably sober and balanced rebuttal of the State Department claim.

5. Again we are back in the area of the US accepting sham reform. In August media censorship was abolished, and theoretically there are independent media outlets, but in practice there is absolutely no criticism of President Karimov or the central government in any Uzbek media. State Department call this self-censorship: I am not sure that is a fair way to describe an unwillingness to experience the brutal methods of the security services.

6. Similarly, following US pressure when Karimov visited Washington, a human rights NGO has been permitted to register. This is an advance, but they have little impact given that no media are prepared to cover any of their activities or carry any of their statements.

7. The final improvement State quote is that in one case of murder of a prisoner the police involved have been prosecuted. That is an improvement, but again related to the Karimov visit and does not appear to presage a general change of policy. On the latest cases of torture deaths the Uzbeks have given the OSCE an incredible explanation, given the nature of the injuries, that the victims died in a fight between prisoners.

8. But allowing a single NGO, a token prosecution of police officers and a fake press freedom cannot possibly outweigh the huge scale of detentions, the torture and the secret executions. President Karimov has admitted to 100 executions a year but human rights groups believe there are more. Added to this, all opposition parties remain banned (the President got a 98% vote) and the Internet is strictly controlled. All Internet providers must go through a single government server and access is barred to many sites including all dissident and opposition sites and much international media (including, ironically, waronterrorism.com). This is in essence still a totalitarian state: there is far less freedom than still prevails, for example, in Mugabe's Zimbabwe. A Movement for Democratic Change or any judicial independence would be impossible here.

9. Karimov is a dictator who is committed to neither political nor economic reform. The purpose of his regime is not the development of his country but the diversion of economic rent to his oligarchic supporters through government controls. As a senior Uzbek academic told me privately, there is more repression here now than in Brezhnev's time. The US are trying to prop up Karimov economically and to justify this support they need to claim that a process of economic and political reform is underway. That they do so claim is either cynicism or self-delusion.

10. This policy is doomed to failure. Karimov is driving this resource-rich country towards economic ruin like an Abacha. And the policy of increasing repression aimed indiscriminately at pious Muslims, combined with a deepening poverty, is the most certain way to ensure continuing support for the Islamic Movement of Uzbekistan. They have certainly been decimated and disorganised in Afghanistan, and Karimov's repression may keep the lid on for years—but pressure is building and could ultimately explode.

11. I quite understand the interest of the US in strategic airbases and why they back Karimov, but I believe US policy is misconceived. In the short term it may help fight terrorism but in the medium term it will promote it, as the Economist *points out. And it can never be right to lower our standards on human rights. There is a complex situation in Central Asia and it is wrong to look at it only through a prism picked up on September 12. Worst of all is what appears to be the philosophy underlying the current US view of Uzbekistan: that September 11 divided the world into two camps in the "War against Terrorism" and that Karimov is on "our" side.*

12. *If Karimov is on "our" side, then this war cannot be simply between the forces of good and evil. It must be about more complex things, like securing the long-term US military presence in Uzbekistan. I silently wept at the 11 September commemoration here. The right words on New York have all been said. But last week was also another anniversary—the US-led overthrow of Salvador Allende in Chile. The subsequent dictatorship killed, dare I say it, rather more people than died on September 11. Should we not remember them also, and learn from that too? I fear that we are heading down the same path of US-sponsored dictatorship here. It is ironic that the beneficiary is perhaps the most unreformed of the world's old communist leaders.*

13. *We need to think much more deeply about Central Asia. It is easy to place Uzbekistan in the "too difficult" tray and let the US run with it, but I think they are running in the wrong direction. We should tell them of the dangers we see. Our policy is theoretically one of engagement, but in practice this has not meant much. Engagement makes sense, but it must mean grappling with the problems, not mute collaboration. We need to start actively to state a distinctive position on democracy and human rights, and press for a realistic view to be taken in the IMF. We should continue to resist pressures to start a bilateral DFID programme, unless channelled non-governmentally, and not restore ECGD* [Export Credit Guarantee Department] *cover despite the constant lobbying. We should not invite Karimov to the UK. We should step up our public diplomacy effort, stressing democratic values, including more resources from the British Council. We should increase support to human rights activists, and strive for contact with non-official Islamic groups.*

14. *Above all we need to care about the 22 million Uzbek people, suffering from poverty and lack of freedom. They are not just pawns in the new Great Game.*

MURRAY

It is important to understand the background to this telegram. We had just fought a war in neighboring Afghanistan and were gearing toward another in Iraq. Tony Blair had staked all on standing "shoulder to shoulder" with George W. Bush, and the War on Terror and the righteousness of the U.S. cause were unquestionable. I was going way out on a limb.

After I had sent it, I walked through to Chris Hirst's office. Chris was squatting on the floor, going through some documents in a cupboard.

"I know the bastard's here somewhere," he said, standing up. I handed him the telegram, saying he might like to look at it. He looked dubious, but his interest grew as he read, and he became increasingly absorbed. He finished and handed it back, shaking his head.

"Well, what do you think?" I asked.

"Pretty long for a resignation letter," he said.

It was not many days before the attack from my line management came, in the form of a letter from Simon Butt. He was concerned, he wrote, that I was "overfocused on human rights," to the detriment of the balance of U.K. interests in Uzbekistan. He was also most concerned that I was discussing human rights cases in open e-mail correspondence, and making comments about the Uzbek government, in e-mails and on open phone lines, which were likely to be intercepted by the Uzbek security services and thus damage the U.K./Uzbek relationship. My performance was causing concern, and would be closely monitored.

CHAPTER 5

The Ferghana Valley

I WAS DETERMINED TO SET AN EARLY EXAMPLE TO THE STAFF OF GET-
ting around the country, and wanted to get up into the Ferghana Valley.
This high valley, a fertile floodplain where tributaries from the great mountains combine to form the Syr Dar'ya and Amu Dar'ya rivers, nestles in the
foothills of the Himalayas, between the High Pamirs and the Tien Shan,
the Heavenly Mountains.

The valley is heavily populated, home to over ten million people. The
five countries of Central Asia together have a land area six times the size of
Texas. Twenty-five percent of the entire population of this vast area live in
the Ferghana Valley, which is about the size of Vermont.

It is, in a very real sense, the heart of Central Asia. It ought to be the
economic powerhouse of the region. To explain why it is not, I need to
say something about the crazy geography of Central Asia.

The Ferghana Valley is split between Kirghizstan, Tajikistan and
Uzbekistan. The borders of these three countries, and not just in the Ferghana Valley, intertwine and convolute as though they were a jigsaw cut
by a one-armed alcoholic. In the Ferghana Valley there are seven enclaves
of Uzbekistan entirely cut off by surrounding countries.

This is the difficult bit to grasp: the borders are deliberately nonsen-
sical and specifically designed to prevent viable economic units, and to
deny any political, cultural or ethnic coherence. The terms *Kirghizstan,
Tajikistan* and *Uzbekistan* might give the impression that they are the ethnic home of the Kirghiz, Tajiks and Uzbeks. In fact, nothing could be further from the truth. For example, the major Uzbek town of Osh, in the
Ferghana Valley, is over the border in Kirghizstan. The centers of the great
Tajik culture, Samarkand and Bokhara, are not in Tajikistan, but in

Uzbekistan, even though 90 percent of the populations of those cities remain Tajik-speaking—although now subject to drastic Uzbek government attempts to choke out the language.

The Soviet Union was in theory just that—a Union of Soviet Socialist Republics. Kirghizstan, Uzbekistan and Tajikistan were three of them. But Stalin had no intention of allowing the republics to become viable entities or potential power bases for rivals. So they were deliberately messed up with boundaries that cut across natural economic units like the Ferghana Valley. As a result, the valley is a likely ethnic and religious flashpoint.

AFTER TWO WEEKS in Tashkent we had said good-bye to Jamie, who had returned to boarding school in the U.K. This was always a wrench. I was worried about Emily, and very much hoped that the Tashkent International School—largely U.S.-government funded—would prove adequate for her age group.

Fiona was keen to accompany me on trips and see as much of the country as possible. I think she was also keen to limit my chances of sexual adventures while on the road.

I asked Chris to organize the visit. I told him I wanted to call on the local authorities, and to visit major companies, with a special emphasis on businesses in which there was a British interest, and also projects financed by the European Bank for Reconstruction and Development (EBRD). I also wanted to visit any British or EU aid projects and call on consular nationals who fell under my protection. On top of this, I wanted to visit universities, and call on opposition or human rights activists.

This was a pretty tall order for Chris to get organized at a fortnight's notice. The logistics of travel in Central Asia are complicated, and the authorities obstructive. It was plain to me that the embassy had not operated at this level of intensity in the past, and I was interested to see how Chris would perform. In fact, he pulled it all together brilliantly.

I was going to need an interpreter. My Russian was quite good, but my understanding of Uzbek and Tajik was virtually nil. As I was going to be holding meetings outside governmental circles, I would need someone with a good range of language skills.

Normally an embassy will have an in-house interpretation staff. The information assistant would be the usual person called in. But the empty desk in Chris's office was where the information assistant should have been. When I asked Karen, it turned out that this position had been vacant for months, and that there was no recruitment in progress.

The embassy in Tashkent was, in every respect, understaffed and underresourced. At the collapse of the former Soviet Union, we had made a policy decision to set up in the new republics, but never made a fundamental rethink of resources. So these embassies just got by on a shoestring.[1]

What bothered me now was that, within a petty resource allocation, we hadn't even bothered to fill a key position for supporting our political and PR work. It wasn't only interpreting—Chris should have had his assistant organizing my tour, while he got on with other things.

Chris simply said he hadn't felt the need for an assistant. When I pressed Karen to recruit one, she started by saying that Chris didn't like working with people. That was an extraordinary statement. Seeing the look on my face, she amended it by saying that he didn't like having anyone in the room with him.

I replied, "Well, tough shit," and told her to launch a recruitment immediately. To me the conclusion seemed obvious—Karen was older than Chris. She didn't want him working in proximity to an assistant who, given the job description, was more likely than not to be female.

In fact, I was disastrously wrong.

KAREN DID, HOWEVER, tell me that Vakhida, Colonel Nick Ridout's assistant, had been Chris's last assistant and had moved to the defense section. Muttering under my breath about the bloody Ministry of Defense poaching our staff, I went to ask Nick if I could borrow Vakhida for a few days. I found him outside in the embassy garden, puffing away on his pipe, panama on head, wearing red cavalry trousers and a long jacket that looked borrowed from Wild Bill Hickock. He readily agreed that she could join me for the start of my tour, but he needed her back to interpret at meetings. She would have to return with Fiona and Emily when they came back after the weekend for Emily to start school. We would therefore have to find another interpreter for my last few days in the valley.

Finding Russian/English interpreters in Uzbekistan is not difficult. Interpretation between English and Uzbek, Kazakh or Tajik is not easy to get. This is because the educated elite can't speak the native languages, and those who do will rarely have had the chance to learn English, certainly not up to good interpretation standards.

It was a bit of a squash in the Land Rover. Gafur was driving rather than Valeri, who spoke only Russian. Fiona, Emily and I were in the backseat, with Vakhida in front with Gafur. Vakhida was a very pretty girl, with short layered dark hair and a dark complexion. She always dressed smartly in a high-buttoned blouse and skirt with sensible shoes. She came from Karakalpakistan.

We headed out of Tashkent and into the countryside on good, blacktop roads. The landscape was dry and dusty, much of it an angry red. We drove through the dilapidated iron-making town of Angren, and after a couple of hours we were heading up the escarpment, on a sharp, winding mountain road formed from concrete slabs. White water rushed by in the valley bottom below, while the mountains were jagged, inhospitable and largely uninhabited. It had been 104 degrees in Tashkent and wasn't cool here, but the peaks were still snowcapped above us. Our ears popped as the road ran up and up. Finally it dived into low tunnels smashed through the mountain, shortcutting another eight hundred feet of elevation on a twisting climb over the original pass.

At the end of the Soviet Union, when the borders of Uzbekistan, Kirghizstan and Tajikistan changed from administrative internal borders to international borders, the main road from Tashkent to the valley repeatedly crossed the Kirghiz border. That ancient road ran through Khojand and was taken by Alexander the Great after his two-year sojourn in Samarkand, where he married Roxanne. It was on this ancient road he decided finally to stop his incredible drive east, and turned south over the great mountains of the Hindu Kush to India. As he turned he founded in the neck of the Ferghana Valley the city that marked the end of his empire—Alexandria Eschate, or Alexandria the Farthermost.

Nowadays the ancient main route Alexander had trod led through Kirghizstan, so the Uzbek government had upgraded an alternative minor route within Uzbekistan, and cut the tunnels at the top.[2]

Entering the valley, the first thing that strikes you is the sheer weight of military and police presence. We had passed a dozen or more police barriers on our way from Tashkent to the valley, but we had been waved straight through most of them. Here we were held up at both the entrance and the exit of the tunnel while our passports and the car documents were inspected. Then in the valley itself the number of checkpoints was much greater, including the entrance to and exit from all the towns and villages.

The soil was notably darker here, the mountain air fresher and, while it was still warm, the temperature a few degrees lower. Traveling into the valley, the villages consist of trim, single-story, whitewashed cottages fronting onto the street. The roads are lined with flower beds, glowing yellow and red in the summer sun. The fields are filled with endless rows of dark green shrubs. The valley presents a facade of rural contentment.

We stopped in the city of Kokand, which in the nineteenth century was the seat of a khanate ruling over the valley, its power spreading down onto the Uzbek plain. We were met here by local government representatives, headed by the town *hokkim,* or mayor, and we looked over the ruins of the khan's palace, an ancient cemetery and the surviving madrassa, all of which were very fine.

Afterward the local authority representatives took me for my first formal Uzbek meal. I wasn't fully prepared for the sheer volume of food. The table was loaded with grapes, pomegranates, walnuts, almonds, raisins, sultanas, dried apricots, mulberries and plates of cold meat. These were followed by bowls of soup, containing thick hunks of lamb on the bone, then grilled liver, then lamb kebabs. These alternated lumps of meat with great gobbets of fat, crisped on the outside but gushing liquid fat as you bit into them. Finally there was *plov,* fragrant and wonderful. Our hosts had started the meal by breaking the roundels of naan bread and handing it around. This little ceremony was always employed at mealtimes, with the host or father of the family breaking the bread. I realized that when Christ did it, he was not initiating but following a tradition.[3]

I was becoming used to the guarded way that everyone spoke in Uzbekistan. One of the few times the conversation had sparked into life was when we discussed soccer. The *hokkim* said the best teams in Uzbekistan were all in the Ferghana Valley. I commented that there must be great rivalry between the fans. His face lit up, and in a lively voice he

started on an anecdote: "Oh yes, I remember when . . ." Then he recol-
lected himself, the smile left his face and he said in a dull tone, "I remember that the president says that sport is an important factor in building a
healthy nation and uniting our youth."

WE DROVE ON TO Ferghana city itself, police cars in front and behind,
sirens blaring as we approached any crossroads. There were policemen
everywhere, and they all saluted as we passed. Night had fallen by the
time we pulled into the car park of the Zigurat Hotel. A gaggle of men
in black suits were waiting to greet us. While they sorted out the rooms
with Vakhida, we were ushered through to a feast set like the last one.
Had I been on my own, I would have politely sat through it, but as things
were, I explained that we had just been royally entertained in Kokand. At
our hosts' insistence we sat for a little soup, after which we were obliged
to make a show of eating *plov*, but we managed to keep it down to twenty
minutes.

This time our hosts did not sit with us, but a couple of dark-suited
men stood watching us eat. At one stage I got up to go to the bathroom,
and was astonished when one of them followed me inside. He stood by
the washbasins, and then followed me out again. After this dinner, we
took a rickety lift to our room on the fourth floor. Gafur had already put
our luggage in, but our hearts fell when we saw the room. It looked dirty,
decorated in brown and a gray that was meant to be white. A dark patch
spread from the ceiling to the wall, damp to the touch. The bedclothes
felt cold and moist. It had been a tiring day, and we just climbed into the
bed and pulled the covers over all three of us. I told Fiona about the man
following me into the bathroom. She giggled, got out of bed, opened the
door a crack and peeked out. She came back and reported that two men
in black suits were standing at one end of the corridor, and one at the
other end.

"Are we being protected, or watched?" she asked.

"Both," I replied.

The next morning the room looked even grottier, and Emily's feet were
picking up dirt from the carpet. There was no hot water, and only a trickle
of cold. We went downstairs for a breakfast of tea and cold pancakes
stuffed with cottage cheese. The same men in black were still around,

looking like they had been up all night. I had a brief conversation with the receptionist. He spoke excellent English with a slight Liverpool accent. Much to my surprise, he said he had studied there.

Vakhida had come to our room in the morning and explained apologetically that the accommodations were provided by the *hokkimyat*. She would see what could be done about improving them.

We set out for our first meeting of the day, at a large square that hosted a war memorial. Here the regional *hokkim* came to meet us. There were television cameras, and a row of schoolgirls in bright silk costumes. They presented me with bread and salt. As primed, I broke the bread, sprinkled on salt, handed a piece to the *hokkim,* and then ate myself. This was greeted with much enthusiasm and backslapping.

The *hokkim* left us in the charge of one of his deputies for the day. Ferghana is a modern industrial town, of which the oldest parts are the Russian cantonment. There is some splendid colonial architecture, with Russian houses from the end of the nineteenth century, from the ornate governor's mansion down through distinguished officers' residences to rows of barracks. There are also public buildings, including the exquisite pink baroque theater and assembly rooms, now an Uzbek army officers' mess. The parquet flooring inside these buildings is fabulous. I was struck by how universal colonial architecture is. We might have been in Simla or Singapore.

Margilan and Ferghana have grown into one large conurbation, but Margilan is an ancient Uzbek city. It is the center of the silk industry, and twenty-five thousand workers were employed in the textile mills in the early 1990s. The inefficiency of the huge state-run factories, and Karimov's antitrade measures, had reduced output and staff, but the silk industry remained the mainstay of the town.

We were not visiting one of the main mills, but a small private venture that had received assistance from the British Council. The effusive owner greeted us at the gate and proudly showed us his factory. He had started with hand spinning and looming, but had now acquired two power looms, discarded by one of the state mills. We were too late in the season to see the worms feeding on mulberry leaves, but we saw the rows of ladies seated on low stools, boiling and unraveling cocoons and spinning the threads.

The power looms were not yet working, but a large hall housed several dozen hand looms, each producing a strip of cloth about four feet wide. The complex patterns required a great deal of tying and knotting. Sunlight streamed through on the bright strands of silk. The brilliant colors were the product of artificial dyes, but we visited a hut where a happy dyer, his face streaked with purple, sat amid crucibles and bubbling pots, peering into a small kiln. He was experimenting with producing natural dyes from local plants and minerals, a skill that had been lost in the Soviet period.

Most effort went into producing cloth in Uzbekistan's famous atlas design. That is, famous within Uzbekistan—the design doesn't travel well. It consists of very bright clashes of many colors arranged in huge jags across the cloth. This is hard either to export or to sell to tourists. The British Council had paid for designers to work with the factory to produce designs that had more chance in a Western market. The owner proudly showed me some of these—they were single pastel colors with an edging in a complementary shade. Given the high quality of the silk and the prices—$5 a square meter—the factory was now having some success.

They were opening a new carpet-making facility. This was the purpose of the new natural dyes.[4] In the carpet shed, young girls sat in pairs on the floor, in front of looms, knotting intricate patterns. One worked the left of the carpet, one the right. Consulting a cardboard pattern, they threaded silk through a fine cotton mesh and knotted each thread in place before deftly trimming it off with a sharp knife. I looked at the back of the frame, amazed by the intricacy of the work in that half-light.

"Seven hundred eighty-seven knots per square inch," explained the proud owner.

"How long does it take to make a carpet?"

"A small carpet, under five feet in length, will take two girls four months. We can run two shifts, and do it in two months."

"Aren't they a bit young to be working like this?"

"Ah no, they are at least sixteen. They have to have small fingers for the work."

He turned to the crew from the local television station, and beamingly announced that I had agreed to purchase a carpet for $350. This was met with great applause. He later apologized for this, saying that it was expected. He would, however, give me a "special price" of $300.

Emily was loaded down with small gifts, as always happened everywhere we went in Uzbekistan. As we returned to the director's office for formal good-byes, we passed for the third time the company *chaikhana,* or tearoom. There was always a large group of men there, drinking tea, playing board games and lying down on *karpachas*—narrow, thick-quilted blankets. I realized that, except for the dyer, all the workers had been female. I asked whether the men in the *chaikhana* were pensioners.

"Of course not, they are the workers of our factory."

"But they don't seem to do anything. All the work is done by women."

"Ambassador, I am a simple man. I just want to sell silk, not to overturn the natural social order."

IN THE AFTERNOON we took a sightseeing trip to one of the Uzbek enclaves in Kirghizstan, traveling through idyllic alpine scenery to a country residence owned by the *hokkim.* When we returned to Ferghana we found the *hokkim* himself waiting for us on the steps of the Zigurat Hotel.

"I understand that the accommodation here was not suitable," he said. "Pack and we will take you somewhere much better."

Much relieved, we quickly packed and then we all set off again. With our car and escorts now merged with those of the *hokkim,* it was quite a long convoy. All the sirens wailed permanently to underline our new prestige. Policemen held up the traffic at all the junctions, and judging by the queues had been doing so for some time. A short distance outside the city we entered a drive between wrought-iron gates, pulling up at a substantial mansion. White-jacketed staff emerged and carried our bags inside. High ceilings, ornate plasterwork and gilding, imitation Louis XIV furniture, crystal chandeliers and large Oriental carpets: this was the president's residence in Ferghana, and very nice it was too. Gafur was put in the drivers' quarters, but Emily and Vakhida each had their own stateroom, complete with chandeliers, mirrored walls, and Jacuzzis with controls like the flight deck of the starship *Enterprise.* Fiona and I had the presidential suite, which you could get lost in.

We went back into town for a relaxed dinner at a restaurant with our local consular nationals. There were about eleven of them, of whom four were children, which was good for Emily. They were a nice bunch, Australians and New Zealanders, engaged in relief work or teaching for Christian charities. I think they were relieved to find us so informal.

The next morning, gilded furniture was taken out onto the sweeping lawn, where white-gloved attendants served us pancakes, fruit and yogurt. I kissed Fiona and Emily good-bye. Gafur then drove them to the airport to fly back to Tashkent, while I went in the official car with the deputy *hokkim* for a further meeting with the *hokkim*.

We were now entering the business end of the program, and discussed possibilities for British investment in Ferghana, which I had to say were not bright unless the Uzbek government instituted substantial currency and trade liberalization and economic deregulation. The *hokkim* assured me all these were coming. He noted that my program said I would be calling on a local human rights activist, and cautioned me not to believe stories from such an unreliable source. For my own safety, he suggested, I should allow the police to accompany me to such a meeting. I expressed thanks for his concern, but declined the offer.

The *hokkim* smiled and did not press the point; he had fulfilled his duty by this ritual sparring. He added that he thought my program was too full. As my host, he would suggest that I cut out the visit to the university, where protocol would detain me a long time. I said that I was keen to go, as the British Council had given support to English-language teaching there. I would see how the program panned out.

We visited a shoe factory that wanted investment; this used local leather at least in part, and was quite an impressive operation. It had been privatized in 1995, and had reduced its labor force from 4,300 to 300, while doubling production. We next toured a brewery, which had received a loan from the European Bank for Reconstruction and Development for a new bottling line. The loan had been disbursed, but the new plant had not yet arrived. At the time I did not find this particularly suspicious. They used a mixture of local wheat and imported malt. The beer, named Ferghana, was really awful—they did not add hops. Nor did they have a master brewer. There was a chief scientist, and the beer at various stages of production was subject to scientific analysis, but the concept of taste did not seem to be employed at all.[5]

The human rights activist I visited was named Abdusalom Ergashev. Gafur had rejoined me with our car, and he dropped me at his door, the rest of the convoy waiting politely at the top of the street. Mr. Ergashev was a bearded man with a grave manner, and looked Russian rather than Asian. His beard was worthy of comment because they are seldom seen in Uzbekistan, being regarded as a sign of Islamic proclivity and therefore potential political dissent. A beard alone could get you into an Uzbek torture cell and forced to sign a confession of membership in a terrorist group.

Ergashev was plainly suspicious of me. He had himself spent several years in jail after being, he said, falsely accused of charges of sexual assault. I was later to learn that the Uzbek government routinely concocts such sexual charges to silence and discredit opponents, but this revelation made me at first a little wary of him, and our conversation fenced for a while. But I found him considered, organized and impressive, while he also warmed to me. He told me stories of torture and disappearance, and of the more mundane apparatus of repression. In particular, in an economy and society dominated by the state, dissidents and all their relatives would lose their jobs.

I asked Ergashev how many people from Ferghana were being held as political or religious prisoners. He replied about 370 from Ferghana city itself. He had documented most of these cases. The large majority were religious Muslims—about thirty were nonreligious political dissidents. Most were convicted under Article 159 of the criminal code—conspiring to overthrow the government or constitution of Uzbekistan. Many had also been convicted of firearms or narcotic offenses, and of membership in Hizb-ut-Tehrir, a banned Islamic organization.

I asked if we could do anything to help with his work. He said he would appreciate a new personal computer, or help with fixing his old one. I promised to assist.

I should explain something of Hizb-ut-Tehrir (HuT), the Party of Islamic Liberation. This movement started among the Palestinian diaspora in North Africa, but was to find its greatest popularity in Central Asia. The central tenet of Hizb-ut-Tehrir is that a united caliphate should be established to rule over all Muslim lands, as in the early days of Islam. In short they wish to establish a divinely guided theocracy. How they aim to achieve this is unclear. They are against violence, but also against democracy and participation in politics. They seek to obtain their objective by prayer, example and religious proselytizing. HuT supporters in Uzbekistan perhaps number eight thousand, although the large majority of these have no practical contact with the organization.

There is a state-authorized Islamic organization in Uzbekistan that uses about a fifth of the traditional mosques for Friday prayer, at which the mullahs read out messages dictated by the government. Observing the ritual of prayer five times per day is discouraged by the government mosques, as is fasting at Ramadan.

Unsurprisingly, the state religion does not fulfill the spiritual needs of the pious, and there are thousands of underground mosques, normally just a room in somebody's house where a few meet to worship. Possession in private homes of religious literature, including the Koran, is likely to lead to arrest and torture, as is observing regular prayer.

After Uzbek independence, Saudi money paid for a resurgence in religious teaching, but this was suppressed from 1997, and put down with great thoroughness after bombs were set off in Tashkent in 1999. One result of driving the Islamic movement underground was that many of the teachers were not especially educated. In this milieu Hizb-ut-Tehrir started to gain adherents. It was particularly attractive because, in an atmosphere where there is no democratic opposition, no free media and no dissent allowed, Hizb-ut-Tehrir might be the only anti-Karimov voice heard, especially in rural areas. As poverty and desperation increase, given a choice limited to Hizb-ut-Tehrir and Karimov, the religious group starts to look attractive.

So the idea of Hizb-ut-Tehrir spread through the Uzbek countryside like a drumbeat of opposition. Many of those who call themselves adherents have no contact with the central leadership, largely London-based, or with anyone who does. Hizb-ut-Tehrir did not evolve as an organized cell structure in Uzbekistan—it is more an idea than an organization. In consequence, local aberrations in interpretation arose. For example, many HuT adherents in Uzbekistan believe they should have four wives and may smoke tobacco.

Despite all this, HuT has produced a number of followers in Uzbekistan of genuine belief and courage. Avazov and his companion, Alimov, were boiled to death for refusing to recant these beliefs. My best estimate is that about a thousand of Karimov's prisoners genuinely consider themselves adherents of HuT, although over four thousand have been convicted of membership.

Adherents assume a much wider importance because not only HuT themselves but also, paradoxically, the Karimov regime work to exaggerate their role. Karimov needs a radical Islamic enemy he can point to, in order to justify continued repression and to frighten people with the bogeyman of a Taliban-style government. HuT fills this need. Its leaflets are therefore routinely planted on political dissidents of all persuasions.

It is not only Muslims who are persecuted in Uzbekistan—any kind of religious enthusiasm is frowned upon. Baptists and Jehovah's Witnesses are particularly persecuted. Chris and I were to come across a case of a Jehovah's Witness convicted of possession of a store of banned literature. The police listed this literature, chiefly copies of *The Watchtower* and *Awake!* But in the middle of the list appeared several HuT leaflets, which the police had routinely planted on the "extremist" without realizing the contradiction.[6]

After leaving Ergashev, I said good-bye to Vakhida, who left in a police car for the airport. I would be without an interpreter for the rest of the day, but would be joined by a professional one in the morning in Namangan. I judged we still had plenty of time to visit the university, and told Gafur so. He was standing smoking and chatting with the escorting policemen. They looked dubious and called the deputy *hokkim,* who had repaired to a nearby *chaikhana* while I was with Ergashev.

"Please, Mr. Ambassador," he said, "it is late, and it is dangerous to drive to Namangan after dark."

"It's not that late. An hour at the university and we can be away by five."

"But I believe we are not expected now at the university."

My hackles were beginning to rise.

"Well, think what a pleasant surprise it will be for them."

The deputy gave a wan smile, and got back into his Nissan Maxima, which had dark pleated curtains at the windows. I climbed into the back of my Discovery; it seemed strangely empty now, with only Gafur and me in it. The police cars started off and we followed. After about twenty minutes, we were heading out of town.

"Gafur, where are we going?" I asked.

"This is the road to Namangan, Ambassador."

"Is the university this way?"

"No, Ambassador."

"Do you know where the university is?"

"Yes, I think so." I had explained to the embassy drivers that, within reason, they should always reconnoiter the day's calls in the early morning or the evening before.

"Then stop."

"Sorry, Ambassador?"

"*Stop!* We're going to the university."

Obviously impressed by the drama of the moment, Gafur slammed on the brakes and we slowed to a halt. The lead police car and the *hokkim*'s Nissan carried on ahead of us, turning round a corner. The police car behind had to brake quickly, and the doors opened as the police got out to see what the problem was. Gafur, having halted, was turned round looking quizzically at me.

"The university, Gafur. Drive to the university."

"OK, sir."

It was a wide road, and Gafur spun the Discovery round. We sped off, leaving the puzzled policemen standing in the street staring at us. Gafur had worked out we were giving the escort the slip, and drove like crazy through the streets of Ferghana. The escort caught up with us again just as we pulled up in front of the university. I waited for the deputy *hokkim* on the steps. He simply gave me a slight shake of the head. I wanted to go straight to the English department, but he insisted that we should first call on the rector. I was happy to concede that one.

The university building was a large brick edifice that would not have looked out of place in any British provincial university. The rector was sour-faced and unwelcoming, and we endured fifteen minutes of stilted conversation over tea. We then walked down to the English center, our footsteps echoing from the vaulted ceilings. The most striking thing about the university was that it was so devoid of life—there seemed to be virtually no one around.

In the English center I met two charming old ladies who taught there. They showed me with great pride the books they had been given by the

British Council, and explained their cataloging system. The only thing that worried me was that the books all appeared to be neatly on the shelves, as opposed to being used by students. I asked them where everybody was, which brought a moment's silence and no real answer.

The authorities had not wanted me to visit the university because of its resemblance to the Marie Celeste. It was only later that I discovered where everyone had gone: they were all in the fields picking cotton.

Even the massive labor forces held on the state farms are insufficient when it comes to harvesttime. So, more forced labor is drafted in. Staff and students are brought in from colleges and universities, which are effectively closed for the entire autumn term. An able-bodied university or college student will expect to spend three months in the cotton fields. Older schoolchildren will do the same, and even children as young as eight might expect to spend two or three weeks in the fields. Civil servants and factory workers can also be drafted as the size of the harvest and weather dictate.

Conditions can be appalling. The workers sleep in the fields, or in rough barracks. Sanitation is poor, food consists of a bare gruel, and water is taken straight from irrigation canals. The harvest regularly lasts into October or early November, when temperatures can drop below freezing. Each farm and each region had its quota to produce in the five-year economic plan, and managers and *hokkims* were under extreme pressure to fulfill their quota.

Those drafted for the harvest are not paid, but they are, for the most part, successfully brainwashed by constant propaganda on television and radio, in newspapers and on banners and posters about harvesting the nation's "white gold." It is chilling to hear a bedraggled ten-year-old in a field talking about the patriotic duty to pick cotton to fund the nation's independence.

CHAPTER 6

"A True British Gentleman"

THE FERGHANA POLICE CARS WERE WHITE WITH SKY BLUE AND light green stripes, the Uzbek national colors. The new ones from Namangan were light blue with a green stripe, but equally keen on using their sirens and flashing blue lights. We swooped along the road and into the city in the early evening, passing through a very quiet town center, with all the shops shuttered. Climbing a hill we passed through gates, between fortified guardhouses, and entered a large compound. The drive wound through a large equestrian complex, where a number of Arab Thoroughbreds, bays and grays, were exercising in a paddock. The road spiraled up to the crest of a hill, on top of which stood a mansion in classical style. Across an extensive lawn from this stood a large new square brick building, with lines of tall, slim windows. To my disappointment, we swept past the mansion and stopped at the new building.

I climbed out of the car. From this hilltop, lights spread out to the horizon in every direction, a reminder of just how populous the Ferghana Valley is. I was shown to my room.

It reminded me of a student residence hall. The room was tiny, with a cubicle containing a shower and toilet. The bed was less than three feet wide, the mattress thin, the sheets stiff and the tartan blanket scratchy. I looked at the manager in some amazement. He affected not to notice, and told me dinner would be served upstairs in the dining room in half an hour, and the deputy *hokkim* would be joining me.

Gafur arrived with my bag and looked at the room, shaking his head.

"Not good, Ambassador," he said.

"No, but at least it's clean," I said.

I thought for a moment. Why was I worried? I had slept under the stars in Africa often enough, and here I had a bed, shower and bathroom. But I nonetheless felt that more respect should be shown to a British ambassador.

I was glad to take a shower and change, and was looking forward to dinner. I went upstairs and found the restaurant, where a single table was ready. There were just two covers set, each for nine courses. The cutlery was gold-plated. Each cover also had a water glass, vodka glass and four wineglasses of different sizes, all of them crystal and gold-rimmed. A two-foot-high gilded equestrian centerpiece of the Emperor Babur was piled around with fruit. My feelings of neglect dissipated.

The deputy *hokkim* arrived about ten minutes late. A short, ball-shaped man with a fringe of longish black hair around a balding pate, he wore the regulation black suit and white shirt. He patted at the back of his neck with a white handkerchief as he bounded up the steps two at a time. He had a friendly, open face and a broad grin as he held out his hand to shake mine, then realized he still had the handkerchief in it.

"Ah, Mr. Murray! Sorry to be late. I had a meeting with the *hokkim* about the cotton harvest. The president is not happy we will meet our quota. He has sent two presidential counselors here to warn the *hokkim*! Of course, it's seven years since a *hokkim* was last shot for not meeting his quota, and he had been smuggling personally. Or was it his son? I forget. Anyway, things are more civilized now. Still, it's worrying. I am the deputy *hokkim* for Islamic affairs and external relations. Of course, you are an experienced diplomat, so you know that means KGB. Only now we say SNB. Your career has been very good. Did you like Poland? Did they teach you to drink vodka? I served in Poland. Oh, the Polish women! Can we take off our jackets and ties?"

I was rather bowled over by this introduction. There followed one of the most enjoyable evenings of my life. The meal was tremendous, every course of it, and I was hungry, having had a busy day and not eaten since breakfast. The wines were very good, from Georgia—it was the only time I saw wine other than the execrable Uzbek stuff at an official function. There was a superb, well-aged oaked red with the shashlik, and a fine dessert wine served with honey cakes. We had a frank discussion in which I promoted economic reform and he social stability. We then moved on to more important topics—soccer and women—and eventually, after finishing three and a half bottles of wine between us, got on to the vodka toasts.

We started with the queen and President Karimov, and then moved on to the *hokkim* and Tony Blair. We then pledged to friendship between our two countries. My host made a flowery speech about the eyes showing the soul, and that he could see in my eyes I had a good heart. We were getting maudlin by this stage and I was quite touched, though I later found this was a standard Uzbek compliment.

With each toast we drained our glasses in one go. He was quite impressed by my ability to drink vodka, but not by my style. He showed me that the arm should be cocked with the elbow raised to the same height as the mouth, so the forearm is horizontal. You then flick only the hand, without moving the arm, to toss it down. This was the approved Soviet military fashion. You should try it next time you drink with the KGB—they'll be impressed.

The vodka glasses were made of slim-stemmed fine crystal, with the actual container part conical. The meal had been served by three waitresses, blond and not ethnically Uzbek, which is unusual in Namangan. They wore little black skirts with white aprons, and were both efficient and distracting. Every time we drained our glasses in a vodka toast, they were immediately refilled. But four or five toasts in, I noticed something. My glass was always filled right to the brim, so I had to lift it carefully. My host's glass was filled only halfway up—and the glass being a cone, filled halfway it contained about a sixth as much as filled to the top.

We drank a couple more bumpers, and then I had an inspiration. It was my turn to make the next toast. I rose to my feet and said, "I feel we are becoming true friends. Our nationalities and positions are not important. As men, ordinary men, we understand each other. In Scotland, we have a tradition—when we are drinking a toast, we pledge our friendship by exchanging glasses."

I reached across the table and picked up his glass, handing him mine: *"Slainte va."*

We drank, and sat down again. I had, of course, made this story up.

"An interesting tradition," he observed; "perhaps its origin lay in people poisoning glasses?"

"Oh yes, probably," I replied airily. "Dropping like flies from poison all over the place, I dare say. You just can't trust some people."

The waitresses, though, were cute in more ways than one. For the next toast they filled *my* glass halfway, and his to the brim. He then insisted on again observing the Scottish tradition, with a glint of genuine humor in his eye. I decided we should switch to a venue where the dice were less loaded.

"My friend, let's go look at Namangan," I said. "Maybe a bar or night-club, where we can meet some women?"

"You know, Namangan is not Warsaw."

"I know, but there must be somewhere."

"OK, we can try."

He had the obligatory Nissan Maxima, in black. He yelled at the driver to get out of the car, and got into the driver's seat himself. I got into the front seat beside him and we set off into the city. It was only about 11 P.M., but Namangan had the deserted air of 4 A.M. We drove quite a way until we came to an outside bar; the tables and chairs were still out in the courtyard, but the bar itself was shuttered up.

"Shit!" he said, throwing the car into a screeching reverse turn. In any Western country he would have been ten times over the drunk-driving limit. We drove around to two or three more bars, with the same result. Finally he got out his mobile phone and made a number of calls, then turned to me with a smile.

"There is one place, and tonight they have a dancer!"

We drove off again, winding our way through the city. Finally we entered between high walls into the yard of a large house, which loomed above us in complete darkness. He got out of the car and had a piss against the yard wall. I followed suit. We then walked round the back of the building, feeling our way in the darkness. We climbed a short flight of concrete external steps with an iron side railing, he opened a door, and we went in. We passed down a pitch-dark corridor—I was beginning to feel just a trifle nervous. Then my host simply vanished. For a few seconds I felt around, wondering where he had gone, panic just starting to rise, when an arm seemed to come out from the wall and pull me in.

Behind a carpet hung on the wall was an opening, and on the other side a bar. There were about eight tables around a dance floor, with a few disco lights mounted. Besides us was a bar counter from which a grizzled old man with a bulbous nose dispensed beer and vodka. There were about a dozen men in the place, all of them in military uniform. At the other end was a low stage on which a dancer was performing.

I decided to switch to beer. There was a choice of Ferghana and Zolotaya Bochka—Golden Drum. Having tried Ferghana, I decided to give Zolotaya Bochka a go. To my surprise, it was quite good. My companion stuck to vodka.

The dancer was performing Uzbek traditional dance. She was tall and slim, and carried out the complicated arm and wrist movements with neat precision. She wore a long tunic of atlas cloth over pink trousers. The only flesh exposed was hands and face. It was doubtless very good, but involved too many clothes for my taste.

The deputy *hokkim* looked at her raptly.

"What do you think of her?" he asked.

"She's OK, but the costume's a bit dull."

"Don't worry. There will be a new costume for each dance."

I cheered up, thinking we would be in for a prolonged striptease. In fact, her subsequent costumes became increasingly all-enveloping. I half expected her to finish off with her hat and coat on.

Stranger to me were the army officers around us, with whom my host exchanged some good-humored banter. After each dance, the dancer would go off to change, and Russian pop music would blare out, the disco lighting whirring into life. The soldiers would all get up to dance. They were a sight: peaked hats askew, tunics unbuttoned, ties loosened, cigarettes hanging from side of mouth. They stuck their arms out horizontally and then swiveled and banked from the waist, like children playing at airplanes.

This is how Uzbek men dance, the advantage being that it is dead easy if you are forced to join in.

But what I found surprising was that these men danced with each other. There were no women, and I presumed that men dancing together was a product of Muslim culture. But the strange bit was that they weren't just dancing together, but interacting with each other in the dance, just as men and women would do, in a range between the flirtatious and the erotic. That I had not expected.[1]

After the dancer finished work, my host made a good attempt to persuade her to join us for a drink. She declined, and I was a bit disconcerted when asked if I wanted him to compel her. I attempted to say
something gallant, about such a charming lady having the right to choose
her own companions, but my Russian was starting to collapse—it gets
much more fluent after drinking, but after a bit more drinking goes into
rapid decline. I made about four attempts to say this, causing her to laugh
very prettily, and then I just gave up and said, "No."

"I knew it," he said. "I have met a true British gentleman."

He then repeated this observation to the rest of the bar, and suggested
we all drink to it. The suggestion, however, fell on deaf ears, the officers
having drunk themselves into a stupor. Several of them appeared to be
bedding down on the floor for the night.

We felt our way back out through the darkness, and had another piss
against the wall. My clothes reeked of bad tobacco smoke. Then we got
into the car, and drove back to the guesthouse.

I BREAKFASTED AT EIGHT, feeling remarkably good. I was glad that there
was no sign of any police escort. I wondered if this was because the deputy
hokkim was still indisposed. Our professional interpreter had turned up, an
impressive young man. Anyway, we headed out toward the Nestlé factory.

Nestlé had established a plant for producing pasteurized milk in car-
tons, and water in plastic bottles. They had tankers collecting milk from
farmers all over the valley, a welcome injection of private-sector cash into
the economy. The managing director was a likeable Australian, Martin
Woolnough. Their plant was a haven of cleanliness and efficiency.

Pasteurized milk and safe water are both sorely needed in the country, particularly as TB and other diseases were becoming epidemic.
Unfortunately, Nestlé was finding it extremely difficult to market the
milk. Many Uzbek families, even in the heart of Tashkent, have one or
two cows in their courtyards or on the road verges, and if they don't, they
buy their milk from a neighbor who does. To get anywhere close to the
price competition of the informal sector, Nestlé was selling the milk at a
loss while it built up the market.

I was surprised to find that the greatest cost of a carton of milk was
the carton itself—later that day I was to find the same thing true when I

visited an EBRD-funded juice factory. The reason is the very high costs of the patented Tetra Pak technology. The Swedish family that owns the patents is among the top five wealthiest in the world.

Nestlé had found, to its own surprise, that the bottled water was its big money spinner. While the water came from its own boreholes, it was not mineral water and it was treated. But it filled a much needed demand and production had soared, causing Nestlé to open an extra line. Unfortunately, it had stopped working the day of my visit. The new ban on imports meant that it had run out of the plastic blanks from which the bottles were expanded.

Given its huge reserves of hydrocarbons, the Uzbek government had invested in a plant to produce plastics, polythene and polyethylene, from natural gas. It had opened that summer, at a cost of $1.2 billion. The equipment was largely American and Italian, and export financing had come from those countries. The Uzbek government had, however, refused to accept a large number of expatriate experts to run this plant. In consequence, when started up that summer, it had blown up.

We were now to visit another example of economic madness. The EBRD had invested 26 million euro of equity, not loan, in a woolen-textile mill. The total value of the investment in this mill was over 70 million euro (as compared with about 23 million euro Nestlé invested in its very impressive factory). The wool factory was in a small town outside Namangan, housed in a series of huge buildings.

The assistant manager and a small delegation were waiting for me, and took me into a vast manufacturing hall filled with textile machinery. I have always been fascinated by the complexity and ingenuity of such machinery, and there was certainly plenty of it. But there was one major problem—it wasn't doing anything. A single machine in a far corner clanked away rather unhealthily, producing dark brown wiry blankets. None of the combing, spinning, washing, weaving or dyeing equipment elsewhere was working.

The assistant manager was a tall Uzbek with high cheekbones and a good pinstriped suit. He was accompanied by a young Turkish engineer, who represented the foreign investor.

"It's not very busy, is it?" I observed.

"We are running at about ten percent capacity," said the manager.

The young Turk said something in Turkish to my interpreter, who passed it on.

"Really one percent, Ambassador."

I looked around me and observed, "If that."

I pointed to the unappealing blankets. "Is there a customer for those?" I asked in Russian.

The manager replied in Uzbek, through the interpreter.

"The Uzbek army."

"Will they actually pay up?"

"Maybe one day."

I looked more closely at the plant. The spinning machinery had been brand new, but the power looms looked ancient, despite being thickly coated in new green paint.

"The factory is two years old?" I asked. They agreed.

"And this equipment was all sold as new?"

"It is new," said the manager.

"If this lot is new, you must have been paying someone for the last two years to go around hitting it with a sledgehammer."[2]

We went out into one of the big sheds, where bales of wool were being unloaded. There were untidy heaps in the corner of brown, tangled fleeces with the consistency of wire wool. By contrast a truck was unloading big bales of fluffy white fleeces. The manager was beaming with delight.

"Now we will get the factory working properly," he said.

"Is this wool local?"

"No, it's from Australia."

"I beg your pardon?"

"It's from Australia."

"Why don't you use local wool?"

"It doesn't fit the machines."

"But I thought the whole point of this project was to develop local agriculture."

He gestured at the dark fleeces in the corner. "We tried. It doesn't fit the machines."

We went to the factory shop, in which there were bales of suitings, in wool, polyester and blends of the two. These had been produced as samples with imported raw materials when the equipment was first installed. Some of the material was very good, and I thought about buying some. We drank tea, and I felt sorry for the sad assistant manager and his young sidekick. There was a general manager, a tremendous swell who lived in Tashkent on a big salary and never visited the plant. My sympathy for this sad couple elicited more and more of the true story.

They showed me the consultancy report, in English, on which the investment had been based. This said that there were plenty of sheep providing fine-quality wool in the Ferghana Valley, and the plant would take up to 60 percent of the valley's wool production. The truth was, the assistant manager said, that the plant's capacity was three times the wool production of the whole of Uzbekistan. On top of which, the wiry wool of Uzbek sheep was totally unsuited to produce suit material. The young engineer said that it wasn't just a question of producing bad-quality cloth; the machinery wouldn't take the local wool at all, whatever the adjustments he tried to make. Only the blanket-making machine would work, fed with stringlike local yarn.

The feasibility report had been produced by the same Turkish company that supplied the machinery, which was also the foreign investor and part owner of the plant. This was an incredible conflict of interest. However, rather than stay and manage the plant, after the commissioning the Turkish "investors" had disappeared, leaving behind their most junior assistant engineer as a kind of hostage. The poor lad had not been paid for two years.

There were three investors: the Turkish company, the EBRD and the Uzbek government. Obviously, the Turks had made their cash on the supply of overpriced machinery, much of it disguised as new. The project was bogus from start to finish. I was astonished that the EBRD had fallen for this. The young engineer told me that the responsible EBRD desk officer in London, a national of one of the former communist states, had resigned on completion of the project and retired to the Caribbean, which seemed to explain a lot.

But it got worse. The EBRD had now given a new loan of 5 million euros on top of its equity investment of 26 million euros. The loan was to pay for wool to be flown in from Australia to feed the plant. This was commercial madness, but the purpose was political. In May 2003, the

EBRD was going to be holding its annual general meeting (AGM) in Tashkent. Finance ministers from all the world's major countries would be flying in. The EBRD did not want the embarrassment of an obvious white elephant project, so the factory would be functioning during the AGM.[3]

We left the sad factory and went on to a meeting with a representative of Erk, at a village just outside Namangan. Erk was the major opposition party, but had been banned some years previously. The village was intensely rural, and we entered the meeting house through a yard where children were setting out cowpats to dry as a store of fuel for the winter. I met a gentle old bearded man who served me tea from a blue and white porcelain teapot. The women in the village were heavily veiled, and the tea and cakes appeared from behind a curtained serving hatch. This was the first time I had come across purdah in Uzbekistan.

My host said that the Namangan district had long been a center of Islamic culture. It did not have any particular holy sites, it simply represented the culture of its people. He explained that Erk did not want to establish an Islamic state or sharia law. They wished, however, for a state where it was possible for those to follow Islamic customs who wished to do so. He seemed very old, but assured me with a calm serenity that he expected to live long enough to see democracy come to Uzbekistan.

I asked my standard question about the number of people from that district who were religious or political prisoners. He took me aback by saying, from that cluster of villages alone, there were about four hundred. Responding to my look of shock, he said that about one in five of the young men of that area had been taken in. They were kept mostly in Andijon prison. In Namangan province, he believed that about 90 percent of the population would vote against Karimov, given the chance. He did not believe the opposition would turn to violence. This was not due to a creed of nonviolence, but the security forces were too numerous and well armed. But people were getting poorer and poorer, and Karimov's end was coming. He spoke with dignified assurance, and I was left to ponder the mystery of why this grave old man was left alone by the authorities.

WE NEXT HAD an hour's drive into Andijon. This had the air of a much bigger city than the others in the valley, with office blocks and large retail premises, and wide, multilane roads packed with cars. We were headed for the offices of Mercy Corps. This was the site of the British government's largest aid project in Uzbekistan. It cost about £120,000, which was peanuts compared with my previous projects of tens of millions of pounds in Ghana. The money came from the British government's Conflict Resolution Fund, and the project was extremely effective.

As I entered Mercy Corps' office, I encountered several groups of local middle-aged women, wearing brightly colored dresses and head scarves, grinning at me and displaying rows of gold teeth. In rural Uzbekistan everyone has gold teeth. The project offered microfinance—small loans to enable women to set up in business, about sixty dollars on average, but they were enough to purchase a hand loom, or some livestock or some trading goods. The finance worked at a very low rate of interest—about 2 percent—and the repaid money went to start new projects.

Mercy Corps administered the project on our behalf, and it reported that there was a bit of a crisis at present, because many of the loan projects involved trading with nearby Kirghizstan, and the border had just been closed. Others produced products that sold in the bazaars, and they had just been closed also.

The young project leader was most impressive. She timidly suggested we go out and meet some of the loan recipients, and seemed both surprised and delighted when I enthusiastically agreed. We visited a small village outside Andijon. One lady produced hand-loomed textiles, and another embroidered cloths. Both had started from scratch and now employed staff. Another lady had bought molds and sugar to produce boiled sweets, while her neighbor had started a small bread bakery. In total, Mercy Corps believed about fourteen thousand people in three thousand families were dependent on income from this project, and many more received direct economic benefit. It was an astonishing success for such a small investment. Chris Hirst and Karen Moran deserved much of the credit.[4]

Over 90 percent of the loans had performed, but some of this benefit was now put at risk by Uzbek government measures of border and bazaar closures, which appeared expressly designed to bankrupt their own population.

I felt a real anger at the way the regime had just done so much damage to the efforts these ordinary women had made to improve their lives.

The next morning we headed in to Andijon again, where my first meeting was with the *hokkim*. There was again a local TV crew, and the *hokkim* made a flowery speech about bilateral relations. He said that there were seventy-two Uzbek/British joint ventures in Andijon. (We only knew of two, and I presume this was just another propaganda statistic.)

I visited one of these joint ventures next, a company called QuickStop owned by Jitendra Patel. It had a factory in Tashkent, which I had already been round, manufacturing plastic sacks for cement. Its Andijon factory made paper from imported wood pulp. I met Jitendra at the plant, and he explained that they were trying to convert the machinery to operate on local cotton waste. Cotton-made paper is very high quality; banknotes are made from it. He also explained that the company name, QuickStop, came from his U.K. business of food outlets in railway stations.

But Jitendra too had a tale of the problems of business in Uzbekistan. He had founded the Uzbek company with an Uzbek partner, a former minister. Jitendra had later bought out the partner for a very large sum, but the partner had now won a judgment from an Uzbek court awarding him the company. The Uzbek court had refused to accept British court documents certifying that the payment had been made to buy out the partner. This was the first of numerous cases I was to deal with of foreign investors being mistreated by Uzbek courts. I called back on the *hokkim* to discuss the situation with him, and explained that the future of the paper plant was in danger.

The *hokkim* seemed genuinely concerned, and promised to raise the matter with the president. He confided that the difficulty was that the partner was a very important man who had broken the law by accepting payment into a Swiss bank account. This could not be admitted by the court. I was surprised by the *hokkim*'s openness in discussing this.

I next had a lunch appointment with a human rights activist, a doctor from the local hospital. Our arrangement involved meeting him on a certain street. I walked up and down for about fifteen minutes, increasingly convinced this was not going to work, but finally he turned up, a short old man in a threadbare jacket. His two incisors were gold. He insisted on taking me for lunch in a little local courtyard restaurant, and ordered *osh,* which turned out to be Tajik for *plov.*

He said that over a thousand dissidents from Andijon were in jail, but the city had the proudest record of opposition to the government. Compared with Namangan, the people of Andijon were more secular, but their opposition was fueled by economic discontent and by anger at being cut off from the neighboring Kirghiz city of Osh.

I was now convinced that the total numbers of political prisoners in the country were larger than anyone had credited.

There was a remarkable incident during lunch. After we had been there about ten minutes, two men, both wearing leather jackets, came and sat at a table near the entrance.

"I see the SNB have found us," said the doctor. He stood up and walked over to them. He spoke to them quietly in Uzbek, and they got up and left.

"What did you say?" I asked.

He grinned "I said that you were the British ambassador, and you asked that they leave." I made a couple more visits, one to a Christian NGO that focused on health education and the other to a Daewoo car plant that was working at a fraction of its capacity. The next day I returned to Tashkent.

CHAPTER 7

Cry Freedom!

The heavy baggage had arrived, and Fiona had been getting the apartment into shape, although much remained packed as we would be moving again, to the new residence, around Christmas. But we were now able to give our first dinner party, and experimented on the British staff of the embassy and the British Council. This went well, although Galina the cook had been nervous, and Fiona had to do a lot herself.

We were then ready for outside guests, and our first official function was to be a reception for Chevening scholars. All round the world the FCO funds a small number of overseas students to come to the U.K. The idea is to identify future movers and shakers in their country; done properly, it requires a lot of effort, but overall the scheme is very successful. In Uzbekistan we had funding for only three scholars a year, but past scholars included a deputy governor of the central bank and two members of the president's inner office.

It is standard practice to "see off" the new Chevening scholars with a reception, and invite past scholars to it. I decided to augment this by inviting all the UMID scholars, new and past, plus anyone else we could identify who had studied at a U.K. university, plus the staff who were setting up the Westminster University campus in Tashkent, plus our key Uzbek government contacts in the field of education. The British Council was extremely efficient in providing a guest list of several hundred. Many of the past scholars were in the provinces, but about 120 people turned up, which was a tight squeeze as they mingled, drank and chomped canapés in the opened-out space of the ballroom, dining room, and balconies.

Fiona and I had routinely hosted gatherings for many hundreds in Accra and Warsaw, but plainly this was much more than Galina had been used to in Tashkent, and there were a few hiccups. Serving staff were borrowed from the maids of embassy and other families, and off-duty guards were the barmen. They were apparently used to this job, but as none of them knew what a gin and tonic was, I was puzzled about what kind of entertainment had been done in the past.

The Uzbek minister of higher education attended. He passed on one little snippet to me. When the UMID scheme had started, the majority of students had been sent to the United States. However, they had come back "infected" with bad social and political habits. Karimov had therefore decided that most students should instead go to the U.K., where he believed society was more conservative. President Karimov had a very high opinion of the U.K. I wondered what peculiar impression Karimov had of student life in the U.K., which is a great deal more infected with both politics and debauchery than your average American university student's.

Neville McBain, the tall, handsome ex–army major who was director of the British Council in Tashkent, said that the problem was that over half the UMID scholars weren't coming back at all. They stayed in the U.K. as illegal immigrants. This broke the terms of their UMID contracts, under which they had to come back and do government work for five years after graduating.

The parents would be held responsible for their nonreturn. However, many of the parents were from extremely wealthy regime families—the selection process was often corrupt—and they could escape punishment by the same means they obtained the scholarship. Retribution was taken against less wealthy parents, usually in the form of their losing their jobs, but even by working in a Pizza Hut in the U.K., the absconder could easily send back more funds than the family had lost.

I made a little speech wishing our new scholars well, and reminding them that the university experience was much more than formal learning. Social interaction was important too, and I had learned more in the pub than in the lecture theater. Uzbekistan is overlaid with a pompous Soviet culture, and the Uzbeks were amazed to hear someone in authority speak like this.

I was delighted to meet my friend from the Zigurat Hotel again. He had made the long journey to Tashkent by bus. Following our night out, he had been picked up by the SNB and taken in for questioning. They had asked him if he had known I would be returning to Ferghana that evening, and what I said. He replied that I talked a lot about football and chatted up the waitresses in the restaurant. In the marquee, I had said that I preferred Golden Drum to Ferghana beer, and that I quite fancied the belly dancer in the white, but the one in red was too fat.

At this stage, his inquisitor had struck him, declaring that he was lying because ambassadors don't talk like that! They had wanted to know my views on various political subjects, so he had made it all up. He hoped I didn't mind. I assured him I didn't mind at all. It could do little harm to feed rubbish to the SNB.

I presumed they already knew what I thought, because I was pretty open about it anyway, direct with ministers and other contacts. I saw no need to hide my views on Uzbekistan's appalling political and economic system; in fact, the wider they were propagated, the better.

All the policy points I have written of here had been retailed back to London in official classified telegrams. But for many years I had also been used to a close working relationship between London department and embassy by e-mail. I had operated in this way whether posted abroad or in a department. In my previous job as deputy high commissioner in Ghana, I had a close working relationship with the FCO's Africa Department, and would exchange e-mails many times a day in a continuous dialogue.

The Eastern Department was different, and seemed determined to hang on to the stilted working practices of a previous century. Above all, they were obsessed with the need to prevent the Uzbeks from knowing what we were thinking. The Eastern Department was formerly named the Soviet Department, and the old Sovietologists remained steeped in the paranoid culture of the Cold War. I was frequently rebuked for sending communications by unclassified e-mail. I replied that I knew my e-mails were almost certainly being intercepted, and that if the Uzbeks found out this way about my views on the bazaar closures, that was all to the good; it would save me the effort of telling them.

CHRIS NOW RECEIVED the pathology report on the Avazov case, and we immediately distributed copies to the UN, OSCE and the EU, and I started to brief the media. The medieval horror of being boiled to death was so powerful an image that in death Mr. Avazov could play a real part in undermining the terrible regime that had so cruelly killed him.

A new arrival in Tashkent was a formidable lady named Sikeena Karmali, a Canadian of Indian origin. Sikeena was here to open an office of Freedom House, a U.S. NGO devoted to human rights and economic freedom. John Herbst was quick to point out to me that Uzbek agreement to the opening of this NGO was another example of progress. The fiercely bright Sikeena had called on me, and invited me to speak at their opening.

I had been looking for a platform to make a declaration of the real state of affairs in the country. I wanted to fracture what I believed had become a conspiracy of silence by the West on human rights in Uzbekistan, and to outline a distinctively British position in favor of democracy and reform that made plain we did not simply follow the United States. This invitation to speak presented the perfect opportunity.

I sat down and drafted a speech, setting out in stark terms our concerns about human rights in Uzbekistan. I then sent it to the Human Rights Policy Department (HRPD) in the FCO, copied to the Eastern Department. I knew I could expect strong support from HRPD, whose head of department, Jon Benjamin, was a genuine believer in human rights who had joined the service on the same day as I.

In London, the clouds started to gather ominously. Simon Butt decided to trump HRPD by going straight to the top. On October 16, 2002, he e-mailed Sir Michael Jay, head of the diplomatic service, the following:

Michael,

. . . We are fast developing a problem with Craig Murray, who is using unclassified email pretty indiscriminately to fire off criticisms of the Uzbek regime, US policy etc . . . He has also sent the draft text of a speech he is shortly to give at a Freedom House meeting which criticises the human rights situation in Uzbekistan in terms which are bound to infuriate the Uzbeks ("This country has made very little progress in moving away from the dictatorship of the Soviet period . . . no effective brake on the authority of a President who has failed to validate his position by facing genuine political opponents in anything resembling a free and fair election.").

Simon

I later obtained a copy of this e-mail by formally applying under the Data Protection Act. The last five lines were heavily blacked out before the document was given to me, on grounds of national security. But a friend who has seen the whole text tells me that they refer to representations against me from the United States.

Sir Michael Jay's reply, also of October 16, strongly supported Simon Butt:

Simon,

. . . I think your handling is entirely right. I am all in favour of Ambassadors expressing their views to us forcefully. But they . . . need to discriminate between the message & advice to us & the way that message is got across to host governments. That is the basis of good diplomacy.

Michael

It is worth noting here that Sir Michael here presumes diplomacy to be a synonym of duplicity.

Following that exchange, Charles Hill, head of the Central Asia section of the Eastern Department, was charged with formally responding to my draft speech. In a letter of 16 October 2002, he said that he doubted I should make such a speech that risked "antagonising the Uzbek authorities":

Nowhere in the speech is there any acknowledgement of the Soviet legacy Uzbekistan needs to overcome, of the genuine extremist/terrorist challenges it has had to grapple with . . .

I also have doubts about elements that could readily be described as involving a judgement or criticism, when the wording for this judgement or criticism is not taken from something the FCO has said before . . .

My doubts also apply to the sentences in the speech beginning "we believe" as the "we" implies the FCO. So for example the sentence "we believe that there are significantly more political and religious prisoners" is one that I have not seen hard evidence to validate . . .

. . . I also have doubts about the emotional language used elsewhere in the speech and the soapbox tone of the peroration. It would be better to list these concerns with regard to Uzbekistan's international obligations . . . while combining this with a statement of willingness to

engage in dialogue with the authorities, and readiness to offer practical
assistance.

Charles Hill

Plainly, this was a crucial moment. Either I was going to conduct our relationship with Uzbekistan using the traditional quietist approach favored by the Eastern Department, or I was going to break new ground and try to have some impact. This speech would set the tone.

I therefore decided to let Charles have it with both barrels:

Dear Charles,

. . . On the question of fact, I am frankly astonished that you claim to have seen no evidence to back my assertion that there are now more political and religious prisoners than there were a year ago. Have you not, for example, seen [I here named specific intelligence material]? You could not have firmer evidence. I suggest you look at it instantly. And why do you think I am here? I have spoken to a great many people here, including reputable human rights groups, and representatives of a spectrum of Uzbek and expatriate society. I have asked about the August arrests all over the Ferghana Valley. I have met the families of detainees. I know that there are more in political/religious detention now than a year ago.

I can see that you might find this fact politically inconvenient. If you wish me to omit it, then say so. But don't pretend it isn't true.

I will say more sympathetic things about the problems facing Uzbekistan, but you must appreciate that the government ARE the Soviet legacy. I am not convinced, and nor is anyone else here I have spoken to, that the Tashkent bombs were anything to do with the IMU or Islamic terrorism. There are two prevalent theories—either it was the government attempting to blame the opposition, or internal government faction fighting. To mention the Tashkent bombs as one of the government's legitimate security concerns would be considered risible by the audience.

Incidentally I would not be at all surprised to see more bombings of this nature in Tashkent shortly, to justify continued repression and try to take off some of the pressure for reform . . .

On the question of style, of course I agree that the object of being an Ambassador is to maximise my influence. But you don't gain influence by being a pushover. You don't gain influence by never saying anything interesting, by sticking in the crowd. You gain influence by being more informed, intelligent, articulate and outspoken. You gain influence by being formidable, by being a factor that must be taken into account . . .

I find your censures sadly cautious and above all completely unimaginative. Personally I have always regarded the classic public school– and Oxbridge-influenced FCO house style as ponderous, self-important and ineffective. My style is more direct and, in my view, more effective . . .

Uzbekistan is different—the nature of the regime is such that senior individuals have almost never met anyone who dared to disagree with them. They certainly find me a bit of a shock. But I would contend that we have achieved very little in eleven years through the more nuanced approach. It does no harm to actually say what we think.

A speech based on publications is not a good idea. Normally of course we base our lines on what Ministers have said in public, but we have a real problem here because they haven't really said anything—which is something you might usefully seek to remedy. I am sorry you consider the style soap-box. I suspect that lurking behind what you say is a desire that I be so dull that no-one in Uzbekistan notices we have said something on human rights.

Actually I think that outrage is absolutely the correct emotion at learning that someone has been tortured to death with boiling water. If your reaction at seeing photos of this is not to be outraged, but to wonder precisely which UN Convention contains provision against torture by boiling water, then I am sorry . . .

Craig

I made a number of amendments as Charles wanted, including adding sympathetic words about the difficulties the Uzbek government faced. I sent the new draft, pointing out that the speech was to be made the next day, and asking for a finalized text rather than comments.

Tashkent is five hours ahead of London, and I was still involved in these exchanges after midnight. In the ambassador's flat above me, Emily was playing with her nanny, Laura, a Tartar. There are about 600,000 Tartars in Uzbekistan, a population deported by Stalin from the Crimea.[1]

Emily was still awake watching videos; she could twist anyone round her little finger except her mum. Fiona was back in the U.K. for Jamie's half term. Laura was a very pretty girl with a spectacular figure. When I came in they both jumped up and wished me happy birthday.

It was now twenty minutes into October 17, 2002, and I had just turned forty-four years old.

That evening I was due to give the speech at Freedom House at six, and by five-thirty the text had still not arrived. The Eastern Department was negotiating with the research analysts, the Human Rights Policy Department and the Department for International Development, all of whom were fighting hard on my side of the argument. Finally the text arrived just after six, and Karen immediately whizzed off to make a hundred photocopies, while I read it through. I was delighted with the result.

Karen and I climbed into the Discovery, and Valeri raced to Freedom House's new office. We arrived about half an hour late, but I need not have worried; it was a scene of chaos.

The offices were a standard Uzbek courtyard house, and the meeting was planned for the garden, where rows of plastic chairs were set out. Unfortunately, it had started to bucket down rain shortly before our arrival. Indoors, there was not enough space to host a large meeting. After a lot of milling around, it was decided that speeches would be delivered from the large landing, on which an improbable number of TV and radio crews were setting up. The audience was crammed standing behind them, and on the stairs, and in the hall below. This extraordinary setup added to the sense of theater and helped give what happened next its dramatic quality.

The speakers were hemmed in behind a bank of microphones, blinking in the TV lights. Sikeena gave a brief welcome, and then introduced the U.S. ambassador. John Herbst welcomed the Uzbek government's permission for the establishment of Freedom House as a further sign of positive reform. He cited the abolition of censorship and registration of Ardzinov's NGO as more examples of progress, and praised Uzbekistan's cooperation in the War on Terror. The German ambassador next seconded these remarks, in his usual cryptic fashion. Then I was called.

There were a fair number of Uzbek human rights activists in the audience, and they set up an expectant murmur as I walked to the microphone. Because of the cramped conditions, and because some of the auditors couldn't see the speakers, there had been a buzz of background chat. But this died away as people caught the drift of what I was saying, and despite the inelegance of sequential interpretation into both Russian and Uzbek, by a few minutes into my speech you could have heard a pin drop.

This is what I said:

I am most happy to be here today to join in Freedom House's Open House. This is a welcome addition to the resources available to the community which is working to improve basic human rights here in Uzbekistan. The organisers are to be congratulated on the initiative, as are the U.S. government for their assistance with finance.

Ladies and gentlemen, I am a Scot, and proud of my race. Our national poet, Robert Burns, notes in his great poem "The Author's Earnest Cry and Prayer" that "Freedom and whisky gang the gither," which for those whose Scots is a wee bit rusty means "Freedom and whisky together." Well, we all know how difficult it is to find real whisky in Tashkent. It does exist, but mostly on diplomatic premises. There is still a lot of wisdom in old Robert.

It is also a great pleasure to see such a gathering of those promoting human rights in Uzbekistan, both from outside and inside the country, and from both governmental and nongovernmental sectors. I am also pleased to see representatives of the media here today—I trust I will see these proceedings fully and openly reported.

Let us have no illusions about the size of the challenge we face. We must all agree that independent Uzbekistan had a great handicap to overcome in the very poor legacy on issues of freedom from the Soviet Union. But nonetheless this country has made very disappointing progress in moving away from the dictatorship of the Soviet period.

Uzbekistan is not a functioning democracy, nor does it appear to be moving in the direction of democracy. The major political parties are banned; parliament is not subject to democratic election and checks and balances on the authority of the executive are lacking.

There is worse: we believe there to be between seven and ten thousand people in detention whom we would consider as political and/or religious prisoners. In many cases they have been falsely convicted of crimes with which there appears to be no credible evidence they had any connection. Reputable human rights groups such as Human Rights Watch and Amnesty International have brought to our attention specific instances where the same crime is used serially to convict a number of people. There appears to be a belief that such persecution of an individual can be justified by labelling them as an "Islamic extremist."

Now, with the U.S. and other allies, the British government remains in the very forefront of the commitment to the war against terrorism. And we are most grateful for the invaluable assistance rendered to the coalition by the government of Uzbekistan in respect of operations in Afghanistan. We acknowledge that we face the same global threat.

Nobody should seek to underestimate the genuine security concerns of the government of Uzbekistan and the difficulties it has faced in countering those who seek to use religion and the problems of poverty to promote terror. Uzbekistan's strategic situation has put it in the forefront of countries struggling to deal with problems such as terrorism and narcotics trafficking.

But let us make this point: no government has the right to use the war against terrorism as an excuse for the persecution of those with a deep personal commitment to the Islamic religion, and who pursue their views by peaceful means. Sadly the large majority of those wrongly imprisoned in Uzbekistan fall into this category.

But it is not only Muslims who suffer; the British Embassy yesterday observed the trial of a Jehovah's Witness, being prosecuted for pursuing his beliefs. It should not be a crime to practice your religion, nor to tell others about it. And a number of those imprisoned are ethnic Russian human rights defenders, colleagues of some of my audience. I would like to say at this point how deeply I admire you on a personal level. I am very conscious that I stand here in a very privileged position, in the literal sense. You on the other hand daily risk persecution to stand up for the rights of your fellow citizens. You have my deepest respect and one day your countrymen will be in a position to show you their gratitude.

Uzbekistan is to be congratulated on a good record of ratifying key UN Conventions on human rights; unfortunately there appears to be a gap between obligation and practice.

World attention has recently been focused on the prevalence of torture in Uzbek prisons. The terrible case of Avazoz and Alimov, apparently tortured to death by boiling water, has evoked great international concern. But all of us know that this is not an isolated incident. Brutality is inherent in a system where convictions habitually rely on signed confessions rather than on forensic or material evidence. In the Uzbek criminal justice system the conviction rate is almost 100%. It is difficult not to conclude that once accused by the Prokurator there is no effective possibility of fair trial in the sense we understand it.

Another chilling reminder of the former Soviet Union is the use of commitment to lunatic asylums to stifle dissidents. We are still seeing examples of this in 2002.

Nor does the situation appear to be getting any better. I have been told, by people who should know, that there are significantly more political and religious detainees now than there were this time last year. From my own meetings with human rights groups from across the country there appears to be a broad picture of a reduction in the rate of arrests in the first half of this year, but a very substantial increase around August. Just last week saw another highly suspicious death in police custody in Tashkent. There is little sign of genuine positive change in human rights.

And that is what we want to see: genuine change. By that I mean change which actually increases the liberty of Uzbek citizens in their daily lives. Uzbekistan's international obligations require genuine respect for human rights. For example officially censorship has recently been abolished. But you would not tell this by watching, listening to or reading the media which is patently under strict control and contains no significant volume of critical comment or analysis of central government policy.

Let me give you an example. In August the government embarked upon a series of closures of major bazaars in Tashkent, and subsequently across Uzbekistan. I witnessed it happen in Namangan, for example. This is not the forum to address the motive for those closures or the rights and wrongs of this action. But it was a radical action, effected with some degree of physical and moral resistance, and closed off the retail outlets through which the majority of manufactured goods are sold in this country. It directly affected the livelihood of an estimated 50,000 people. Furthermore I have in the last two weeks visited a number of factories in Uzbekistan which have halted production and laid off their workers because their distributors have been put out of business by the bazaar closures.

As I say, I make no comment on the rights and wrongs of this, though I note that the IMF has recommended that these issues be reversed, not least because of the resulting increase in inflation. But everyone in this room knows this has been a burning political issue in the last two months. Yet one could have watched Uzbek television or listened to Uzbek radio solidly throughout this period, and read the newspaper every day, but still have gathered almost nothing of the flavour of what I have just told you. There is little reporting of basic facts and almost no free debate. I trust that the proceedings of this event will be fully and fairly reported.

What then are the components of the real change we wish to see? They are not difficult but they require political will. I believe that people are born with an instinct for liberty and that freedom and democracy come naturally to people everywhere, once they are given the chance.

Giving people freedom does not mean that anarchy and instability will follow. Indeed, it is repression which by allowing no outlet for pressures in society, risks causing resentment, alienation and social tension. Uzbekistan's partners and friends want to see a country which is stable, free and prosperous. For that to come about there needs to be change—releases of political prisoners; registration of political opposition parties and human rights groups; the opportunity for people to express their opinions in free elections and through a free media and the right to free assembly; and to practice their religious beliefs without fear of persecution. Deeper economic reform is needed also. We are ready to support that process of change, and by embarking upon it Uzbekistan will be able to transform its standing in the international community and earn the goodwill and increased support of partners whose engagement is at present limited by the problems I have addressed today.

I thank you for your kind attention.

This was stuff that just didn't get said. The diplomats wouldn't say it, and if any of the Uzbeks present had made a speech like that they would have been put straight into the torture chamber. As I had been making the speech, I had glanced occasionally at John Herbst, and watched his facial muscles grow increasingly rigid. I had in effect contradicted everything he had just said, and challenged the whole carefully constructed U.S. illusion about Uzbekistan.

In case you think I am exaggerating, it is worth quoting David Stern, a seasoned U.S. reporter on Central Asia, who was present:[2]

Three months after British Ambassador Craig Murray delivered a speech in Uzbekistan, diplomats and analysts are still debating how Murray has changed the tone of relations between Britain and this former Soviet republic. Murray caused a sensation for doing one small thing that very few people seem to have done here: he told the truth.

Ambassador Murray, with top Uzbek officials and diplomats present, delivered the diplomatic equivalent of a salvo . . .

The shock value of these statements, as well as others discussing widespread torture in Uzbekistan and the government's refusal to convert its currency or foster cross-border trade, cannot be overstated. In one fell swoop the British diplomat stripped away the euphemisms that characterize much of the West's relationship with Uzbekistan . . .

Analysts point out that what the ambassador said was in essence nothing new . . . Most of Murray's statements are common currency among foreign diplomats and businessmen in the privacy of their homes and workplaces. Yet his speech stood so far apart from official parlance that it struck some listeners as provocative. "You could have cut the tension in the room with a blunt knife," said one of those present.

The irony of Murray's speech, some say, is that it caused friction between the US and British embassies, the two foreign representations that are most concerned with democracy and human rights in Uzbekistan. US Ambassador John Herbst was present at the Freedom House function and had delivered, according to observers, a typical American take on human rights in Uzbekistan, that problems exist but progress has been made. After this predictable address, Murray delivered his broadside. "The British ambassador's speech was an embarrassment for the United States. It showed up the crack in the shield and many thought that he upstaged [Herbst]," said someone who was present . . . Even if that analysis proves accurate, though, the stridency in Murray's words has emboldened some other critics of Karimov. "To me the fundamental question is not why did he say this, but why the other ambassadors didn't?" said one Western observer.

I had achieved precisely what I set out to do. I had irreversibly shattered the conspiracy of silence and brought to international attention the brutality of the Karimov regime. I had also made it plain that British foreign policy in Central Asia was not subservient to U.S. foreign policy.

At least as long as I had my job.

THE U.S. REACTION was immediate. They had already been trying to undermine me through official channels in London. They now set about a full-frontal attack. Another journalist present at Freedom House was Michael Andersen from Danish Radio, who reported:[3]

> Many Western diplomats in Tashkent were disgusted with the US policy, but their governments kept them "on message." That is until Craig Murray arrived . . .
> In October 2002 the US ambassador gave a speech in which he praised the close relations between the US and Uzbekistan and argued that Uzbekistan had made "some progress" on "democratic reforms and human rights." The broad smile he bestowed on his new British colleague as he handed over the microphone quickly disappeared. "Uzbekistan is not a functioning democracy," said Craig Murray, adding (and contradicting what his US colleague had just said), "nor does it appear to be moving in the direction of democracy." He then described, in detail, the case of the two boiled prisoners.
> "Murray is a finished man here," one US top diplomat told me over lunch the next day. "A shame that Blair could only find an alcoholic to send here," another remarked.

Karen had done an excellent job of dishing out texts. After the speeches, the other ambassadors left, but I stayed on for wine and nibbles, and went out to a restaurant with some U.S. NGO staff afterward. When I got home, I turned on BBC World TV to see the news, and was amazed to find that my speech was the third item. It had been a busy couple of days, and I kissed Emily good night, then went to bed exhausted. I still hadn't opened my birthday presents.

I was shaken awake at 6:30 A.M. and shocked by the appearance of a bearded man looming over me. I got on my spectacles and, as my brain started to find its gears, realized that it was Richard Conroy. Richard was a pleasant but rather shy Englishman, now an Australian citizen, who ran the UN office in Tashkent.

"Craig, wake up. Wake up, Craig," he said. "Where's the speech?"

"I'm sorry, Richard?"

"Your speech last night. I need a copy. Where is it?"

"I don't know. Karen had the copies. Hang on . . ."

Richard turned his back as I got out of bed and pulled on a dressing gown. He was apologizing incoherently for the intrusion. I wasn't bothered, though surprised.

Kofi Annan was flying into Tashkent that morning. He had been visiting a neighboring state, and last night had seen my speech reported on BBC World. He had asked for a copy to be ready for him at the airport, where he would be arriving in just under an hour.

The only copy I had was the one I had read from. It wasn't in my jacket, and we found it lying scrunched up on the kitchen table. On Richard's inspiration we ironed it. I then opened up the embassy downstairs and we photocopied it, resulting in a passable copy.

"I could kiss you!" yelled Richard as he dashed for his car. Fortunately he didn't.

That evening there was a state banquet in honor of Kofi Annan at the Durmen residence. I attended in my kilt. The ambassadors were all in their places as Kofi and Karimov walked to the top table. Then, remarkably, Karimov stopped at my table, pushed past several people and sternly held out his hand for me to shake, making the gesture more theatrical by standing well short of me so I had to take two paces forward to grasp his hand. He then returned to his march to the top table. He didn't acknowledge anyone else.

After the banquet I was besieged by other ambassadors asking me what this meant. I could only surmise he was demonstrating publicly, or specifically to Kofi Annan, that he could take criticism.

The banquet finished at ten. Only undrinkable Uzbek wine had been served, so I decided to try the Ragu. This was renowned as the expats' bar, but I had not been there yet. As I entered in my kilt, I saw there was only one other customer, seated on a bar stool at the end of the bar. I asked the two pretty bar girls for a pint of Murphy's Irish Stout. They giggled and ran into a back office.

Some months later the owner of the bar, Raj, told me about this. "They called up and said that a man in a skirt had just come in and asked for a drink, and what should they do?" he said. "I told them if his money's good, I don't care if he's naked."

CHAPTER 8

The Embassy

THE NEW BRITISH RESIDENCE WAS BEING LEASED FROM THE UZBEK ambassador to Azerbaijan. It was a large, imposing building that looked like it should be in Dallas, with a white balustraded double staircase sweeping up to the large double entrance doors. The garden was enormous, and contained a substantial swimming pool. The FCO had leased the house before it was built, and had accordingly had a say in its design. One of my more flippant inputs had been to request a water feature. This had been provided, with a fountain spouting continuously from the mouth of an amphora lying on its side. The fountain splashed into a pool, which cascaded down a series of terraces until it narrowed into a channel and drove a large waterwheel. The water then continued in a narrow stream running down the center of the garden, crossed by a picturesque arched wooden bridge, until it concluded in a pond and moat surrounding a decorative pagoda.

It was lucky that the garden was so impressive, because much of the entertaining would have to be done there. The biggest drawback to the new residence was that the lounge and dining room were small. They would hold about sixty people maximum. They opened through onto a large marble terrace, which then led down to the garden. I had been told that you could entertain outside eight months a year, but now in mid-October, evenings were already a bit chilly.

The lounge, dining room, kitchen and study were on the ground floor. There were two floors upstairs, containing five bedrooms, all with en suite bathrooms. Three of the bedrooms had large dressing rooms adjoining. Downstairs the basement was enormous, extending under the terrace. Here there was a large second kitchen, ideal for functions. There were storerooms and a laundry, and a big room we used as a playroom. There was also a Turkish steam bath, with marble floor, walls, ceiling, benches and fittings, and a separate large sauna in pine, together with associated showers and plunge pool and an eight-person Jacuzzi. Outside there was an external or "summer kitchen," containing large gas-fired *plov* boilers.

A practical drawback was a lack of bathrooms. There were eight loos in the house, but five of these were in bedrooms and a sixth was a staff bathroom off the downstairs kitchen. There was only one on the ground floor. Even pressing into use the one at the bottom of the basement stairs, two loos was not enough for a large function.

There was also no cloakroom. Tashkent is very cold in winter, and sixty people coming to a cocktail party strip off a lot of heavy gear. We had to press the sauna into service as a cloakroom on occasion.

The house was built by a local contractor but it was being finished, in terms of boilers, air conditioners, generators, wiring, alarms and other technical aspects, by a Northern Irish contractor named Alex Platt. He, with his team of Irish and Polish workers, was a welcome, cheerful presence on the social scene. They introduced me to a pleasant little bar just around the corner from the embassy, called Lionheart. It was basic, serving just beer and vodka to a local clientele, mostly of student age. You could take your own music to play on the hi-fi, and I took in Queen, Supertramp and the Beatles.

I met two interesting girls there. One Russian girl named Lucy was an extremely talented artist, who sold delightful miniatures around the bars. They had whorls of pattern that were almost abstract, but would include fire, a phoenix, pine trees and other items that, while forming part of an overall pattern, were individually painted in meticulous detail. Lucy also designed and made her own clothes, which were original and striking, running from a plain, open-sided white silk tunic tied with an orange sash to a purple net blouse with balloon sleeves. She was nineteen, liked vodka and flirting, and would use her powers of seduction on American soldiers to sell her paintings, teasing outrageously until she had clinched a sale, and then pulling away rapidly. This was a high-risk strategy, and I had to rescue her at least twice from soldiers who had understood they would get more than just a painting for their money.

Lucy was a tremendous pool player, and would rook money that way too. I can see her now, winking conspiratorially at me as she bent sensuously over the pool table for the benefit of her next victim, pretending she didn't know how to hold the cue. She had a delicious upturned nose and wide smile. That Christmas she was to declare to me that she'd painted a picture for my present, but found an unexpected customer and sold it to him instead. So she had decided to sleep with me. Looking at me from the side of her eyes, she said that usually she charged three hundred dollars for sex, which was much more than she got for the painting, so this was a better present.

I laughed and told her that I would rather wait till she had a painting for me, and she giggled and hugged me. Sadly, I saw Lucy deteriorate over the next two years; she sold less paintings and more sex. Her face bloated and her eyes got redder and narrower. She drank more and the sparkle left her. I never did get that painting.

The other girl I met was Nilufar. She was short, beautiful and vivacious, with a perfect figure in skintight jeans and T-shirt. She seemed a fixture in the bar, sat there at the end of it, cigarette in hand, chatting to Yuri the barman. Yuri had long dark hair, wisps of beard and sported a red bandanna. He affected a cosmopolitan air, but had never left Tashkent.

Nilufar was extremely intelligent and very much her own woman. The first three or four times I offered to buy her a drink, she turned me down flat. In the end, I had to buy the whole bar a drink, in which she didn't object to participating. I thought Yuri and Nilufar were an item, but was most surprised when she introduced me one evening to her fiancé, Bob. He was a fifty-year-old American, short and balding with a potbelly. He worked for a company called Premier Executive that operated commercial flights in support of U.S. operations in Uzbekistan. Two of his colleagues also drank in the bar; they were essentially ground crew. Their company ran small executive jets. This did not surprise me at all, as I could think of numerous ways that kind of logistic support would be needed by the large U.S. presence in Uzbekistan, with its major construction projects at the new embassy and K2 airbase. I was surprised to learn that they sometimes flew Uzbek prisoners back to Tashkent from Baghram airbase in Afghanistan.

Nilufar was extremely feisty, and determined not to be impressed by my being an ambassador. She came from a wealthy Uzbek family, and her father was a retired KGB colonel. Nilufar and I used to argue a lot about politics. She took me aback by saying that things in Uzbekistan had gotten much worse since Soviet times. I argued, saying that she was romanticizing the Soviet Union. Communism had been an awful system, and the Soviet Union had collapsed simply because it didn't work.

I had been strongly ideologically opposed to the Soviet Union, and while I had recognized how awful the Karimov regime was, I had not yet fully come to understand that indeed this was something much worse than the Soviet Union. Since independence, there has been steadily less personal freedom in Uzbekistan, while living standards have plummeted as Soviet institutions have collapsed, without any compensating individual economic freedom. The brain drain of professionals and Russian nationals has been disastrous, and positive aspects of the Soviet legacy, like universal literacy and good roads, are fast collapsing.

A number of Nilufar's student friends were taking part in this conversation. One tall ethnic Russian, with striking long ash blond hair, was just completing her Ph.D. thesis in mathematics. She told me that her worry was the examination on the works of President Karimov. I was astonished. She explained to me that every educational course in the country, from elementary school to Ph.D., included compulsory study of Karimov's execrable books.[1] She added that she had to submit a paper titled "What the Independence of Uzbekistan Means to Me." She said, with a bitter smile, that what it meant was that the police had been able to rape her three times in the last year. Yet again, I was astonished.

This was seldom commented upon. Of that group of five girls, four had been raped by the police, some several times. The police did it because they could. People were continually stopped by police for their papers, and pretty girls were fair game. There was no justice or redress in Uzbekistan. An alleged problem with her documents, a threat to plant narcotics or charge her with prostitution, was enough: the police had a girl to play with. This evil was extraordinarily prevalent. It had become accepted as one of the standard hardships of life in the country. Nobody even seemed to get very angry about it. They were more concerned to hide the shame—a girl must be a virgin to marry.

There was an incredible practice prevalent throughout Uzbekistan.

Girls had their hymen sewn back up before marriage, so that the blood-spotted bedsheets could be displayed. This was not an urban myth—the World Health Organization estimated that 40 percent of urban Uzbek girls had their hymen stitched up, and I met a British anthropologist researching it. I also met a gynecologist who performed the operation, but 90 percent of such procedures were "back-street" jobs, carrying a serious risk of infection.

All of which gave me some pause for thought. I had been fortunate to have a number of extremely enjoyable relationships, ranging from a few hours to several years, with a number of beautiful and fascinating women, on my travels. Some of these had been genuine long-term relationships, as complex as any other in their mixture of intellect, romance and physicality. I was always prone to falling head over heels in love.

But these relationships had one thing in common. Whether in Central Europe, Russia, the Caribbean, Asia or Africa, there had always been a startling economic gap between the girl and me. I was much richer than they, or anyone whom they might normally meet. Plainly beautiful girls do not normally fancy graying, potbellied weaklings with bad teeth. Was this a continuum—to what extent was what I might do with these Uzbek girls before me equivalent to what the Uzbek police had done to them? Is voluntarism the only criterion, or do you have to consider the motives behind agreement? On the other hand, have not wealth and authority always attracted women to men?

The question troubled me. That conversation with those Uzbek girls resulted in a distinct change in my social behavior, to be less sexually predatory.

ON THE POLITICAL front, all was quiet for a couple of days after the Annan visit. Then on Sunday morning I received a summons to go immediately to the Ministry of Foreign Affairs (MFA) to see Foreign Minister Komilov.

I called Karen to accompany me. I was fully expecting to get declared persona non grata and asked to leave the country. We arrived at the Uzbek foreign ministry and squeezed into the tiny lift. It was a typical Soviet administrative building, with rows of identical doors leading off long, straight corridors.

I had paid a courtesy call on Komilov before my call on the president. He had given me scarcely five minutes, and barely shook my hand before leaving to a meeting, before I had a chance to sip my tea. Now I had his attention. Anyway, they didn't chuck me out of the country. I returned to the embassy and sent back the following report, which Karen (who understood these things) kindly typed into comms and sent off:

Restricted
Fm Tashkent
To Deskby 211030Z FCO
Telno 123
210733Z October 02

INFO Priority Cabinet Office, DFID, MODUK, HM Treasury, Bank of England, OECD Posts, NATO Posts, UKDEL EBRD London, UKDEL IMF/IBRD Washington, OSCE Posts, Pretoria, Capetown, Harare, Abuja, Lagos, Santiago, New Delhi, Security Council Posts, Islamabad, CIS/Baltic Posts, Washington

SUBJECT: UZBEKISTAN: REACTION TO HUMAN RIGHTS SPEECH

SUMMARY
1. Public display of friendship from President Karimov followed by Sunday morning summons to MFA. Foreign Minister Komilov notably more friendly than at my introductory call but no meeting of minds. Requests increased dialogue. Uzbeks will try again in London to test whether our line holds.

DETAIL
2. At the State banquet for Kofi Annan on 18 October, as is the custom here Karimov and Annan swept in and out to the top table, past the assembled guests without acknowledging them. Except that on departure Karimov made a small sideways plunge to shake my hand, holding the pose silently for a while before sweeping on. I took it as a theatrical display of openness for the UNSG.

3. Annika Savill of the UN Secretariat told me that Annan had read the speech through and included the major points in his discussions on human rights with Karimov, who had been notably terse. In the press conference Karimov had exploded at the BBC correspondent, Catherine Davis, who had asked Annan whether he thought it was sensible for donors to be pouring aid into countries with such a poor human rights record. Annan had given a reasoned though non-committal reply. Before the next question Karimov had called Davis back to the microphone and upbraided her repeatedly for asking incorrect questions. Another journalist present described him as incandescent. Savill commented that the nature of the regime had already become pretty plain to the UNSG before then.

4. I subsequently was called in to the foreign ministry at 11am on Sunday 20 October to discuss the Freedom House speech. Foreign Minister Komilov and Deputy Foreign Minister Safayev were present. Karen Moran (DHM) accompanied me.

5. In sharp contrast to my introductory call on first arrival, when Komilov was bewilderingly rude and walked out after five minutes, he was at pains to be friendly and the meeting lasted about an hour. He was this time speaking Russian and using an interpreter. As his English is fluent— better than the interpreter—this was strange until I noticed he was speaking from a script which was written in Russian. Plainly he needed to be able to say that he had stuck to the letter of the script from a higher authority.

6. Komilov said the government of Uzbekistan took issue with the speech but trusted this would not affect other areas of co-operation between us. He noted the speech had caused debate in the media. We must realise the sensitivity and ambiguity of the issues involved in fighting the danger of Islamic fundamentalism. 80% of Uzbekistan is Muslim and it would be suicidal for the Uzbek government to act against Muslims. He did not agree that there were any political prisoners or that there was religious persecution. He had heard such accusations from journalists, but never from the Ambassador of a major country.

7. I was a new Ambassador. The speech had come to the attention of the President and would reflect on the relationship with the Ambassador and the Embassy. He thought the tone of the speech different to the tone of his discussions last month in the FCO where there seemed to be a different view. They would be seeking to contact the FCO again for further talks to confirm this.

8. He admitted there were isolated incidents of abuse—they awaited the visit of the UN Special Rapporteur on Torture to discuss these. But he noted the different approach of our two governments to Hizb-ut-Tehrir. Recently hidden arms had been found in Kirghizstan and Kazakhstan which showed this group was not peaceful. They had already shown us HuT leaflets calling for Jihad and advocating the kamikaze use of aeroplanes. They had been aggressive against the Embassy in London. So when they find material calling for political change, these people are not political prisoners, they are criminals. However he re-iterated he wanted our relationship to be co-operative and not based solely on contentious issues. He would welcome increased dialogue.

9. I thanked Komilov for his views and welcomed the idea of detailed and regular dialogue. I hoped he had noted the passages in the speech thanking the government of Uzbekistan for its assistance in the conflict against terrorism and noting the very real security threats which Uzbekistan faced. I noted what he said about a perceived difference in tone but wished to make it quite plain that every word of my speech had been cleared, and much of it written, by the FCO. It was a considered speech of which he should take account.

10. The fact we had gone public showed the strength of our concern about the human rights record of the government of Uzbekistan. The repressive approach to dissidents, including those who want a more Muslim state, was breeding real grievance. There was no legal political opposition and in the absence of legitimate outlet this build-up of grievance could lead to further terrorism. We feared the Uzbek approach was counter-productive, in addition to not meeting international standards on human rights.

11. We were also concerned that apparent improvements praised by the international community had not materialised in practice. The abolition of censorship was an example. As Komilov had noted, the speech had much play in the international media. It must be important or we would not be spending a Sunday morning discussing it. And yet not one word of the content of the speech had appeared in the Uzbek media, although they had all filmed and taped it. So censorship still seems to be as effective as ever, despite its abolition.

12. Another example was the arrest and conviction of three officers last year for prisoner murder. This had been heralded as betokening a change of approach, but many such cases had occurred since with no sign of further prosecution. We were looking for real, practical, structural reform in human rights.

13. Komilov said with other governments they prefer to deal in concrete instances, not alleged thousands of prisoners. He wanted concrete facts. Uzbekistan is a large sovereign country and entitled to do things its own way. In particular no country had a right to tell it to become a less secular state.

14. I said we had not and would not comment on how secular a state Uzbekistan should be; that was for the people of Uzbekistan to decide, preferably through a free and fair political system. But just advocating a less secular way of life ought not to be cause to be locked up and mistreated.

15. Komilov said again they would only discuss individual cases. We disagreed fundamentally but dialogue should continue. While unlike the IMU, HuT was not ostensibly violent, did we expect them to wait for HuT to commit a terrible atrocity before acting? I agreed these are difficult issues; we had plenty of experience in dealing with the so-called political and paramilitary wings of movements. But a large number of those detained appeared to have no definite connection with either IMU or HuT. We, and I individually, had witnessed the courts in action and how poor the level of justice was in political trials. Reputable international human rights groups had built up a large volume of evidence on this.

16. Komilov said again they wanted hard facts and cases. I said being Sunday morning I had not arrived with a portfolio, but the EU still awaited a response to its demarche on the two prisoners who had been scalded to death in Jaslyk prison. That would be a good case to start.

17. Komilov said he stood by his own opinions and had given me the formal position of the government of Uzbekistan. They would seek in London to clarify the British government position.

COMMENT

18. The Uzbek government had felt that by joining the coalition against terrorism they would secure a respite from serious international pressure over their repressive and dictatorial regime. As Kofi Annan left

Kwasniewski arrived and Karimov was looking forward to a bit of international limelight. It has not gone off as planned.

19. The timing of the speech on the eve of Annan's arrival was entirely fortuitous, and if it had not appeared on BBC World he would never have known of it. However neither Savill nor UNDP [United Nations Development Program] *resident rep Richard Conroy has indicated that Annan found it anything other than helpful. We are seeking a wider briefing on the Annan visit to report separately.*

20. I confess to not being sure just how violent or not HuT is. The planting of HuT leaflets on prisoners is standard practice here—in one recent trial in Ferghana where our Electronic Court Reporting is in use, allegedly a prisoner taken from bed in his underpants had some hidden in them. To move from planting leaflets to creating your own featuring heightened violence is a small step. I would be grateful for a read-out on how much we can authenticate on HuT's views.

21. I should also be grateful for guidance on how we view the Uzbek government's appeal to the doctrine of pre-emption. I didn't respond on this occasion because I don't know what our line is. As I understand it there is a well-established right to act against conspiracy, but presumably acting against people you think might be going to conspire is still pretty contentious?

22. On Komilov's desire only to discuss individual cases, this chimes with the German approach here. The German Ambassador told me they prefer not to make a public fuss but to work on getting key individuals released who are then given political asylum in Germany. He referred to two journalists and a number of writers and artists. I told him this approach seemed wrong-headed. The answer was to improve Uzbekistan, not ship good Uzbeks to Europe. He replied we should concentrate on the possible.

23. I trust Komilov will be disappointed in hoping to hear a substantively different message in London.

MURRAY

Foreign Office telegrams are an art form in themselves. They are normally beautifully phrased and say very little, being lengthy exercises in temporizing, with an extra emphasis on special pleading on behalf of the host government.

My telegrams were so different that I was now receiving many congratulatory e-mails and letters from colleagues, including from ambassadors much senior to me. One message ran: "Well done! In these dangerous and difficult times, it is our duty to call it as it is, not say what others want to believe." A simpler message read: "You must have balls like a sperm whale."

One fellow ambassador sent me a postcard of Oscar Wilde, with a Wilde quotation: "Anyone who tells the truth is bound to be found out sooner or later." That proved to be prescient. His message began, "We have been reading your telegrams with equal measures of astonishment, agreement and enthusiasm."

Suddenly, my stock was very high. Being British ambassador had not cut much ice when I first arrived. In my first fortnight, I had accepted an invitation to a dinner to celebrate the sixtieth anniversary of the state tractor factory. All the ambassadors were invited, but I was the only one to turn up apart from the Belgian honorary consul. We were completely ignored, and left to find our own place on the bottom of many tables. I learned that the rudeness shown to the diplomatic corps at Independence Day was typical. The Uzbek authorities were as contemptuous of the outside world as they were mindful of minute hierarchies among their own members. Just as in Soviet days, who appeared in official lineups with the president, and in just what position, mattered minutely. The third assistant engineer at the Nukus cotton ginnery outranked any ambassador. In consequence, other ambassadors had stopped going to all noncompulsory events.

They missed some treats. I was invited to a concert at Tashkent Conservatoire, and enjoyed a superb performance of both Gershwin's "Rhapsody in Blue" and "An American in Paris," featuring a young Uzbek pianist who had won that year's Conservatoire competition. The orchestra was first-class, and I was amazed to learn that these were the first performances of Gershwin in Uzbekistan.

I was again the only ambassador to turn up. There was nothing prepared for me and I was left to find a place in a concert hall that was overfull. I had made the mistake of going to the main entrance, whereas the concert hall is entered by a side door. It was six-thirty and just getting dark. A very pretty young student, with long red hair and bright red lipstick, saw me looking confused. She wore jeans and denim jacket, while everyone else was in either Western formal or Uzbek traditional clothing.

She took me by the arm and led me round the great modern building. It was quite a walk, but in her company most enjoyable. She spoke almost no English, and was a native Uzbek speaker whose Russian was not fluent. She told me that her name was Kamola, and she was studying concert piano and composition. Her father was professor of traditional music at the conservatoire. As I had plans to use music in my diplomatic effort, I was glad to meet her. I was even more so when the great romantic climaxes swirled up in "Rhapsody in Blue," and her bosom heaved while she looked at me with wide eyes.

After my Freedom House speech I discovered I was suddenly somebody. I was quickly on the top table wherever I went. Komilov came and sat next to me at functions.

More to the point, I started to be able to get things done. The assault on the private sector continued, with new bans on cash transactions. These forced transactions through the state banks, which quite simply stole people's money. Any transaction over $500 would bring a visit from the tax police, who had a whole heap of antienterprise weapons. It became clear that there was a definite intention to eliminate private wealth and economic autonomy outside of the regime families.

Part of this was an assault on foreign investors. Jitendra Patel, owner of QuickStop, was typical in facing attempts by the Uzbek courts to take his company from him. At least eleven British companies were in similar positions. One U.K. company owned a 60 percent stake in a cottonseed plant in Jizzak. They now found the doors locked against them; without their knowledge, a court had reassessed the asset value of the joint venture, and awarded a 70 percent stake to the local government. Other foreign companies were being deliberately bankrupted, for example, by not being allowed to export products. The government would then claim the assets.[2]

The extraordinary thing about my new hard-man status was that I could intervene in such cases, and actually be listened to. In most cases the local *hokkimyat* was the key government entity dealing with investors. I was soon zooming round the country in the Discovery, meeting with *hokkims* and shouting at them. The browbeating seemed to work and I was able generally to suspend the action against British firms. After 10,000 miles in its first three years, the Discovery put on another 25,000 miles in my first three months. All this activism on behalf of British business was to prove crucial to me in my coming trials.

The head of the Center for the Organization for Security and Co-operation in Europe (OSCE) was a Turk named Ahmet Erozan. The OSCE had originally nominated a British candidate, Simon Hemans, but the Uzbeks had refused to accept him, as they did not want the OSCE to be active on human rights. The OSCE had then rather spinelessly produced a panel of candidates for the Uzbeks to choose; they plumped for a Turkish diplomat, thinking he would be most unlikely to trouble them.

They could not have been more wrong. Ahmet Erozan was a big, hearty man with a naughty grin and a great passion for life, a passion for his work and a passion for helping ordinary people. He took over the office from a Romanian who had no obvious interest except in sleeping with his staff. Erozan transformed it into an effective and hard-hitting unit, and did so remarkably quickly.

Now he sat in my office, savoring his tea, stretching out his legs before the sofa, hands in pockets, grinning his broad grin.

"You see, my friend, you have balls. They don't expect that in an ambassador. The others crawl to them. Of course, I have balls"—he patted them expansively to illustrate the case—"but no one expects them in a British diplomat. Of course you are Scottish—*Braveheart!*

"I am a Turk," he went on. "You know, my people are close to the Uzbeks. I can understand their language, it's like old country Turkish. And I understand their culture. I know their mentality. Other diplomats are polite and listen. They may try to explain but not to argue. I tell you this—the Uzbeks have nothing but contempt for the ambassadors in this town. They despise them. They think they are weak!"

Can't say I blame them, I thought, but just tried to maintain a noble William Wallace–type bearing.

"But you are different. You just refuse to play by their rules. You tell them to their face what you think. You know, you would be surprised at some of the people in this town who admire you. Believe me, I know. Of course, you realize most of your Western colleagues hate you."

Ahmet obviously needed no lessons from me in straight talking. He carried on: "I hear you told Azimov to his face that his statistics were lies?"

"Pretty well," I said.

"You probably don't realize just what you have done. All their lives, nobody ever dared talk to these people like that. Uzbeks would be beaten and imprisoned, Western businessmen are groveling for favors, and diplomats simply don't. Take Azimov. You know as leader of the Uzbek Communist Student League he denounced his fellow executive members. Some of them disappeared completely. No one has stood up to him since he was eighteen. He's been spouting his rubbish for years. No one ever challenged him. Then you. This society is based on raw power. Suddenly they find you've got the big balls, and you're pushing them around."

I had been wondering about this. "But what's my leverage? Is it just bluff and psychology? Or do they want something I am threatening? They don't seem too bothered about an IMF loan, for example."

"Mostly it's just basic psychology. They respect the bigger balls. But Karimov cares about international reputation, and they are very keen to host the EBRD AGM in May—that's a big prestige thing for them."

Reputation was bringing businessmen with problems, and ordinary Uzbeks whose relatives were imprisoned or tortured, flooding to my door. Every NGO and journalist was coming to me for straight-talking analysis of the situation, and I was making friends among members of the Uzbek elite, many of whom were engaged in political bet hedging. All this was enormously helpful to me in picking up information on the country.

I was getting very busy. A small triumph to savor was when, before some official event, I received a call from the Ministry of Foreign Affairs protocol department. Ambassadors had been instructed to be in their seats over an hour before the function started. But I could turn up ten minutes before, as long as I didn't tell anyone else!

I was learning that I had seriously underestimated Karen. She had concentrated on commercial work and, with the help of the excellent Lena Son, she had an encyclopedic knowledge of the workings of the Uzbek commercial sector. With Dave Muir tied up continuously in immigration work, Karen also kept much of the mechanism of the embassy turning over and coped with the appalling burden of bureaucratic returns back to London. She could handle any task with tremendous energy and dispatch. Chris also was a great support, as he seemed to welcome the new tempo I brought to the embassy's work. He was very capable, though lacking in confidence. For example, he had not been allowed to send off his own telegrams on politics and human rights before. I gave him his head, and he was very good.

On the other hand, working relationships in the embassy were poisonous. Dave obviously hated Chris and Karen, while the relationships between U.K. and Uzbek staff were strained and formal. I had the impression the Uzbeks were treated with scant respect. This was a pity, because they were good. Part of the trouble was the lack of the normal senior and middle-level British staff in an embassy. To put it at its most basic, Colonel Ridout and I were the only university graduates among the U.K. staff. The Uzbek staff were almost all graduates, even most of the guards. Relationships seemed to be ruled by mutual contempt.

In early November we had a trade mission visiting from the London Chamber of Commerce. This consisted of a dozen or so representatives of companies hoping to export to Uzbekistan, ranging from British Aerospace to a one-man trading firm. We provided an excellent program of meetings, and managed to get everyone who wanted in to see the senior minister in charge of their sector, an unheard-of level of access.

We held a reception for the mission at the unfinished new residence, in the garden, on November 5. It was getting pretty cold for this, but on an inspiration I had ordered large gas-fired patio heaters, which were spread around the terrace. We had about 250 guests, including senior Uzbeks and contacts relevant to the specific business of each company. The evening was a great success, and being Guy Fawkes night, concluded with a fireworks display.

All this was proving too much for Galina, whose nerves couldn't cope with catering on this kind of scale. I learned from Alex Platt that the original residence cook was Galina's sister, a first-class professional chef. She had married Alex's foreman, and moved to Northern Ireland. The job had then passed to Galina, a teacher who couldn't particularly cook. As my predecessor's needs were simple, that hadn't much mattered. Unfortunately, Galina now resigned. We replaced her with Lena, a short, bouncy Russian who could cope with pretty much any demand.

*   *   *

THE TRADE MISSIONERS introduced me to a person and to a place. Both had a major effect. One businessman invited me to dinner with his key Uzbek contact, an oligarch named Zokirjon Umarov. He lived in a village outside Tashkent, off the Samarkand road. I had not realized how far away it was, down narrow country lanes. Dinner was well advanced by the time I arrived, but I could not help but be entranced by the huge villa tastefully furnished with modern oil paintings and antiquities. These included wooden carvings from Khiva, illustrated volumes of poetry from Samarkand and ceramics from Afrosiyab. He was a genial host, speaking broken English, and insisted he would invite me again.

The other introduction was to the Safar Club. Right above the Lionheart bar, this was a nightclub where the clientele sat in curtained booths, eating and looking out at the dance floor where showgirls belly danced, or occasionally pole danced in bra and knickers. The belly dancers would go round the tables, squeezing into the booths and performing right in front of you, while you tucked a note into their bra or knickers strap. It was all very demure compared with Western lap-dancing clubs—it became a regular haunt of mine, and I never saw so much as a nipple. But you could invite the dancers or waitresses to sit in the booth with you. The drinks and food were reasonably priced, but certain items—nonalcoholic cocktails and chocolate—were ludicrously expensive. The girls would request these, and get a 10 percent commission on them. The unwary could spend an evening with a girl and feel confident she had drunk only fruit juice, and then get a bill for several hundred dollars. The answer was to buy the girl beer and slip her ten dollars direct. This was fine with the girls, but sometimes the management could get shirty.

Some of the missioners took me out to this club, where we had a very jolly table. There was a ten o'clock curfew on bars, and you entered the club by knocking on a nondescript door. It opened a crack, and if the doorman ascertained you were safe, a beautiful girl would lead you down a corridor and up two flights of steps, the pitch darkness broken only by the flicker of her cigarette lighter. You then pushed through heavy felt curtains and emerged into the bright lights of the club. A couple of the businessmen knew the pitfalls of what to order, and warned the rest of us. It was a fun time.

* * *

ONCE THE TRADE mission left, I was immediately confronted by two staff crises. The first was astonishing. I received a letter from Chris and Karen's Uzbek neighbors. They alleged that Chris had set his dog upon their children, thrown the children's bikes into a ditch, kicked down the door of the family home and threatened the father with an iron bar.

Chris and Karen had a large rottweiler named Lalka. It was a terrifying beast, 130 pounds of pure muscular strength. They had been unfailingly kind to my children, and visiting their home one day I was appalled to see Lalka pulling Emily around the tiled floor as Emily clung to her tail. Emily was enjoying the game and the dog seemed to do so too, but the dog weighed three times Emily and could kill her in a moment. Karen saw my face and hastened to assure me that Lalka was very docile, but I wouldn't let Emily go to their house again.

So the allegation that Chris had set the dog on children really worried me. I remembered my predecessor's enigmatic warning, called Chris and Karen in to my office and showed them the letter.

They denied it flat. Chris said the children had been in an apricot tree overlooking their courtyard, throwing stones at Lalka. Chris had simply gone round to remonstrate with their father. He had neither kicked the door down nor threatened, though he had been angry. I asked about the bikes, and Chris said he had needed to move them to get to the neighbors' door, but had not thrown them.

Karen said she had been there and could confirm that Chris was telling the truth. But I noticed tears were welling in her eyes, and she turned away from me as one started to trickle down her cheek. My instincts told me she was lying.

Later that day David Muir stopped me in the corridor. "You're not going to do anything, then?" he said.

"Sorry, Dave. About what?"

"About Chris."

"Well, I don't see that I can."

"Really?" He smirked, not entirely pleasantly.

"Someone has made an allegation. Chris denies it flatly, and Karen says she was there and backs him up. I can't say two colleagues are lying without more evidence."

"Can't you?" David raised an eyebrow.

"Not unless you can tell me something more."

"I'm saying nothing."

"Look, David. You either know something or you're trying to imply that you do. Now, I'm tired and I need help."

"Well, this isn't exactly the first time. I know loads of expats in Tashkent, and the only one who ever has problems is Chris Hirst. Now, what does that tell you?"

David headed back to the visa section, leaving me with food for thought.

The next day, I called Chris and Karen again.

"Look, I've been thinking about this. I am told it's not the first time you've had problems."

"Some of the neighbors are really difficult," said Karen.

"I think it's a provocation by the SNB," added Chris.

"Well, I don't think your house is large enough to do the scale of entertaining I want my deputy to be taking on. And we'll need a new house anyway as presumably, when you leave next year, you'll be replaced by two separate officers, not a couple. So let's find a new house and move you to another district."

Chris seemed enthusiastic; he jumped at the idea. Karen looked unhappy, but didn't argue much. After they left, I said out loud to myself: "And then I'll find out if it was the neighbors, or if it's you."

AN EQUALLY EXTRAORDINARY problem hit me the next day. Valeri had asked Nafisa, the accountant, for a false declaration of salary for Zhenya and himself. Families earning below a certain level get free schooling, while Zhenya and Valeri had to pay a small contribution, a few dollars a month. Nafisa refused to issue a false certificate, and so they had produced one themselves, on embassy paper.

Karen brought me the news. She seemed triumphant rather than sad. Zhenya and Valeri admitted it—Zhenya arrogantly, Valeri quietly and shame-facedly. I reluctantly agreed to Karen's assertion that this had to be a sacking offense.

I would miss Valeri, but had to admit I hadn't warmed to Zhenya. She had been recruited direct from the KGB, and maintained some of those attitudes. I wasn't sure how far I trusted her.

I now needed a new secretary, and I decided we would get two people, one for me and one for the visa section, rather than split the job as Zhenya had done. My office and the visa section were both getting exponentially busier. We advertised the jobs in the local papers—another new departure for the embassy—and got a tremendous response. Karen and I selected a dozen secretaries for interview, and we set aside a day to do it.

Within minutes of the first candidate walking in the door, she had the job. She spoke near-fluent English, typed and took shorthand, and had previously worked for a Turkish commercial company. She also had the most extraordinary classical beauty, a perfect face framed by long blond hair. Karen agreed she was the best candidate, which I found a useful defense when Fiona first set eyes on Kristina.

To replace Valeri we promoted one of the guards, Yuri, to driver. He was a slight but handsome man. Karen worked out a new shift roster to try to reduce the overtime. This meant that there was no longer a designated flag car driver, though in fact Gafur became more and more "my" driver. We eventually ended up hiring a third driver, Sasha, as the embassy got increasingly busy. I also had a personal driver, Konstantin, paid from my own pocket, to drive my private car, a Mitsubishi Montero, and to look after Fiona.

Fiona was also increasingly busy. We were averaging three functions a week at home, ranging from afternoon tea through dinner for sixteen to cocktails and canapés for three hundred. In addition she had taken on the job of chairman of the board of Tashkent International School. This was no sinecure. With the greatly increasing presence of U.S. government personnel, the school was rapidly expanding and needed new premises. Acquiring property in Tashkent was complicated, and the scheme was likely to involve a multimillion-dollar contract for building and/or renovation. Fiona was tackling all this with her usual mix of energy and brusque acuity.

Meanwhile we received a welcome addition to our British staff in the shape of Sergeant John Agnew of the RAF, as assistant to Nick Ridout. It now became still more urgent to get the defense section out of their cupboard, and we anxiously awaited the completion of the new residence so that the embassy could expand into the apartment above.

CHAPTER 9

Merry Christmas,
War Is Coming

EVENTUALLY THE EU MECHANISM CLICKED ROUND, AND IT WAS finally agreed that EU ambassadors would deliver a démarche over the boiling deaths and the Khuderbegainov trial. Komilov had been kicked upstairs from foreign minister to be a presidential adviser, and his smooth deputy, Safayev, had been promoted to foreign minister. Safayev had been Uzbek ambassador to Washington, and the U.S. embassy viewed him as a reformer, though I never saw the slightest evidence of it.

EU démarches were normally delivered by a "troika" of three nations. As there were only four EU ambassadors in Uzbekistan, we all went.

Jacques-Andre Costilhes, for the French presidency, delivered the démarche in a tour de force of Gallic insouciance. Every nuance of tone, every scrap of body language, spelled out a plain message: "I am very sorry to waste your time with this, Minister, and this has nothing to do with me, or with France, but I have to read out this rather embarrassing statement. We are civilized people and I will do this quickly, for form's sake, then you can reply while I listen politely, then we can all go home."

Safayev said that in the case of Avazov and Alimov, an official investigation had revealed that they had died in a fight over a samovar, which explained the scalds. As for Khuderbegainov, he was astonished that the European Union concerned itself with a violent terrorist.

Before we left, Jacques-Andre asked if any of his colleagues had anything to add. I said that in the Khuderbegainov case, the problem was the lack of any kind of fair trial, whether he was a terrorist or not. In particular, the allegations that the accused and witnesses had been tortured were not taken seriously by the courts. We were worried about the prevalence of torture in general and the reliance of the legal system upon confessions. Over 99 percent of trials ended in conviction, which threw doubt on the fairness of the system.

"Ambassador, all our countries have different legal systems. Your system is perhaps very clumsy. Unfortunately, in the United Kingdom many innocent people are accused and, of course, acquitted. Under our system, only the guilty are accused. That is why they are not acquitted. You must allow us our own tradition."

My French and German colleagues laughed obsequiously at Safayev's little sally. They had been shifting uncomfortably when I was speaking.

The lack of fair trial was a continuation of the Soviet system, although the use of physical torture had increased. The KGB had largely used the most intense psychological pressure—brute physicality was a hallmark of the Uzbek regime. More and more cases came to me. Plain beating was commonplace, as was smashing of limbs by a blunt instrument, and application of electric shock, generally to the genitals. Drowning was pretty common. More so was asphyxiation, and one technique was widespread throughout the country—they would strap on a gas mask and then block the filters. I presume that the advantage of this was that it would suffocate without bruising. I also came across several cases of the use of chlorine gas.

Most common of all was rape and sodomy. Any young woman arrested was very likely to be raped, whether she confessed or not. Men were most often raped with objects such as bottles, though they could be brutally sodomized as well. Rape of family in front of a detainee is a very common method of extracting a confession.

Homosexuality is taboo in Uzbekistan, where it is illegal. Gays are seldom prosecuted but often brutally beaten. Many are blackmailed by the police. But I could not understand how macho policemen, who would hate gays, could then rape prisoners, not just with objects. I asked Zokirjon Umarov to explain this.

"They don't see it as sex. It is power. To humiliate and give pain."

"But these policemen come."

"Yes, but it's not sex, it's power. It's not a man, it's just a hole. They are not gay. Call one gay and see what they do to you."

I was unconvinced—plainly there was a lot of weird repression in this society.

CHRIS HAD PUT A huge amount of effort into a court-reporting project. There were no transcripts of trials in Uzbekistan, so the British government had paid for computers to be installed in courtrooms to make an untamperable recording of proceedings. We employed the American Bar Association and an NGO called Central European and Eurasian Law Initiative (CEELI) to manage the project. A pilot had started in the Ferghana Valley, and was due to be rolled out across the country. I was skeptical.

Chris organized a meeting with the ladies from the American Bar Association to persuade me to support the next phase. Their hearts were all very much in the right place, but I asked, "So, how many trials have been monitored so far?"

"Over a thousand now, Ambassador."

"And how many acquittals have there been?"

Consternation.

"Well, it is difficult to be completely certain, but we don't believe there have been any actual acquittals. But the point of the equipment is to provide a record. It can be used for appeal."

"Well, how many have been acquitted on appeal?"

"Well, none yet, but probably most of them haven't completed the appeals process. We believe the existence of the equipment in the court may be leading to a change in courtroom behavior, with more respect paid to the defense. There could be a reduction in the severity of sentences, and in the use of the death penalty."

"Can you quantify that?"

"No, Ambassador, not yet."

I concluded it was too early to justify spending on the next stage. What particularly worried me was that the scheme was being quoted, not least by the Uzbeks, as evidence of reform, while it was giving nothing but a veneer of respectability to an unjust system. Better sham trials seemed of limited use, and arguably pernicious.

PROFESSOR THEO VAN BOVEN, the United Nations special rapporteur on torture, was paying an investigatory visit to Uzbekistan. Everyone was somewhat baffled as to why the Uzbeks had agreed to let him in. It was understood that the U.S. had persuaded Karimov that a well-managed visit would burnish the country's image.

There appeared to be little to fear. Van Boven's program had been negotiated with the Uzbek authorities. But much of it depended on input from Chris, direct to Van Boven's office, on the most notorious torture centers to visit.

Van Boven arrived in the late afternoon and his official program started the next morning. But that first evening, we gave a reception for him in the residence, to which we invited human rights defenders and relatives of torture victims. It was harrowing. The facade of cocktail party did not last long, before Van Boven's team got out their notebooks and started taking down case histories. Soon little knots were forming all over the apartment. Fiona switched the supply of drinks to relays of coffee, and I bustled round directing staff to interpret. Under gentle and expert questioning, details came out which I had not heard before. I found tales involving children especially harrowing; at one stage I retreated to my office to recompose myself. I learned of the placing of healthy dissidents into TB wards so they catch it. Uzbek prisons are riddled with drug-resistant TB. I recall Dilobar Khuderbegainova giving details of her brother's case to a researcher, seated at Fiona's dressing table, he perched on the edge of our bed, notebook on knee.

When Van Boven eventually left, the researcher with Dilobar had still not finished his notes of this case. He needed a few more minutes, and Chris offered to run him back to his hotel when he finished. Chris and I agreed that, after hearing all that horror, we both needed a drink, so I went along too. It turned out neither Chris nor the visitor knew which hotel he was in, and Chris drove his Land Rover to several, cursing under his breath, until he found the right one.

After we finally got rid of our visitor, Chris headed for the Lionheart bar and, on the way, something quite extraordinary happened. He put his foot down and started driving in a manner I can only describe as manic. He gunned the Land Rover up to full speed, ignoring red lights and causing one car to swerve violently to miss us at an intersection. Even more worrying, he drove straight at a Lada moving quietly along in front of us, traveling about fifty miles an hour faster than it was. Just when it seemed we must hit, he slammed on the brakes and slowed inside it, missing it by inches. Having passed it, he pulled back sharply in front and slammed on the brakes, bringing the Land Rover screeching almost to a halt. The whole time he stared ahead, his face purple, his pupils contracted to pinpricks, his knuckles white on the wheel.

"Fuckers," he spat out, "fuckers fuckers fuckers fuckers. Fuckers fuckers fuckers fuckers. Uzbek fuckers."

This was counterpointed by my attempts to break in. "Chris!" I yelled. "Chris! Chris! Speak to me, Chris!"

I put my hand on his arm. He slapped it away, leaving his hand on my chest. He was much more powerful than me. But he seemed to see me, and he brought the car to a stop, in the fast lane.

"Yes, what is it?" he asked tetchily.

"Are you OK? You seemed to get madly aggressive."

"I don't know what you're talking about. Do you still want that drink?"

"Yes, but calm down."

"OK. Lionheart bar, isn't it?" He drove off sedately. "I think Van Boven learned a lot today."

He's not the only one, I thought. But I said, "Yes, the evening went very well. Thanks for all the slog you put in."

We pulled up at the Lionheart bar, but Chris lost it again. I bought him a drink, and he turned to me and said, "This place is full of bloody Uzbeks."

I smiled an apology at Yuri, who shrugged. But Nilufar had heard.

"I'm a bloody Uzbek," she said.

"Fuck off, I don't talk to prostitutes," said Chris.

Several people stood up. I put my arm round Chris. I could feel his muscles flexing.

"Chris, you're tired, go home," I said.

"Do you want to go to Safar?" he asked.

"Good idea," I said. At least I might get him out of there before a fight started. But once we were out the door, I discovered that he didn't mean the Safar upstairs, but Safar in the park. There had been five of these Safars, under the same ownership, though they were getting closed down one by one by the Uzbek government. The one in the park was reputed to feature actual stripping. I told Chris I didn't want to go to the park. He stormed off into the night.

I went back into the bar to apologize. Nobody held it against me. I paid for the beers poured for Chris and me, gave them away to a couple of students and made the short walk home. I was really worried about what I had seen from Chris, and couldn't understand it. He normally had an old-fashioned Yorkshire courtesy, but I had seen this mad rage. I made allowances because I too had been emotionally affected by a difficult evening. But how could you explain someone who seemed to work with a genuine commitment to human rights, and the next minute could sound like an aggressive nutter?

The next day I pressed Karen over plans for them to move. If there were problems in a new district I would know, as I now suspected, that Chris was the problem. What would then be the solution was another question.

VAN BOVEN'S VISIT was stunning. Against the protocols, the Uzbek authorities refused to let him enter the SNB holding center in Tashkent, the most notorious of all the torture sites. He visited Jaslyk gulag, but the Uzbeks deliberately messed around the transport so a day's inspection was shortened to an hour. We obtained definite intelligence material proving that the Uzbeks deliberately delayed and obstructed him. I pointed out to London that we were about to invade Iraq based on much less concrete evidence of obstruction of United Nations inspectors.

Van Boven produced a report that said that torture in Uzbekistan was "widespread and systemic," and "used as a routine investigative technique." The Uzbek government was furious, and the Americans much embarrassed. John Herbst argued that it was a mistake to report in such strong terms, because now the Uzbeks would be wary of such visits. I suggested that visits which pulled their punches were of no use anyway. The diplomatic climate was changing in my favor. The diplomatic corps could write off reports from Human Rights Watch as unreliable; they were not a part of official reality. But a UN report certainly was.

The OSCE was preparing a workshop to be held in the Intercontinental Hotel. It was a teach-in on the international legal position on torture, which is banned in all its forms, much as is slavery. The course included the definition of torture, and how judicial mechanisms might be used to prevent the infection of the justice system by torture evidence. Uzbek ministries and law enforcement agencies were all supposed to participate at a senior level, but they all sent low-ranking representatives. Here I met Professor Douwe Korff, who teaches international law at London Metropolitan University. He gave a powerful presentation, setting out that it was against international law to obtain or use information gathered under torture.

Just before this, I had been most concerned by intelligence material we were receiving from SIS (better known as MI6). I had been reading the regular flow of this material, and as I got to know the country, I had been increasingly concerned at the gap between this material and the truth.

Numerical codes showed me that this was CIA material, sourced from the Uzbek SNB, which the CIA shared with MI6, who issued it to customers such as British ministers, the Eastern Department and me. I now saw two items that seemed to sum up my concerns about these intelligence reports. The first claimed that Islamic militants were gathered in camps in the Tajik hills just above Samarkand, ready to swoop upon the city. I discussed this with Nick Ridout, and we agreed it was nonsense—there were, physically, no such camps there.

The second piece of intelligence purported to give information that certain Uzbek dissidents were linked to al-Qaida, and had traveled to Afghanistan to meet Osama bin Laden. This closely resembled the statement of the old man at the Khuderbegainov trial, and I recalled his desperate outburst: "It's not true. They tortured my grandchildren in front of me until I signed this."

Mostly the material just said it came from "a friendly security service." Sometimes, but not always, it specified "from detainee debriefing." I had seen enough of the routine methods of the Uzbek security services to be pretty sure that this stuff was hot out of the torture chambers.

After meeting Douwe Korff, I was convinced that what we were doing was not only wrong, but illegal. That provided the leverage I needed to get us to stop it. The trick, I decided, would be to get the question above officials, and put squarely before ministers. A telegram from an ambassador expressing concern that ministers were acting illegally would have to be put before them, rather than filtered out by officials who prepared the ministers' "red boxes" of daily material.

Before drafting a hard-hitting telegram, I wanted to make quite sure I was on firm ground and would not be making a fool of myself. I therefore asked Karen to go see her U.S. opposite number, David Appleton, to check with him that the CIA did not have procedures in place to ensure that any material they received from the Uzbeks could not come from torture. She returned and reported that David was not available, so she had met another senior member of the mission. My recollection was that she reported to me that she met the head of the CIA station, but I have since been informed that it was Larry Memmot, political counselor. He had said that yes, come to think of it, the intelligence probably did come from torture. He had not thought of that as a problem before, and he commented to Karen that it was an indication of how far 9/11 had shifted moral perceptions.

So, confident I was on safe ground, I sent off my bullet. I can't reproduce the telegram, because it was classified top secret. But it said that we were obtaining intelligence material from the Uzbek security services. It was probably obtained through torture, which the Americans, who supplied it to us, were not denying. We should stop getting it on legal, practical and moral grounds.

Legally, we were in contravention of the UN Convention against Torture, Article 4 of which banned "complicity" in torture. To obtain such intelligence on a regular basis undoubtedly made us complicit. I said that in supplying this intelligence to ministers, I was afraid we might be putting ministers at risk of breaking U.K. and international law.

Practically, I said the information was useless. It was not just wrong, it presented a deliberate distortion. It all had a common theme: it aimed to exaggerate the Islamic threat to Uzbekistan, with the aim of justifying continued support of the Karimov regime.

Morally, the argument was self-evident. Torture is simply wrong. In resorting to receiving information through torture, we were demeaning ourselves and abandoning the very values we claimed to be defending in the War on Terror.

My intention had been to get attention at the top of the FCO. I succeeded. Foreign Minister Jack Straw, head of the diplomatic service Sir

Michael Jay, and head of MI6, Richard Dearlove, held meetings to discuss it. But I had seriously miscalculated when I had believed that British ministers would not want material obtained through torture. What I achieved was to increase to sizzling point the hostility toward me at the senior levels of the British government, and particularly from the intelligence services.

I had failed adequately to take into account that I was only seeing the torture material from Uzbekistan. In the War on Terror it had been decided to relax our taboo on torture, and we were accepting material from the torture chambers of Egypt, Pakistan, Jordan, Saudi Arabia and a number of other countries, including the Sudan and Syria. The British government was even going to court for the right to use torture material as evidence in court. The government won this right in the Court of Appeal in November 2004, but lost to a unanimous judgment of seven law lords on December 8, 2005.

I had not accounted for the possibility that Blair would return the U.K. to Tudor standards of barbarity. I am glad that the law lords upheld the values of civilization, but I still find it incredible that the government was prepared to argue, before the highest court in the land, for the use of torture material.

Samarkand was the target for my next regional visit, and I would be setting off with the new team of Yuri and Kristina to accompany me. On the way back, we would be visiting the town of Jizzak. It was a dark, cold, late November day. I had wanted to leave at noon, but the pressure of work kept me back. When I finished work it was about 4 P.M., and beginning to snow quite heavily. Several of the staff advised me not to go, but I didn't see any great danger in the late-autumn weather.

The road to Samarkand ran through a bit of Kazakhstan, and with the border closures, a fifty-mile section had been closed off. Ordinary traffic had a two-hour detour, but diplomatic vehicles could still get through, and it was an easy three-hour drive. As we joined the main Samarkand road from a slip, I realized the snow was getting heavy, and the light had taken on an ominous purple tinge. Already there was a foot of snow on the verges, and with little traffic, the slush on the highway was substantial.

By thirty miles outside Tashkent, we were in pitch blackness, and the wipers could not cope with the weight of snow piling on the windscreen. Yuri had slowed to about twenty miles an hour.

"Yuri," I said, "we'll have to go quicker or we'll just get snowed in. Take a chance on it."

Yuri sped up to around fifty miles an hour. The snow was falling just as heavily, but at that speed the rush of air blew it past the car. We got along fine, bar the odd skid. Poor Yuri had huge difficulty in working out where, in the tumbling chaos, the road was. Again and again, our luck held.

Then it didn't. Suddenly light pierced the darkness and a military guard post loomed, one of the permanent checkpoints on the road, this one marking the boundary of Syr Dar'ya and Jizzak provinces. By the time we saw the floodlit checkpoint through the snow, we were less than a hundred yards away. Yuri slammed on the brakes, and as we were now traveling on top of a thick carpet of snow and ice, that was a big mistake.

The wheels locked and the vehicle slowed round. It continued on the same trajectory straight down the highway, but now speeding along sideways like a one-ton curling stone, having hardly lost any speed and with nothing we could do about it.

The checkpoint had concrete barriers to funnel the westward traffic into two lanes and make sure there was no route around the side. The lanes were divided by concrete barriers set along the lane markings. They were four feet tall, twelve feet long and just six inches deep, with a broader base at the bottom. We were now hurtling at forty miles an hour into the six-inch concrete edge, which was going to strike exactly at the rear passenger seat. The broad base would slip under the car chassis, meaning that the full, massive impact would be concentrated on that narrow edge. Time seemed to slow down.

Kristina was seated on the left side of the rear seat, and that concrete edge was hurtling straight at her. She screamed. Instinct took over, and I unclipped my seat belt and threw myself on top of her, bracing myself against the door that would take the impact, my feet pushing her across to the other side (not much, she still had her seat belt on). I cursed myself—what a stupid way to die.

Land Rovers were famous for their flimsy bodywork, which offered no protection in a roll. But the new Discovery must be fearsomely well built. The concrete edge slammed into the rear passenger door, which jack-knifed, bending outward. But the side protection absorbed the shock, and the door only came in some inches, pushing me on top of Kristina, by no means the worst thing that had ever happened to me.

The left side windows had smashed. We were shocked but unhurt. I felt embarrassed about my unnecessary heroics.

"I was worried I was going to lose you there, Kristina," I said. "It was a lot of money and effort to recruit you. I'd hate to have to go through that again."

Kristina grinned fetchingly, but Yuri was now in tears. With windows missing and the door not closing, it was suddenly incredibly cold. I got out into the storm and looked round the car.

"It doesn't look too bad," I said, "unless the chassis's twisted."

The soldiers had not appeared out of their hut, presumably safe in the knowledge that no one would be traveling on a night like this. They had left the barriers open. Yuri was still sobbing. Kristina was getting into the front seat to comfort him. I stopped her and first swept the shattered glass off the seat with a copy of the *Economist*. I had presumed Yuri was just in shock, but when I got back in my place and asked him to try starting the engine, he whispered quietly to Kristina. She looked back at me.

"Yuri's sure he'll be sacked for wrecking the car," she said.

"Don't be stupid," I replied. "It was entirely my idea, both risking the storm and traveling so fast. Yuri has done a great job. Anyway, it's only a car and we're still alive. Yuri, stop worrying!"

The storm was so fierce the soldiers still hadn't noticed we were there, only twenty yards from their hut. I plowed over and banged on the door. The soldiers were eating sausage and drinking vodka. They were cheery and full of concern. They got the door shut, and taped plastic fertilizer sacks over the broken windows. We set off again into the night.

I decided we would give up on Samarkand and head for Jizzak, which lay a few miles north of the main road, about thirty miles ahead of us. It was a long thirty miles. The car's heating coped better than I expected, though ice was forming on the inside of the damaged door.

Just after we turned off for Jizzak, the car slowed to a halt. It had been misfiring for a while. Yuri was completely dispirited. I knew nothing about engines. Plainly, it had snowed very heavily here, but now just tiny crystals were falling, sparkling like diamonds in the headlights. The road temperature gauge had been showing minus eighteen.

The orange lights of Jizzak glowed tantalizingly on the horizon, reflecting vividly off the glittering white landscape. Yuri got the hood open. I realized we had a couple of minutes to get the car started before the diesel froze solid. I opened the carburetor and poured Kristina's lighter fluid into it. I had seen it done in Chicago and, amazingly, it worked. The engine started with a bang, but wouldn't engage gear. Still, we had the heating on and big jerricans of diesel; we could survive the night here if we had to. Kristina had her luggage open and was trying to put on all her clothes.

She had an idea, and phoned human rights activists we were to meet in Jizzak. They readily offered to come out to the rescue.

Forty minutes later they were with us, in a battered green Lada. Rescuing an ambassador was a great adventure, and they were very cheerful. Their leader was Bakhtiyor Hamroev, a pleasant, short man in a quilted Uzbek gown and lacquered hat. They made light work of getting the vehicle going again. Bakhtiyor said there was a private hotel in Jizzak, and we followed them through the deserted streets, snow banked up against the low houses. I was skeptical, but the Bek hotel was a delight. It had about eight large bedrooms. There was no gas, and the city's district heating and hot water plant was down, but the rooms had electric fan heaters and individual immersion boilers.

It was still only 10 P.M. I telephoned Lena Son at home in Tashkent and asked her, provided snow wasn't still falling heavily, to get Gafur down to us with a replacement vehicle. I also asked her to start work on canceling the morning's Samarkand program and bringing forward my Jizzak appointments.

The bathroom had new Italian fittings and tiling and I ran a deep bath, unscrewing all the little shampoos and gels and tipping them in. I then closed my eyes, and soaked.

I emerged to find what looked like every policeman and official Jizzak in the lobby, and three formula-one pit crews and the engineering corps of the Uzbek army outside working on the car. Amazingly everyone, including the city officials, seemed to be taking direction from

Bakhtiyor. Who needs breakdown insurance when you have human rights activists? I was whisked through to the restaurant, where we had a very good meal indeed, with French wine and real whisky. I was amazed.

Yuri was still considerably shaken and a bit tearful. He still couldn't believe he wouldn't get the sack. Kristina was getting distinctly tactile with him. Lena called back to say Gafur would set off at first light. She had already had considerable success in changing programs.

I slept very well. Lena had arranged for us to call on the *hokkim* of Jiz-zak at ten. I was at breakfast at nine. By 9:45 neither Kristina nor Yuri had appeared. I called Kristina on her mobile, and she and Yuri appeared together just after ten. I hustled Kristina quickly into a car the *hokkimyat* had kindly put at my disposal, and we left Yuri to await Gafur.

The *hokkim* was very welcoming. He was the youngest *hokkim* in Uzbekistan, the same age as me. We exchanged pleasantries and then discussed the problems of the disputed cottonseed factory. He started by saying it was all down to independent courts. I told him straight that I wasn't interested in playing games—I knew as well as he that the courts weren't independent. Unless he got a grip I would be raising the matter with the president. This distinctly worried him.

I was interested in two other factories in Jizzak that had received EBRD loans. One was a pipe extrusion plant, to which the *hokkimyat* took us. It wasn't working because of the failure of the huge polymer project, but it did exist. Which was more than you could say for the winery. The *hokkim* looked completely blank when I asked him about it, and called in his director of industry. He confirmed there was no winery in Jizzak, nor had there ever been. There were no grapes in the province's agricultural production plan. This was pretty weird, as the EBRD loan for this nonexistent winery had been given out in full some two years previously, and interest was being repaid on schedule.

We had lunch with the *hokkim*, after which we went back to the hotel and met up with Gafur, who had turned up in the old dark green Toyota Land Cruiser, which he preferred in the snow for its greater wheelbase and wider tires. Gafur cheerfully set off back to Tashkent in the damaged Land Rover. It looked awful, but the chassis was basically OK.

After lunch we met Bakhtiyor and other human rights activists at his flat. This was in a standard Soviet block, about eight stories high, built of stained concrete. I walked gingerly over sheet ice to the entrance, and up the dank, crumbling stairs. The bottom couple of flights were covered in ice. The tiny flat currently had no heating, water or electricity. The electricity had only been off a couple of days. The apartments of Jizzak had no public heating, or gas or running water, and little electricity, all that winter.

About two hundred dissidents had been arrested in Jizzak in the previous few months. They had documented eighty-four of these cases. Jizzak had long been a center of opposition, and while they didn't want to estimate the total number of political prisoners from there, it certainly amounted to several hundred.

We set off that evening for Samarkand, passing through the Gates of Tamburlaine, a pass where he allegedly installed massive iron gates to guard the major road from Tashkent to Samarkand, Bokhara and Balkh.[1]

We arrived in Samarkand, where there was not so much snow, but the cold was incredible. We were booked into a small hotel, the Malika, which had no heating in the absence of gas. It was late when we arrived, and so we just had dinner and went to bed.

We called the next day on the *hokkim* of Samarkand, Mirzaeyev. Again I had to wait after breakfast for Kristina and Yuri to turn up late. The day before I had made allowances, but now I made plain that this was not what I expected. Although we arrived at the *hokkimyat* some ten minutes late, Mirzaeyev was later. We were shown into a reception room, where we waited in extreme cold for perhaps twenty minutes. Eventually Mirzaeyev turned up, having evidently come from somewhere heated. We went into a meeting room and sat down at a long table, with Mirzaeyev flanked by five or six officials on one side, and Kristina and me on the other. There were small bottles of mineral water on the table that had frozen solid. On some the tops had been forced off and sat atop little columns of ice rising from the bottles; on others the bottle itself had split, and ice was frozen to the sides like wax on a guttering candle.

Mirzaeyev was in a fur-trimmed long leather coat, and kept on his Soviet-style military fur hat. I wore my gray cashmere coat, climbing boots and sheepskin-lined leather gloves. Kristina's beautiful face was framed by a huge fur collar. It was all pretty surreal, especially as Mirzaeyev launched into a thirty-minute speech. This was not the normal *hokkim*'s speech about the regional economy and investment opportunity. It was rather Karimov's "paranoid" speech, with a piece added on at the end about the impossibility of privatizing the cotton industry. Some specific points in this were plainly direct responses to my meeting with Azimov. The government of Uzbekistan is an efficient despotism.

I had two specific points to push, one on tax problems affecting British American Tobacco's factory in Samarkand, the other requesting support for the festival of British music I was planning to hold in Uzbekistan in May 2003. I wanted Samarkand to be the second city for this. I was asking the *hokkim* if they could provide the venue, publicity and meet local costs of accommodations and food. He readily agreed, saying he was delighted at this example of cooperation. He would make sure there was a full audience for every concert.

Something about the way he said this alarmed me. I said that we were not intending an admission charge, but we needed to publicize the events in local media, so people could come if they wanted. We didn't want an audience to be compelled. The *hokkim* smiled and said he understood.

Mirzaeyev spoke with great energy, occasionally striking the table with the open palm of his gloved left hand. He had the assured swagger of the bully. He had previously been *hokkim* of Jizzak, where he had been responsible for the most notorious of Uzbekistan's human rights abuses before the boiling deaths. Several old ladies, involved in an agrarian protest, had been mown down by combine harvesters. In 2004 he would be promoted to prime minister of Uzbekistan.

We then went on to the Agricultural Institute, which had some links to U.K. institutions. The institute had a weather station, which we visited. We learned that the current temperature was minus twenty-five degrees Fahrenheit. The strange thing is, minus twenty-five doesn't really feel any colder than zero Fahrenheit. Some of the effects, like breath condensing to ice on your chin and upper lip, are pretty spectacular, but extreme cold does not make you more uncomfortable in the way extreme heat does. I rather hoped that the temperature might lead our hosts to cancel the tour of the agricultural machine park, but I was wrong.

In the evening we had an invitation to the home of Professor Mirsaidov, to meet with a group of Tajik dissidents.

* * *

THE TAJIK CIVILIZATION of Samarkand and Bokhara was one of the world's great cultural flourishings, producing *The Thousand and One Nights, The Rubáiyát of Omar Khayyám,* the invention of algebra, the medicine of Avicenna and the astronomy of Ulugbek. Over 90 percent of the population of Samarkand still spoke Tajik. But they were falling victim to Karimov's nationalist Uzbek policies.[2] Over eighty Tajik schools had been closed down in Uzbekistan since independence. There were now only twelve left. The Tajik newspapers had also been closed, and Tajik radio broadcasting stopped.

All government positions now required Uzbek-language examinations, as Uzbek replaced Russian as the state language. Legislation had been passed, with deadlines reserving different grades and categories of public jobs to Uzbek speakers at different times. University teaching in all subjects was to be in Uzbek by 2005, a major problem when the large majority of lecturers were ethnic Russians and Tajiks. Fewer than 40 percent of university lecturers were native Uzbek speakers.

There was a deeper problem. The cultured population of the cities had always been Tajik. The literary heritage of the region was almost entirely Tajik. Printed Uzbek literature was, historically, almost nonexistent. There was very little to found a culture on. There were only 140 books in print in the Uzbek language. Six of these were by Karimov, and another forty were propaganda publications of his government. Many of the rest were educational textbooks or public health literature, much of it donor funded. Of Uzbek literature per se, the bulk was Soviet propaganda material of execrable quality, including poetry, plays and some terrible operas. There were three Uzbek novels in print, all of which fell into the propaganda category. Of modern Uzbek plays, seven times as many were banned as were currently available. The best living writers in the Uzbek language were all long-term political prisoners.

This was a major disaster. A Soviet achievement was that 99 percent of the Uzbek population was literate in Russian, and most had some familiarity with Pushkin and Gogol. Now a significant proportion of young Uzbeks, especially in country districts, scarcely understood Russian. Bringing Russian literature into Uzbekistan was illegal. In 2003 the Uzbek government refused a gift from Russia of 4 million school textbooks, in a variety of subjects. There were dilapidated street stalls selling books in Tashkent but, in what used to be the fourth-largest city of the Soviet Union, there was now no bookshop. Karimov was leading his people into the deepest ignorance on the planet.

Professor Mirsaidov was a retired professor of Tajik literature at the University of Samarkand. He and his friends had wanted to start a Center for Tajik Culture, where the language, music and heritage could be celebrated. Naturally, this had been banned. He had gathered in his home to meet me a selection of a dozen dissidents from Samarkand, all of whom seemed to move in and out of jail regularly. The plates of steaming soup were welcome in the biting cold, as was his traditional Tajik wine made from raisins. It tasted sweet, nutty and complex, rather like a good Madeira.

I was told that Mirzaeyev had redoubled the crackdown on Tajik. School closures had started again, and a community newspaper published by one of the guests had been shut down, the printing equipment confiscated. There was a purge of teachers at Samarkand's universities. Trade and employment had been badly affected by border and bazaar closures.

An impressive young local from the Institute for War and Peace Reporting, a British NGO that did invaluable work within Uzbekistan, had much-documented material on recent arrests. He also told stories of the cotton harvest. The previous year, not only the doctors and nursing staff, but all the walking sick from Samarkand's hospitals had been sent out into the fields, resulting in several deaths.

Time and again, I was struck by how delighted such dissidents were to meet me. Trapped in a world of crippling injustice, the idea that anyone outside cared at all was a great relief to them. Whether or not in practice we could do anything to help remained to be seen.

THE NEXT DAY we paid a call on a local medical NGO that occupied a crumbling courtyard house in the center of the city. There was a lot of building rubble, and several empty or part-plastered rooms. They were doing up the premises as funds came in, which was slowly. The embassy had given money previously, as had Chris Hirst from his own pocket. There were pictures of Chris on the wall.

I was shown a newly but sparsely equipped operating theater, the pharmacy and a couple of wards containing women swathed in bandages. The center was a cross between a hospital and a women's refuge, but there was something deeper that the director, a female surgeon, was not telling me. After the tour we sat hunched in our coats in the director's office. There was no heating or water, and the diesel for the generator was almost finished. Temperatures throughout the hospital were a long way below freezing, and the patients had been hunched under thin blankets. The very bread and fruit I was offered in the office were frozen solid. I immediately handed over what cash we had, both mine and the embassy's, and Yuri was sent with a hospital staff member to search for diesel and electric heaters.

I had to become brutally direct with my questioning to get the full story from the director, but this is it.

The hospital dealt with victims of self-immolation—women who had tried to burn themselves to death. Generally they covered themselves in blazing cooking oil in the kitchen. This was the traditional means of female suicide throughout southern Uzbekistan. This center alone had dealt with 230 cases, just from Samarkand, in the past year.

Only a minority of such cases got to the center. Most such attempts were successful. If they were not, the family would either quickly kill off the woman, or leave her to die slowly in the home, to avoid the disgrace. The government hospitals would not accept such cases, nor would the government acknowledge the existence of any such problem in Karimov's Uzbek "paradise."

In Uzbek culture, marriages were arranged. From the wedding, the girl became effectively a domestic slave to her in-laws. The mother-in-law would immediately retire from all housework once she had a daughter-in-law. The girl would have to rise at 4 A.M. to milk the cow, clean the house and prepare breakfast. Then she would go work in the fields, weave or do whatever else supported the family economy. She would probably be regularly beaten, severely, by any member of her husband's family. In the evening she would have to prepare a large meal, and would frequently be subject to rape, not just by her husband, but by the other men of the family.

I was appalled at this picture. The director said that these were traditional features of Uzbek life, but had been worsened by a general brutalization of society by Karimov, following the destruction of traditional societal mechanisms by the Soviets.

The scale of the thing was just awful. The director estimated that, if 230 found their way to the center, over 1,500 tried suicide this way in Samarkand alone every year. Across Uzbekistan it might be many thousands.

It is difficult to conceive. Just how miserable do you have to be to set yourself on fire? And if thousands reach that stage, how many tens of thousands or hundreds of thousands of women lead absolutely dreadful lives, but cling on to them? I left the center with a feeling of real despair.

OUR NEXT PORT of call was the British American Tobacco (BAT) factory just outside the city. It felt very solid, new and clean. It had its own heat and electricity and water, and was providing them free to local communities. It was ridiculously comforting to sit in an office with British square pin plug sockets.

We were taken on a tour by the Chilean production manager. It was a large, standard cigarette factory. I like going round such places—I find the dexterity of the machinery astonishing. I have never smoked, but I like the smell of raw tobacco.

BAT was the largest foreign investor in Uzbekistan, having put in $300 million of their own cash. They were also the country's biggest taxpayer. They had never made an operating profit, let alone any return on capital, and in 2001 had to write off, in their U.K. accounts, $48 million of *sum* earnings they were not allowed to convert into hard currency. They were now trying, unsuccessfully so far, to avoid further operating losses and sit things out, hoping for better times.

Their biggest problem was competition from smuggled cigarettes, which weren't subject to tax or duty. Over 60 percent of cigarettes sold in Uzbekistan were smuggled, nearly all from Korea. Given Uzbekistan's tightly controlled borders, this would be impossible without official complicity, and indeed, cigarette smuggling was controlled by the Karimov family together with Almatov, the minister of the interior, and Gafur Rakhimov, the leader of the Uzbek mafia. This was a coalition of the most powerful people in the land, and regular murderers to boot, so BAT had problems. What was worse was that the Uzbek government were

deliberately trying to bankrupt BAT Uzbekistan (UzBAT). Gulnara Karimova, the president's daughter, had already done a deal for a joint venture with the South Koreans to take over BAT's factory when they were
gone. I had at least half-serious discussions with the management about
how to destroy their machinery and still get safely away.

BAT had other problems. Their cigarettes were made with 90 percent
Uzbek tobacco, with imported varieties used to blend. The Uzbek tobacco
farmers all had plots leased from state farms. Even though the farmers paid
for the lease of the land, UzBAT was only allowed to pay 40 percent of
the tobacco price to the farmer. The other 60 percent had to go to the
state farm and *hokkimyat,* for the senior officials to steal. This meant that
it was very difficult for the farmers to cover the cost of their leases.

UzBAT had in 2003 just managed to negotiate the amount paid to
the farmers up to 50 percent, when the Uzbek government brought in a
regulation that the payments could no longer be made in cash, but had
to be made through a state bank. This gave yet another avenue for state
officials to rob the farmers, and indeed, at the 2004 harvest, six months
after UzBAT had made the payments into the state bank in full, not one
farmer had received a single cent.

I got to know the UzBAT staff well, from the head, Rene Ijsselstein,
an expressive Belgian, down. Without exception, they were passionate,
not just about making the company successful, but about tackling
poverty and injustice and improving the terrible lot of the Uzbek farmers. It is deeply unfashionable to say something positive about a tobacco
company, but that is the truth.

We headed off back to Tashkent. About twenty miles outside Samarkand, we stopped at a small town where DFID had put money into assisting a cooperative of private farmers with marketing strategies.

In the mid-1990s, Uzbekistan had embarked on some limited agricultural privatization. Azimov had claimed to me that about 40 percent of
the country's agricultural output was now privately produced. That was,
as usual, a large exaggeration, and I had learned at BAT something of the
reality of "private" farmers' lives. Here, I was to learn more.

In this town, several hundred farmers had been allowed to lease plots
of twenty-seven acres each. But they were told what they had to grow
on 95 percent of the land, and given quotas of how much they were

expected to produce. On the remaining 5 percent of the land they could, in theory, grow what they wanted. But the quotas were almost impossible to meet, so they had in practice to devote all their land for this. The fines for not fulfilling a quota could exceed the payments for what they did produce.

In the last year, they had been ordered to produce cotton, tomatoes and wheat. The payment for the cotton had not materialized; that was usual. The tomatoes were to be delivered to a puree plant that was a joint venture between the *hokkimyat* and a Russian firm, Baltimor. After they delivered, the *hokkimyat* had taken over the plant from the joint venture, saying it had gone bankrupt, and that the new company did not owe them anything. For the wheat, they had been told they would be paid not in cash, but in fertilizer. This they had to collect themselves from a state plant in the Ferghana Valley, over three hundred miles away in the mountains! They had no means of doing this and knew, even if they turned up, there was no chance of their docket being honored by officials without hefty bribes, which they didn't have the funds to pay.

All this was explained by a dignified and well-educated lady, paid by DFID to organize the cooperative. I asked how on earth people lived. She pointed to the frozen vegetable patch in the garden. The farmer next to her just grinned and pulled back his sleeve, to show his emaciated arm.

BACK IN TASHKENT, it was time to organize the staff Christmas party. There were over sixty staff plus partners, guards being the largest contingent. We couldn't afford a restaurant for so many, and decided to hold it in the new residence. This was almost ready. The embassy was in the poshest bit of Tashkent, near the homes of Karimov's daughters, so it always had heating, electricity and water. In the rest of Tashkent these were in short supply that winter. This included the new residence, which had no gas for heating. I went down two days before the party. It was thirteen degrees actually inside the building—and that was at midday.

Packing so many people in would warm it up, I decided, and there would be lots of hot food and plenty to drink. The kitchens weren't yet fully operational, so we had arranged for the Intercontinental to deliver eight turkeys while we did the vegetables and puddings. Fiona and Lena the cook went into overdrive.

The day before the Christmas party, I was approached in my office by Lena Son and Atabek. The local staff would not come to the party, they said, if Chris and Karen did. I knew relationships were bad within the embassy, but this was amazing.

"Look, Lena," I said. "This has been an incredible three months. We have all achieved so much. Now it's Christmas. I am inviting you. And I am inviting Chris and Karen. Nobody is forcing you to come. But if you don't, I shall be, personally, very insulted."

Everyone did come, and we had a great evening. Even though the temperature inside never did get above freezing, coats were removed and there was a lot of dancing. Jamie came for Christmas, Emily was delighted to see him, and we spent a happy Christmas Day. Hugo Minderhoud, a bright Dutchman with ABN AMRO bank, and his wife and children were our guests.

I RECEIVED INSTRUCTIONS to call on Safayev, outline the weapons of mass destruction dossier for him and seek his support for an invasion of Iraq. Fortunately, I did not have to say anything about WMD, as he was positively eager to express unconditional support for an attack on Iraq. I left him a copy of the dossier I didn't believe in, wondering what the New Year would bring.

CHAPTER 10

Iron in the Soul

IT WAS A HARD WINTER. THROUGHOUT THE COUNTRY THERE WAS no gas and no district heating, and intermittent power cuts.[1] My immediate concern was for the embassy staff, many of whom had no alternative heating or cooking facilities in their homes. I instructed David Muir to get in extra stocks of diesel for all the domestic generators, and order several dozen electric heaters to be flown in by air.

I had to fly to London for a conference of ambassadors, which was a waste of time. It was just a PR exercise in the lead-up to the Iraq war. The main purpose was the television news pictures of Tony Blair and Jack Straw addressing the massed ranks of their ambassadors. But it was nice for me, because it was like slipping into a warm bath of backslapping and handshakes. My punchy telegrams, and criticism of the War on Terror, had been going down well with most of my colleagues.

I had two meetings while in London. The first was with Linda Duffield, whose FCO title was director of wider Europe. She was Simon Butt's new boss and the woman who would countersign his staff reports on me. Linda was a severe, dry woman with short gray hair. I had arranged to call on her, and when I entered her office Simon was there too. A heavy atmosphere hung in the room.

"Sit down, Craig," she said. "Simon tells me that he has areas of concern about your performance and, from what I have seen, I must say I am concerned too."

"OK. Nice to meet you, incidentally."

This was ignored. Simon started up.

"I think our worry is that you are antagonizing the Uzbeks to the stage where they will pay you no attention. You are also causing real damage to our relationship with Uzbekistan. I was most concerned, for example, that you told Komilov that every word of your Freedom House speech had been cleared with London."

"Why not? It was."

"You know that's not the full story. You railroaded that speech through junior staff."

"That's simply untrue. I sent the draft to you and to John Macgregor [Linda Duffield's predecessor]. I even copied in Michael Jay on the correspondence. In fact, I seem to recall you complained I was going over your head."

Linda came to Simon's rescue. "I want to make myself perfectly clear. Had I been in this position at the time, I would not have allowed you to make that speech."

Her head shook and she seemed to tremble with suppressed outrage. "No ambassador should ever make such a speech. That is the job of politicians. Your job is to administer U.K./Uzbek relations, not to undermine them. You seem to lack any sense of proportion. Human rights is only one area of our work, and by no means the most important. You are neglecting your commercial duties. I understand there are management problems inside the embassy."

Simon was smirking. I was really getting angry.

"I am sorry," I said, "you are completely wrong on all points. I put much more effort into commercial work than into anything else, and we have transformed the performance of the embassy in that regard. And we are not losing influence with the Uzbeks, we have more than ever before. Standing up to them is important—they take no notice of conventional diplomacy. I think you've been very badly briefed." I looked at Simon. "Look, Linda, why don't you come out and visit Tashkent and see for yourself."

She flinched. "I have a very large area of responsibility, and because of you I am already spending more time on this than I can afford. We have decided that Simon will come out to visit shortly. He will report back to me."

Plainly my difficulties were going to get still worse.

I had organized a meeting in the personnel department to discuss the problems with Chris Hirst. Karen seemed to be deliberately stalling on moving to a new house, and I wanted to know if I could compel them to move. The meeting was chaired by a nice man with the splendid name of Rufus Legge, and included staff of personnel, health and welfare and security departments.

The answer was yes, I could compel them. But I also explained that part of my intention in moving them was to work out if the problem really was bad neighbors, or whether it was Chris. Since I had proposed the move in November, further direct observation had led me to worry. Rufus said the personnel files indicated that Chris had a short fuse. There had been allegations of domestic violence while Chris had been posted in China. They promised to get back to me on this.

A couple of days after I got back to Tashkent, I received an e-mail from Mike Balmer in the security department. It stated baldly that Chris Hirst had a documented ten-year history of alleged violence. I was astonished. How has this been allowed to go on so long? Why had my predecessor been sent a telegram from the FCO congratulating him for defending Chris against allegations of violence, when the FCO knew his history? Why had I been told nothing apart from Chris Ingham's veiled comments? Even these had emphasized that the policy was to defend Chris. I told Karen I wanted them to move very quickly indeed.

A MAJOR NEW British commercial interest in Uzbekistan was a company called Oxus Mining. They owned a 50 percent stake in a joint venture with the Uzbek government to open a new gold mine.

Uzbekistan was the world's seventh-largest producer of gold. This was produced by a huge state-owned conglomerate, the Kombinat, which also produced uranium and other metals. The gold came largely from the Murantau mine.

Oxus were planning to open their new mine at Amantaytau, some forty miles south of Murantau. They had, however, run into difficulties raising the cash they needed for the project.[2] Time was running out and things were looking very hairy for Oxus. A visit by the British ambassador would enhance their prestige, show political support and help disguise the desperate scramble for finance going on beneath the surface.

It was a tough two-day Land Rover journey to Amantaytau, in the middle of the Kizyl Kum desert. There I met Richard Wilkins, the enthusiastic Welsh director of Oxus. I was accompanied by Lena Son and driven by Gafur. Richard had started up a successful gold-mining joint venture in Tajikistan, but this was bigger potatoes. He was under a lot of pressure, and kept breaking off for long, anxious phone calls. The mine site was a series of cabins in the middle of the scrubby red sands of the desert. There was a small, friendly staff of British geologists and mining engineers. They were all extremely enthusiastic about the prospects; their investigations of gold yields had got them really excited. Several of them had been working on this dusty site for years.

I met the head of the Kombinat, Mr. Kucharski, an ebullient Ukrainian miner. The Soviets had brought in Ukrainian engineers, who dominated the senior ranks of the Kombinat. Many of them had been there for thirty years. With Kucharski, I visited the Murantau mine. The second-largest hole in the world, it is visible from space. Watching the giant ore carriers wend their way down the slopes of the great crater, until they became tiny specks far below, was fascinating. They were extending the pit down to over a half mile, and starting to build great bucket conveyors to bring out the ore at an angle of forty-five degrees.

Still more spectacular was the ore mill. In a hall whose scale makes the brain reel, you stand on a gallery and look down on huge cylindrical mills turning, pounding the ore inside against their load of heavy spherical steel balls. This hall was a mile long, and contained thirty-six of these giant mills in a line. The noise was unbelievable. You feel it can't be real: it must all be done with mirrors. As you walk along and discover the true scale, it becomes disorientating.

The control panel was a giant wall of polished marble, in which twinkled the lights of the inset instrumentation. It all looked like the spectacular set for the climax of a James Bond film. The mine produced one and a half tons of pure gold every week. They let me push around a dozen new ingots on a trolley; sadly, they were too heavy to make a realistic dash for the exit.

The mine was so large that it is worth the while of the world's largest mining company, Newmont, to operate a joint venture with the Kombinat just to process the tailings. These were spoil heaps of ore that had been processed, but were still rich enough in gold to be worth reprocessing. Newmont moved this powdered deposit from the huge spoil heaps, bulldozing it onto conveyors that ran for miles, and piled it into a great hill. Cyanide was pumped through this hill, leaching out the gold for processing from the resultant cyanide lake.

This was another EBRD-funded venture, and indeed, loans totaling $165 million made it the EBRD's biggest investment in Uzbekistan. I was therefore keen to see it before the EBRD AGM. But the project raised a lot of questions in my mind.

The EBRD called it "the lowest-cost, most efficient secondary mining operation in the world." That was true. It produced thirteen tons of gold a year. But it was only a tailings operation—the expensive mining had already been done. The technology was cheap and basic. The claimed total investment was over $300 million, with $140 million put in by Newmont. I just couldn't see it. I couldn't even see that the capital cost would amount to the $165 million loaned by the EBRD. Oxus were building an entire new mine and mill, not just a tailings operation, for $40 million. I suspected serious padding in the Newmont project cost.

I gave a dinner for the Oxus staff at the sports stadium in the mining city of Zarafshan.[3] It was a jolly affair—the long-term engineering staff's guests included one British, and several local, wives. The experts all agreed that the capital costs of the Newmont joint venture were massively overblown, and seemed delighted that I had noticed.[4]

My good friend Sir Sam Jonah, then chief executive of Ashanti Goldfields, had given a dinner for me when I left Ghana. He had investigated the Murantau scheme as a possible investment for Lonmin (Lonrho Mining). The investment had not gone ahead.

"You see, Craig," he said, with his usual mischievous twinkle, "it was too corrupt for me—and I'm an African!"

I was beginning to see what he meant.

After dinner that night, Richard Wilkins lost his company. The phone calls had been getting more intense, and this normally shrewd but affable man had started sweating heavily. He continually went outside to talk. After dinner we found him leaning on the fence of the stadium car park, swearing softly and staring into space.

It was just after 10 P.M. in Zarafshan, five hours earlier in London. Oxus had failed to raise the $21 million required that day. In consequence, it had now fallen to a hostile takeover by a South African company, which Oxus ironically had intended to employ as a contractor to carry out the excavations. This company had raised the cash needed from South African sources. It had bought out the minority shareholders—the key that day was when my friend Jitendra Patel had gone over to the South Africans.

Richard was convinced, with good reason, that the Amantaytau project would be massively profitable. He had worked on it for many years, and done the extremely difficult negotiation to bring the Uzbek government on board. To lose it at the moment the deal should have been completed was very bitter indeed.

The chairman of Oxus, Roger Turner, was out on his ear. Richard and he had started Oxus's adventures in Central Asia ten years previously, and Richard was terribly upset for his friend. Richard was being kept on as a front man.

The next day I checked with British Trade International. We were still considering Oxus a British company. The South African company that had bought it had a British office. Oxus HQ would still be in the U.K. My visit therefore took on a new priority—persuading the Uzbeks that the change of ownership did not affect the joint venture.

This may sound simple, but it wasn't. Kucharski and the Kombinat had never been keen on the joint venture, arguing that it could develop Murantau itself, which was certainly true. But it had been pushed into it by the State Geological Committee, which owned the gold reserves. Kucharski could use the changes at Oxus as a pretext to try to break the deal, particularly as the new Oxus planned to use secondhand rather than new equipment. The reduced Oxus investment could lead to demands to change the share percentages of the joint venture. Also Uzbekistan was not used to the private sector, and the notion that a company is a public institution, irrespective of the owner, was particularly difficult. In the former Soviet Union, where there had been some privatization, the oligarch was the company. Kucharski might consider his deal to be with Roger Turner, rather than an entity called Oxus.

The next day we visited the mining operation at Uchkuduk, and looked at a revolutionary piece of technology patented by the Kombinat for mechanically grading lumps of ore by gold content. Uchkuduk is right at the end of the roads and water pipes into the desert. Some of that water is put to good use, because here the Kombinat has built its own brewery. Using the finest imported malt, and Czech and German equipment, it produces a range of beers including dark, live ones. We drank an excellent strong winter ale called, in English, Old Nick. It was a strange thing, sitting in the middle of the Kizyl Kum drinking real ale.

We traveled on through the desert and visited the weird moonscape of the Kombinat's phosphate operation, where massive digging machines crawled over the scarred white earth. It was well below freezing, and a vicious wind whipped across this wasteland, coloring the desert with white dust for fifty miles around.

We then saw something of the uranium mining operation. I don't pretend I understood this. Over a huge area of desert, water is forced into the sands through vertical pipes. There is a great web of these all over the Kizyl Kum. The water running through the sands picks up the uranium, which is then processed out. The bit I don't get is how water dispersed into the sands of the desert, over a great area, can ever be collected again.

Our discussion with Kucharski was held over a long formal lunch. Kucharski was flanked by his senior staff, and I by the managers of Oxus. In Uzbekistan, no enterprise is possible without government support. Kucharski therefore may have given much more weight than it merited to my declaration of British government support for Oxus. By the end of the lunch, the ice had been well and truly broken and we were into jokes and vodka toasts. It had been a fascinating few days, and effective in helping see Oxus over this crisis.

The sales of gold and uranium of the Kombinat had no bearing on its revenues. It received a budgetary allocation from central government. The gold and uranium produced were sold on the international market; the quantity of output and the revenue from sales were both secret. The revenue went not to the company but to the Ministry of Finance. The state budget was itself a secret, so this was all completely unaccountable. The Kombinat simply received a budgetary allocation, unrelated to the sale of its products, to pay its staff and cover its costs, as though it were a government department.

* * *

ON RETURN TO Tashkent I accepted an invitation from Zokirjon Umarov to dinner at his palatial home. I was glad I did. We had a sumptuous meal and got on very well. At this meeting, and others with his friends over the next few weeks, I learned a great deal.

Zokirjon is an Uzbek aristocrat. His family used to own much of Bokhara. It was an important family before the Russians came, and moved effortlessly from emirate to tsarist service. In his hall Zokirjon had an oil painting of his great-grandfather, a distinguished man in a turban and an oiled beard, wearing the glittering star of a tsarist order on his breast. The move from tsarist to Soviet service had been less smooth initially, but ultimately successful. Zokirjon had been number two in the KGB operation in Afghanistan during the Soviet/Afghan war. The Soviets had used Uzbeks against the mujahideen, in exactly the same way the U.S. used the Uzbeks of the Northern Alliance against the Taliban ten years later.

Zokirjon was full of good stories about this. At one time he had been caught with a group of officers and an important Soviet general in an advanced post pinned down by Afghans. The officers had drunk their way through a crate of vodka. When it was finished, the general called an aide de camp and ordered him to send back a helicopter for another crate.

"But, General," said the orderly, "the hills are full of mujahideen with Stinger missiles. That is why we aren't taking you out by helicopter. It could be shot down."

"Good point," said the general, "better send three helicopters to bring a crate of vodka each. One should get through."

Zokirjon told me much else that was of more practical use. He and many others in the Uzbek elite were thoroughly fed up with Karimov, who was making the business climate more and more impossible for the private sector. Zokirjon himself had his major business interests in Russia and Germany and his family in the U.K., but when in Uzbekistan he faced a constant stream of supplicants from his extended family, his village and others with a claim on him who were unemployed and in desperate straits.

He told me that Karimov's personal fortune came chiefly from 10 percent of the production of the Murantau mine, which he had been taking for more than a decade. He took his cut as ingots, flown to Rothschilds bank in Switzerland. Meanwhile his daughter Gulnara was taking an increasingly firm grip on the range of government contracts, and had been the chief beneficiary of what privatization had occurred, for example, in telecoms.

Karimov was keen that Gulnara should succeed him. She could control her father, and she was concerned that any other successor would break agreements and take her business and property empire from her. Karimov had decided firmly against economic liberalization and would be increasingly distancing himself from the U.S. He was looking to Russia and China for investment. Uzbekistan's massive gas reserves remained the key asset, and these would mostly go to Russia's state-owned Gazprom. The Gazprom executive in charge of investments outside Russia was an ethnic Uzbek called Alisher Usmanov. He was a major oligarch in his own right (indeed, I knew of him, as he had recently bought a major stake in Corus, the Anglo-Dutch company incorporating what used to be British Steel). Usmanov and Gulnara were putting together the deals in Moscow. Putin would have a stake, controlled through his private secretary, Piotr Jastrzebski, with whom Usmanov had shared a flat as a student. Usmanov had gifted Putin a major share in Mapobank, an important Russian business bank for the oil industry. Again this deal was fronted by Jastrzebski.

Zokirjon was open about his motive in telling me all this. He wanted the West to see through Karimov, stop supporting him and start to push Uzbekistan toward a capitalism that would allow Zokirjon Umarov and his friends to make money.

Our embassy in Moscow didn't like my report of this at all. They reported back that Jastrzebski was a good friend of the ambassador and highly respected. The ambassador was sure he was not corrupt. Our Moscow embassy also said they had never heard of Alisher Usmanov, which I found very strange. He was easy to Google.

OUR AMBASSADOR IN Tajikistan, Michael Smith, sent a telegram reporting information he had picked up that alleged that the Islamic Movement of Uzbekistan had decided to kill John Herbst and me, and had in fact already dispatched a twenty-five-man team of undercover operatives from Afghanistan, specifically in order to kill me. I replied, in a widely copied telegram: ONLY 25? I AM INSULTED.

This spread like wildfire throughout British government circles and did more than anything to enhance my reputation. I still get reminded of it occasionally. In fact, it had been a pretty easy gesture, as I had never believed in this information anyway.

But I also sent a more serious telegram saying that I was worried about the new residence. The embassy and the old apartment had bulletproof windows. The new residence didn't. It had many very large windows, and was substantially overlooked by other buildings and nearby hills and mounds. I received an astonishing telegram in reply. There was no money for bulletproof glass. I should therefore: PLANT QUICK GROWING CONIFERS . . . TO SCREEN THE HOUSE.

I wondered just how fast they thought conifers grow, and had a mental vision of al-Qaida coming to get me, while I backed up the garden planting trees in front of them. I went back with some rejoinder, and received further advice to keep the curtains closed.

Much more important, I had not received a substantive reply to my telegram about torture and intelligence. In February I saw yet more dodgy intelligence, specifying it came from detainee debriefing, so I sent a further telegram repeating the arguments.

At the start of March I was attending an EU meeting in Brussels to discuss policy toward Central Asia. I received a pretty terse summons to travel to London afterward to attend a meeting on the torture intelligence question. This I did.

I was firmly expecting to get sacked. I had concentrated hard on the Brussels meetings and I had, in any case, a useful facility for putting off apprehension; sufficient unto the day is the evil thereof. Unfortunately the day came, and when facing an unpleasant meeting, I probably feel more scared than most people. I hope that I hide this beneath a veneer of sangfroid, but I doubt it. My hands don't shake, but my palms go horribly sweaty.

I walked over from my London hotel to a small café, named Le Club, next to St. James's tube station. Here I had sausage, bacon, fried eggs, fried tomato, toast and tea for about £5. The order was taken at the counter by a particularly chirpy Italian in a white chef's tunic, and when I wandered over to collect it a few minutes later a very pretty girl, with long sandy hair tied back, insisted I go back to my table while she brought it over. She spilled tea on me, but the thought was nice. I read the *Guardian* and watched the crowds scurrying out from the Underground, heading for work. The breakfast was excellent, but I could not shake the anxiety that gnawed at me. "The prisoner ate a hearty breakfast" kept piercing into my train of thought.

I really did not mind losing my job, from the point of personal position. Britain was about to enter an illegal war in support of extreme right-wing, corrupt American Republicans, and to the advantage of the oil and weapons industries. Did I want to represent this? No, I didn't. But the cliché position of so many married men in middle age came home. I was trapped. Trapped by my need to provide for Fiona, Jamie and Emily, not to break their happiness. If I left the FCO, how would I make money for them? Jamie would certainly have to leave his private school, with his O grades looming. Fiona did not have my experience of personal poverty and I did not think that she would take to it.

I discovered to my surprise that I had started off being scared of being sacked, and my train of thought had wandered to the opposite position of musing about resigning.

My brain started to race—the excuses for staying on piled up: the individuals facing persecution I might be able to help, the need for someone on the inside arguing the case for integrity.

I found myself gazing idly through the window at the passersby with a vague kind of love. They were a mixed bunch, these Londoners going to work, ethnically, religiously, sexually, politically mixed. I loved my countrymen, their tolerance, resistance. As often, the legacy of my upbringing kicked in and I started thinking about the Second World War, how proudly, how indomitably we had stood up to fascism. Those Londoners had the hell bombed out of them, nightly, as they had in Coventry, Birmingham and elsewhere. The U.S. had stood by and watched for two years. Only when they themselves were attacked at Pearl Harbor did they join the war against fascism. Why then had we rushed uncritically to instant support the moment they had been attacked from the air in the Twin Towers? The death toll did not equal Coventry, let alone the London blitz.

I pulled myself up. I did not like this line of thinking. The resentment was perhaps natural, but the logic poor. If they had behaved badly then, should we behave badly now? What were the parallels between the war on fascism and the war on al-Qaida? Let me think. Yes—the point was that Saddam Hussein had nothing to do with al-Qaida, and I knew, as did so many others in Whitehall, he did not possess weapons of mass destruction. There was no line of justification from the Twin Towers to attacking Iraq. And in the wider War on Terror, there was no excuse for torture, for abandoning human rights, for betraying the values we claimed to be fighting for. And that is what we were doing.

I glanced at my watch. Wow! I had been in the café more than an hour, lost in this reverie. It was five to ten; I would be late. I paid quickly, leaving the startled pretty girl a tip of what I had saved by not breakfasting in the hotel—it might, I mused grimly, be my last chance to afford to be generous. I hurried across the park to the Foreign Office and found myself queuing for a pass behind a large number of people arriving for a conference of some kind. I had forgotten I would need to get a pass to get in, and certainly had not allowed for the fifteen minutes it took. So I arrived late at Linda Duffield's office. She was waiting at the top of the three stairs that led up from the third-floor corridor to her office, cheeks sucked in and looking even crosser than usual beneath her severe haircut.

"You're late," she said.

"Yes, I'm sorry," I replied meekly.

"The parliamentary undersecretary apologizes," she said brusquely. "An urgent meeting has come up and he can't now see you this morning. He has asked me to brief you."

She led the way into her room. Two people were seated at the round, polished mahogany table.

"You know Matthew and Michael."

It was a statement, not a question. I did not in fact know Matthew, although I knew of him. Matthew Kydd, head of the Whitehall Liaison Department, the link between the FCO and MI5, MI6 and other shadier organizations. A long-nosed, sharp, refined face. Impeccable grooming, neat, whitening hair. Firm handshake.

Now, Michael I did know. Sir Michael Wood, FCO legal adviser. A friendly face I was particularly glad to see at that moment.

Michael is highly deceptive. Curly hair cut short, small spectacles on a string round his neck, a pedantic manner, smooth and rounded. Fastidious and extremely careful and accurate in speech. A prissy, almost effeminate manner, a bit like a maiden aunt. Not only does this hide a muscular shrewdness, it also hides the only man in the FCO who can drink me under the table.

I had worked closely with FCO legal advisers on efforts to bring the monumentally important UN Convention on the Law of the Sea into force. This is little recognized but one of the UN's greatest achievements, setting the international legal framework for use of the resources of the oceans and for navigation, for the delimitation and exploitation of continental shelves, and much else besides. It is of incalculable environmental and commercial importance and was bitterly opposed by Reagan and Bush Senior.

Presumably Bush junior will get round to attacking it sooner or later.

One day after work in New York, Michael and I adjourned to a bar. We then adjourned to a great many other bars, drinking very large whiskies. Michael's knowledge of Manhattan was phenomenal, focusing heavily on Irish bars. He seemed well known, with a huge collection of down-to-earth friends, including some very pretty girls. As the evening went on the bars got dingier and dingier, and some of them aggressively Fenian. This was ironic, as our mission to the UN had given me a handout for official visitors that stressed that we should avoid Irish bars for fear of antagonism or violence. Like many people who have lived in poorer bits of Scottish cities, I can sing "The Sash" or "The Jolly Ploughboy" as occasion demands, so I wasn't worried. Michael seemed totally at home. By midnight we had been drinking for seven hours, but I definitely remember entering one establishment through an unmarked dirty fire door, past the bins into a restaurant kitchen, then through into a cozy parlor that seemed peculiarly domestic in the foot of a huge Manhattan building. Then it definitely does get blurred. I recall singing, not being able to walk and Michael manhandling me up to spend the night in one of many spare bedrooms in his huge Manhattan flat. Then around 7 A.M. he appeared, fully clothed and immaculate, again the prissy lawyer, and told me where to get breakfast and to let myself out once my hangover had calmed.

Yes, I was very pleased to see Sir Michael.

The atmosphere in Linda's room was tense and unpleasant. Even

Michael did not look me in the eye. Everyone was seated ramrod straight. The mirrorlike varnish on the mahogany was misting around my sweaty hands. Linda started in formal, clipped tones: "The PUS asked me to say that he considers it unfortunate that you did not raise these matters, as invited, in person with William Ehrmann when you were back for the Heads of Mission Conference. The PUS does not think it is wise to commit such matters to paper."

I said nothing. Linda went on.

"The PUS wishes me to assure you that your concerns have been given full consideration at the highest level. He has discussed this with Jack Straw, and C has given his views.[5] Both the FCO and MI6 have taken legal advice on the question that you have raised. Michael, could you outline the legal position?"

Michael looked distastefully at the papers before him.

"I am not an expert on the UN Convention on Torture, but I have studied it quite carefully in the light of Craig's telegrams. I cannot see that we are in material breach of any provision simply by possessing, or indeed by using, information obtained under torture and subsequently passed on to us.

"It does appear that under Article Fifteen such evidence would be inadmissible in a court of law, but that is the only restriction on the use of such material arising from the convention. I therefore see no legal obstacle to our continuing to receive such information from the Uzbek security services. Arguably we are further distanced from any acts of torture by the fact that the material comes to us via the United States."

He coughed discreetly. "That is my view of the legal position. I make no comment on the morality of the case."

"Michael," I asked, "a number of prominent public international lawyers have told me that in this case, when put as a hypothesis, possession and use of such material would be in breach of the convention. I have spoken to, among others, Françoise Hampson and Douwe Korff. Why would they take that view?"

"It is hard for me to say," said Michael. He took off his spectacles and held them in front of him; he studied them, screwing up his eyes, as though they might hold the answer to this question. "There is certainly nothing on the face of the convention that I can see, and I am not sure I have seen anything published that would cover the case. But I haven't heard of this man Korff—he can't be much of an authority."

"But you know Françoise?"

"Of course."

"Speak to her."

Linda interjected, her mouth set so firmly that wrinkles appeared all round it.

"I think we have the legal view and that is very plain. Michael, could you be so kind as to write to Craig and confirm it?"

"Certainly."

"Good. Now, Matthew, could you give the view of the security services?"

Matthew purred, "Certainly, Linda. The view of the security services is that this is high-quality intelligence material and plays a very important role in the War on Terror. It would be a major loss if we ceased to have access to it. It would also cause unprecedented practical problems for the U.S./U.K. intelligence-sharing agreement, which we are anxious should not be disturbed."[6]

"But it's nonsense," I interrupted. "The intelligence is crap. It exaggerates the strength of the IMU and is full of false information about so-called links to Bin Laden. It's just stuff the Uzbeks want the Americans to believe so that they will continue to give the Karimov regime military, financial and political support."

"On the contrary"—Kydd again, still more silken—"I can assure you, this has been considered at the very highest level, and there is no doubt that this is operationally useful material."

"Thank you," said Linda, still more clipped, "I think that clears this up. We needn't detain you gentlemen. Could you stay a moment please, Craig?"

After Michael had slouched and Matthew smirked out, I stood. I was not in the mood for any cozy chats. Linda went on

"The PUS wants you to know that he realizes these are difficult times for many in the service. He discussed your telegrams in person with the secretary of state and with C. This question of torture is very difficult. He wants you to know that both the secretary of state and he lose sleep over it."

"Look, I am at the sharp end. I see the twisted limbs, meet the parents who have seen their children raped and murdered in front of them. I don't think they are that bothered about Jack Straw's sleep pattern."

"We really do understand why you are upset. But we need to know that you are on message: Do you understand the position? You are a civil servant and I should not have to remind you that you act on behalf of the secretary of state and in accordance with policy set by ministers."

Suddenly I felt very weary.

"Don't worry," I said, "I understand the position perfectly."

I walked to the lift in something of a daze. But as I came out into the daylight of the FCO quadrangle, I was struck by a revelation. It had been a carefully planned and rehearsed meeting designed to put me in my place. But they were more scared of me than I was of them. This meeting had been a defensive exercise. They were in the wrong, and they knew it.

I FLEW BACK TO Tashkent, deeply depressed and worried. The meetings in London had had a profound impact on me. I had served my country for twenty years, proudly, in the belief that being British entailed certain fundamental decencies of behavior. Rejecting torture was one. I now found that I was mistaken, and either the British government had never stood for, or had ceased to stand for, those basic values. I was deeply disillusioned. The whole purpose of my working life seemed to have evaporated.

A few days after my return I received by fax the promised written clarification from Michael Wood:

From: Michael Wood
Legal Adviser
Date: 13 March 003
cc: PS/PUS
Matthew Kidd
Linda Duffield

UZBEKISTAN: INTELLIGENCE POSSIBLY OBTAINED UNDER TORTURE
1. Your record of our meeting with HMA Tashkent recorded that Craig had said that his understanding was that it was also an offence under the

UN Convention on Torture to receive or possess information under torture.
I said that I did not believe that this was the case, but undertook to re-read
the Convention.

2. I have done so. There is nothing in the Convention to this effect. The
nearest thing is article 15 which provides: "Each State Party shall ensure
that any statement which is established to have been made as a result of
torture shall not be invoked as evidence in any proceedings, except against a
person accused of torture as evidence that the statement was made."

3. This does not create any offence. I would expect that under UK law
any statement established to have been made as a result of torture would
not be admissible as evidence.

> *Signed*
> *M C Wood*
> *Legal Adviser*

So there we had it. Torture by proxy for intelligence purposes was
legal. If the so-called evidence that resulted could not be used in a court,
that was of little worry—the government had instituted indefinite detention without charge in the U.K., on the authority of the home secretary,
citing "intelligence material."

I returned to Tashkent the next day and, that evening, deeply depressed,
I went back to the Safar Club to unwind. The girls were delighted to see
me again, as I had a reputation as a generous and respectful customer. I
drank Chivas Regal, and ate some chicken. Dilya danced for me and two
or three of the girls came to sit with me. Normally I laughed and joked with
them, but this evening I felt down and distracted. Then, gazing out of the
booth to the dance floor, I saw her.

She wore matching embroidered purple knickers and bra. Her body
moved sinuously as she danced, her upper and lower torso wonderfully
articulated by a slender, supple waist of extraordinary flexibility. Her
body shape was perfection itself. All the girls in that club were great
dancers, but she made the rest look clumsy and contrived. She was like a
swan among ducks, a comparison all the more apt for her long, graceful
neck and proud carriage.

She had a shaggy mane of highlighted hair, and she looked out at me
with large, dark eyes. As I caught her glance, I felt she was drawing me

into her very soul. Her lips shone with a liquid gloss, and they were parted in a way that was both sexy and innocent. She looked lost and anxious, like she really didn't want to be there.

I had been chatting with a nice hostess called Lena, a heavily built and down-to-earth girl who managed the floor. I asked her who the girl was.

"I had noticed you looking," said Lena. "She's new. Her name's Nadira."

After finishing her solo dance, Nadira came belly dancing around the booths. I gave her twenty dollars. She then returned to join others on the dance floor. She was intensely distracting—my eyes were going back continuously to her. Eventually, one of the girls drinking in the booth with me stood up and firmly drew the curtains, blocking the dance floor from view. Nadira was looking directly at me as the curtains closed her out.

I couldn't get her off my mind, and eventually prevailed on Lena to get her to join me. Lena agreed in return for a playful kiss, which left me covered in bright red lipstick. I later learned that the management had to prevail heavily on Nadira to come to me, and she was pretty horrified by this lipstick-smeared man when she did.

She told me she was an English-language teacher from Samarkand. She had quit because her teaching job paid a theoretical $21 a month, but the pay seldom arrived. On top of which the director of the school was trying to force her into sex. She hated working at this club, but had little choice. Her parents were actors, working for a state company, and had not been paid for months. They didn't know where she was working. She also had two younger brothers to support. One was at school; the other had worked in the bazaars before their closure, and was now unemployed.

All of which sounded like a line, but proved to be true. I never doubted her. My instinct told me this was a girl I could trust, who would return the love that was overwhelming me. She refused to give me her address or phone number.

I asked, "Where can I find you?"

She smiled, and replied, "Here."

I astonished her by saying that I wanted her to give up the club and be my mistress. I explained I could not marry her, as I was married, but would keep her. I gave her my card, and urged her to phone me.

The next day, I told Kristina and Shakhnoza, the young student from Westminster University we had employed part-time on reception, that if a girl called Nadira phoned, they should put her through straightaway, whatever I was doing. They looked suitably mystified. All morning I stared at the phone, but it rang less than usual, and it was never her. It was a terrifically busy time at the embassy, as we prepared for the British music festival, the EBRD AGM, the queen's birthday party and a visit by a British minister, Clare Short. I didn't get a chance to get back to the Safar for a few days. When the opportunity finally came, Nadira was not there. I bumped into Hugo, who seemed to find it difficult to understand why one girl was not as good as another, but eventually we succeeded in persuading Lena to find Nadira's phone number for me.

I rang this several times, but nobody ever answered. I did not know it, but after she heard I had come back asking for her number, Nadira had started to telephone me. She rang several times, but had not been able to get put through, as my protective staff demanded to know what her business was before interrupting their ambassador. I was really itching to meet her.

In fact, Nadira had decided she would see me again only after being persuaded by her flatmate, Nargiza. Nargiza wasn't sure what an ambassador was, but was pretty clear that I must be rich, and she pointed out that it would soon be Nadira's birthday. At the least she might get an expensive birthday present out of me. If I was boring, or tried to insist on sex, she could drop me. On this basis Nadira decided to meet me again. We were finally able to get together, but not until I had dealt with Simon Butt's arrival in Uzbekistan and the astonishing events that followed.

BY THIS STAGE the British government was hell-bent on war. This must have been pretty obvious to everyone from the rhetoric and the newspapers, and obviously over a million people from all over the U.K. realized it with sufficient urgency to travel to London to demonstrate against it. In the FCO we had known George Bush was planning to attack Iraq, even before September 11, 2001. The only question had been when.

Despite being in Tashkent, I was seeing a great deal of internal government communication on the issue, copied to me because Uzbekistan was viewed as one of the few highly dependable allies the U.K. and U.S.

had, and particularly valuable as a "Muslim" state that could be claimed to support the war. But I also knew of the hollowness of the claims of weapons of mass destruction.

From August 1991 for a year, I had been head of the FCO section of the Embargo Surveillance Center. For much of that time I literally lived, slept and ate in an underground bunker in central London. Our job was the real-time monitoring of Iraqi attempts at arms procurement. We reported every morning directly to Thatcher and later Major. I knew what we could and could not know, and how tightly we had sewn everything up. We had a handle on not just the demand for weapons but on potential supply, physical movements of gear and transfers of money all over the world.

This was ten years earlier, but I had never lost my interest or contacts. Before going to Tashkent, I had a chance to speak with the outgoing head of the Middle Eastern Department, Bill Patey, a fellow graduate of Dundee University, later to be ambassador to Iraq. The dodgy WMD dossier had just been published. I had put to him that surely we could not support the stuff in the dossier—it was a mix of the unlikely and the unknowable. He replied, with proper Dundonian bluntness, "Of course not, it's bollocks."

He was telling the truth. Ministerial desire railroaded the civil servants into producing what they knew to be rubbish on the Iraqi threat. Some civil servants were (and are) scared. Some cynically didn't care if it was true, so long as it helped their career. Others, perhaps the majority, took the view that they were civil servants and it was their job to give the democratically elected government what it wanted. Almost nobody took the view that there was an overriding obligation to tell the truth, particularly if the consequence of lies would be a war in which tens of thousands of people, the large majority completely innocent civilians, would die.

More people in the Foreign and Commonwealth Office had difficulty with the notion of going ahead with military action in the absence of United Nations authority. It was hard to disguise the fact that this represented acceptance that the United States, as the sole superpower in the world, can disregard international law and institutions whenever it pleases; a situation which I fear will last until a resurgent China begins to flex its gigantic muscles, about 2015. Then, of course, it might get worse.

Both the Americans and the Uzbek government in Tashkent had an increasing swagger as the troops built up in the Gulf and war loomed larger and larger, now dictated by a military timetable. Robin Cook published an excellent account of the cruel machinations in London in this period.[7] As I watched with horror from Tashkent, I was struck by the increasing gap between the official telegrams I was receiving and the obvious reality. The Foreign Office chose to salve its conscience over the catastrophic demolition of the authority of the United Nations with a collective act of self-delusion.

One telegram in particular I will never forget. Sent to all concerned diplomatic posts, shortly before the UN was expected to meet to consider a "second resolution" on Iraq authorizing the use of force, it was an almost incredible exercise in deluded optimism. It said we were confident of obtaining the "second resolution." It suggested that Putin and Chirac would pull back from threats to veto, because they didn't want to damage the authority of the United Nations. This was an argument Tony Blair was continually deploying at this stage. It was appallingly hypocritical. It was the rapist's argument: "I am going to do it by force anyway, so why don't you consent," or Hitler's argument in securing the Munich Agreement to annex Sudetenland.

Anyway, the telegram breezed confidence that Chirac and Putin would defer. There was a short period between this hopeless telegram telling us that a second resolution would be forthcoming, and the explanation that it had been miraculously discovered that one wasn't necessary after all. Apparently a combination of the "first" resolution, specifically not authorizing force, and thirteen-year-old resolutions authorizing force in the first Gulf War would be good enough. This remarkable bit of news was not accompanied by the actual legal opinion that set out this doctrine.

I considered the criticism I would have come under had I made such a great error of judgment as lay behind that telegram stating that we were confident of obtaining the "second resolution." It had been spectacularly deluded, and had quickly been objectively proven to be so, as we had to give up even trying to put the resolution forward to the Security Council. I was daily under threat from the FCO for errors of judgment that were debatable and, even if true, insignificant by comparison.

I seriously considered sending a sarcastic telegram, quoting back in detail the optimistic phrases about obtaining a second resolution, and asking what had happened. I started drafting, but in the end decided to bite my tongue.

Events now unfurled in astonishingly quick time and I found myself watching in horror the "shock and awe" bombing of Iraq, graphically displayed on our TV screens. I knew enough, from my insider's view of the first conflict, not to believe the propaganda about the clinical accuracy of our weapons. Thousands of women and children were dying, as the world now knows. The doublespeak amazed me—one news bulletin had an expert explaining that, unlike last time, weapons were now so accurate they could take out military targets and miss civilians next door. Much lower down in the very same news program, it was reported that two of our missiles, aimed at Baghdad, had hit Syria by mistake.

In the early stages of our invasion I saw on BBC World a speech by George Bush justifying it. Having seen what I had seen of the real motives and methods of U.S. foreign policy, I was appalled at the sanctimonious crap. I could contain myself no longer, and the next day fired off another telegram to Jack Straw, copied widely to our embassies around the world:

Fm Tashkent
To FCO
18 March 2003
SUBJECT: US FOREIGN POLICY

SUMMARY

1. As seen from Tashkent, US policy is not much focussed on democracy or freedom. It is about oil, gas and hegemony. In Uzbekistan the US pursues those ends through supporting a ruthless dictatorship. We must not close our eyes to uncomfortable truth.

DETAIL

2. Last year the US gave half a billion dollars in aid to Uzbekistan, about a quarter of it military aid. Bush and Powell repeatedly hail Karimov as a friend and ally. Yet this regime has at least seven thousand prisoners of conscience; it is a one party state without freedom of speech, without freedom of media, without freedom of movement, without freedom of assembly, without freedom of religion. It practices, systematically, the most hideous tortures on thousands. Most of the population live in conditions precisely analogous with medieval serfdom.

3. Uzbekistan's geo-strategic position is crucial. It has half the population of the whole of Central Asia. It alone borders all the other states in a region which is important to future Western oil and gas supplies. It is the regional military power. That is why the US is here, and here to stay. Contractors at the US military bases are extending the design life of the buildings from ten to twenty five years.

4. Democracy and human rights are, despite their protestations to the contrary, in practice a long way down the US agenda here. Aid this year will be slightly less, but there is no intention to introduce any meaningful conditionality. Nobody can believe this level of aid—more than US aid to all of West Africa—is related to comparative developmental need as opposed to political support for Karimov. While the US makes token and low-level references to human rights to appease domestic opinion, they view Karimov's vicious regime as a bastion against fundamentalism. He—and they—are in fact creating fundamentalism. When the US gives this much support to a regime that tortures people to death for having a beard or praying five times a day, is it any surprise that Muslims come to hate the West?

5. I was stunned to hear that the US had pressured the EU to withdraw a motion on human rights in Uzbekistan which the EU was tabling at the UN Commission for human rights in Geneva. I was most unhappy to find that we are helping the US in what I can only call this cover-up. I am saddened when the US constantly quote fake improvements in human rights in Uzbekistan, such as the abolition of censorship and Internet freedom, which quite simply have not happened (I see these are quoted in the draft EBRD strategy for Uzbekistan, again I understand at American urging).

6. From Tashkent it is difficult to agree that we and the US are activated by shared values. Here we have a brutal US sponsored dictatorship reminiscent of Central and South American policy under previous US Republican administrations. I watched George Bush talk today of Iraq and "dismantling the apparatus of terror . . . removing the torture chambers and the rape rooms." Yet when it comes to the Karimov regime, systematic torture and rape appear to be treated as peccadilloes, not to affect the relationship and to be downplayed in international fora. Double standards? Yes.

7. I hope that once the present crisis is over we will make plain to the US, at senior level, our serious concern over their policy in Uzbekistan.

MURRAY

I was fully aware that this telegram would be met with great hostility within the Foreign Office establishment. It was the only widely copied internal FCO document that questioned our uncritical support for Bush, and the true motives behind U.S. foreign policy. Though carefully drafted to reflect on U.S. policy in Uzbekistan, and thus stay within my legitimate sphere of comment, it was correctly interpreted as an attack on the morality of the invasion of Iraq itself.

The initial reaction was muted. I received a telegram from Peter Collecott, head of FCO administration, instructing me not to copy my telegrams so widely, allegedly because of complaints from Gulf ambassadors. Otherwise, he threatened, telegram minimization procedures would be activated. This meant I would be electronically prevented from sending on the FCO network.

It is worth noting that thus far, and indeed until the attempt to get rid of me the following August, my concerns had not appeared in any media, nor had I said anything in public not specifically approved by the Foreign Office. I was exercising my duty to give my views on policy, and warn of the dangers I saw brewing, by internal FCO communication. Only those close to me knew I was deeply troubled by our support for Bush and the turn the War on Terror was taking. It was not I who chose to make my views on all this public. I was still operating as a conscientious civil servant, to the best of my ability.

CHAPTER 11

Murder in Samarkand

Two days before the end of March 2003, Simon Butt came out to visit Tashkent. I had been keen to show him some of the reality on the ground, in the hope that I could convince him of how bad Karimov was, and of the dangers of supporting him. I was also keen that he should learn firsthand, particularly from the British business community, how much more active the embassy had become. Fiona and I had decided that we had best invite him to stay in the residence, although I had warned her that on a personal level he was unlikely to be a pleasant guest.

He had declared that his two interests for the visit were continuing the dialogue with key Uzbek ministers and visiting the archaeology of Samarkand. He had "done" the Ferghana Valley on a previous visit. He also wanted to check on the morale of staff in the embassy.

I held a meeting with him on the morning of his arrival, and briefed him in particular on the situation with Chris and Karen, who to my pleasure had finally moved. Since the Van Boven visit, there had been no further worrying symptoms from Chris, or complaints against him. That evening Chris and Karen would hold the first reception in their new home, for Simon to meet Tashkent human rights activists. I also briefed him on the more positive aspects of U.K./Uzbek cooperation, knowing this would interest him most, including the forthcoming British cultural festival, the support we were lending to Westminster University and our efforts to encourage female participation in the Chevening scholarships program. He said very little, but recorded what I said in minute handwriting, apparently word for word, on little pieces of card.

Simon had a separate meeting with members of locally engaged staff, without me present. I had been concerned he would be trawling for complaints about me, but that was not the result of the meeting. Rather to my surprise, the LE staff presented him with a list of complaints of bullying and harassment against Chris Hirst. They produced accounts of verbal and racial abuse, while Atabek claimed that Chris had thrown a file at his head. Vakhida explained why she had moved to the defense section in similar terms. It was notable that all the specific accusations related to events that occurred before my arrival, but Simon instructed me to give Chris a written warning on his conduct toward locally engaged staff.

Simon met a series of ministers that day—including Trade Minister Ganiev, who gave him the usual stream of ludicrous figures: vast increases in economic growth, imports, exports, private agricultural production, state agricultural production, automotive production, textile production. In fact, an economy could never have done so well. I was concerned that Butt meticulously recorded all of this guff with great seriousness, as though it had some meaning—I even saw him write down the claim that U.K. exports to Uzbekistan equaled $420 million in 2002. Our own figures were about 10 percent of that. Butt failed to challenge any of this; he said we were concerned by trade restrictions and border closures, but did not question Ganiev's assertion that trade was booming and that the borders were not closed. In all, he could not have been more meek and attentive—he had all the presence and command of a swotty schoolboy taking notes from a teacher he had a crush on.

This was even worse in his meeting with Foreign Minister Safayev. Throughout this meeting Butt's pen scratched away as he filled acres of card with his tiny, detailed notes. Safayev gave the standard Uzbek spiel that reform should not go too fast in Uzbekistan's precarious geographical position, surrounded by enemies and a true bastion against the evils of drugs and terrorism. Butt could not have been more uncritical in his response. He lauded Uzbek assistance in the War on Terror and regarding Iraq, and all the help they had given the coalition. He was delighted with their cooperation on counternarcotics. We had, he said, noted improvements in human rights and in some areas of economic reform, but hoped that the pace of liberalization might increase. He then assured Safayev that finds of weapons of mass destruction in Iraq were sure to be imminent. He also confirmed that Clare Short would be arriving in May to chair the AGM of the European Bank for Reconstruction and Development, and said that this senior ministerial visit was evidence of the good relations between the U.K. and Uzbekistan. He hoped that Safayev would soon be able to accept Jack Straw's invitation for an official visit to the U.K.

Safayev seemed delighted by this easy ride, as indeed he had good reason to be. The British Foreign Office sees no distinction between diplomacy and brown-nosing. I told Simon Butt in the car as we pulled away from the Uzbek Foreign Ministry that this kind of performance undercut my position; that I had given clear messages on human rights and the urgent need for economic reform, but that he was giving the impression London did not place much weight on this. He replied that he felt he had been quite firm in saying we would like to see quicker political and economic reform.

By FCO standards, perhaps he had.

That night, after dinner at the new residence with members of the British business community, Simon indicated to me that he wanted a one-on-one talk. I led him to the armchairs at the end of the lounge. He sat down and reached for another cigarette; he was smoking a phenomenal number, but I noticed each was only smoked halfway down.

"Now then," he said heavily, "there is serious concern about you in London. That telegram you sent really made people very angry, right at the top of the office. It is pretty off to send a telegram of disagreement just as British troops are about to go into battle. Bluntly, the view in London is that you are unpatriotic."

I offered no response, so he continued, fiddling nervously with his cigarette and taking quick puffs between tightly pursed lips.

"I was asked to send you a pretty stern reply, but I told the PUS that there was no point in initiating a correspondence. I thought it better to warn you in person that you really are pushing things too far. I have told you before that you must make more of an effort to adapt yourself to the current priority of security cooperation. If you can't do that, maybe you had better leave Tashkent."

"Well," I began, "I am not in the least going to apologize for the telegram. It needed to be said, and indeed, a number of British ambassadors from around the world have contacted me to say so. As for lack of patriotism, I am British, not American, and that telegram was largely a critique of U.S. foreign policy. I didn't sign up to promote U.S. foreign policy."

"But you did, like it or not." Simon was lighting a cigarette from the previous one, and his hands were visibly shaking with nervous excitement. "The prime minister has made it plain that we stand shoulder to shoulder with the U.S. in the War on Terror. We are embarking on a war, and London has better things to do than to read overemotional telegrams from you."

Now I was getting angry, and my voice grew steadier and more deliberate: "I am sorry if I get emotional about people being boiled to death, or children being raped in front of their parents," I said. "I don't know how else to react. If you don't get emotional about it, I feel sorry for you."

"I really think," said Simon coolly, "that if you cannot understand the wider picture, we will have to withdraw you. In the meantime, your telegrams are likely to be stopped by the communications center. There is a war on and the systems are busy."

"I am telling truths you don't want to hear. U.S. policy in Central Asia is disastrous. It's crass to prop up Karimov while claiming the need to topple a dictator in Baghdad. It is my duty to report back my analysis and advice, and I will continue to do that."

"You have lost the attention of the top of the office. Nobody cares what you think anymore."

"That is a pity. But I am still going to tell it as I see it."

I stood up to go to bed, rather taking Simon by surprise. I waited for him at the lounge door. He stood and followed me, taking a few steps before, turning back, he picked up the ashtray and took it with him up the stairs to the guest suite.

THE NEXT MORNING was crisp, cold and bright. Simon and I were meant to leave for Samarkand at eight, so I took breakfast with Fiona at seven-thirty. It appeared that the sea-green, the incorruptible Butt had a defect—he couldn't get up in the morning. For the second day running he was late, and appeared about eight-fifteen. As we sat waiting, the electricity flickered and the generator automatically coughed briefly into life before normal power was restored. Fiona suggested Simon was recharging himself from the mains.

Rather than watch Simon eat breakfast (and partly from an urge to rub in his lack of punctuality) I went outside to where the car waited, with Gafur tramping up and down in his big quilted jacket, and Kristina standing by the back of the car in a thick white jumper with a large roll-up neck that framed her beautiful face. It was now past eight-thirty. Gafur came up to me with his customary opening in English: "I'm sorry, Ambassador, but . . ." This was always followed by a stream of Russian. This morning he was getting worried—our first meeting was with the regional *hokkim* of Samarkand at 11 A.M. Less than two and a half hours to Samarkand was really pushing it.

Simon came out the door carrying his case—he would be going on to Tajikistan by road. Michael Smith, our ambassador in Dushanbe, would be making the mountainous journey to Samarkand to pick him up. I was looking forward to seeing Michael, a thoroughly decent man. I knew he would relish a visit by Simon Butt as much as I did. Simon's case went into the back, joining the overnight bags for Kristina, Gafur and me, plus the jerricans of diesel, the satellite phone, the medical kit with its sterile needles, gauzes and blood plasma, and the emergency rations of champagne, mineral water and tinned corned beef that I always carried on journeys.

We set off, with Kristina in the front passenger seat, I behind her and Simon behind Gafur. As the guards swung open the heavy gates, Gafur positively gunned the engine and roared out down the narrow lanes. As he bullied his way through the morning traffic and out of Tashkent, I felt Simon stiffen with disapproval beside me.

This got worse as we hit the divided highway. Gafur got the speedometer up to ninety-five miles per hour, which took a fair amount of cranking in a Tashkent-maintained Discovery fueled by Uzbek diesel. He mercilessly tailgated anything in the fast lane, almost making contact on numerous occasions, particularly with the passenger-crammed minibuses, which were, as ever, oblivious to what was happening around them. At the numerous police and army checkpoints we slammed on the brakes with a terrific screech and burning of tire rubber, not to stop but to go through slowly enough so they could work out who we were, and hopefully not shoot us. Simon was sitting unnaturally rigid. I rather like this sort of thing and I had a great deal of confidence in Gafur's ability. Kristina was preoccupied in changing the radio channel every time she didn't like the next track, which was often.

We arrived at the *hokkimyat* at 10:55, a feat for which I loudly congratulated Gafur, who gave a great beam of pleasure and repeatedly clapped his own shoulders, to loosen joints stiffened by driving. We were taken to a waiting room, where Simon and I sat while Kristina bustled off to organize things. Simon took the opportunity to tell me to reprimand Gafur about his driving—it was very bad for the image of the embassy to be seen to drive recklessly. I replied mildly that we had set off rather late. Simon said he had been surprised that I had not said anything to steady Gafur in the car. I said that in local culture it would not be acceptable to shame Gafur in front of Kristina. Besides, I added, I had not really noticed the driving because I had been giving profound thought to Simon's sensible words of the night before. Simon looked at me quizzically but I affected not to notice, gazing upward as though once again engaged in this improving meditation.

About eleven-fifteen the *hokkim* arrived with a small group of accompanying officials. We all shook hands and went through to the same conference room where Kristina and I had met him in late November. Mirzaeyev launched with characteristic energy into a fulsome introduction. He said he was delighted to see me again—I was the "good friend" of Samarkand. It was also good to make the acquaintance of such an important person from London as Mr. Butt. Turning to me again he said he hoped my last visit had convinced me what a progressive city Samarkand was. I replied that I had promised him I would return in the spring, and indeed here I was—although spring had failed to make it. But while I was sure we would meet many times, this was a visit for Simon, who had much he wished to discuss.

There followed a discussion similar to the one I'd had three months previously, with Mirzaeyev talking of great strides in farming and industrial development. Simon prompted him with nonchallenging questions, and the meeting had very much a sense of going through the motions.

The Registan of Samarkand is breathtaking. Lord Curzon, who knew a thing or two about grandeur, declared it to be better than any of the great squares of Europe. It is marvelous in the literal sense. I can't look at it without my jaw muscles slackening. The verticals appear so effortless that you are unaware of its great height, and the superb blue domes appear almost to float, while the beautiful tilework dazzles the eye.

It consists of three great buildings around a central square. You approach it from the fourth, open side, and soon the great decorated fronts of the buildings, the *ivans,* loom high above you, completely covered in brilliant, decorated tilework that sparkles and glints in yellows, blues and browns, featuring complex floral motifs and beautiful Arabic scripts. At the top of the *ivan* of the right-hand madrassa, two great symbols stand out, meeting in mirror image. A figure of a tiger under a rising sun bearing the face of a chubby, benign god. This was the badge of Tamburlaine—Amir Timur Lenk—whose children and grandchildren built this great Muslim complex, in which it strikes a completely un-Muslim note. Living things are not supposed to be depicted in Muslim art, and the sun symbol harkens back to the Zoroastrian religion of fire worship, which had long predominated here, while the god's face seems an echo of the earlier great flourishing of Buddhism along the Silk Road.

The left-hand madrassa as you enter the square was built by Timur's grandson Ulugbek. A great mathematician and astronomer, Ulugbek built this in effect as a university where medicine, mathematics and astronomy were taught alongside religion. This period saw the tremendous cultural flourishing that brought the medical discoveries of Abu Sinna—known to Renaissance Europe as Avicenna, and the mathematical breakthroughs of Al Khorezm, who invented logarithms. Samarkand was the heart of Islamic culture at its zenith. It was in Samarkand, not Baghdad, that Scheherazade first wove her tales. This is where Omar Khayyám wrote his poetry and pondered mathematics.

When you see it, you can understand why Samarkand came to occupy the Western poetic imagination as an almost mystical place of exotic Eastern luxury. You need also to remember that, at the height of its medieval greatness, the Registan was surrounded by other great domes and buildings, glorying in bright tile, decoration and gilding. The palaces and pleasure gardens have all gone, and only a few sites remain to give you an idea of the splendor, but not the extent, of that glory.

After a brief tour of the wonders of the city we drove off to meet with Professor Mirsaidov and his Tajik dissidents.

The professor was beaming with pleasure as we arrived, waiting expectantly outside his house, surrounded by his numerous family. He led us inside to where the table groaned with the familiar weight of food, and an extra-large amount of the homemade wine that I had so praised last time.

I had warned Simon that this was likely to be a two-dinner day, as the professor's insistence on providing hospitality was most unlikely to be diverted by Kristina's explanation that we were having dinner later in the evening. Some ten other representatives of the Tajik community were there to meet us, though a slightly different group from the one I met last time. I hoped the professor would realize the need to be brief and to the point in his comments.

In fact, the meeting went very well. The professor's opening spiel was to the point, and his associates gave their tales of linguistic discrimination and political repression effectively and with convincing detail, which stood up well to Simon's sometimes cynical questioning. The recent dismissal of the rector of the university in Samarkand, one of the city's leading Tajik figures, featured. There had been a student protest demonstration, the largest in living memory in Samarkand, and in consequence the parents and other family of many of the student protestors had been dismissed from their jobs. The role of the *hokkim* in the increasingly repressive atmosphere in Samarkand was well highlighted.

We had arrived at the professor's house at about 4:30 P.M., having not eaten much breakfast and done a lot of traipsing around. The wonderful spread of walnuts, almonds, dried apricots, sultanas, pomegranates and sweet pastries was very tempting. Inevitably it was followed by soup, then kebabs and then *plov*, and I left sated. I think there was also a genuine warmth among myself and the professor and his friends, and that Simon had been given pause by what he had heard.

We arrived at the guesthouse where we would be staying, checked in, and immediately Michael Smith's Toyota Land Cruiser drew into the courtyard, comprehensively dirty from its long, mountainous journey from Dushanbe. We soon drove out again, to the Tomaris restaurant, where we were booked for dinner. Michael was replete with hair-raising stories of landslides and precipices negotiated on his journey. We sat on a horseshoe-shaped couch with a central table, and I contrived to get myself and Kristina as far away from Michael and Simon as possible, with the drivers in the middle. It was a shame not to be able to easily converse with Michael, but after two days I thought he should take over the burden of making conversation with Simon.

This did not prevent Simon from raising his voice across the table to make plain his admiration of Mirzaeyev. He regarded the regional *hokkim* as energetic and go-ahead. I had a much less favorable impression of his tub-thumping, bullying style and I found his claims to be a modernizer as unconvincing as his glib flow of statistics.

We ordered drinks and local wine—on this occasion the Uzbek wine, despite having precisely the same label as the drinkable stuff I had before, was just awful. I switched to whisky and asked to see the bottle, to check what I was purportedly getting, having far too many experiences with fake scotch in Uzbekistan. It was Chivas Regal and the bottle, at least, looked genuine.

"What are you doing, Craig?" Simon interrupted from across the table in a schoolmasterly tone.

"I'm having a whisky. Just checking it's genuine."

"I see. I hope you're not buying the whole bottle. These are public funds."

I was tempted to say yes, I am going to buy the whole bottle with public funds, then I'm going to drink it, murder some babies and dance upon their graves. But I replied patiently, "No, I'm just having a glass. I was just checking it's the real stuff."

Michael chipped in, affecting to have just noticed the subject of conversation. He was a well-built man with glasses, an almost permanent smile and a cheerful, bustling manner.

"Whisky, eh? Let's buy the whole bottle. Or at least have a few stiff ones."

I could have kissed him.

Michael and I certainly had quite a few stiff ones, and told some good stories across the table as the evening went on. Michael was a keen fan of Scottish music and was amazed to hear that we had the Battlefield Band coming out for a tour as part of our British Days festival. He could not see any way to find the funding to get them to Dushanbe as well, but promised that he would personally get over to Samarkand for that gig.

At the end of the dinner I proposed we move on to the Blues Bar.

Simon quickly and Michael reluctantly declined. They were making a start at first light for Dushanbe, while Kristina and I had nothing to do the following morning until our ten o'clock call on the city *hokkim* (as opposed to the more senior regional *hokkim,* Mirzaeyev). It was around eleven, and in the Blues Bar we drank some pretty rough Uzbek "Koniak." We listened to the old Russian in his red shirt and black waistcoat who played Gershwin with as much calm sophistication as you would get in any penthouse cocktail lounge in New York.

We stayed less than an hour before returning to our beds. It was an innocent enough close to the evening, but enough for Simon Butt to note in a minute to Sir Michael Jay dated April 16, 2003, that: "I ought perhaps to mention, without further comment, one further aspect of Craig's unconventional style. After a dinner in Samarkand, the rest of the party returned to our hotel. Craig, in the company of our young female LE fixer, went off in search of a jazz club."

The drip, drip of innuendo against me was moving toward full flood. A jazz club with a young female, eh? Shades of Sodom and Gomorrah.

OUR RETURN JOURNEY the next day was without incident and I got back to the embassy at about three-thirty. It had been presumed I wouldn't be coming in, so there was some scurrying as crosswords and mobile phones were put away and everyone pretended to be working. Kristina arrived about half an hour later. I got up from my desk to ask her something. I walked about three paces when CRACK!

I pitched forward onto my face, my spectacles spilling onto the carpet ahead of me. Bloody hell! I had been attacked from behind and stabbed or shot in the back of my left leg. I had actually heard it break. It was agony. I rolled over, peering around and scrabbling for my glasses. No one around. I must have been shot.

I tried to stand up; I couldn't bear to put any weight at all on the left foot. But no sign of blood. What on earth was happening?

I called Kristina, and soon with Gafur and Yuri under my armpits I was being carried out of the office and back into the car. We drove to the international clinic, where an orderly was waiting for our arrival with a wheelchair—Kristina had plainly recovered her usual efficiency.

* * *

DR. REIMERS, the cheerful doctor from the Marshall Islands, was looking at my left calf muscle. "Mm, looks swollen."

A tape measure was produced—it was two inches greater in circumference than my right calf muscle.

"Something wrong there. Can't take any weight at all? Does it hurt if I—"

"AAAAGH!"

She had flexed the foot at the ankle. "Mmm. That's not good. Need any pain relief?"

"All I can get."

She gave me an injection of morphine or something similar, and then got out her textbooks. That she was willing to look things up in front of you, rather than pretend omniscience, increased my confidence.

"I think you've snapped a calf muscle. It's more like a sports injury and I'm not expert. What does it say here? 'Typically the patient pitches forward. An audible snap may be heard. Very often the patient has the initial impression of having been struck forcibly from behind.'"

"Yes, that's a perfect description."

"Thought so. One more thing to check. This may hurt."

"AAH! It did."

"Well, the important thing is, your Achilles tendon is OK—it's the muscle, not the tendon. The tendon would have been much more serious. What you need is to rest it, and tight support with an elastic bandage. Oh, and for the next twenty-four hours, lots and lots of ice."

While an assistant was bandaging me, Dr. Reimers left and reappeared with two crutches, tall and aluminum, of the traditional under-the-shoulder model.

"You'll need these."

"How long?"

"Oh, about eight weeks."

I got back to the embassy toward six o'clock, expecting everyone to have gone home. To my surprise, Karen, Chris, Lena and Kristina were lined up on the steps waiting for me. I expected some wry comments on my crutches, but they looked stern and worried. Karen spoke.

"It's Professor Mirsaidov," she said. "His grandson's been murdered."

* * *

EARLY THAT MORNING the body of the professor's eighteen-year-old grandson, Shukrat, had been dumped in the street outside the family home. The professor had been trying desperately to contact me while still in Samarkand, but had presumed I had been staying at one of the big hotels. He had got through to the embassy and spoken with Lena. The simple facts were these: the grandson had left the house at around 8 P.M., shortly after Simon Butt and I had departed. His body had been dumped from a truck in the street in the early hours. The professor believed the young man had been killed as a warning, in response to our meeting with the dissidents.

They told this to me as I stood braced on my crutches at the foot of the embassy steps.

"Oh my God!" I said. "Does the professor blame me?"

"No, not at all," said Lena. "He says that he knows you will bring justice."

I hobbled a step backward and levered myself on my crutches back into the Discovery. I put my head in my hands for a minute or two. We then went back into the embassy. I delegated Chris to phone the Foreign Office, while I drafted and sent a telegram outlining the bare facts as we knew them. I made a point of being plain that Professor Mirsaidov's meeting was with Simon Butt, not just me. London would take that more seriously. Simon himself would still be on the tortuous road between Samarkand and Dushanbe.

The response from London was immediate and alarmed—plainly a scandal like this could affect the hosting of the annual general meeting of the European Bank for Reconstruction and Development, due to take place in Tashkent under U.K. chairmanship barely one month later. I was ordered to get down to Samarkand immediately and ascertain what exactly had happened, and in particular whether the murder could be positively pinned on the authorities, and if so whether it could be linked to our meeting with Mirsaidov.

It was now after dark and I was pretty tired, and in pain from my leg, so I told Gafur to be ready to go down to Samarkand with me at first light; Lena was to accompany me as interpreter. I didn't want to make Kristina leave her child again so soon. I then had to explain to Fiona that I would be leaving straight away again. I did this hurriedly on first arrival, as soon as I met Fiona in the living room. Only after I finished did I realize that I had not explained my appearing on crutches with a bandaged leg.

Fiona was sympathetic, but reckoned I should have told the Foreign Office I had hurt my leg and could not go back to Samarkand.[1]

The next day my leg hurt even more as I eased myself into the car, and all the many potholes on the Samarkand road caused agony. I clenched my teeth and made light conversation with Lena. Around 10 A.M. we arrived at the professor's home again. A more somber family group greeted us as old friends. I stumbled taking my shoes off to enter the house. Professor Mirsaidov then led us to an upper-story room—going upstairs on crutches is not too bad, apart from the rubbing under the shoulders. I had not been upstairs in the house before.

The body had been buried immediately, in accordance with Muslim custom. But they had managed to take extensive photographs of the corpse before burial, and even make a video. The photographs showed that the elbows and knees had been smashed, and the back of the head stove in. In addition, the right hand looked like cooked chicken, with skin and flesh peeling away from the bones. I recognized this, and the tide line around the wrist—immersion in boiling liquid. There was also matted blood around both eyes.

Professor Mirsaidov showed me the official postmortem report, which noted none of this physical damage, but gave cause of death as asphyxiation by vomit as a result of an overdose. It was not possible, the professor declared, pointing to the photos. I tried to be exact and rational in the face of the old man's dignified grief.

"Well," I said, "there could have been a drug overdose as well, but, if so, it wasn't necessarily self-inflicted."

I went outside to speak with Gafur. A small crowd had gathered in the narrow street, mingling with the neighbors and family who had come to console. I asked Gafur, who was a Tajik speaker, to see what he could pick up from them; perhaps someone had seen or heard something. I then returned to the professor, who confirmed that his grandson had simply left the house in the evening and been dumped back in the early hours, tortured and dead.

He said there had been a lot of blood around the body. So he was either still alive or very recently dead when he was dumped. After the body was found—about 5 a.m.—the police had come. They had hosed away the blood, swept the street and taken the body away for autopsy, before returning it some hours later. The family had moved the body inside, and had taken the photos I had seen, before the police arrived. No one had seen the police make any investigation of the scene before washing and brushing away any evidence. The police had not taken any photos. I asked whether the family had called the police, or whether they had just turned up. The professor was uncertain. He hadn't called the police; he didn't know whether anyone else had. To the best of the professor's knowledge, nobody had seen anyone abduct his grandson.

I asked whether the lad had any history of drugs. The professor told me something I was to hear again and again that day. Samarkand was directly on the main route for heroin trafficking out of Afghanistan. It came to Samarkand either straight from the border crossing at Termez, or through the mountains of Tajikistan. Heroin in Samarkand was substantially cheaper than beer. The grandson, Shukrat, like the large majority of his age group in Samarkand, was unemployed. He had scratched a living from the international bazaar trade before the government closed it down four months previously. He was not a *narkoman,* but had probably tried heroin. Almost every young person in Samarkand had. There were now two or three young people with desperate addiction problems on this very street—and the same was true on any small street in the city. I asked if this led to HIV and AIDS problems. The professor's jaw muscles tensed, and he added a curt *"da."*

He then expounded a bit more. Opium had been part of traditional Tajik and Uzbek life for generations. It was drunk, in small quantities and very dilute form, in tea. It was used for headaches and menstrual pain, and to provide mild recreation. Only in recent years had Afghanistan started to export predominantly heroin rather than raw opium, and the culture of injecting heroin was a completely different one. It was devastating his community. He grew misty-eyed, and I observed that he could articulate his grief for his community in general, but was so tightly buttoned-up over what must be a profound grieving for his grandson in particular.

I asked if he had been concerned about his grandson and drugs. He said not particularly—he had said that it was likely his grandson had tried them because they were so prevalent. He had not said that he definitely had. I asked if he had ever noticed injection marks; he said no, definitely not. I asked whether he had noticed injection marks on the body; he said no, but given overall levels of damage, it would be hard to tell. I thanked him.

It may seem stupid to be asking these questions about drug abuse in such an obvious case of murder, but I knew that I would have to prove to London that I had given due consideration to the official Uzbek autopsy explanation, no matter how laughable I might think it.

I asked the professor if I could see the last person to see Shukrat alive. I looked again at the photographs. He was a thin lad, with surprisingly blond hair. Given the agonies of his death, the face was restful. Looking at the shattered legs, I recalled childhood images of the Passion. My eyes started to feel hot and tears began to well. Lena squeezed my hand.

In came a small child, looking graceful and grave in his long velvet *chapan* and square black lacquered skullcap. He bowed and salaamed, and sat in the chair on the side of the table opposite me, his large, beautiful black eyes looking at me seriously, though with no obvious sign of emotion. He was Shukrat's little brother, and was eight years old.

Lena checked that he spoke adequate Russian, and asked why he had come to see us. Because, he replied simply, he was the last person to see Shukrat.

He explained that he had been in the bedroom with Shukrat that evening. They had been sleeping—the rest of the family had been busy all day preparing for my visit. He had been hungry, he said, because the family had spent all their money on the banquet for me. He said this in an even tone, without accusation or petulance, and continued to look me straight in the eye. He had asked Shukrat for some money, but Shukrat had said he didn't have any. Then Shukrat had dressed and gone out.

I asked what time.

About seven-thirty.

Had he dressed casually or carefully?

Carefully; he had washed and shaved.

Had he said where he was going?

To see Nigina.

Nigina?

His girlfriend.

Girlfriend? I had been told he was newly married.

Yes, the child replied, as though to someone very dim. He had a wife. But Nigina was his girlfriend.

Had he said anything else?

No, he had said he was off to see Nigina, and gone out. He had not seen his brother since. They had not allowed him to see the body. At this last, the child's extraordinary composure cracked for the first time; his lip began to tremble and tears to form in the lower rims of his eyes. Slowly and with visible self-control, he got down from the chair, bowed again, turned and left.

I was close to tears again too. Hell, I would never have made a policeman.

I turned to Lena. "He went to see a girlfriend? Well, that's a whole new factor."

"Yes," she said. "You know, it could be the girlfriend's family. Maybe her brothers . . ."

"It might explain the brutality. I should have asked if Nigina was married. Maybe his wife's family?"

"No." Lena sounded pretty definite. "It's not considered that big an insult to the wife or anything. But Nigina's family, possibly. Depends who she is."

I asked to see the professor again.

"Who is Nigina?" I asked.

"She's a very bad girl. I have made an official complaint to the Mahalla committee about her. They have spoken to her parents. But she wouldn't stop seeing my grandson."

"She was his regular girlfriend?"

"He had known her for many years. He had told her it must stop when he married, but she kept calling him."

"You know that he said that he was going to see her when he left?"

"Yes, I know."

"Could her family have killed him?"

"No. She was a very bad girl. They knew it. We know them. They don't think it was Shukrat's fault."

I did not find this exactly convincing, but decided to move on. I asked to see Shukrat's wife.

She entered in her *maraka* mourning dress. She wore a light blue long gown, with a long white veil over her hair and falling over her arms to her waist, with the bottom of her face covered by a piece tucked over. Her eyes were red and raw from crying. Lena continued to interpret, but there was a flicker of understanding in those eyes when I spoke English.

I started by apologizing for intruding upon her grief. I explained that the professor was convinced that her husband had been killed by the authorities in connection with my visit. She nodded. I then leaped in feet-first.

"You know that the last thing your husband told his brother was that he was going to see Nigina?"

This brought on a paroxysm of tears. What did I expect? But what else could I have done?

I did not get a direct answer as to whether she already knew this, but she said that she knew of Nigina, that Nigina had been her husband's girlfriend before their marriage, and that she knew he still saw her. He had stopped seeing her for a period after their marriage, but Nigina kept phoning and inducing him to go back to her.

I asked whether Nigina's family might have killed her husband. Taking a deep breath, I added the question of whether her own family, or someone concerned with her interests, might have taken action against her husband because of Nigina.

She smiled wanly. No, that was impossible. Besides, she knew who had killed her husband.

Really? I sat up straight, and soon wished I hadn't, as any movement was now causing me great pain in my left calf. Sweat was forming on my upper lip, and my shirt felt soaked, bunched and uncomfortable at the small of my back.

She reached into the folds of her gown and produced a photograph of her husband. He was sitting in a restaurant, small, thin, open-shirted and, in this photo, mousy-haired. He had a silly grin on his face. He stood out among the group of four men, sitting behind their table, arms around shoulders, with Uzbek champagne and vodka bottles and party detritus before them on the white tablecloth, cheap wood paneling behind. The other three were much heavier and broader built, with sallow complexions, broad faces and a more Asian cast to their eyes.

They wore leather jackets, chunky watches and gold jewelry. Gold teeth shone.

"They killed him."

"Who are they?"

The photograph had been taken at a birthday party, just a couple of weeks earlier, for one of Shukrat's schoolmates, and many of the old class had been invited. She indicated one of the group. He was SNB—secret police. The other two were drug dealers. They had befriended Shukrat, who had known them at school, but she said Shukrat had told her they had not been special friends. In the last two weeks he had been out with them several times to expensive bars and restaurants, and they had paid for him. She had begged him not to trust them, but Shukrat had told her not to worry. Now, she concluded simply, they had killed him.

I asked why, and she said she did not know. But she was sure it was them. She stood up to leave. On an impulse I asked her if she had Nigina's phone number. She did not flinch, but calmly wrote it down for me.

"Looking for a girlfriend in Samarkand?" Lena inquired, after she had gone. We needed some gallows humor, and it was appreciated.

"I take it you mean Nigina and not the widow?"

"Of course."

"No thanks. I wonder if Nigina's crying her eyes out now too? My leg's killing me. I need a drink."

As if by magic the professor entered bearing a bottle of his homemade wine, followed by two ladies of the family with tea and mineral water. I looked out to the spreading grapevine, supported on horizontal wires to shade the whole courtyard, now budding with new life. After they left I turned to Lena.

"What do you make of all this, Lena?"

"Well, the SNB connection could add weight to the professor's claim of a political killing."

"Yes, but on the other hand, there's a drug connection again. Of course the two could be linked—maybe he had learned too much about the authorities' involvement in drug smuggling? Maybe they hadn't realized his family links to the opposition until I came, and then they had to get rid of him? I don't know."

The dead man's mother came to see us next, of her own volition, but she kept bursting into tears and beating her breast, and did not appear to have anything new to add, so I was anxious not to upset her further. Finally I saw the neighbor who had discovered the body. About 4 A.M. he had been awoken by the sound of a truck in the narrow alley. The house across the street rented out PA systems for parties, so quite often large vehicles would come at strange hours, and he hadn't thought much about it. About 5 A.M. he had opened the gate of his courtyard and seen the body. He had touched it; still warm and not stiff. There was a great deal of blood, mostly from the back of the head.

We spoke with Gafur—he had picked up that the whole neighborhood knew of the affair with Nigina, but nobody seemed to think that was connected with the death. He had also learned that there was a major drug problem in the community, but that Shukrat was not thought to be involved. A son of the man who found the body was an addict. He confirmed that when the police arrived, they had very quickly hosed down any evidence. They had taken great care to brush away any tire tracks—one of the neighbors said that he had asked a policeman why they were spoiling this evidence, and had been asked by the policeman whether he wished to die too. The neighbors were sure that the authorities had done it.

I stayed to eat *plov* with the family, which was done in heavy silence. Then I took up my crutches and hobbled away. The professor's parting words were: "Karimov is truly the heir of Amir Timur as he claims. My grandson died as a warning to his opponents."

I HOBBLED PAINFULLY to the Land Rover and we went to the Afrosiyab hotel. I lay on my bed for a couple of hours, in which time the hotel failed to find any ice for my leg. We sent Gafur to find some and he returned with the boot of the Discovery filled with a great block. I asked him to smash some in pieces and put it in a cloth. He said something I did not understand and I asked Lena what he had said.

"He suggested that he chisel a hole through the middle and we stick your leg through it."

By the end of the afternoon I felt up to confronting the authorities. Professor Mirsaidov had given me the address of the district procurator dealing with the case, and we drove there. At the reception counter, I showed my green Ministry of Foreign Affairs diplomatic accreditation card, and after being checked by about six officials in ascending order of seniority, I was finally shown in to the district procurator himself.

He wore a gray and blue military camouflage uniform, and was a sharp-eyed man of strongly Asian features, with bushy eyebrows and a lined forehead. He looked me in the eye.

"It is most unusual for an ambassador to honor a mere district procurator with a visit. To what do I owe this honor?"

"I am here in connection with the murder of Professor Mirsaidov's grandson."

A flicker of recognition—he certainly knew of the case.

"I was not aware that the professor had such powerful foreign friends."

"I think you will find he has quite a strong international reputation."

"Really. Samarkand should be proud of him. I did not know the outside world took such an interest in Tajik literature."

His eyes narrowed. He continued, "The death of the grandson is most unfortunate. A drug addict, you know. Very sad case. An overdose. Very sad. It seems to have turned the old professor's mind."

I lost my temper. Coming ungainly to my feet on my crutches, I took the photographs of the body from Lena. I slammed down a photo of the smashed back of the skull on the desk in front of him. I positively shouted at him, "Perhaps you can explain how that happens as a result of a drug overdose?"

I slammed down more photos, slapping my palm hard on the desk each time. Concerned officials started to arrive behind me. As each photo hit the desk, showing boiled hand, smashed arms, broken legs, I yelled, "Explain that! And that! And that! And *that*! Go on—tell me that's a drug overdose."

I stood over him, and the procurator motioned for me to sit down, which I did.

"Ambassador," he said, "to an amateur the sight of any dead body is grotesque. You can easily misinterpret."

"Procurator," I replied, "since I came to Uzbekistan, I have seen more of these kinds of photos than I would have ever imagined. This evidence is pretty plain."

He shifted his ground. "This dead young man was not British; why do you care?"

"We have a strong interest in human rights in Uzbekistan. Besides, I had a meeting with Minister of the Interior Almatov last December. It was very friendly and he invited me to visit any police station or prison at any time, and inquire into any case."

"Unfortunately, this office is under the procurator general, not under Mr. Almatov. I am not authorized to speak with you."

"Are you personally in charge of the case?"

"Yes."

"Did you attend the scene?"

"Yes."

"Why were the police allowed to wash away all evidence at the scene?"

"It was not necessary to conduct forensic investigation."

"If you persist with this story of drug overdose, I will make you known as a liar throughout the world. This could affect the holding of the European Bank AGM in Tashkent."

I saw the first flicker of fear in his eyes.

"Are you calling me a liar?" he blustered.

"If this case is closed, yes."

Suddenly he was all comradely bonhomie.

"But who said it was closed? My investigation is just beginning. You and I know how governments work."

He winked and leered.

"I will report your interest to my authorities. Who knows what will happen? And when this case is . . ." he paused, collected the photos from his desk and handed them back to me, ". . . buried, you will come back to Samarkand and we will drink together."

It was the best I could do that day for the professor. I left my card and said I would get back to him.

BY EVENING I WAS feeling a bit better and we did the discos of Samarkand—well, all three, to be exact, one of which had no booze and no customers but insisted on a ten-dollar entrance fee. Lena was great company and we had much fun with the local youth and my crutches. It was desperately needed light relief.

The next day we went back to Tashkent. I reported to London that it was impossible to be certain why the professor's grandson had been killed. Plainly the autopsy report was a sham. That combined with the efficient destruction by the police of evidence at the scene showed the authorities were deliberately hiding something. This would give weight to the professor's view that the murder was done by the authorities themselves, to discourage dissidents from meeting British embassy staff.

On the other hand, the victim's tangled love life might be the motive. Or it could be connected with his new friends and the drug trade. The authorities were up to their necks in narcotics trafficking throughout Uzbekistan, and might have ordered both murder and cover-up from that motive. At this stage, it was impossible to be certain. I could investigate further, for example by visiting Nigina and her family, or by going to Shukrat's old school, identifying the three men in the picture from the school reunion and questioning them.

London did not want me to investigate further. Even though I was doing so on their direct instruction, they seemed to think I had investigated too much already. They were satisfied that there was enough area of uncertainty to allow them to proceed with chairing the EBRD AGM. I was, however, allowed to make a protest to the Uzbek Ministry of Foreign Affairs about the discrepancy between the autopsy report and the photographic evidence. I did this but as usual received no practical response.

About ten days after my return from Samarkand I was attending a state banquet, I believe for a visiting president of another former Soviet state. As I was milling around in the general gathering over drinks, the Russian ambassador, Dmitry Ryurikov, pulled me aside. He asked me what London made of the death of Mirsaidov's grandson; the professor was telling everybody it was connected to my visit.

I said that it was certainly possible; the autopsy was plainly a fraud and there had been no proper investigation. Something was being covered up.

Ryurikov lowered his voice. There were, he said, many ethnic Russians still in the SNB. The Russian embassy still had excellent contacts with the SNB, who were furious at the killing, regarding it as pointlessly sadistic and counterproductive. It had been done by the Samarkand *mil-*

itsiya on the direct orders of the regional *hokkim,* Mirzaeyev. He was determined to stamp out Tajik dissidence in Samarkand.

I thanked him. It was food for thought. It certainly seemed to fit with Mirzaeyev's explosive style: the school closures, linguistically based job purges and the removal of the Tajik university rector. What is more, Mirzaeyev was credibly credited with several deaths in his previous job as *hokkim* of Jizzak.

I considered what I knew of Ryurikov and his character, his motivation for telling me the truth or for misleading me. I considered whether the SNB might have misled him, and why. I considered what was known of Mirzaeyev and of Mirsaidov. My conclusion was that Ryurikov, whom I believed to be a good man, was telling me the truth. The most likely explanation of the death was that Mirzaeyev ordered the killing to intimidate Samarkand dissidents. It fit all the known facts.

That leads me to conclude that, in a sense, I was responsible. Had I not arranged to visit Mirsaidov and the other dissidents with Simon Butt, the lad would probably still be alive now. I continue to worry away at it, but it is some consolation that Mirsaidov does not blame me. As he points out, totalitarian regimes terrify you into inaction by the threat of violence against you, or still more effectively, against others. If for that reason we give in, totalitarianism will always win.

I can appreciate that intellectually, but emotionally I still experience waves of guilt. Sometimes they hit me in the supermarket or on the subway. I think I will still see in dreams those images of Shukrat's corpse, horribly tortured yet peaceful, until the day I too die.

I reported back to London what Ryurikov had told me, and that I believed him, but they did not seem that interested. In fact, from about this time my influence with the FCO appeared to vaporize; they simply ignored almost anything I had to say.

At the state banquet, as he moved away, Ryurikov motioned toward the glass of champagne in my hand.

"If I were you," he said, "I wouldn't eat or drink too much here."

I thought he was being melodramatic, but I put down my glass and found a bottle of Nestlé water with the seal still intact, which I stuck to throughout the evening. At the state banquet each course was brought individually plated and put in front of you. Members of the visiting delegation, who comprised a third of the guests, were continually leaping up from their seats and heading off to fine-tune speeches, handle press queries or deal with logistics for the next day's program, all tasks I knew very well. I contrived to keep taking courses from their empty seats, depositing my plates on a side table.

Anyway, I had no bad effects from that evening. But later I had much cause to dwell on Ryurikov's warning.

CHAPTER 12

Pinafore, Battlefield and Baseball Bat

I WAS FEELING PRETTY LOW. GETTING SO CLOSE TO THE DEATH OF Mirsaidov's grandson, and a nagging sense that it was my fault, had hit me hard. My sore leg was causing constant pain. I had lost my faith in my own country and in the job I was doing. The issues of torture and intelligence were causing me a real crisis of conscience. I was facing unmistakable personal hostility from my immediate management. Intellectual company was in short supply, and I didn't have any sympathetic senior colleague with whom I could talk over these problems. I had to cope with this while living in the landscape of human misery caused by one of the worst regimes on earth.

In novels, people survive a whole series of dramatic and traumatic events and come through them all, guns blazing. They never crack up under the strain. I suppose that's why they are heroes, and why it is fiction. Anyway, I couldn't crack up yet, as I was about to enter the busiest period of my professional life. So were the rest of the embassy staff.

In the next four weeks our tiny staff had to prepare for chairing the EBRD AGM, to put on the British Days festival in five cities, organize a visit by a senior British minister and to run the queen's birthday party with a guest list of over two thousand. I had miscalculated one vital factor. I had been used to working with teams of dynamic and ambitious young graduates, wedded to the job and prepared to give their everything at all hours. Now I was having to bring along lower-flying, less ambitious staff who were not easy to inspire. I ended up doing much more myself than I expected. I also found it was the local staff who best rose to the challenges.

There had been changes in staff. Dave Muir had left and been replaced by Steve Brown, another ex-army man, and his beautiful ethnic Russian wife from Kazakhstan. Jackie had left and been replaced by Angela Clarke. Angela was a single mother with two young sons, and she had taken on a lot by coming to live somewhere as difficult as Tashkent.

I had initiated a major program of new and better staff housing. We had also taken on quite a number of extra Uzbek staff. Steve Brown had two new assistants, Ulugjan and Lilya. I had finally persuaded Chris to take on an assistant, an earnest young man named Talat. I had signaled to London that, if I was going to stay in Tashkent, they would have to put the embassy on a better funding basis and update the communications equipment. One of the issues that had prompted this was a complaint from London that the embassy was not following all proper procedures in accounting, procurement and recruitment. Quite simply, the embassy had never had enough staff to carry out the FCO's bureaucratic requirements.

I AM A GREAT FAN of cultural diplomacy—reaching the population of a country, and presenting them with a connection with the U.K., through popular events. Given modern communications, with satellite television promoting popular culture worldwide, this may seem anachronistic. British soaps are watched, and British pop music heard, all round the globe. But not in Uzbekistan, where the media are tightly controlled and the large majority of the population—all except the wealthiest city dwellers—have no access to satellite television.

As the fourth-largest city of the Soviet Union, Tashkent had a great tradition of classical music, opera and ballet. I invited the great former ballerina Bernara Karieva to dinner on a couple of occasions, and much enjoyed her stories. But she was very sad about the decline of the arts in Tashkent.[1]

If you see Uzbekistan as a postcolonial state, having thrown off Russian occupation, then it is only natural to expect that the colonizer's art forms should disappear. But it was still sad. The opera and ballet continued, though with sharply declining standards. The new conservatoire still provided excellent teaching, but the balance was shifting evermore toward Uzbek traditional music, which has a very different tonal base. In the Soviet tradition, this "folk" music had been cut off from its roots in communities and was presented in a stultified and joyless, state-approved form.

Some wonderful classical musicians remained in Uzbekistan. The national symphony orchestra was absolutely first-class, though rather weak in the brass section. But the orchestra seldom got to play. There were no public orchestral concerts. Very occasionally the government decided to bring out the symphony orchestra on a state occasion—for example, a concert in honor of the EBRD AGM. But the orchestra was wilting through neglect. Its members received theoretical salaries of about twelve dollars a month, but they seldom arrived.

My idea, based on my experience in Poland, was to put on a music festival using local musicians to play British music. We couldn't afford to bring an orchestra out from the U.K., but using the Uzbek orchestra could be both effective and cheap. What we could afford to bring out was a folk band. I chose the Battlefield Band, in my opinion the best and certainly the most enduring of the Celtic revival bands. I had found that Scottish music has a universal international appeal, except perhaps to the English. The final element came together when I was invited to a concert— Handel's *Messiah*—by the local Silk Road Chamber Choir. Privately sponsored by South Korean businessmen, they were excellent, of the highest musical standard. I am a great fan of Gilbert and Sullivan operettas, which I think are ludicrously underrated in the U.K. They too travel well internationally. This choir could tackle one.

So in October I had put the plan together. There would be three elements. The Battlefield Band would play in Tashkent, Samarkand, Navoi, Ferghana and finally Tashkent again. The orchestra would put on a program of accessible British light classical music in Tashkent and Samarkand, followed the next day in each venue by the musical *HMS Pinafore.* The embassy would pay for the performance fees, scores and U.K. costs. We would ask the Uzbek authorities to cover venue, transport and accommodations.

None of the music in the festival had ever been heard in Uzbekistan before. This would be the first-ever production of Gilbert and Sullivan in Central Asia. It would need the willing cooperation of the infamously truculent Uzbek authorities. Not one of the proposed cast of *Pinafore* could speak English. The orchestra had never so much as heard the music. We needed to make sure that concerts were carried on radio and television to meet a much wider audience.

Kamola, the young student pianist I had met at the Gershwin concert, was to prove invaluable, becoming pretty well an extra, unpaid member of staff. She introduced me to her father, Ilios Luftullayev, a professor at the conservatory. Between them they did a tremendous amount to spread the word and excite the local musical community about the festival. Ilios invited Fiona and me, with the children, to a lovely traditional meal in his house, after which he got out his *dutar*—a long-necked two-stringed instrument. I have spent a lot of time with excellent musicians from many cultures, but Ilios's playing was incredible. I would have thought it impossible to get such range from just two strings, and to combine melody with a compulsive underlay of insistent rhythm, counterpointed by percussive effects produced by striking the body of the instrument with a fingernail. It was impossible to follow his fingers, and the music, sometimes lyrical, sometimes surging, was superb.[2]

Karen had organized to hire the Uzbek National Orchestra—the rate was fifteen dollars per player per performance, plus $100 each for the conductor and director. The orchestra as an institution would get to keep the scores, which were worth a couple of thousand pounds. The initial contract was to play at the queen's birthday party, at two orchestral concerts and two performances of *Pinafore*. We were using a sixty-three-piece orchestra, and the fee for all this was approximately $6,000. I was very excited when, accompanied by Kamola, I attended the first orchestral rehearsal. The orchestra were excited too, because they seldom saw new scores.

The conductor, Vladimir Neimer, kindly ran through the whole program for me at the first two rehearsals, before getting down to serious work. He was a tall, gaunt man of few words, and a fantastic musician whose services were in demand throughout the former Soviet Union. He was dedicated to his orchestra, and spent huge effort on individual tutoring. His father had been a conductor at the Volksoper in Vienna, so he took easily to the spirit of this light music. He could be fierce in rehearsal, and would bark at the musicians when they didn't give the tone he wanted. I worked closely with him, in particular on the tempos, and we forged a firm friendship. I got to conduct the orchestra in rehearsals once or twice; there is no more exhilarating experience. Under Neimer's direction the orchestral concerts were quickly on track, and indeed in the event were nothing short of superb.

HMS Pinafore was much more difficult. From the start I had intended that it would be a concert rather than a staged and costumed performance. We invited the entire choir and the orchestral section leaders to listen to a recording in the residence, which aroused great enthusiasm. But getting the choir to sing successfully in English was difficult. They had done a lot of singing in German, and so pronounced everything with heavy German accents. Stopping the *w*'s from being *v*'s, and the *j*'s from being *y*'s was hard work, and the vowel sounds were awful. I spent more time working on the pronunciation than on the music.

THE QUEEN'S BIRTHDAY party was to be held on April 28 at the new residence. Previously these had been held at the back garden of the embassy, for about three hundred people, and had been a simple cocktail party. The French, Germans and others did much more, and I was determined that we would now use the occasion to confirm the new, higher-profile role of the British embassy. I wanted about twelve hundred guests, so we would need to invite about two thousand people.

I had announced this to a stunned staff in November. I said that the first hundred names on the guest list should be the most famous people in Uzbekistan, be they actors, sports personalities, newsreaders, singers or whomever. I wanted people to leave saying, "Wow! Did you see who was there?" This idea was greeted with some skepticism—Atabek said the mafia held a third of the top hundred places—but gradually they warmed to it. I then wanted the heads of the hundred biggest companies, state or private, the *hokkims* of the regions and the big cities, all our commercial and political contacts, every consular national for whom we were responsible. Every British company was to have the chance to nominate guests useful to them. We should invite not only ambassadors but key diplomats from other embassies. Oh, and all the neighbors.

I wanted a program of entertainment that would start at 3 P.M. and finish at nine. This would kick off with the full symphony orchestra in evening dress playing the British light music program on the marbled terrace by the swimming pool. It would conclude with a concert by the Battlefield Band, playing to a banked corner of the garden where we would set out three hundred chairs in a natural amphitheater. Food would be substantial. There would be eleven thousand canapés, three thousand shashliks and one hundred pounds of *plov,* served over six hours. There would be two large bars, plus a Pimm's tent, a British beer bar and a British cheese stall. British Airways would fly out much of this. Getting it through customs would be a tussle. Lena the cook and sixteen helpers would prepare the food, while the Sheraton would provide bars, glasses and forty-six serving staff. We would buy and import marquees. The *hokkimyat* would provide chairs and tables for six hundred, to be spread round the garden. Twelve policemen would organize the traffic, and we would hire a nearby stadium for parking for three hundred cars—it would overflow. Thirty-six soldiers would secure the perimeter. And of course, there would be fireworks to close. I love fireworks.

It was a hell of a lot of work. Just collating guest lists and writing invites was a massive task. The Uzbek post is completely unreliable and all the invitations had to be hand delivered all over the country. Karen, Kristina and Fiona produced miracles of organization.

It was lucky that Karen and Lena Son were so active, because Chris had effectively stopped working. One lunchtime he had come in dirty and bruised with a bleeding leg. He had, he said, been walking by the canal when a Lada drew up, and four big men with crowbars got out to attack him. He had, however, beaten them off.

Chris told the story with no conviction, then returned home and essentially stopped working from that moment. He turned up occasionally and slouched around sulking. I was left pondering Dave Muir's comment that these attacks had never happened to anyone else. That was true. An expatriate told me at this time that he had seen Chris walking in a park with his rottweiler, and apparently raising a metal baseball bat to threaten a passing local, who ran away.

But now we were seriously firefighting, and I had no time to think of Chris.

The next day Karen told me she had sacked Shakhnoza, the receptionist. I was pretty taken aback, as I had found Shakhnoza both efficient and pleasant, but Karen maintained that she was just not good enough in English on the telephone. It seemed to me that the last thing we could afford at this minute was to lose a member of staff. But even less could I afford just now to fall out with Karen, so I let it go.

On the afternoon of Friday, April 25, Kristina brought me the following letter, from a Mr. Burkhanov, a partially sighted and registered disabled man. It had been delivered by hand to the embassy. He wrote:

On April 25 2003 at 7.10am when I was going to my work along the Ankhor river bank, which flows along Bainal Minal Street (International), an unknown man with his dog was coming towards me. The dog, without a muzzle and collar, was running 20 metres in front of its owner. The animal came near me and attacked me. It bit my thigh and ankle joint of my right leg, my trousers were torn. I lost consciousness, could not protect myself and felt very bad. I am third category disabled.

The owner of the dog unhurriedly approached me. Instead of giving me the first medical aid, he on the contrary suddenly pushed me aside and went on past as though nothing had happened.

Some time later I regained consciousness and . . . called the ambulance.

The letter went on to give Chris and Karen's address. I sent Ulugjan to the hospital to check out the story.

Handing me this, Kristina told me that Shakhnoza had told her by telephone that another letter about another attack by Chris and his dog had been delivered to reception a few days previously. Shakhnoza had been translating it for me when Karen had taken it off her, saying that she would pass it to me. Later that same day Karen had suddenly told Shakhnoza she was sacked, and ordered her to leave the embassy.

The weekend of April 26 and 27 was spent setting up the residence for the queen's birthday party, briefing all the staff involved, dealing with late requests for invitations and rescuing supplies from customs. At 2:30 A.M. on April 28, the day of the queen's birthday party, I was at the airport welcoming the Battlefield Band, along with Talat. He had assured me that there would be a bus from the hotel waiting to take the six of them and their large amount of equipment. There was no bus, and we crammed them into the Land Rover and two taxis, arriving at their hotel toward 4 A.M. It was the same private hotel that Van Boven had stayed in—and it wasn't expecting the Battlefield Band. What was more, it was fully booked. Three days from the start of the EBRD AGM, so were all the other hotels.

Except for one. The Uzbek government had built or refurbished several huge hotels to provide the thousands of beds needed for the EBRD. They then gave management contracts to international hotel chains, in effect paying to use their names. The old Tashkent Palace Hotel, an original imperial building, had been refurbished in marble and was just reopening that very day as the Meridien. We turned up just after four and were their very first customers on reopening. I left the band so they could grab some sleep, and went to get a little myself, before the eleven o'clock gathering of staff to prepare for the queen's birthday party kickoff at three. Before I went to bed I loaded two thousand bottles of beer and many hundred bottles of wine and soft drinks into a series of large chest freezers, to get cool by the afternoon. I got to bed around 7 A.M. and was up again at nine-thirty.

Ulugjan arrived early with Steve Brown. He confirmed to me that he had seen the partially sighted man in the hospital, and had no doubt he had been attacked by Chris's dog and then roughly shoved down by Chris as he had tried to get off the ground. Shortly thereafter Chris and Karen arrived. Chris quickly argued with Fiona, and then went and sat at a table by the wall, where he remained all day, contributing nothing. I had determined that he was going to have to be sent home as soon as we got through these very intensive few days. I think he realized I knew. Karen worked incredibly hard that day and maintained a forced brightness; her pleasant parents were visiting. My heart sank when I thought I was also going to have to do something about Karen over her treatment of Shakhnoza and the letter she had intercepted.

THE DAY OF THE queen's birthday party was, in conventional terms, the high point of my career. I have said that I had obtained more influence than other diplomats in Uzbekistan. That day gave proof of it. The Uzbek government would always nominate a single full minister to attend every embassy's national day. You might get a few deputy ministers thrown in. The Americans were the sole exception; they might get two or even three full ministers. We had seven, which astonished the diplomatic corps— including me. Even more unheard of, we had the president's daughter.

Gulnara had never been to a national day, before or since, but she came to that one.

She appeared in midafternoon, as the orchestra was in full swing. Fiona and I had spent the first hour greeting guests in the living room as they passed through to the garden. Kristina had been standing by us to interpret when necessary, and there had been some difficult moments, as Fiona insisted Kristina stand respectfully behind, whereas quite a lot of the guests had dealt with Kristina and wanted to shake her hand.

After an hour we had gone into the garden to circulate, and I was called back into the house some time later to greet Gulnara. I led her out into the garden. Every chair and table was taken and I sent a message for Karen and Chris to vacate theirs, feeling guilty at moving Karen's mum and dad. But Gulnara decided in any case she didn't want to sit, and we stood talking on the little wooden bridge over the stream. Then thirty-one years old, she was charming and girlish, giggling delightedly at my light conversation.

A particularly drunken guest came up to me. A fat, gray-haired man, he was the deputy *hokkim* of Navoi, and rather full of his own importance. Earlier he had asked me for ten minutes of my time. I had said I should be delighted to give it to him, but not on this particular day. Now he was back, drunker and more persistent. He interposed himself between Gulnara and me.

"Mr. Ambassador," he said, "I have something very important to speak to you about."

"Not just now, my friend," I said. "I am really busy."

He turned and leered at Gulnara. She shrunk back, and I sensed several security men move closer.

"Are you an interpreter?" he demanded.

I grabbed his arm.

"No, she's not an interpreter," I said. "I'll come and talk to you in a little while."

He turned back to Gulnara, and pushed her hard in the shoulder.

"But you speak English, yes? You can interpret?"

Gulnara was shaking her head at one of her security men, telling him not to intervene. Michael Timke, the South African honorary consul and a businessman, came past. I put my arm round the nuisance and shoved him toward Michael.

"Why don't you have a drink with my good friend Michael?" I suggested.

Michael is a large, well-built man. He is also quick on the uptake, and he firmly but chummily led him to the bar. I turned back to Gulnara.

"I am so sorry about that," I said.

"Do you think I could get a job as your interpreter?" She giggled. "Sounds like it might be fun."

It is of course a truth universally acknowledged that no woman can resist flirting with a man in a kilt. Nevertheless, how many presidential children would react so prettily to being pestered by a drunk? (The deputy *hokkim*, not me. Pay attention.) It was difficult to reconcile the young woman and her reputation. Her simple dress belied the $4.5 million of personal jewelry listed in her U.S. divorce settlement. But there didn't seem to be obvious darkness behind her laughing eyes. Was she really behind the corrupt acquisition of all those businesses, the closing down of rival companies, the massive bribes from huge energy deals?

Then there were more sinister interests. She owned, jointly with a younger son of the emir of Dubai, a travel agency. But this agency paid the airfares of its clients. It trafficked thousands of Uzbek girls a year into the sex trade of the Middle East. Most prostitutes in Gulf hotels were of Uzbek nationality. The agency offered the whole package—it even had the right to issue UAE visas. I was left wondering to what extent Gulnara did these things, and to what extent they were done in her name. But she must, at the very least, have been aware of them.

EVERYTHING AT THE party went perfectly. The orchestra was superb, and the Battlefield Band got everyone up and dancing. They were joined by Uzbekistan's most popular musician, Sherali Juraev. This was received with wild enthusiasm because he is banned by the government from public performance, for criticizing the president—but on diplomatic premises they couldn't stop him. Nor could we, and the music wound up around ten, even then only because I started the fireworks display.

Gradually people left, and by eleven the party was basically over. Maybe a dozen close expat friends and their wives and girlfriends remained, having a quiet drink and musing over the day. Some pretty American and Canadian girls, from the human rights organization CEELI, stripped down to their underwear and jumped in the pool. Two or three others joined them, including Richard Wilkins's partner, a member of his Uzbek staff who went further and took off her bra. This was going a bit far for the circumstances, so Fiona took her a towel to cover herself. I got to bed about 1 A.M.

The next evening the Battlefield Band held their first public concert, in the opera house. It was packed to the rafters, and the music was incredibly well received.[3] They had the audience going wild, and received a massive standing ovation and several encores.

The next day I had to make a speech to the Institute for War and Peace Reporting on persecution of writers in Uzbekistan, and chair a number of EBRD preparation meetings. The day after that, we had the arrival of the British government minister, Clare Short, a full day of meetings, the official opening of the EBRD conference, the final Battlefield Band concert at the Railway Palace and a late-evening reception at the residence for three hundred Brits involved in the EBRD conference. These included the British delegation, EBRD staff, the visiting press corps, NGOs attending the meeting and local businessmen. By now I was exhausted.

On Wednesday, Fiona and I were due to leave Tashkent at lunchtime to attend the orchestral concert in Samarkand. But I received a phone call from a Mr. Yusupov saying that I was to call on Foreign Minister Safayev at 4 P.M. I said that I couldn't, because I had to be in Samarkand. It was made plain to me that this was compulsory. The MFA would, however, arrange a police escort to get me to Samarkand afterward.

Every time I was summoned to the MFA, I worried they had decided to declare me persona non grata. I consoled myself that that couldn't be the case this time, or they wouldn't escort me to Samarkand. I arrived at the MFA with Fiona and the luggage ready in the car. The meeting with Safayev did not take long. He said that it was a grave matter: Chris Hirst had been attacking people in the street. A formal complaint had been made to my predecessor, but no satisfactory action had been taken. He said he had a dossier listing twelve attacks, including ones on an old lady who had suffered permanent brain damage, and a twelve-year-old girl who had been dragged by her hair down the street by Chris.

These new and terrible details amazed me. I said I was deeply ashamed. I had at first found the stories unbelievable, but now found them to be true. I would ensure that Chris Hirst left Uzbekistan straight away. Safayev, who had been prepared for a fight, looked astonished at my reaction. I noted that among the papers he handed me was a note from the Uzbek MFA of September 18, eight months previously, which I had never seen.

I sped straight from that meeting to two days in Samarkand for the music festival. On return I had the difficult task of tackling Karen. She was tearful, but said that she was relieved it was over. She admitted she had been intercepting letters of complaint about Chris, preventing them from reaching me. This included the Uzbek note. She said that while Chris had not struck her, she had suffered from relentless bullying and intimidation. I asked if she had hidden the papers Chris Ingham said he had left for me. She denied this, and said he had not left them for me, but to her. She proved this by producing them, still in a sealed envelope addressed to her by him. I opened it, and saw for the first time his telegram of January 28, 2002, to the FCO. It began:

> Note from Uzbek MFA accuses Chris Hirst . . . of beating two Uzbek citizens and setting his dog on them. Appears to be distorted account of incident in which Chris was himself assaulted.

I sent back a telegram outlining developments. London replied, instructing me in effect to get Chris Hirst on the next plane out. For several days his behavior had been moody and strange. I believed that there was a real danger he might react violently to the news. I called Chris to the residence. My brother Stuart was visiting and he, John Agnew and Steve Brown—all of them large men—were hidden within easy reach as I talked to Chris.

I told Chris that there were more complaints from the MFA that he had been involved in violence, and that I had come to believe the complaints. I thought he needed help, and he was to return to London in the morning. I didn't think he would come back to Tashkent.

Chris breathed heavily and stared straight in front of him, saying nothing, for a very long and tense five minutes. Then he said, "I suppose that's it, then."

I handed him his air ticket, and he left.

The next morning, I went with Karen and Chris to the airport, to make sure he got on the plane. Both Karen and I tried to make light conversation, which Chris ignored. He still had that fixed stare, but he went quietly enough.

My telegram to London said that I believed Chris might be mentally ill and need treatment. I certainly believed he was dangerous. I could not explain it. His commitment to human rights was apparently genuine, and he worked hard at it. But then he was attacking people on the street.

The European Bank for Reconstruction and Development held its AGM in Tashkent on May 4 and 5. The decision had been made some years previously, when reform had been expected to go rather faster in Tashkent than it had. As things stood, the EBRD AGM had acquired enormous significance. The Uzbek government saw it as a tremendous boost to their international image. For the international community, and for NGOs in particular, it had become a litmus test for how the international institutions should deal with recalcitrant dictatorships that refused to reform.

On a more mundane level, for me it also meant a great deal of work. Not only was there a visiting U.K. delegation to look after but also extra liaison duties fell on our small embassy because the EBRD is London-based. Furthermore, Clare Short, then secretary of state for overseas development, was coming out to chair the conference. Any visit by a cabinet minister puts a great demand on an embassy in terms of extra communications with London, bilateral meetings and press conferences to arrange, and numerous logistics to provide for the minister and their staff.

SOME OF THE arrangements the regime made for hosting the conference verged on the incredible. Four new five-star hotels were built and six substantively renovated, at incredible speed and a cost to the Uzbek people of well over $300 million. Management contracts allowed them to be called the Radisson, Meridien, Sheraton, Intercontinental, etc. Roads were repaired, tramways restored or ripped out. False shop fronts were put up to cover empty buildings on key routes. Rotten concrete buildings from the Soviet era were given facades of blue glass.

The charade to fool the delegates got still more extraordinary. Bazaar stalls and key shops were instructed to display goods at one-third the true price, to give the visitors a false impression of living standards. They had to sell at that price to anyone who looked like a foreigner, though locals got short shrift.

I had been at the airport at 2 A.M. to greet the minister on her arrival at the newly refurbished VIP side of the airport, known as Tashkent 2. It glittered in marble and gold leaf. More than thirty ministers and at least four heads of state were expected for the conference, each with their own delegation, plus thousands of delegates, EBRD staff, businessmen chasing EBRD contracts, journalists, NGOs and lobbyists. This really was an event on the grand scale.

It was also an event conducted in true Soviet style. It was after 2:30 A.M. that British Airways arrived. I met Clare Short and her small staff on the tarmac and drove with them to the terminal. The senior official accompanying her was Jessica Irvine, a friend whom I had worked with on West Africa, and who had been a house guest with us in Accra.

At the terminal Elyor Ganiev, the minister for foreign economic relations, was waiting to greet Clare. He shook hands and led her into a sumptuous side lounge while the baggage was collected. We sat around a marble-topped table, piled with fruits and nuts.

Ganiev is a heavily built, slow man who looks every bit the ex–KGB operative that he is. He has an unalloyed Soviet style, but I didn't expect to be treated to it at 2:30 A.M.

He rose ponderously to his feet and addressed Clare Short in Russian. He paused for interpretation after every phrase.

"Minister," he began, "you are most welcome to Uzbekistan. We greatly value our alliance with the United Kingdom. We are proud to be working with you on Iraq, and we have the greatest respect for the leadership shown by Tony Blair to the whole world in the War on Terror. As your esteemed ambassador knows," he nodded cumbersomely in my direction, "Uzbekistan was already fighting this menace before the events of 2001.

"This is a strong country and we believe that our economic achievements deserve recognition by the international community. We have always met our obligations on debt repayment and never requested restructuring. For this reason, we now believe our currency is strong enough to sustain convertibility. We have devalued the *sum* by over eighty percent in the past eighteen months, and will move to full convertibility by June.

"The basis of our economy is a strong industrial and agricultural base. GDP growth in 2003 is projected to exceed eight percent. It is worth noting that in seven years the Republic of Uzbekistan has seen GDP per capita increase by a total of fifty percent.

"At a minimum, three hundred twenty-seven enterprises will be privatized during this year. Wheat production is increasing by eighteen percent, while the percentage of agricultural production from private farms will increase from thirty-two percent to thirty-six percent. In the automotive sector—"

Clare Short stood up and smiled. In her strong Birmingham accent she said, "Thank you, Minister. That's all very interesting. But it's two-thirty in the morning, we're very tired and we're going to bed." She then turned round and walked out of the room, while we scurried to catch up.

I had been disappointed that she had decided to stay in the hotel where the conference was being held, as she was chairing it, rather than in the residence. As we drove to the Intercontinental, she turned to me.

"Is he always like that?"

"No, usually he's worse."

"Bloody hell! Was any of it true?"

"No, this year there has been a growth in fake economic statistics of one hundred eighty-two point seven percent."

IN THE OPENING session of the EBRD conference, Clare Short and EBRD president Jean Lemierre both put forth strong criticism of Uzbekistan's economic policies, and the lack of human rights and democracy. Karimov had viewed hosting this conference as a massive propaganda coup and endorsement of his regime. Banners and Uzbek media coverage had been trailing this line for months. He sat at the top table, on the stage of the great Hall of the Peoples' Friendship, flanked by the presidents of Kazakhstan, Georgia, Kirghizstan and Tajikistan. He was hosting them, and senior ministers from almost every Western country. It was the ultimate display of his prestige. And now, at the height of his success, he was being criticized in unmistakeable terms by Short and Lemierre.

He had been president of the Uzbek Soviet Socialist Republic and then president of Uzbekistan for fifteen years. Nobody could do this to him. And this was being broadcast, live and uncensored, on all main Uzbek TV and radio channels, with a massive audience that he himself had ordered drummed up to watch his apotheosis.

I cannot overstate the drama of that moment. Clare Short's points were piled up relentlessly. Lemierre was sharp and expressive, his tone redolent of Gallic contempt. Karimov first went ashen-faced. Then he ostensibly removed his earphone and tossed it away. Then he placed his head in his hands, covering his ears before slowly moving his hands round to cover his eyes, then allowing his head to slump forward until it almost rested on the table. He remained in this extraordinary posture for ten minutes. At one stage Nursultan Nazarbayev, president of Kazakhstan, put a consolatory arm around him.

All this was captured on Uzbek TV, so well that the producer and director were sacked as soon as the conference delegates had left. But that broadcast was a defining moment. It did more than anything to break Karimov's grip on his people—his carefully cultivated image of perfection was stripped away. It was the moment when the boy shouted out that the emperor had no clothes.

Why did he react so badly in public, rather than put a brave face on it? I can only think it was a mixture of shock and disbelief. But, as my friend Ahmet would say, it gave room for doubt about the size of his balls.

There were so many presidents and ministers in town that mere ambassadors were a long way down the pecking order, and I had a long walk to my car after the session. I had to pass a taxi stand. A gaggle of taxi drivers who had been listening to events on the radio recognized me. They mobbed and hugged me, offering me vodka, and a small crowd gathered to cheer, "*Gaspadin,* Craig."

I hosted a lunch for Clare Short to meet human rights activists. These included Tamara Chikunewa. She told of her son, who had been sentenced to death. She had gone again and again to the prison asking to see him. She had been repeatedly denied, but one day she had been bundled into a room and ordered to wait. She hoped that she would finally see her son. Then she heard a single shot. The guard returned and told her, "You won't see him now, we've just shot him in the head."

The lunch worked well in presenting just how grim the situation was. Sikeena Karmali was particularly forceful and impressive, a fact which Clare Short noted to me afterward. She also made an acid observation that I had invited all the men to speak before any of the women. I had arranged a speaking order by subject, and was not aware that it had this effect. I felt quite guilty.

In the car, Clare Short said to me, "Jessica tells me that you're getting problems from the Foreign Office."

"To say the least," I replied.

"It takes ten seconds to tell what kind of government this is. But if we support Bush . . . Anyway, tell me if you need any support. Not that I'll be in much position to give it!"

I was slightly mystified by this last phrase. After the EBRD meeting closed, along with several other ministers, Clare Short flew on to a meeting in Kirghizstan to discuss development in Central Asia. Ganiev was also present, and was there when the Kirghiz government showed the delegates the bridges across the border river in the Ferghana Valley, recently destroyed by Karimov to seal the borders to trade. The separated families and the harsh economic consequences had been all too obvious, and apparently Short had absolutely exploded at Ganiev. Good thing too.

That evening she returned to London. The next day she resigned from the government.

CHAPTER 13

Love in a Hot Climate

I FELT MORE AND MORE ISOLATED FROM LONDON. THEY HAD, IN effect, sent me to Coventry. I simply stopped receiving any reply to my telegrams, letters and e-mails. But as the world blackened around me, I had one major solace. I had fallen profoundly in love.

I had obtained Nadira's phone number, but my attempts to get through to her had not succeeded. She finally answered her mobile on Monday, April 7. Her voice was so gentle and sweet on the telephone, and I was elated when she told me she also had been trying to telephone me. We agreed to meet at 8 P.M. the next day in the Ragu bar. I came from a meeting at the residence where we had been wrestling with the logistical problems of the queen's birthday party. I was in good spirits, and as we looked round the garden I several times vaulted the stream on my crutches, to general applause and amusement. Steve and Ulugjan came with me to the Ragu. There was a camaraderie among men in Tashkent, pretty much all of whom had girlfriends as well as wives. Steve did already.

Nadira arrived on time. She looked terrific in sky blue jeans and a clinging cotton blouse, and I was taken aback anew by just how spectacular her figure was. Steve and Ulugjan grinned their approval. She asked for an orange juice, and I persuaded her to remove her baseball cap, which she was reluctant to do, as her hair was dirty. She told me that two days previously she had quit her job at Safar, which cheered me up. But she also said she could only stay for one hour, which didn't cheer me up at all. I couldn't shake her from this—she said her flatmate Clara was ill at home, and she had to look after her.

The hour passed quickly, and then I insisted on leaving with her. She said that she lived in a bad area, that her flat was poor and dirty, and that it would be hard for me to get up the stairs on my crutches. She then appeared to get annoyed, and said that I was only coming with her because I didn't believe she was really going home. But I was not going to lose her so quickly, and we went to her flat in a smelly, crumbling block at Zhemchuk, one of the worst bits of Tashkent. Prone alcoholics and staring drug addicts littered the yard. It was hard to get up the staircase on crutches in the pitch dark. There was almost no furniture in the little flat, and the tiling in the bathroom was cracked. Clara was a pretty girl with long, lustrous hair. She looked pale and ill and lay stretched out on a sofa under a blanket. Nadira's fifteen-year-old brother, Sanjar, eyed me distrustfully from deep dark eyes under a mop of blue-black hair. The other inhabitant of the flat was Nargiza, a plump, traditionally dressed girl with a wild clump of hair and black spectacles. She kept making jokes in Uzbek and occasionally bursting into song. I was a lot more tolerant of this than her flatmates. We drank tea and chatted. Nadira kept flitting around. Clara was, of course, a captive audience, and I talked with her a lot. Nadira had a beautiful short-haired Siamese cat, which sat on my lap as I stroked it. It was two days after Nadira's twenty-second birthday.

I felt I had found a refuge from my troubles. I was particularly entranced by the way Nadira made the green tea. In traditional Uzbek style she three times poured tea from pot into bowl, then back into the pot, to brew it. She then handed me a bowl of tea with her right hand, her left placed over her heart in a gesture of respect. I had seen it many times, but she did it with such deft grace and natural feeling, I was really moved by it. I left around midnight.

I phoned Nadira again the next day, but she said she couldn't come out because of Clara, and that I couldn't come to see her, because they'd had a power cut. There was really no reason why that would stop me, but she so evidently didn't want me to come that I decided it might be counter-productive. I was off to Samarkand and Bokhara for a few days, so I didn't have the chance to see her again until the following Thursday. I gave a speech to the American Chamber of Commerce, which was hard-hitting and well received by an audience that included all the major foreign investors, American and otherwise. I had been invited to dinner after-ward with Zokirjon. I went to Nadira's flat first and swept her off with me to the dinner.

Zokirjon was delighted to see me, and pleased that I had finally got a girlfriend. He was convinced that I needed a lot of sex to help me cope with the stress of my job. He had many times offered to set me up, but I respectfully declined. I think he had started to think I might be gay. For her part, Nadira was worried about meeting Zokirjon. In Uzbekistan, such obvious opulence could mean only one thing—mafia—and Nadira had few illusions about what could happen to girls in places like this.

Zokirjon was in good form, and we had a pleasant dinner. I had brought wine, and he had a bottle of Johnnie Walker Blue Label he had bought specially for my visit. I didn't like to tell him I prefer Black Label at about a fifth of the price. We also drank vodka with pickled tomatoes, which is a great deal nicer than it sounds.

After dinner Zokirjon retired with his companion (he always had a different beautiful girl with him every time I called). He showed Nadira and me to a luxurious bedroom suite on the ground floor. Nadira was now very scared.

"I'm a virgin," she whispered, once we had closed the door. I put a hand around her tiny waist and kissed her on the forehead.

"It's OK, we don't have to have sex," I said. "But I don't want Zokirjon to know that."

We sat on a large sofa and chatted, just lightly kissing a few times, and occasionally throwing cushions at each other. After an hour or so we said good night to Zokirjon—we had to shout this through the sauna door.

Zokirjon had been most worried about my appearance on crutches. He insisted I should go to see his doctor the next day, and he got out a mobile and made an appointment there and then. I felt I had been treated very well by Dr. Reimers at the international clinic, and I was reconciled to another six weeks on crutches. I didn't think an Uzbek doctor would be able to help, but Nadira persuaded me to give it a try. The following lunchtime I got into the Land Rover with my crutches (at which I was getting pretty adept), and gave Gafur the address for the doctor, telling him to swing by Nadira's flat on the way.

We drove to Chilanzar, another cheap, dusty suburb of dreary Soviet apartment blocks. My faith diminished further when I found the doctor was based in a small apartment in the middle of this estate. I struggled up the steps to the first floor. An extraordinary little man in a velvet gown opened the door. Short and wiry, with his long, wispy beard he looked like the old Chinese sage in a kung fu movie. He led me through to his front room, largely filled by what seemed to be an old enamel-topped morgue trolley.

He gestured toward Nadira and said to me, "Zokirjon told me you were like him."

He then placed a towel and a pillow on the trolley, and indicated I should take off my clothes and get up on it, which I did. He gently unwrapped the strapping from my left calf, and then felt up and down it, pushing his fingers between the layers of muscle. It was intense agony. Then he went out of the room, quickly returning with a candle in one hand, and in the other a cylinder that smelled strongly of alcohol and held two dozen foot-long needles, with wooden handles. Bloody hell! Acupuncture! What had I got myself into?

Only the desire not to let Nadira know what a coward I am prevented me from getting up and walking out. Plainly the needles were in alcohol, and before inserting each one he sterilized it further in the flame of the candle, so the risk was limited. I decided to go with it.

I had imagined that acupuncture involved sticking the needle in a little way. Not at all. These were going in several inches, and quite a few being pushed right in and out the other side. I watched from the corner of my eye, transfixed in horror, as the first needle went into the right side of my neck. The next went through the right elbow. It was pushed into the inside and, amazingly, passed through the joint and came out about four inches on the other side. The next one went right through the top of my left thigh. I didn't know much about acupuncture, but I had presumed it didn't hurt much because it was cunningly directed at nerve points, or something similar. I was swiftly disillusioned. It hurt every bit as much as you might imagine having a large needle stuck through you would hurt. Once the needle was in position, it became uncomfortable rather than painful. But then would come the next needle.

I lay on my back with the needles in me for about five minutes. Then he removed them and motioned I should turn onto my stomach. He put needles into my back and buttocks. He now seemed to be trying to maneuver each to touch a precise spot within me. When he hit it he would twist the needle. He then passed a series of needles into and through the affected calf muscle. After this set of needles was withdrawn, he massaged the muscle strongly and deeply; it felt like he was pulling away tendon from bone, but this time it didn't hurt.

The entire session lasted about an hour. When he finished he told me to get up. I reached for the crutches, which were leaning against the wall, but he motioned me not to. He wrapped up my bandage neatly and handed it to Nadira. I stood to dress and gingerly put some weight on my left leg as I pulled on my underpants. It seemed OK. Once dressed, I slowly and carefully started to walk toward the door.

As I got to the door, he stopped me. He indicated he was worried about something, and he spoke quietly with Nadira.

"He thinks you are starting a big problem with your heart," she said.

He motioned me to unbutton my shirt. He felt between the ribs, just to the left of my breastbone, and then pushed in and withdrew a needle in an incredibly quick movement. It penetrated the chest cavity and went in a good three inches. It only lasted a second, but it was indescribably painful, and I was really shaken. He spoke again to Nadira. She looked a bit put out. I was worried.

"What is it?" I asked her.

"He says you have many difficulties, and it will hurt you. To give strength, you should sleep with young girls. At least two."

"Well, let's go and make a start."

"No, younger than me. Maybe sixteen years old."

Great stuff, I thought. It ought to be available on the National Health Service.

I WALKED OUT THE door and down the stairs, Nadira coming behind carrying the crutches. Gafur gave a whoop of joy when he saw me walking. My calf muscle was completely healed, and behaved normally from that moment. It had been ruptured, a fact that had been confirmed by ultrasound. I have no way of explaining how acupuncture fixed it.

I met Nadira again several times over the next week, for a quick drink in the evening, and once for dinner. She came with me to a couple of orchestra and choir rehearsals. But the pressure of work was too great to devote the time I would have liked to developing an affair, and we were in danger of becoming just good friends.

Nadira, Dilya, Sanjar, Clara and Nargiza went to all the British music festival concerts. For a week or so in the countdown to the festival, I had been seldom able to call Nadira, and when I did she didn't answer. After the opening Battlefield Band concert, I was due to meet her outside to go for a drink. But the concert was such a success that the band were besieged by autograph hunters, and packing up all the gear took longer than anticipated. By the time I emerged, Nadira had given up and gone. My heart ached for not having seen her for so long, and I went to her flat to look for her. Sanjar answered the door and said she had been called away to nurse a sick aunt. I was worried she was angry with me, so I insisted on entering to check she wasn't in the flat. She wasn't.

In fact Nadira had been playing me along, and my passionate desire to be with her was scantily reciprocated. Nor was she nearly as sexually innocent as she looked. She was indeed a virgin, but had done pretty well everything that could be done otherwise. She had a regular boyfriend, a diplomat at the Turkish embassy. He had bought her the Siamese cat, and the clothes she was wearing the night of our first date at the Ragu. She was meant to have dinner with him that evening, which is why she had told me that she had to leave at 9 p.m. She had been in despair when I went with her to her flat. Clara wasn't ill, just a good actress. The phone call I thought was to her father in Uzbek was to her boyfriend in Turkish.

She had another boyfriend called Lee, a GI serving with the U.S. forces in Afghanistan. He had been sending her money from his pay packet for months. He was not the first GI to be her boyfriend, or to ask her to marry him. He had come to Tashkent on leave the week before our musical festival. While I had been fretting about neglecting her, she had been living with him in the Sheraton Hotel, making a determined attempt on the world oral sex record. This continued when she was supposedly nursing her sick aunt.

But I was in love, and didn't find out any of this for more than another year. When I did, I felt terribly betrayed, which just goes to show what a hypocritical bastard I am. I had told Nadira I was married and could not have a permanent relationship. Yet I expected complete loyalty in return. Nice if you can get it. I suppose we deserved each other.

*   *   *

BACK IN THE EMBASSY I had the problem of what to do about Karen. I had advised London that I personally was inclined to credit her claim that she had been bullied by Chris, and that this explained her actions in covering up for him. Who knows just what a woman might suffer in an abusive relationship? I had in fact gone out on a limb in telling Karen that I would ensure that no further disciplinary action would be taken against her. This was to involve fending off Simon Butt and creating still further bad blood with the Eastern Department. But whether she should stay in Tashkent was another matter.

She was due to leave that November anyway. She was desperate to stay until then. My initial reaction was to ask her to leave, but the more I thought about it, the more attractive it was to let her stay. She was very good at the job. But in the end I was swayed by a vehement approach from the Uzbek staff, supported by both Steve and Angela. The Uzbek staff said, in effect, they would not work with her anymore. So I asked Karen to go. That was, I think, a major error on my part.

Chris, Karen and I had been the only British resource doing the main work of the embassy—that is, political, economic, commercial and information work. With all three of us there, we had been seriously under-resourced. Now I was going to be doing it all myself for the next three months, as well as taking on the substantial administrative and managerial burden Karen had borne. And I was already exhausted.

One of the reasons for the bad blood between Karen and the local staff was her involvement in so many summary dismissals. The last of these had been Talat, briefly Chris's assistant. One thing was plain—with Chris and Karen gone, I was going immediately to need more Uzbek staff to keep the embassy going. There was no time for a recruitment process, and nobody to organize one, so I got on the phone.

Shakhnoza didn't want to work again, so I got in Nilufar from the Lionheart bar to reception. She proved to have charm and efficiency, and is today the ambassador's personal assistant.[1] I put Leonid Kudryavtsev from Radio Grand into the information section, but effectively gave him large wodges of Chris Hirst's job. Leonid's English was superb and I had met him at a number of cultural events. He was a former pop singer and TV presenter, now in his late forties, who loved and was fascinated by the U.K. I judged him to be bright and capable—and it turned out to be a great appointment. As his assistant I got in my Russian-language teacher, Victoria Belyarskaya. A journalist, she proved to have somewhat too much initiative, and that appointment worked less well. But Yulya Usatova was a brilliant young economist and an important addition to the team. I broke every recruitment rule in the book (which was to be used against me), but I had a functioning embassy again in twenty-four hours.

My mother and brother had come out to visit for several weeks. It was great to see them, and provided some much-needed relaxation. Nadira and I were becoming comfortable together, meeting perhaps three times a week. The relationship was still pretty chaste, but it provided what I needed at that time.

On Thursday, May 22, Catherine Davis from the BBC and Matilda Bogner from Human Rights Watch contacted me about another human rights case. The body of another torture victim, Orif Eshanov, had been returned to his parents in Yangiyul, a village some thirty miles outside Tashkent. His case was particularly interesting because he was from Hizb-ut-Tehrir, and had been beaten to death in Karshi, where the U.S. base was situated.

I dashed down to Yangiyul to see the victim's family, taking with me Catherine Davis. The family were traditional Uzbek, living in a low mud-built house, and they greeted me with great courtesy. Over tea we discussed the condition of the body, including the fact that the fingernails had been pulled and genitals mutilated. Catherine Davis recorded the entire meeting, and it had quite an impact when it was broadcast on the BBC World Service.

Eshanov had been forty-six years old and a father of three. One of the ironies was that his father, a stooped, bearded old man, had been an officer of Stalin's KGB. He discussed precisely what had been done to his son with a disconcerting dispassion.

That evening I again had dinner with Ilios Luftullayev, again followed by wonderful music. My mother and Stuart were entranced. This time Kamola and her sister played Rachmaninoff together on the piano.

Ilios's dream was for Kamola to study in Europe. The first step was for her to improve her English. The family had been saving and borrowing money from relatives. But they were still short a few hundred pounds. I had arranged for Kamola to attend a British Council–approved language school in London for two months, and to stay with Stuart. I rather hoped that romance would blossom (Stuart was recovering from a painful divorce).[2] I gave Kamola the extra money needed.

The day of her departure, Kamola came to the office to see me, in some distress. She didn't put it that way, but she had spent several hundred dollars of the money on clothes (mostly on one leather jacket) and now was short. I was rather annoyed, but I gave her the needed cash, and a hug good-bye. This too was to be used against me.

I had to travel down to Jizzak again for a further meeting about the cottonseed factory. This was Nadira's hometown, so I took her with me. I had lunch with her parents at their flat. Like most of the city, they had had no running water for about a year, but the flat was notably better furnished and equipped than other Uzbek flats I had entered. This reflected all the money Nadira had been sending back to her family.

As we pulled up outside the block, dozens of street urchins had come pouring out of the flats, calling "Nadira! Nadira!" She had burst into a great grin, and lifted one or two of the smaller ones up into the air. She explained that, since her early teens, she had looked after the children of the flats, sitting in the courtyard and making up fairy stories for them as they sat at her feet. As we trudged up to her parents' flat on the fifth floor, young and old appeared at their doorways to embrace her as she went past. This spontaneous effusion of affection toward her was quite astonishing.

Nadira told her parents that she worked with me as an interpreter, though I am not sure they were much taken in. Her father was a jolly, mustachioed man who seemed happy to meet me. Her mother fussed anxiously over the food, of which there were massive quantities. Her father was a playwright, actor and theater director, her mother an actress. Various friends of theirs, mostly writers and actors, kept dropping in during the meal to look at me. After lunch we went up into the mountains on the Tajik border and saw the beautiful shrine at Bakhmal'. Here a crystal clear stream bubbles out of the foot of the mountain, into a beautiful rock-cut pool. Holy fish feed on the nutrition carried up by the stream, and disappear into the fissures from which the water flows. There are five of these, and they have cut five channels in the basin, said to have been the imprint left by the hand of a prophet. An ancient wooden mosque still stands on a site whose superstitions predate Islam.

I held Nadira's hand. As I looked at that pure mountain water, and then my gaze swept down the fields of grain lying sun-basked in that fertile high valley, my heart rose within me, and I thought: What a great place to make whisky.

I can't help it. Genetic imprinting.

A FEW DAYS LATER, first thing in the working day, Sikeena from Freedom House sent another victim round to see me. His name was Mr. Atayev, and he was a small farmer from the town of Kitab, south of Karshi. His story was that he and three of his brothers had leased land from the state farm, or *kolkhoz,* there. The *kolkhoz* had wanted it back. The brothers had refused. As a result one of the brothers had been murdered and a second jailed for seven years. The third had gone into hiding in Tashkent, and was with me now. In the past week his mother, who was eighty-four years old, had been beaten up by a mob, and their apple orchard cut down. The local authorities knew he was in Tashkent seeking help. They had told the family that no foreign embassy could affect what happened in Kitab.

I decided we should prove them wrong. I yelled to Kristina, "Go home and pack. We're off to Kitab. Tell Gafur to get ready."

Kristina immediately got up and walked to the door. She paused, turned back and said, "The farmworkers probably won't speak Russian. Do you know if they speak Uzbek or Tajik down there?"

"Tajik, I should think." I conjectured, "It's near Shakhrisabz. Does Leonid or Victoria speak Tajik?"

"No, I don't think so. Shall I try to find an interpreter?"

"No, there's no time. Let's take Nadira—she can speak Uzbek and Tajik, and every other known language, as far as I can tell."

"Shall we pay her as an interpreter?"

"You mean my company's not payment enough?"

"Not for me, it isn't."

"But you're not Nadira."

"Thank God. You're difficult enough as a boss. As a boyfriend you must be impossible."

Kristina gave me that incredibly beautiful smile, and disappeared to get ready for the trip.

Two hours later we set off from Kitab. Just round the corner from the embassy I was amazed and delighted to see a small group of human rights demonstrators outside the procurator general's office. I got out of the car and shook their hands. They were all friends of mine, led by Talib Yakubov. They knew about events in Kitab and, when I said that was where I was heading, gave a small, ragged cheer to send me off.

IT WAS A FIVE-HOUR drive to Karshi. Uzbekistan was in the grip of a diesel shortage, and after Samarkand we had to head into a farm, where for a bribe they siphoned diesel from a tractor for us. We arrived in Karshi after 3 P.M., checked into a hotel and then sped on to Kitab, another hour's drive. I had to quell a rebellion by the rest of the party, as none of us had eaten all day, but I insisted we didn't have time to stop. I bought bread and cheese for the car. We arrived after 5 P.M. Driving into the deep countryside, we looked for our small farm. Eventually we found it. There was no longer much to see. The cattle stalls were broken and abandoned, the fields overgrown with weeds. There were three cottages close together. One had belonged to the murdered brother, one to the imprisoned. The womenfolk now lived all together in the third.

When we met them, they started pouring out their stories all at once, and it was difficult to grasp anything coherent. It turned out they spoke Uzbek rather than Tajik. One thing they did say was that the *kolkhoz* had moved recently retired military personnel into the vacated cottages. They had been carrying out a campaign of violence and intimidation.

This was rapidly borne out. We stood talking in a field when three swarthy men came up to us, carrying farm tools in a menacing manner. One stepped forward and prodded me twice round the face, hectoring me. I didn't understand him, but it was plain he was telling me to go away. He poked me in the chest again so I slapped him across the face, hard but with an open palm. Surprised, he backed off for a moment. Gafur was out of sight in the car, and I was alone in the field with Nadira, Kristina and the three Uzbek women. Suddenly Nadira was in front of me, yelling angrily in a throaty language and seemingly threatening the three men who stood facing her with mattocks in hand, but looking uncertain whether to use them.

I put a restraining hand on Nadira's shoulder and asked her what had happened. She was shaking with fury, "He said they would beat you dead and rape your women."

Kristina, who had not previously understood the Uzbek exchange, started to look very nervous and to back down the path. I thought that was psychologically dangerous so I stepped forward and pushed what seemed to be the leader in the chest, saying loudly that I was the British ambassador. I had no hope he would understand me, but thought that the unknown tongue might give him pause. My heart was in my mouth, and it was not helped when one of the Atayev women said something that Nadira translated: "She says these are the men who murdered her husband."

Great. Typical of my planning—end up miles from anywhere in a field, in a slanging match with three brutish murderers, accompanied by two gorgeous women.

Although they looked like they would murder their mothers for a plate of beans, fortunately they were not quite certain if they were meant to murder me. I decided to shout a bit more, and they shrugged their shoulders, turned their backs and walked across to the far side of the field. There they sat on the fence and looked at us, occasionally hefting their mattocks menacingly from hand to hand.

As we talked on with the women, we were joined by two male cousins of the Atayev family and with them an earnest young Russian who had been sent to the village by a Samarkand human rights group. The story was as I had been told it in Tashkent. The family had leased land from the *kolkhoz* in the brief spring of liberalization in the mid-1990s. For a while it had flourished, with cattle and apples. Then the *kolkhoz* had decided they wanted it back, and what had followed was violence, intimidation and theft or destruction of livestock and crops.

The brother who had been jailed was convicted of stealing his own apples, as the court ruled they should be the property of the *kolkhoz* who owned the land. The fact that the brother had paid for a lease was ignored by the court. The family invited me to go into the village and meet the grandmother who had been beaten.

We were not the only group that had been expanding. The three thugs had been joined by others, and shortly a white Nissan Maxima pulled up. Three men in suits and sunglasses got out, and joined the small crowd at the other side of the fence looking at us. Kristina had gone to get the car, and Gafur pulled up for us to drive the mile or so to the grandmother's house. But I decided to make a statement. Our group of cottages was at the end of the village, which straggled a mile or so along the road. We had to go to the other end, and I decided to walk. The women all got into the car. I started the long walk down the road between rows of low white cottages, our three new male companions walking alongside me. The Discovery followed just behind. Twenty yards behind that came the three thugs walking, followed by the Nissan Maxima, followed by a small crowd of unfriendly looking men. The sun was setting directly behind me, and the entire village came to their doors and gates as we walked by. Some ducked inside and closed the door as we reached them. I was being deliberately melodramatic and milking the moment, but it did feel exactly like a Western.

There was a point to this. I was openly defying the *kolkhoz* authorities in a little world where they were gods. I was showing that even in Kitab, twenty miles off the Karshi to Shakhrisabz road, the British embassy could reach.

It had been 105 degrees that day. It was still very hot and the walk seemed long. We eventually reached the old lady's home. She was standing in her courtyard. She showed me her destroyed vegetable patch, and then took me inside the little house with its plain walls of mud and dung. It was totally bare—everything had been stripped by her attackers. Then in the courtyard she astonished me by pulling down her dress. Her shriveled breasts, arms and upper torso were covered in huge, livid blue and purple bruises, some of which were bleeding. She had been beaten mercilessly with clubs three days earlier. She was eighty-four years old. She stood there defiant, half naked, having moved beyond shame. I was boiling with rage.

We then walked around the corner, and my eyes were struck by an even more arresting sight. It was the Atayev family's orchard. A field stretched down the hill as far as the eye could see, and row upon row of felled apple trees, perhaps thousands of them, lay in terrible death, their black and gnarled limbs looking like a great litter of charred and twisted bodies. The leaves were coming away, and here and there great sweeps of late blossoms were browning and giving off the sweet smell of decay.

Over each corpse stood, for a headstone, a golden-topped stump. That wanton destruction of so much goodness, that loss of so much potential, seemed a metaphor for all the cruelty and waste of Karimov's Uzbekistan.

I turned to one of the men with me.

"Who did this? Who cut them down?"

"The *kolkhoz*."

"I know it was the *kolkhoz*. But someone had physically to cut the trees. It was a lot of work. Who did it?"

He looked at me as though I were simple. By now most of the village had gathered at the top of the field to see the fun. He gestured toward them.

"Why, the people of the village, of course."

"Why? Why would they do that? Why chop down their neighbors' trees? For Christ's sake, in a village like this, half of them must be related to your family."

"Certainly. But it's not their fault. They are poor. The *kolkhoz* paid them two hundred *sum* each to do it."

So there you were. Society was so debased that for twenty cents, some-one would cut down his neighbors' trees and ruin their life. I was deeply depressed. How could you help such a people, who were devoid of any feelings of mutual solidarity and support? I felt that I was trying to save a people without a soul.[3]

It was certainly true that they were poor. The wage for the sixteen thousand workers on this huge *kolkhoz* was 2,000 *sum*—that's $2—a month. They lived on the vegetables and livestock they could produce in their own little courtyards, usually about forty-foot square for a family. Before I entered the orchard I had entered a home, asking permission of the astonished lady of the house. There was an old tin stove, a short table, two wooden benches and a few cooking utensils. They slept on mats on a beaten mud floor.[4]

I addressed the villagers in Russian, saying that this destruction was a crime against God and nature. I also said that the world was changing, as my appearance in Kitab demonstrated, and neither the regime nor the *kolkhoz* would last forever. One day those who now attacked their neigh-bors would answer for it.[5]

I asked the family whether they hadn't tried complaining to the local procurator. The attack on the old woman, for example, was plainly a

crime. I was told that the procurator had actually been here and insti-
gated the attack. When they had tried to get him to investigate the
brother's murder, he replied that if they caused trouble, he would have
them all killed. He was the law in Kitab, and there was nothing anyone
could do about it. I decided the procurator deserved a visit.

The local human rights monitor plainly felt this was all much more
than he had signed up for, and declined to join us. But we squeezed in
two of the Atayev family ladies who had witnessed the district procurator's threat to kill them all, and Gafur, Kristina, Nadira and I set off with
them in the Discovery into Kitab town, to find the procurator's office.

Kitab was a pretty little town, with streets lined with trees providing
shade. We entered the district procurator's office, where we were confronted by an aggressive young man in military uniform, demanding to
know who we were. It was about 8 P.M., but Uzbek government offices
worked long hours to keep that great bureaucracy churning. I explained
I was the British ambassador, come to see the procurator. He said that the
procurator was not in, as he had gone to the site of a bus crash with the
deputy procurator of Uzbekistan.[6]

I replied that it was good that the deputy procurator general was
around, because I was sure he too would be delighted to see the British
ambassador. I spotted an office with the district procurator's name on it,
opened the door, walked in and seated myself behind the desk with my
feet on the table. My rather bemused party followed me in.

After we had been waiting half an hour or so, a young man entered
with tea. Shortly thereafter, a simply dressed man with heavy gray stubble arrived. He introduced himself as the managing director of the
kolkhoz. He asked why I had come, and I said I was investigating allegations against him of murder and violence against small farmers. He
retreated to the corridor and fished out a mobile phone, then returned
and gave me the message that the procurator could not make it back that
evening, but could see me in the morning at 8 A.M. I decided this was as
good as we could get, and agreed. I gave the Atayev ladies money for a
taxi, and told them to rendezvous there again at 8 A.M. the next day. I was
a bit worried about them, but felt that with me obviously around and
proactive, they were unlikely to be bumped off overnight. They were giggling with delight. They were astonished that anyone could be in a posi-

tion to behave this way toward the local authorities. I hoped that the general effect might offer them a bit more protection in the village.

The *kolkhoz* manager asked if we would join him for a beer and shashlik to talk over the problem. I could virtually hear Nadira and Kristina salivate at the mention of food. I decided there was no harm, and I might get beaten up by my own people if I refused, so I accepted. We walked across the street in what was now complete darkness, and sat under a tree on the rough wooden benches of a shashlik stall.

Our host said I shouldn't get too worried about the problems of the Atayevs. The *kolkhoz* was a huge institution—it had thirty thousand acres. The welfare of the whole was much more important than the welfare of three families. It was one of the top cotton farms in the country, and the head was personally appointed by Jurabekov.[7] I asked, if the farm was so huge, why was the Atayevs' small portion—less than a tenth of a percent of the farm—so important? He said it was because it was the patch that surrounded their village, and the *kolkhoz* needed to expand that village for housing for more workers. The Atayevs had been offered better land elsewhere in exchange, but they had refused. The violence against them was regrettable, but nothing to do with him. Of course if they were interfering with the well-being of the *kolkhoz,* the *kolkhoz* workers would get angry. He couldn't control that. As for the murder and imprisonment, well, the law must take its course, the judiciary were independent—at which I said, "Look, there is no point in talking such bollocks to me," and he grinned. As for the destruction of the apple trees, well, they were going to build housing there, so they had to go.

He concluded by saying that if I came back to Kitab, I should let him know, and stay with him. Looking lasciviously at Kristina and Nadira, he said he could organize the kind of hospitality and entertainment that might be to my excellent taste. But he then added, "But I don't suppose you will come back to Kitab. Nobody ever does. Tomorrow evening you will go away, and I will still be in control here. That is what matters."

He got up, and ostentatiously pulled a wad of large-denomination bills from his pocket, giving one to the astonished shashlik vendor, who literally fell to his knees and cried in gratitude. When he had gone, we agreed our host had made a convincing murderer.

"It is true, you know," said Kristina, "tomorrow you will be gone and he will be here."

"Keep chipping, chipping, and you'll crack the marble," I replied. It had been a scorching-hot day, and Kristina asked if the sun had got to me.

WE TRAVELED BACK slowly in the blackness of the winding country roads. Every now and then we passed an illuminated nodding donkey, slowly and tirelessly bringing up the oil, and orange flares lit up patches of sky toward Karshi. In the middle of nowhere we came across a service station that was both open and had diesel. I rummaged in the little plug-in fridge in the trunk, and got out a bottle of champagne. We sat under the stars on a fence and drank from the bottle, thinking over the day. We got to the hotel at midnight. It was fifteen hours since Gafur and Kristina had started work, and I apologized to them.

Gafur astonished me.

"We all love you, Ambassador," he said. "There will never be another like you."

I quickly left and walked away to my bedroom, so they wouldn't see me cry. When I got there, I realized I had turned my back on Nadira and left her with the others. Shortly there was a quiet tap at the door, and she came in. She wiped my tears and kissed me on the forehead. She said, "I didn't know about you. I didn't understand what you did. Nobody ever cared about or tried to help such country people. May Allah protect you. I will say *dua* for you."

She slipped out and I was left alone with my thoughts. I seemed to be engaged on a hopeless personal crusade. I was trying to assault a massively entrenched dictatorship by hurling myself against it. What was the point?

The point, I decided, was that it had to be done. Think William Wallace. On the other hand, when they tortured him to death they forced his own testicles down his throat.

With that less-than-comforting-thought, I fell asleep.

THE HOTEL AIR-CONDITIONING was not working. I was so tired I nevertheless slept well, but I awoke with the bedsheets drenched in sweat. I then found there was no running water either. All I could do was towel down briskly. Kristina and Nadira appeared for breakfast around six-thirty, but there was no sign of Gafur. I checked his room, but he had upped and packed. By seven o'clock I was getting worried, but he reappeared in the lobby, covered in oil. The air-conditioning in the car had broken down; he had found a mechanic, but they had been unable to fix it.

This was seriously bad news. We set off back to Kitab, and even as we arrived just after eight it was swelteringly hot. Our two ladies were waiting for us in reception, and we all entered together into the procurator's office. The district procurator was there, an untidy, old-looking man, together with the deputy procurator general, a much younger and better-groomed man, with a great deal of gold braid on the shoulders of his green uniform. The two men were sitting at a long table.

There were no greetings or handshakes, and the district procurator opened aggressively: "What do you want, Mr. Ambassador? We are extremely busy here. I can give you five minutes."

Plainly I needed to wrest the initiative.

"Get out of this office!" I shouted.

He was stunned.

"What did you say?" he asked.

"Get out!" I replied. "Get out of this office! These two ladies will testify that you threatened to kill them. I believe you are already implicated in the murder of one man, and were present at the beating of an old woman. You are not a procurator, you are a criminal. Now get out!"

He faltered.

"But this is my office!" He looked appealingly to the deputy procurator general for support, but the latter stared fixedly ahead of him. The district procurator stood and picked up his cap.

"I have other business to attend to," he said, and left.

My approach had not been premeditated, but this was a stunning result. This local tyrant had been humiliated in front of these women and the gaggle of staff and others who were revealed, standing in the corridor, as he opened the door to leave.

I sat down at the table, unbidden. Kristina joined me. Nadira and the two ladies took a seat on chairs that were standing against the wall.

"An unusual way to behave," remarked the deputy procurator general. "Tell me, Ambassador, what is your locus in this matter?"

I had got used to answering that one.

"Uzbekistan, along with the U.K., is a signatory of a number of international conventions guaranteeing human rights. As a lawyer I am sure you realize that a state party to a convention has the right to urge compliance on another state party."

I was relieved he didn't ask me which clauses of which convention I was referring to, because I could never remember that stuff. But he simply nodded, and asked, "And is this an official complaint from the government of the United Kingdom?"

Oh well, in for a penny.

"Yes."

"And what precisely is the nature of the complaint?"

"Yesterday I met an eighty-four-year-old woman who had been beaten by thugs from the *kolkhoz*. Perhaps these women might tell you their story."

And they did, the deputy procurator general apparently taking notes of what they said.

"I know of the case," he said. "I will look at it when I get back to Tashkent, and send the ambassador a report."

"Look," I said, "we all know the system and how it works. Sadly, there is going to be no major change in the structure of Uzbek agriculture anytime soon. But for local officials to get so ridiculously brutal with a small farmer is just going to bring in people like me, and cause you a great deal more trouble than the disputed land is worth. Think about it, and tell them to leave these small farmers alone."

The DPG said something noncommittal, then the district procurator returned, now all false bonhomie. When I got back to Tashkent I tried to persuade Atayev to go back to Kitab and look after his womenfolk and his farm, saying I was pretty confident I had put the *kolkhoz* off any further radical moves in the short term. But he was too scared, and claimed asylum in the United States instead.

We did get the other brother out of prison, which was an excellent result.

Returning from Kitab to Karshi, we visited the U.S. Air Force base at Khanabad. I learned a lot of stuff there, but I can't tell you about it, because it's secret. The scale of the thing, and particularly of the civil works in progress, was vast. I was made very welcome, but plainly they were even happier to see Nadira and Kristina. Can't say I blame them.

We had a late lunch at the base, and then driving through Karshi again I stopped at the SNB headquarters, where, a week previously, Orif Eshanov had been tortured to death. I registered my interest, while wondering if it was one of the men I met who had yanked out his fingernails. We then embarked on quite an ordeal of our own.

The drive from Karshi to Samarkand takes about three hours and passes through serious desert. The heat was searing—the car's thermometer was showing an external temperature of 126 degrees. Inside it was still hotter. Even at the U.S. base, they had been unable to fix the car's air-conditioning. I had stocked us with a crate of mineral water, and we were soon drinking it from the bottle at a temperature that would have been hot for a bath. Even with all the windows open and my head intermittently stuck out of one, I soon began to feel giddy and faint and have a blinding headache. More worrying, so did Gafur. We parked for a while and rested in the shade of a nodding donkey. After drinking a great deal of hot water, we headed off again. We arrived at the Afrosiyab hotel after dark. The air-conditioning wasn't working in the hotel either, but it seemed deliciously cool.

The next morning we left at first light to get to Tashkent before it got really hot. As I pointed out, this had the great advantage that we could still do a full day's work when we got there. Kristina and Gafur didn't seem to share my enthusiasm.

CHAPTER 14

Hammer to Fall

CHRIS AND KAREN'S EXTRAORDINARY DEPARTURE HAD SHATTERED morale in the embassy, while the Uzbek staff's suspicion and distrust of the British staff seemed to have transferred seamlessly to Steve Brown and Angela Clarke. I had the strong impression that the British embassy had existed, on a shoestring, without a great sense of purpose. To try to tackle all of these problems, I decided that we would have an Embassy Away Day.

We headed off to the spectacular new resort on the mountain lake at Chimgan, owned, unsurprisingly, by Gulnara Karimova. There we had morning and afternoon workshops where I outlined the global mission statement and objectives of the FCO. We then discussed these areas of activity, for example, trade promotion, democratization and narcotics control, and applied them to our work in Uzbekistan, ending up with a decent set of detailed objectives for the embassy. I would never have got the Uzbek staff to open up and play a full part if we had held that discussion in the embassy, but in this environment they relaxed and got involved.

The second workshop finished at 4 P.M., leaving plenty of time to enjoy the pool, Jet Skis on the lake, mountain bikes and other diversions. Then in the evening we had a group dinner with plenty of wine, and an impromptu disco.

It was on this occasion that we took one of the Land Rovers down the terraced steps that ran within the resort from the hotel to the swimming pool area. The vehicle was driven by Gafur, who was not only sober but a teetotaler. Colonel Ridout got down and checked the ground clearance first.[1]

* * *

WE HAD IN A year brought more international attention to the horrors of the Karimov regime than had been achieved in the previous ten years of Uzbek independence. The Bush administration was extremely unhappy about the exposure of its ally, and was about to strike back. The first blow was unexpected.

I had been pleased to be invited to lunch by Jennifer Windsor, director of Freedom House, visiting from Washington. I had worked closely with Freedom House on a number of occasions, and cooperation with Sikeena had been first-class.

I said as much to Jennifer Windsor, a former senior State Department official, over lunch. She said that she appreciated my input, but there would be a change in Freedom House's operations in Uzbekistan. She explained that a number of influential members of the board of Freedom House approached these issues from a vantage point on the right of the Republican party, and they had expressed concern that Freedom House was failing to keep in sight the need to promote freedom in the widest sense, by giving full support to U.S. and coalition forces in the War on Terror.

I asked what this meant in practice. Jennifer said that it meant they would be stopping "advocacy"; that is, they would no longer be making public statements on human rights in Uzbekistan, or publicizing individual cases of abuse. They would be careful not to work with political opposition figures. They would be "emphasizing human rights over democracy." The primary activity from now on would be working with the Uzbek authorities, training them on how to respect human rights, rather than standing outside and shouting at them.

I said we were ourselves trying to start some work with the Ministry of the Interior in the same way, and hoped we could cooperate. But the Uzbek government seemed competent at playing along the international community while having no intention of intitiating genuine change. The cooperation programs could then become fig leaves to cover horrors. That was much more of a danger if you simultaneously stopped criticism, as Freedom House was about to do.

This conversation worried me, so that evening I phoned Sikeena. She stunned me by saying that she was packing to leave Uzbekistan. I asked what was wrong. Had she been sacked? She said no, of course not. She was going back to Canada to finish a book. She sounded poised as ever, but there was a catch in her voice. I never saw her again.

ONE AREA WHERE the Karimov regime was protected by its alliance with the United States was narcotics trafficking. The United States, Germany and the United Kingdom bilaterally, and the UN and European Union, had all put money into narcotics control. At Termez, where the Friendship Bridge crosses into Afghanistan, they had provided Uzbek customs with every modern facility, from sniffer dogs to giant X-ray machines that could scan an entire container.

United Nations famine relief vehicles were sometimes stuck for weeks at this border, waiting to get into Afghanistan. But if you stood there for a little while, you would start to notice the convoys of Mercedes with black windows, and of military six-ton trucks, which were waved onto a track around the customs facilities, and never stopped. They carried 40 percent of Afghanistan's heroin production. Mostly it was then placed into cotton bales and sent up the railway to the Baltic at Riga and St. Petersburg, for shipment into Europe.

The Afghan end of this trade was controlled by General Abdul Rashid Dostum, the leader of the U.S.-backed Northern Alliance, which did the bulk of the ground occupation against the Taliban, following on the heels of U.S. carpet bombing. General Dostum had a predeliction for tying opponents to tank tracks and driving on, and for locking prisoners in metal containers in the searing heat and leaving them to bake to death. He thus had the same kind of hobbies as President Karimov. The vehicles that were never searched ran between Dostum and Karimov, bringing narcotics out and arms, money and chemicals for heroin manufacture in.[2]

Like human rights abuse, this was one of those things that just never got mentioned. And everyone was engaged in antinarcotics cooperation with the Uzbek government, providing expensive equipment and training, and pretending they were tackling the problem. In fact, the few interceptions of narcotics by the Uzbek authorities were best characterized as removing private sector competition.

Customs and Excise in London argued to me, with a straight face, that because the Uzbek authorities intercepted negligible amounts of heroin, that proved very little comes through the country. In Tajikistan next door, a great deal was intercepted, so that must be the major route. Of course this argument was bonkers. The big league avoided Tajikistan precisely because it had effective interception.

In general, I have the highest respect for the Customs and Excise Special Investigations Division. Unlike MI6, they are intrepid, reliable and put themselves in personal danger. But they didn't even have anyone in Uzbekistan. We were covered by Stuart, who would turn up about one day every three months from Turkmenistan. He was good fun, and we would always have a drink together.

I HAD ASKED personnel command to send out someone on a pastoral visit, to cope with the aftermath of the Chris and Karen affair, and see if it could recommend anything on the continuing British/Uzbek staff divide.

A pleasant young Scot, Colin Reynolds, was sent out. He held an opening meeting, at which I urged everyone to be open and cooperate fully with him. He then held individual meetings with virtually all of the staff.

Something extraordinary started to happen. First Nick Ridout, then Steve Brown, then Kristina, came to see me immediately after seeing Colin. They were mystified. He had asked them almost nothing about Chris and Karen or relationships within the embassy, but had instead asked repeatedly how much I drank and whether I was sleeping around. One by one, virtually the entire embassy staff came to see me after seeing him, all pretty angry, and anxious on my behalf.

Colin came to see me at the end. He said he was concerned that not all proper procedures were being followed. I said they never had been because the embassy hadn't been resourced to do them. Steve Brown and I were making a real effort to improve on this, but obviously the loss of Karen and Chris had disrupted things a bit. I then said that the staff had been telling me he had focused on asking personal questions about me. If I was under investigation, it would have been polite to have let me know.

Colin said that he had been asked to investigate allegations against me, including that I was alcoholic and that I was, together with an expatriate, renting a flat in the town for shagging purposes. The Eastern

Department had shown him an article in an Uzbek newspaper that covered the Chris Hirst affair. It said I had covered up for Chris Hirst because he and I used to go drinking and womanizing together.

I said all these allegations were untrue. Colin said he agreed, but had wanted to check out the evidence with the staff before talking to me.

I should say something about drink. I have recounted several drinking sessions, because they were memorable. I have always had the ability to drink a great deal, to hold my drink, and to get up and go to work the next morning. I did not drink every day by any means—on average, I should think I drank on three evenings a week, and two of those moderately. Sometimes I might go a couple of weeks without a drink at all. I was never drunk in the office or at work.

But now, the strain of doing the jobs of Chris and Karen as well as my own was getting to me. I found shortly after Colin's visit that I was having a drink when I got home to relax the tension. I had never used alcohol in this way before, so I went to see Dr. Reimers about it. She said I was massively stressed and greatly needed a holiday. But with Chris and Karen gone, I just had too much work to do.

For months I had received virtually no communication of any kind from the Eastern Department. It may be illogical to ascribe a quality to silence, but this was a hostile silence. I did not know that, following his visit to Tashkent at the end of March, Simon Butt had already initiated this attack. On April 16, he had written a minute to Linda Duffield and Sir Michael Jay:

From: Simon Butt, Eastern
Date: 16 April 2003
To: Linda Duffield
cc: PS/PUS

SUBJECT: CRAIG MURRAY, TASHKENT
    I visited Tashkent from 30 March–1 April. I briefed you orally on my return on discussions with Craig on his performance, and we met with the PUS [Sir Michael Jay] yesterday. This is to record the position more formally . . .
    I discussed with Craig his telegram on US policy, sent and widely copied

on the eve of the hostilities in Iraq, and another example of his accustomed, rather emotional style. (He has since been instructed, with some of our other ambassadors who have the same predilection, not to copy their reporting quite so widely, following complaints from Gulf Posts.)

Craig was unapologetic. What he had said needed saying. He had again received congratulatory emails from a number of other posts which had received the telegram. These were issues about which he felt strongly, and which needed to be aired . . . He was not prepared to compromise on principles to further his career . . .

I ought perhaps to mention, without further comment, one further aspect of Craig's unconventional style. After a dinner in Samarkand, the rest of the party returned to our hotel. Craig, in the company of our young female LE fixer, went off in search of a jazz club. I have heard from others that he has patronised strip clubs in Warsaw (where he encountered Andrew Mackinlay MP) . . .[3]

Simon Butt

So in mid-April, Sir Michael Jay, head of the Diplomatic Service, was already holding meetings that were setting out the problem: Craig Murray criticizing U.S. foreign policy, and refusing to stop, even if it threatened his career—and the potential solution: attack his personal life. This was followed by that period of hostile silence, then the attack in the shape of the visit by Colin Reynolds, primed with stories about me.

Unfortunately for them, Colin Reynolds was perceptive, experienced and honest. His report on his visit included the following:

While some of the staff said that they were initially surprised by Craig's more relaxed style, none said anything about activities outside of the office which would cause us embarrassment. All the staff said they felt Craig's profile was high, and that while his style was undoubtedly unlike any ambassador they had had before, they all said how much they enjoyed working for him and how much British businesses respected and liked him.

Why was Colin Reynolds asked to investigate my private life? A campaign had started against me, which was an early symptom of the fact that while we continued to advocate human rights in public, in private the government was deciding to abandon the concept of fundamental rights, as an interference with the War on Terror. It is now pretty open about it, but in 2003 it was still schizophrenic, and I was caught in the middle of that schizophrenia.

The other factor was the Americans. The rumors about me that the Eastern Department was passing on to personnel command, about the source of which Colin Reynolds was deliberately obscure, were being produced by the U.S. embassy in Tashkent. After twenty years in the diplomatic service I had a lot of friends, particularly in the lower grades. A junior member of Jack Straw's private office has told me that what happened next was that Sir David Manning, Tony Blair's foreign policy adviser, came back from a visit from Washington with a message that the U.S. wanted someone to rid them of that troublesome British ambassador in Tashkent.

The *Observer* columnist Nick Cohen has told me that in the autumn of 2003, he had lunch with an FCO minister who said that the instruction to get rid of me came from Number 10. Michael Andersen, the distinguished Danish journalist and Central Asia expert, has published that in autumn 2003: "Sources in the Foreign Office told me that 'a systematic campaign' was waged against Murray, partly directed from Downing Street."[4]

I had a holiday in Canada with the family booked for the end of July. I desperately needed this holiday, but who was to take over? Daniel Grzenda had been appointed to replace Chris Hirst, and it was agreed to bring him out early to do this. It was extraordinary that he would get to be in charge of the embassy after a day of his first posting, but we decided it would be so quiet in August in Tashkent, it should be all right. In retrospect, I should have been suspicious that the Eastern Department seemed so anxious for me to get away for my leave.

Fiona and Emily had returned to the U.K. a few weeks ahead of me, at the start of Jamie's holiday, and I had been able to spend a lot of time in the evenings with Nadira. We had really gotten serious. I was sorry to say good-bye to her for a month, but was looking forward to Canada with the children.

I had seen Colin's report and felt that I had fended off the Eastern

Department's attacks for now, although there was no change in their frostiness in the month between Colin's visit and my getting away on leave.

I had one day in London before we left for Canada. I used it to call on Simon Butt, Linda Duffield and Alan Charlton, the director of personnel. If I had any illusions that the hostility had died down, they were quickly dispelled.

I received astonishing news. Kristina, Lena Son, Atabek, Yulya and Nafisa—my five senior members of locally engaged staff—had all been suspended from duty and asked to leave the embassy. This had actually happened the moment I left the embassy building, as I was on my way to the airport. I was astonished and livid, demanding that they be reinstated.

Dominic Schroeder was on the phone to Jessica Irvine of DFID. She plainly was furious—Atabek was a DFID, not an FCO, employee. I stepped into Dominic's office.

"Is that Jessica?" I asked. "Tell her it's nothing to do with me, and I want him back."

Dominic gave me an unconvincing smile and a thumbs-up, but didn't say this. I repeated it. He was telling Jessica there would be a full investigation, and again didn't pass on my message. I decided to do so myself, but though I tried several times that afternoon, I could achieve no more than a message on her answering machine.

Simon Butt denied all prior knowledge when I met him. He said they would investigate it and I should go on holiday. I said I wanted it fully understood these were valuable members of staff.

The rest of my conversation with Simon was even more worrying. He said that he had been appointed the investigating officer in the Chris Hirst case, and that disturbing facts had emerged. He said he had interviewed Chris and found him convincing. Chris had said that he had the baseball bat purely so he could hit a ball a long way for the dog to chase. He denied all the assaults. Furthermore, Chris claimed I was harassing him because of my personal dislike of dogs.

There were further allegations. Both Chris and Karen counteralleged that I was drinking in bars, and had taken Chris to a strip club after the Van Boven reception. Also, at the queen's birthday party, there had been nude swimming in the pool. That alone could constitute gross misconduct, Simon said. He then said that Karen alleged that I had no respect from the British business community.

I couldn't believe it. I had no doubt the charges against Chris were true. Karen had admitted it, we had checked a case in the hospital and got further information from others, including the lawyers representing the woman left brain-damaged. There had also been an assault on a Polish diplomat, confirmed by the Polish embassy.

I had stressed in writing to the FCO that, without treatment, I was concerned Chris could be a danger to the public in the U.K. But now it became all too clear that the FCO were much more interested in using Chris Hirst to substantiate allegations of me having a drink, than in repeated and potentially murderous assaults.

I replied to Simon, describing the events after the Van Boven reception. I suggested that, in the circumstances, counteraccusations from Chris might be considered with a little more skepticism. As for the queen's birthday party, it had finished and a few friends had stayed on for drinks and a swim. Richard Wilkins's guest had briefly removed her top.

Simon said he thought this was a major problem.

Profoundly depressed, I told both Linda Duffield and Alan Charlton that I was considering asking to leave Tashkent. The policy differences were making it difficult for me to continue in conscience, and seemed to be feeding through into persecution. Neither tried to dissuade me; both told me to make my mind up quickly.

We flew to Toronto the next day.

All my instincts were screaming at me to give up the holiday and get on the next plane back to Tashkent. Plainly something strange indeed was happening, and I was convinced that the removal of my key staff was the start of an attack on me while I was on leave. But I was both physically and mentally in desperate need of a holiday. It had been a draining year, and I had not had a break of longer than four days in the preceding three years. Fiona and the children were hugely looking forward to the holiday in Canada, and we weren't all together as a family very often.

So, fatally, I went.

FOR THE FIRST few nights I couldn't sleep. I had a profound worry about what the FCO was up to. It grew to a constant subconscious nag, an awareness of facing an implacable hostility. Every now and then the hairs on the back of my neck would rise and I would be overcome by a despairing consciousness that people were acting against me, thousands of miles away. It wasn't a psychic phenomenon—it was my mind working on a perfectly rational analysis of the situation, and forcing it to my attention, while I was constantly struggling not to think about it. I tried not to show any worry, especially to the children, but I think the strain did show, and Fiona certainly noticed I couldn't sleep. I kept telling myself that, as the holiday unfolded, I would get less stressed, but it didn't work—the feeling just built and built.

Which is a shame, because it was a wonderful holiday. Toronto, Niagara Falls, Fort Henry, Quebec, Sunwapta Falls, Vancouver. It could not have been better for the family.

In Vancouver, having crossed the continent largely by road, we were staying at the Royal Towers casino hotel. I had found it on the Internet simply as a good-quality hotel offering an excellent deal. The casino was incidental; it did not bother us and we did not bother it. The room was cheap—eighty-five Canadian dollars a night—presumably because they expected you to spend money in the casino. The family were happy and bubbly as we checked in, although as I signed in I noticed the hotel address, New Westminster, and wondered just what hostile plan they were up to in the FCO. I had no idea that my marriage would end in that hotel.

At first we were in a cramped room with two double beds. I looked up the Internet booking printout, and went down in the morning to do battle with reception. They upgraded us with great promptness and courtesy. A porter helped move the luggage. By now we had a huge stack, full of souvenirs from all our points of call and presents for all the Uzbek staff. They put us in a beautiful penthouse on the ninth floor.

We went to the tourist information center, looking for a play or film to see that evening. It had free Internet access, and Fiona logged on to our family address. There was an e-mail for me from Howard Drake in the FCO personnel department. It was peremptory. I was to telephone him immediately.

Howard was my "grade manager." He was responsible for the career progression of the senior grades of the diplomatic service. The next morning I went to our consulate general in Vancouver. The consul general, a nice man named Laurence, was slightly bemused but lent me his office. I got through to Howard Drake.

I knew Howard slightly. I had once taken over a job from him, either as head of the Cyprus section or head of the maritime section of the FCO, I forget which. He had big hair, a careful blond coiffure like that of a minor American politician. We had had a week's handover of the job, and got on well. He had a generally pompous demeanor, but not above the Foreign Office norm. Now he sounded uncomfortable indeed.

"Thank you for phoning, Craig. How are you?"

"Very well, thanks, Howard. How are you?"

"I am fine, thank you, Craig. And how is your wife? Fiona, isn't it? And the children?"

"All fine, thank you, Howard. We have had a good, much-needed break."

"Yes, I am sure. Well, Craig, the thing is that you called on a number of people before you left for, er, Canada, and you said that you were thinking of quitting in Tashkent."

"Yes, that's right. I said I'd think about it over the holiday."

"And did you?"

"Yes, I did. I think I was just exhausted. I am ready to soldier on now. Actually, I'm looking forward to going back."

"Oh. That could be unfortunate."

"I am sorry, Howard?"

"Well, Craig"—he audibly swallowed—"the thing is that it has been decided here that Tashkent would be better off without you."

I remember that phrase precisely. *Better off without you.*

"Well, I don't agree. Have I been withdrawn?"

"Not yet, no. What are your travel plans?"

"Well, we fly back to Tashkent in a couple of days."

"Are you coming to London first?"

"Only to change planes."

"Well, Craig, I have to be quite clear. You are not to return to Tashkent. That is a direct instruction from Sir Michael Jay. You are to come back here immediately and to see me. I have to tell you that there are serious disciplinary allegations facing you."

"What allegations? Who from?"

"I can't say any more on the phone. How soon can you be here?"

"I don't know. I'll have to see a travel agent. Will the office pay the extra costs?"

"I don't know. I suppose so."

They didn't.

TASHKENT TIME IS about ten hours off Vancouver time. The hotel staff were very helpful when I explained I had to make some urgent international business calls at 4 A.M., and didn't want to disturb my family. They gave me the key to an adjacent suite, activating the phone and asking me not to use the bathroom or disturb the bed.

I quickly got through to Daniel. I explained to him briefly that London had told me I would not be returning to Tashkent. His strangled "What?" indicated genuine surprise. I asked him what could have happened to precipitate this—now that Chris and Karen were gone I thought things were running OK. Daniel sounded pensive and worried.

"Well, I think some things were said when Dominic Schroeder came out."

"Dominic came out? Why did he come out? And what things were said?"

"He came out three weeks ago to investigate the suspension of local staff. He asked a lot of questions about you."

"And what did people say?"

"Well, I think some people thought you could give them more support, and back their judgment more in management issues."

"Well, that hardly sounds enough."

"Look, I think we all just said we should talk it through with you when you returned and sort it out. No one wanted you kicked out."

A suspicion crossed my mind.

"Daniel, Dominic came out in response to the suspension of local staff. Now whose idea was that?"

"It was my decision as chargé d'affaires."

"Yes, of course. But what happened exactly?"

"Well, Steve brought me this e-mail from Atabek, which was mocking my authority. We looked it up in *Diplomatic Service Procedure* and decided it was gross misconduct. It said that suspension pending investigation was the first option. So I did that. Look, I said to London that if anyone could show me what I did wrong according to *Diplomatic Service Procedure,* I would take the blame. As far as I'm concerned, I just followed it."

"No doubt. Daniel, I am really not worried about that—I have been in the service for twenty years now and I haven't opened *Diplomatic Service Procedure* yet. But you didn't know, following Dominic's visit, that I wouldn't be coming back?"

"No, we didn't think that was the outcome at all. We said we had some management issues, but just wanted to put them on the table with you to improve relationships."

"OK, Daniel. Thanks. Don't worry about it."

"OK, Craig. Look, I'm sorry. What shall I tell the others?"

"Nothing yet. Good night, Daniel."

"Good night, Craig. Sleep well."

I didn't. At six o'clock in the morning, I woke Fiona and we went into the bathroom to talk where the children wouldn't hear us. I told her everything I knew. I also told her about my relationship with Nadira. I couldn't think what else the office could be going to throw at me. I didn't want Fiona to hear about it from anyone else. Fiona was obviously furious, but icily calm. She asked if I was prepared to give Nadira up, and never see her again. I said I didn't think I could promise that; I was in love. But neither did I want to split up our family. Fiona told me not to be so childish and to grow up. If I didn't end the relationship with Nadira, the marriage was over anyway.

Despite her fury at me, Fiona saw clearly that the desire of the FCO to remove me from Tashkent had nothing to do with Nadira. Marital breakups in the diplomatic service are extremely common, and my personal history had plenty of entanglements that had never threatened my career. I told Fiona we were most unlikely to be going back to Tashkent.

We couldn't fly back to London the next day, and so would be returning only a day ahead of schedule, which the children didn't even notice. We tried to keep things as normal as we could for them the next day. We went out in a large inflatable on a whale watch trip around the islands.

We didn't see the promised school of whales, but every now and then glimpsed the distant hump of a lone minke whale. The guide tried to assure us that a lone minke was a much rarer sighting than a whole school of more common whales, but we weren't convinced.

It is a long flight from Vancouver to London, especially if you call in at Chicago. It was a fourteen-hour overnighter, and I didn't sleep a wink.

CHAPTER 15

One Step Ahead of the Shoeshine

I WENT STRAIGHT BY TAXI FROM HEATHROW AIRPORT TO THE FCO, while Fiona drove home with the children and the luggage. I arrived at the Old Admiralty Building off the Mall, and searched through its maze of corridors for Howard Drake's office. I went to the bathroom to splash cold water on my face, to try to snap my brain back into gear. Looking in the mirror at this man in crumpled clothes, with reddened, narrow eyes and two days of stubble glinting gray and russet, I thought I could not have made myself look more disreputable if I tried. It was August 21, 2003.

I was first introduced to Kate Smith, a young lady from my union who was to accompany me to the interview. The union, the Diplomatic Service Association, has since changed, but at that time it represented only the most senior members of the Diplomatic Service, so it was hardly the most radical organization in the world. It was probably the only organization accredited to the Trades Union Congress, the majority of whose members attended private schools. It tended to the view that the FCO administration, composed of a fair proportion of its own members, was probably right in most instances. Like me, Kate Smith was on a fast-track career. About thirty, she had a key role in the Iraq unit. She sported the usual short-cropped hair, flecked with premature gray. Her smile is warm and her features elfin, but at this first meeting she was viewing me with ill-disguised reserve, like a barrister defending a mass murderer he is pretty sure is guilty.

We went in together to see Howard Drake.

"Hello, Craig," he said. "It's been a long time."

The hair was still big, but thinner, and the blond color had dulled.

"Ten years?" I suggested.

"Your career has gone well, eh? Ambassador?"

"Well, it *is* only Uzbekistan."

"Still, you've done better than me." Suddenly his mouth clenched and facial muscles tightened, and he said as if by a great effort, "Look, this isn't very pleasant, but I might as well launch into it." He then started speaking from prepared notes, and as he progressed his voice took on a tone of active hostility. He was getting into the part. He didn't look at me much.

I will give you the official record of Howard's opening remarks, written by Howard Drake himself. Like all official records, it elides some of the spikiness, and Howard perhaps makes himself out to have scored better than he did. But despite the dead hand of officiousness, you can get a good idea:

Craig Murray, HMA Tashkent

1. At my request, Mr. Murray came to see me on 21 August prior to his return to Tashkent following a leave absence . . .

2. I explained both Personnel and Wider Europe Directorates were now of the view that he should withdraw from Post on operational grounds. We had very serious concerns about the way the post was being run under his leadership. There were also a number of very serious allegations which had been made about Mr. Murray's personal conduct. We were bound to investigate these allegations (as yet unproven). Some of them also raised concerns on security grounds, which SSU would be exploring given that Mr. Murray's Direct Vetting was coming up for review in any case.

3. I handed Mr. Murray copies of the reports by Colin Reynolds and Dominic Schroeder following their separate visits to Tashkent. I recognised that Mr. Murray had seen neither of these before (the Schroeder visit took place after Mr. Murray had departed on leave, but the contents of the Reynolds report had been discussed in full with him) and so invited him to take them away and consider them . . .

5. In addition to these major operational concerns, Dominic Schroeder had reported a series of very serious allegations from members of the

UK-based staff in Tashkent. The FCO was duty bound to look into them, and determine if there were a disciplinary case to answer. Some of the allegations related to potential vulnerabilities from a security point of view, and SSU had been concerned given the very explicit warnings given to Mr. Murray prior to taking up post on his conduct.

6. I said that Mr. Murray should be in no doubt that this was a very serious matter. We were asking Mr. Murray to agree to withdraw from post as soon as possible ie return to Tashkent to pack up and leave during September . . .

7. I invited Mr. Murray to comment, adding that given the circumstances (he had come directly to the meeting after an overnight flight from Canada, and was en route back to Tashkent) he was free to add to anything he might say at our meeting when he'd had time to consider the details more carefully.

8. Mr. Murray made the following points:

a) Mr. Murray was shocked and would try not to be emotional. If the Office wanted to suspend him while the disciplinary issues were investigated, fine. But he was not going to leave post on the grounds I had outlined . . .

Howard was plainly shaken by my refusal to resign. He positively went white. The FCO is a very collegiate organization, in which those few in the top levels who don't come from a private school and Oxbridge background survive by acting as though they did. This meeting was a bit like the old films where the army officer is left the revolver on his desk and asked to do the decent thing. I picked it up and started shooting at the bastards. I countered the specific management points made, and then:

g) Mr. Murray said that the move to get rid of him was being conducted by Eastern Department. Personnel Directorate needed to consider whether policy disagreements were leading to a bias against Mr. Murray. Mr. Murray acknowledged that he was not the usual FCO personality, and that he asked difficult policy questions (by way of illustration, he described in outline a highly classified telegram concerning intelligence obtained via torture). Mr. Murray firmly

believed that policy differences were at the root of all this: he had
clearly got up the noses of senior management . . .

This minute has five close-typed pages, and reading over it I am astonished how coherent I was. It had just passed 1 A.M. in Vancouver, and I'd
had virtually no sleep for the previous seventy-two hours. But I pointed
out the major discrepancies between Dominic Schroeder's allegations and
Colin Reynolds's report of just four weeks earlier, and I rebutted in detail
the claims about my mishandling of the Hirst/Moran affair. I also asked
why none of these points on management had been made to me when I
had called on Simon Butt, Linda Duffield and Alan Charlton only three
weeks earlier.

It became obvious to me that nothing I said was having any impact
on Howard. So I stopped and asked him if anything I said might change
the mind of the office, and he said no, and there was no point in our talking about it. So I asked why they did not, in that case, simply instruct me
to leave, rather than ask me to resign. He recorded his reply: "I reiterated
that our hope was that he and we would agree that withdrawal would be
the right step. We also had in mind his well-being and dignity."

When Howard handed me the allegations, I didn't have time to take
them all in, but what I read hit me like a bullet. Offering visas for sex,
being an alcoholic, financial corruption. How on earth, after twenty
years' service, could they produce such lies? These people actually knew
me. But why were they so keen to browbeat me into resigning? I drew a
simple conclusion. They couldn't sack me. They knew as well as I that
these allegations were bullshit, and they must have been warned off by
their lawyers. As soon as I got back to Tashkent, I would start to marshall
witnesses in my defense.

Howard read my thoughts.

"If you do go back to Tashkent," Howard said, "you are not, under
any circumstances, to mention this meeting, these allegations or the
request that you resign, to anybody at all. Is that plain?"

I could hardly have been given a more sinister instruction.

"Plain but not fair. How do I establish a defense?"

"You don't. The FCO will appoint an independent investigator to
determine the facts."

"In which case I want it noted that I have no confidence in the fairness of the procedure."

Howard was not open to reasoning, and was just carrying out instructions from the top of the office. But I had changed one mind. Kate Smith and I retired to another room immediately after the meeting, and she was plainly perturbed at what she had just heard, and realized that something strange was happening here. I was asked to resign on the basis of a series of points acknowledged never to have been put to me before, and told it made no difference what I might answer. I suggested to her that the Eastern Department had failed to get what they wanted from Colin Reynolds, so had gone out to do the job themselves. The suspension of my key staff while I was still on my way to the airport looked like a put-up job to get Dominic out there to do the business.

I returned to Tashkent with Emily, who had to start school. Fiona was remaining in the U.K. a couple of weeks with Jamie, until he returned to Glenalmond College near Perth. From Tashkent I maintained a correspondence about procedure with Kate Smith, who got ever more helpful, and Tessa Redmayne, acting for the administration. The hostility from London was unabated. So I decided to address the infamous FCO allegations against me. On August 27, I sent an e-mail to all who had received Howard Drake's minute.

From Craig Murray, Tashkent
27 August 2003

Craig Murray—Disciplinary Allegations
   It has become clear to me that the allegations contained in Dominic Schroeder's minute of 6 August are colouring opinions in London against me, even though they have not yet begun to be investigated. I would therefore like at this stage to give my initial response, which may also help to get the investigation off to a flying start, and go some way to help remind those in London not to prejudge me:

Allegation 1
   That he had facilitated visas for girlfriends, paying money for air tickets, receiving sexual favours in his office in return.

I have never had a sexual relationship with a visa applicant. I have never indulged in any kind of sexual activity in the office. Even in the broadest sense of the term, I have "facilitated" no more than perhaps six visa applications in a year in Tashkent. I have never seen a Head of Mission in a visa post do less.

Allegation 2

That he regularly turns up at the office drunk or hungover and late before going home to "sleep it off," then returning to the office at 16.50 demanding people start work with him.

Completely untrue. I have never been drunk in the office. I would put my average arrival time between 09.10 and 09.15. I generally work a week of around 65 hours including receptions and officially directed out of office activity.

I have held over 700 meetings with perhaps 1200 visitors over the year. Nobody has ever claimed they found me not sober and on the ball.

In the course of the year I have returned to the Residence during office hours on perhaps 7 or 8 occasions. Three of these were to attend staff meetings in the Residence on queen's birthday party organisation. One was to give a TV interview and one to prepare the staff Christmas Party. I once went home feeling unwell—not hungover—and once to attend to some frais accounting. It is possible that on one of these occasions I returned at 4.50 and asked for some important work to be done, but I have no recollection of it.

If I regularly returned home during the day it would show in the flag car log.

I believe there are medical tests now which show background or long-term alcohol abuse. I would happily take one.

Allegation 3

That he took a girlfriend as an interpreter on an up-country trip after which no note was produced.

I roped in a friend, Nadira Bekhanov, as an interpreter on a (particularly gruelling) visit to Kitab to investigate human rights abuses against private farmers there, which had received widespread publicity on the BBC. It was alleged further acts of violence were imminent so we went at short notice. As we were visiting deep country areas around Shakhrizab where Russian would not be understood I needed interpretation potentially for Uzbek and Tajik. The Embassy was very stretched as we had lost the DHM and 3rd Sec (Chris Hirst and Karen Moran) while visa section was very busy and needed their interpreters. Kristina Ozden, visits officer and social secretary, was accompanying me and she cannot interpret in Uzbek or Tajik. I therefore persuaded a friend fluent in the relevant languages (and with a master's in English) to come with me.

We held meetings with the farmers affected, with the local prokuracy, with the head of the collective farm, and with the national Uzbek deputy prokurator-general . . .

We left at 10am and reached Kitab around 3pm. We first met the victims, then toured vandalised fields, then met the head of the collective farm. We returned immediately to Karshi to our hotel and did not reach it until midnight—a very gruelling day and spent largely outdoors in 45C. The next morning we were up at 7am to return to Kitab. We met the local and deputy state prokurators. These were tense and difficult meetings . . .

It is true no single note was produced, but the visit was mentioned in our telno 55 and elsewhere, and particularly in discussions with our OSCE and US colleagues. It resulted directly in a major success—the release of an innocent man from jail. Leonid Kudryavtsev has been working on this case and can confirm this. Kristina Ozden can confirm my account of the trip, including that Bekhanov was needed for translation, and that this was a very hard-working trip. You can also check the hotel bills and see that our party of four (inc driver) had four bedrooms.

I will not continue to give my response to each allegation, but you get the general idea. The rest of the allegations were:

Allegation 4

That he authorised the purchase for £4,500 of the sound system of a band (made up of his friends) which played at the queen's birthday party. The equipment is in the MO's cellar, never likely to be used. That $80 bottles of whisky were drunk by the band and paid for by local budget.

Allegation 5

That at an away-day Craig encouraged drivers to take Embassy vehicles down staircases.

Allegation 6

That he belittles UK-based staff behind their backs before denying a problem when approached by the officers directly concerned.

Allegation 7

That he has told the DHM not to be serious about an MCS review due in mid-September "We'll promote everyone and they'll be happy."

Allegation 8

That he "knows" the SBU [local intelligence service] are watching him but doesn't worry because he is open about his behaviour. But he is scared his wife will "find out" and divorce him, taking the children.

Allegation 9

That certain LE staff "dollybirds" are employed in e.g. visa section at double normal rates "because he says so."

Allegation 10

That staff were warned not to co-operate with Colin Reynolds during his recent visit because Craig "had something" on the FCO.

Allegation 11

That he has twice asked the management officer to issue a warning to his own personal assistant which has been rescinded without explanation once the personal assistant has spoken to Craig.

Allegation 12

That he frequently takes the flag car out (with driver) until 02.00–04.30.

Allegation 13

That the May account is not yet signed off.

Allegation 14
    That a 5 % overspend of local budget in the first quarter is "laughed off."

Allegation 15
    That no meetings are held, notwithstanding Craig's assertion to Simon Butt that they are.

Allegation 16
    That he turned up at the first Commercial contacts meeting three hours late at 21.30, claiming to be the only UK-based officer who did any work, but was "covered in lipstick."

Allegation 17
    Claims to UK-based colleagues to send e-mails to "wind Simon Butt up," then complains about Simon's response to Linda Duffield.

Allegation 18
    "Admits" to writing "exaggerated" letter to Peter Collecott about conditions at Post.

Dominic's minute simply stated each allegation, without expanding on it, and claimed that each was supported by at least one member of the U.K.-based staff.

Most of these allegations had no basis in fact whatsoever. I suggested that some of the problem might arise from the fact that for the past three months I had been working with just two FCO staff, both of whom had the very lowest substantive grade in the service, well below diplomatic rank. They simply didn't understand what I was doing. But I didn't believe these allegations had all genuinely been made in the form Dominic put them. My refutation concluded: "They also show a distinct tendency to malicious gossip and unpleasant innuendo. How much of this will be supported by open statement we will have to wait and see. I suspect that Dominic Schroeder may have himself put a spin on certain comments in his manner of compiling and presenting them."

I was to get further evidence to support the possibility that this is what had happened. Many months later, Angela Clarke told me that she had been sitting having a coffee in a Tashkent hotel, when Dominic Schroeder joined her and asked, "What's the gossip about Craig Murray, then?"

He had seemed jovial, and she had told him some gossip, without any intention of certifying it as true, just in the way people like to indulge in a little mildly vicious gossip against the boss. She recognized it as the germ of some of these allegations.

The large majority of the allegations could have been cross-checked and dismissed by Dominic Schroeder, or anyone else in Tashkent, in a couple of hours at most. But the truth was not the aim. The aim was to force my departure.

There is a manuscript note on a minute dated September 1, from Sir Michael Jay to Jack Straw, the British foreign minister. It reads: "Updates our conversation last week. Gareth Evans has now spoken to me, and written to you. Tony Crombie is content for the arrangements for the enquiry ie Craig Murray to stay away from the Embassy. Perhaps we could discuss again at our next bilateral on 3 September."

In his own hand, Jack Straw replied: "I agree with this approach."

This is significant. It proves that Jack Straw was minutely guiding the attempt to get rid of me, and regularly discussing it at meetings with Sir Michael Jay. In fact, my "Deep Throat" tells me there were seven such meetings. Yet to the media and to Parliament, Jack Straw has repeatedly denied that he had any involvement with the disciplinary allegations or attempts to remove me from Tashkent.

Jack Straw was lying through his teeth.

When Howard Drake had first handed me these allegations, I had been severely shaken. It was hard to believe that the organization I had worked for, very successfully, for nearly twenty years was now acting against me with such appalling malice. Then I started to cheer up; the allegations were so far removed from the truth, they must be easy to fight off. As I left the building I was whistling Simon and Garfunkel to myself:

> *I've been slandered, libeled;*
> *I've heard words I never heard in the Bible,*
> *But I'm one step ahead of the shoeshine . . .*

But once back in Tashkent, it was difficult. Because I wasn't allowed to mention the allegations to anyone, I could do nothing to prepare a defense. And Dominic Schroeder had sent his minute to every member of the British staff, so they all knew exactly the hymn sheet from which the office wished them to sing. They all had their careers to think of, and were jumpy. It was hard for them to deal with a boss who they knew was hated at the top of the organization and likely to disappear any minute. They were at the same time anxious individually to indicate to me that none of them had wanted this to happen. They had made some individual management points, when they had been trawled for complaints, not knowing they were feeding into a devastating and unwarranted personal attack alleging corruption.

I was getting more and more agitated about my inability to defend myself. On August 26, I e-mailed Kate Smith:

> . . . For example, one completely untrue accusation against me is that I am habitually late for work and drunk or hungover on arrival. This is easily disproved—I can call as witnesses the cook who prepares and serves my breakfast, the drivers who take me to work, the gate guards at each end of the journey who know what time I leave and arrive, the staff I work closely with. But I am not allowed to contact any of these potential defence witnesses. As I understand the office intends me to leave Uzbekistan very shortly, and as it will be very hard indeed to build my case from outside Uzbekistan, this prohibition seems completely unfair. This is especially so as it does not apply to Eastern Department, and Dominic Schroeder is continually on the phone to the British staff to exhort them to back up his allegations.

I think it is fair to say that Kate was now convinced, and started to work hard on my behalf, which was to be crucial. Howard Drake had given me the deadline of August 29 voluntarily to resign. I had to communicate my decision to Dominic Schroeder. If I didn't jump, the office would decide whether to push me, and Howard had left me in little doubt as to the outcome.

I left my office on August 27, 2003, convinced I would never see it again. I was clearing out, and had to explain to Kristina that I had been banned from the embassy, and expected to be asked to leave Tashkent permanently the following day. I gave her a brief description of the nature of the allegations against me. She was first incredulous, then reduced to tears. Fifteen minutes later Kristina, Lena Son, Yulya, Atabek, Nafisa, Leonid and I were all in my office, and all in tears. I had now broken the instruction not to tell anyone about the allegations. I had been punished for that before I had done it, by being banned from the embassy, so I wasn't too bothered.

I left with the declaration ringing in my ears from the staff that they would fight this. As I left for the residence, they got to work.

That very afternoon Jack Straw and Sir Michael Jay received a letter signed by 90 percent of the Uzbek office staff of the embassy.

28 August 2003
His Excellency
Jack Straw
Secretary of State
Foreign & Commonwealth Office
London

Your Excellency,
. . . Ever since he arrived in Tashkent, Craig Murray had been the most active and outspoken critic of the Uzbek government's poor human rights record and lack of economic progress. His famous speech at the opening of the Freedom House was the first public criticism of the Uzbek Government and its anti-reform policies in the run-up to the EBRD Board of Directors in the Annual Meeting in Tashkent. He has been the main agent for raising the profile and support for civil society reforms and promoting political and economic freedom in this complex environment. Notably, his voice was heard and respected not only by international community but more importantly, by host government. It goes without saying that any positive changes however small and hard fought, bear personal contribution by Craig Murray. He is considered here as the undisputed star of the diplomatic corps and renowned leader of the international business community.
He is not only seen as the most active promoter of democratic and civil

society values but also as an ardent supporter of economic liberalisation and regional economic co-operation and integration. His frequent visits to the projects managed by UK businessmen are highly praised both by foreign and local entrepreneurs who in all honesty are not used to seeing Ambassadors in their premises. He is the first high ranking diplomat to combine effectively his human rights and economic/political duties.

Craig Murray commands sympathy and the respect of the Embassy staff and British commercial circles in Uzbekistan. He is admired for his professional abilities and a great sense of humour.

We strongly feel that his departure from this post will not only lower the morale of Embassy staff but also reflect negatively on the Embassy image in local and foreign institutions present in Uzbekistan.

Sincerely Yours,

Atabek Sharipov	*Gafur Gafurov*	*Kristina Ozden*
Lena Son	*Leonid Kudryavtsev*	*Nafisa Nasyrova*
Nilufar Ibragimova	*Ravshan Salidjanov*	*Shahida Akhunova*
Sasha Babulaev	*Umid Abudallaev*	*Victoria Belyavskaya*
Yulya Usatova	*Yuri Yelkov*	

That seems pretty powerful, especially as the unhappiness of locally engaged staff was one of the four reasons Howard Drake had given that I had to be removed from Tashkent. But the FCO was too subtle for this. Personnel directorate sent a handwritten note to Michael Jay on a copy of this letter: "This is potentially valuable as evidence that Murray has put pressure on staff. It therefore justifies your decision to ban Murray from the Embassy. There is no reason to suppose that these are genuine views of the local staff."

No reason except, of course, Colin Reynolds's report of six weeks before, which stated: "The LE staff were uniformly positive about Craig during my visit."[1]

The FCO might have been pleased that it managed to twist the staff letter into evidence against me, but just two hours later the fax whirred again in Michael Jay's and Jack Straw's offices, and a letter arrived in my support signed by fifteen British businesses in Tashkent, including British

Airways, British American Tobacco, QuickStop, Oxus and Trinity Energy. The letter stated that: "Craig Murray is without doubt the British Ambassador who has put the most effort into promoting British commercial and economic interests, and the only British Ambassador who has had real clout with the Government of Uzbekistan."

The moment this letter arrived, the wheels came off the plan to sack me. Plainly I could not be an incompetent alcoholic. The attempt to force me out on that pretext failed when the effort to keep it all quiet failed.

The Foreign Office had failed to hush up the stitch-up.

But the political imperative to be rid of me was still there. Tessa Redmayne telephoned to say that, irrespective of the outcome of the eighteen allegations, I would now face a nineteenth serious disciplinary allegation: I had broken the instruction not to tell anybody about the allegations.

Meanwhile, those fax machines kept churning. Individual letters of support started pouring into Jack Straw's office, including from former Australian foreign minister Gareth Evans, now president of the International Crisis Group, Hartley Booth, the head of U.K./Uzbek trade promotion, and a range of companies operating in Uzbekistan.

29 August 2003

Dear Jack,

I have learned that you are considering recalling your ambassador to Uzbekistan, Craig Murray. I would normally not even think of commenting on a matter so clearly within HMG's competence but the case is unusual. The man in question is a most prominent diplomat in a specially sensitive area where ICG is deeply involved, and it is the perception of our people on the ground—whose judgement I highly respect—that such a move has the potential to be quite damaging for the British government's image in Uzbekistan and perceptions of its wider foreign policy goals and ideals.

ICG's Central Asia staff based in the Ferghana Valley have considerable experience in Uzbekistan and a good understanding of the activities of the UK Embassy. Murray has a reputation in the country as one of the few diplomats able and willing to make strong representations to a notoriously obdurate government on a wide range of issues, from human rights abuses to economic reform. Of course he has run into considerable opposition from the authorities but he has been extremely influential in gathering support around a more coherent international policy towards Uzbekistan that is shared by at least most European governments, the IMF, World Bank and other international organisations. His forthright approach has been a useful balance to some perhaps overaccommodating aspects of US foreign policy.

    The allegations against Murray that we are aware of—and of course we cannot be as well informed as you and your department on all the internal dimensions of this matter—are considered either trivial or unsubstantiated by my senior ICG people, who have personal knowledge of the man and his work in the difficult Tashkent environment. The risk under these circumstances is that his recall would inevitably be viewed by the Uzbeks and many internationals as intimately connected with his strong support for human rights, democratisation, and economic reforms, all avowed aims of UK policy in the region. Murray has been particularly effective in promoting the image of the UK among Muslims in Uzbekistan, at a time of growing suspicion in that community of Western interests.

    My people on the ground consider Murray the best informed ambassador in Tashkent. He has taken considerable pains to understand how the system works, and has travelled widely throughout the country. He has won influence among Uzbek elites and has been the most prominent member of the diplomatic community for some time. He has significantly raised the profile of the UK in Uzbekistan and gained considerable respect among international organisations, other diplomatic missions and the local population. He has also been, I should frankly acknowledge, extremely helpful to the ICG in helping us cope with some of the pressures to which a key member of our locally-engaged staff has been subjected by the Uzbek authorities.

    Ambassador Murray has been a very effective advocate for British foreign policy goals during his year in Tashkent. His recall, for whatever reason, so early in the normal tour of duty certainly carries with it some risks—in both policy and political terms—which I thought it proper to convey to you from ICG's perspective. I simply ask you to ensure that the

considerations I have raised are fully taken into account before any
irrevocable action is taken.

Sincerely,
GARETH EVANS
President
International Crisis Group

Of course, it was correct but not really helpful of Evans to note that
I was providing a useful balance to U.S. foreign policy. It was because of
this that Straw wanted rid of me. The British government didn't want
U.S. policy balanced, they wanted it unquestioningly backed. This was
the War on Terror, black-and-white, with us or against us.

A letter from Hartley Booth, former Tory MP and now the official fig-
urehead for U.K./Uzbek trade promotion, was addressed to me and
copied to the FCO:

7 September 2003

Dear Craig,

I have been informed that there are questions about your performance
as British ambassador in Tashkent. I am horrified, to say the least. As both
the chairman of the official British Uzbek Trade & Industry Council and as
chairman of the British-Uzbek Society, I have had opportunities to see you
in operation on behalf of Britain. You have three unusual and special
qualities, in my observation and based on the reports I have received.

1. You have quickly grasped the most complex issues of the posting and
formed accurate and sound judgements on them—a quality not always
immediately found in outposts such as Tashkent.

2. You have been fearless and most helpful to British interests in
Uzbekistan by your pursuit of the logical conclusion from your judgements
inside the Uzbek government.

3. You have gone out of your way to provide help for the brave frontline
of British interests that I too am in post to defend and promote. All
businessmen I have met and with whom I have had occasion to discuss you
over the past year have said that you have been the best ever British
ambassador in Tashkent from their standpoint.

Please show this to whom it may concern. I will attempt to have this passed to the Head of Department FCO and am happy to give confidential advice to anyone in appropriate authority.

With Best Wishes
Dr. V E Hartley Booth

AGAINST ALL DIPLOMATIC procedure, letters of support came from staff heading the UNDP, EBRD and European Commission headquarters in Tashkent. The American Chamber of Commerce wrote in my defense. The reviews were great and just kept pouring in:

I have been in the country for nine years now . . . During this period I have known three British ambassadors before the present incumbent, and I can say without hesitation that Mr. Murray is easily the most effective of all four . . .

Construction Contracting Consultants Ltd.

We have welcomed the honest, open and direct approach that Ambassador Murray and his staff have shown when dealing with the Uzbek government . . . The Uzbeks do choose their battles carefully and will avoid conflicts with stronger parties. It is therefore essential that UzPEC continue to receive the strong and active support of Ambassador Murray . . .

Uzbek Petroleum Enhancement Company Ltd.

. . . Mr. Murray contributed to the ongoing dialogue with the government to improve the foreign investment climate and he supported foreign and local businessmen in their efforts to do business in a very difficult economic environment. Mr. Murray is a "breath of fresh air" in the diplomatic community . . .

ABN AMRO Bank

I have had the privilege of personally knowing all Her Majesty's ambassadors who have served in Uzbekistan so far and I have found H.E. Mr. Murray to be the most capable and professional ambassador. He is very compassionate and friendly and always available to promote British business interests in Uzbekistan.

DIL International Ltd.

. . . Mr. Murray dealt with our issues directly. With his personal involvement he successfully convinced the governor of Jizzak region not to overuse his authority against British personnel. Working on "Jibri" joint venture in Jizzak, in another case, with his help we restored our share in "Ohangaron Rangli Sement" JV after it was taken away by the State Privatisation Committee of Uzbekistan.

Eurocommerce UK Ltd.

Dear Ambassador,
I would like to thank you for your assistance in terms of lobbying the interests of our venture "UzCase Tractor" with the government of Uzbekistan, thereby resulting in a $1 million export contract from the UK.

Case Tractors UK

The role of the British Embassy in supporting British businesses and improving Uzbek-British relationships has significantly increased with the arrival of His Excellency Ambassador Murray . . . he had been highly effective.

Carthill Investment Company Ltd.

The role of the . . . Ambassador Mr. Craig Murray during the last nine months has been significant. Without the strong support and backing of the ambassador we would not have achieved the very positive results, which we have achieved today and continue to achieve . . .

Trade Development

British Mediterranean Airways started operating their flights to Tashkent on 31st March 2003. Mr. Craig Murray, British ambassador, played a great role in this . . .

British Airways

. . . Craig made a valuable contribution to establishing the ethos of the University. After free and fair elections Craig hosted a reception for the entire student body . . .

University of Westminster

The current ambassador, Craig Murray, has been particularly active in . . .
assisting British companies with their activities in Uzbekistan.

Oxus Mining

Our efforts in Tashkent have resulted in significant business for us. I have
had the pleasure of personally discussing our activities with the ambassador
Mr. Craig Murray and have received continued support from him
throughout this time.

Geest Overseas Ltd.

The current ambassador has been proactive in helping this British company
to lobby the government of Uzbekistan for liberalisation of the economy
and to resolve many company-specific issues.

British American Tobacco

The above represent just extracts from a selection. I calculate Jack
Straw's fax machine received at least eighty-seven pages of letters in support of me from those with a direct interest.

Plainly the weight of this material clearly contradicted the story that
I was an incompetent drunk who didn't turn up to work and did not have
the respect of either his staff or the local British community. If the senior
management had genuinely been reacting to reports initiated from below,
it is inconceivable that, faced with all this, someone at a higher level
would not have started sending minutes querying whether Simon Butt
and Dominic Schroeder had got their assessment of me right. That this
did not happen can only mean that the "Murray must go" line was indeed
instructed from above. In fact, yet again the only senior reaction to this
correspondence was not to consider the content on its merits, but to
accuse me of conspiring to conduct a campaign.

So the office introduced a further refinement. Tony Crombie, formerly of our embassy in Moscow, had been appointed to conduct the
investigation. I was informed by Tessa Redmayne this would be a purely
internal affair. Crombie would not talk to, or consider evidence from,
anybody not employed by the British government.

The deck was being loaded still further against me. My feelings of
helplessness were starting to spiral toward despair. The injustice of it all

stunned me. The common theme running through the letters was that I was better than other British ambassadors. But if I had done very little, and been quietly inactive, the FCO would have been perfectly happy with me. They didn't want me doing stuff. I was meant to be ornamental, not effective.

The twenty-ninth came; I had to resign that day. I said I was tired and would like another day to think about it. They said no, I couldn't have another day. Still I didn't reply until the thirtieth, and then I said no, I won't go, I've done nothing wrong, you'll have to sack me.

After that it all went eerily quiet. I was extremely busy anyway. The lord mayor of London was visiting with the lady mayoress and the sheriff of London and his wife. They had a full program, including meeting Karimov himself, Deputy Prime Minister Usmanov and the ministers of foreign economic relations and industry. I hosted a number of functions, including a briefing lunch with British companies, and an evening reception for four hundred. For this the residence garden was beautifully illuminated with thousands of fairy lights and flaming torches, and the entertainment included a chamber orchestra, jazz band, dancers and acrobats.

The lord mayor could be rather brusque. He continually asked more and more detailed questions about such subjects as rates of corporation tax and changes in import tariffs. Luckily I could answer. He also was good at assimilating and presenting all this various material. He put firmly to the Uzbek authorities the need for economic liberalization to promote foreign investment, and he even succeeded in interrupting the famous Karimov "paranoid" forty-minute introductory speech. For some reason all the Uzbeks, from Karimov down, were effusive in their praise of me. They all raved, about the music festival in particular, with such uniformity that plainly it was part of a central script.

The local business community made sure that the lord mayor knew of my problems, and what they thought of them. One of the mayor's ports of call was British American Tobacco. As we left, Rene Ijsselstein, the manager, came up and grasped my hand as I was about to get into the car.

"Look, Craig," he said, "try not to worry too much. Anything we can do, anything at all, just let me know."

At this stage it was expressions of kindness that I found most difficult; I had learned to cope with unremitting hostility. My lip was trembling and I turned my face to look out the window. Gavyn Arthur said to me, "Ambassador, you should know I saw Rene's gesture, and I know what it is about. I have noted your complete support from the British business community, and I will make sure my views are known at the appropriate level in London."

I had a new deputy now, Carl Garn. He was pleasant and efficient, but not decisive. He found himself thrown into the middle of an impossible situation. I had to run the whole mayor's visit while trying to disguise the fact I was banned from the embassy and couldn't approach my own office.

ONE OF THE FIRST things I had done on arrival was visit Nadira and tell her that I wouldn't be able to see her for a while, as I was under investigation, and it was even possible I would suddenly leave the country and never see her again. She found this impossible to accept. I had seemed so solidly wealthy and powerful to her, she didn't believe it could vanish, and she presumed this was just a brush-off after I had reconciled with Fiona on holiday.

Nadira had been having a particularly nasty time in my absence. She had twice been raped by the police. On one occasion she had pleaded with the policeman not to take her virginity, and he had raped her anally. On the second occasion, which had been in a Nissan Maxima, the policeman was a senior one. He had ignored her pleas and used violence as well as coercion, but luckily he had been unable to sustain an erection.

Nadira was hurt that I had been away, not contacted her from Canada, and was saying I wouldn't be in touch now I was back. I was confused about the rapes when she explained the circumstances to me. It in no way excused the policemen, but in one case she had voluntarily entered his flat to go to a "party," and in the other had voluntarily entered his car for a lift from a bar. Sexual assault is never justified, but I didn't view her behavior as sensible, and I felt she had been behaving in a way that showed she was not serious about starting a genuine, permanent relationship with me. So our meeting was an occasion of mutual hurt, misunderstanding and anger. I reacted by withdrawing still further into self-pity. Nadira responded by going out partying with other men.

On September 5, when, to my surprise, I was still in Tashkent, I went to her flat, on the twelfth floor of a block at Zhemchuk. I told her I was going away, perhaps for a fortnight, perhaps longer, and gave her $300. I went out to the balcony and looked down. I felt an overwhelming desire to jump. I was saved by a chance remark from Nadira, who said that from here she saw Karimov drive past every morning. That brought my mind back to the struggle against dictatorship, to which I still had much to contribute.

I somehow came through the lord mayor's visit. I recently met someone to whom I spoke at my reception for the lord mayor, and he says that he found me lucid and outwardly fine. But inside I was falling apart, and I have little memory of that fortnight in Tashkent. The lord mayor having flown off on the sixth, and with Fiona returning on the eighth to look after Emily, I could give up the terrible effort to soldier on. I collapsed completely, mentally and physically. The feeling of helplessness, that I was crushed by an unrelenting hostility with no course of action to defend myself, manifested itself in physical helplessness. I lost the use of my muscles, and cried continually. Someone got a doctor to me, and they flew me back to the U.K. the next day, Dr. Reimers beside me. I did not positively want to kill myself, but I had lost the desire to live. It was the viciousness and injustice of the allegations, combined with not being allowed to fight them.

In London I was treated for depression, including ten days spent on suicide watch. This involved a burly male nurse watching your every move twenty-four hours a day, and even following you into the bathroom. I can promise you, if you are not suicidal before, you will be suicidal after such attention.

But things started to turn slowly in my favor. Tony Crombie started on a painstaking four-month investigation that eventually would result in my being cleared of all the ridiculous charges against me, though I was to be reprimanded for allegedly talking to my staff about them.

More important, the media started a massive campaign in my support. Initially it was the FCO that leaked the story to the media, to get me smeared as an alcoholic and sexual predator. At least four journalists told me that they had been warned by the FCO not to support me because I was a hopeless drunk and that, when the truth came out, they would look foolish.

My own friends in journalism have been invaluable in relaying such information back to me. It was at this time that I learned that a Foreign Office minister told one of the country's most senior columnists that the pressure to remove me from Tashkent had not been initiated by FCO ministers, but by the prime minister's office.

I was already well known to a lot of senior journalists, and they simply didn't believe the allegations against me. Virtually every British newspaper sent a journalist to Tashkent, and they crawled all over the bars and hotels trying to dig up dirt on me. This included the tabloids, who would have loved to run an "ambassador sells visas for sex" story. But, without exception, the media concluded from their own investigations that there was no truth in the allegations, and that they were trumped up because of my concerns about the human rights record of an ally of the United States in the War on Terror. Every British paper not owned by Rupert Murdoch was eventually to carry an editorial calling for my reinstatement.

CHAPTER 16

What Dreams May Come

IT WAS MID-NOVEMBER 2003. I COULD HARDLY BELIEVE I WAS really going back to Tashkent. The investigation had not concluded, but enough had been done to make plain there was no evidence. More important, journalists' own investigations had shown this was a story not about any crimes by me, but about crimes by our allies in the War on Terror. The Foreign Office had backed down. I had won!

Most of the serious newspapers covered my pending return as a victory over the Foreign Office, and they were right. The great support from the NGO and business communities, from the British public and media, and from individual MPs and MEPs had foiled their quiet little stitch-up. I also felt clear that, once back in Tashkent, I could face down any false accusations

The plane was pretty full, but the British Airways flight to Tashkent calls at Yerevan, and the large majority of the passengers are only going to Armenia. On this occasion about thirty were going on to Tashkent, and once the Armenia mob had left us, people began to pick me out and congratulate me on my return, with a steady trickle through the curtain that divided business class from economy. One young Uzbek man had a *Daily Telegraph,* which he flourished in my face, pointing to an article about me. He then grasped both my shoulders and hugged me.

Business class was very comfortable. I had been able to lie down and sleep a bit on the London-to-Yerevan leg, and I read an Ian Rankin novel between Yerevan and Tashkent, getting up occasionally to stretch my legs. The flight was eight hours in total. We had been due in to Tashkent about 4 A.M., but with the Heathrow delay we arrived about six-thirty.

When my legs touched Uzbek soil again I sighed audibly. I hadn't thought I would make it back. Even the greeter from the Uzbek Ministry of Foreign Affairs had a cheesy grin as he formally welcomed me. Entering the VIP lounge, I went to the customs area and looked past it to where Gafur was waiting, positively beaming at the sight of me and giving little skips of delight. With a look that brooked no interference from the customs officials, he hustled past them and clasped my arms.

"Ambassador! *Ja ochin rad, ochin ochin rad!! Leonid tozhe, i Kristina, Yulia . . .*"

His voice tailed off, then, collecting himself, he retreated back to his place behind the customs barrier.

Even the little man deputed to collect my luggage seemed to have a spring in his step, and he must have made a positive effort to gather it for once. He reappeared with the bags in only thirty minutes. He wheeled them out to the car, I following, with Gafur leading the way carrying my briefcase. He took the Union Jack from inside the Land Rover and fitted it over its silver mast, commenting that it was good to be flying it for the "real" ambassador again.

I had no Uzbek money on me, so when the porter had finished loading the bags in the back Gafur tipped him. I said I would pay him back, but he replied jovially, "*Ni nada,* Ambassador, *ni nada.*"

Gafur refusing money! This really was a red-letter day.

It was a crisp, bright Saturday morning in November. We hurtled round the city bypass at speed and in style, before turning left across the tram tracks and then shooting down a warren of twisting alleys between low houses, as we entered the Mahalla of the residence. Gafur beeped the horn joyfully as we approached the big green gates and they swung open, a sturdy guard on each. As I got down from the car, the guards came rushing forward to shake my hand and slap me on the back. They had not even waited to close the gates first, which was a serious security breach, but it didn't seem to matter on this glad morning.

Lena the cook, Reiapa the cleaner and Alijon the steward hurried down the steps to join in the general jollity. My bags were taken and carried up the steps as I went in to the lounge, where Fiona was waiting for me. She regarded me hostilely as Lena entered the room with me, taking my order for tea and porridge. Once alone, I embraced Fiona, but she glared at me defiantly through reddened eyes.

"Well?" she demanded. "What have you decided?"

"Fiona, darling, I am only just back. Let's talk about this later."

"No," she said firmly. "I want to know where I stand. Are you going to give up this floozy?"

"Look," I said lamely, "I can't just give her up. I haven't seen her, or you, for months. I need time to think things over."

"You've had plenty of time!" Fiona was shouting now. "If you're not prepared to give her up, I want a divorce. It is that simple."

"Look, I really don't see why we have to get divorced over it. I've had girlfriends before. And I can't just drop Nadira."

"Oh, no! I am not going through that again! I bet everybody in the embassy knows. Don't they? *Don't they?*" By now Fiona was screaming. Lena opened the door to bring in the tea, but beat a hasty retreat back to the kitchen.

"You don't know how horrible it is, everyone laughing at me behind my back. And all your little groupies thinking, 'Oh, Fiona, she's just stupid, Craig doesn't care about her.'"

"Darling, I don't think anyone thinks you're stupid."

By now Fiona's face was crimson, hot tears coursing down her cheeks.

"I must be bloody stupid to have put up with you. I can't stand it anymore."

She sank down in a chair and curled up, looking utterly defeated. I felt like a complete bastard. I knelt and put my arm around her, but she shook it off. Fiona lay there like something broken. I knew that I could mend her, end her nightmare, by simply vowing to give up Nadira.

But that was the only thing I could not do. If I let Nadira go, she would fall back into something even worse than Fiona was experiencing. And I was convinced that my one chance of personal fulfillment lay with Nadira. Even to think of her name gave a dull, deep echo from the base of my heart.

Why did Fiona need everything to be so black-and-white? Why was she forcing on me a choice I wanted to put off, when I was just off the plane? An unjust resentment made me feel peevish. I didn't want clarity. For the last ten years my personal life had been swathed in ambiguity, comfortably cocooned in gray mists of vaporous duplicity. I had a wife I loved, and wonderful children, a comfortable and well-ordered home.

And I had wonderful, madcap, booze-fueled evenings out, full of wit and wrongdoing, and a string of mistresses. It was like living inside *Die Fledermaus*. It was cosmopolitan and somehow both sophisticated and adolescent. It had all worked so well for me. But only by Fiona's indulgence, her willingness to swallow small lies, to look the other way, and to forgive me when caught out.

Now a very public crisis had hit, one that could not be papered over. I was confronted with the reality of all the agony I had brought Fiona over many years, now come to a head.

The door opened, and Emily put her head around it.

"I thought I heard mummy crying." Then she saw me.

"Daddy! My daddy! My daddy!" she screamed, and came running toward me, arms outstretched, the tails of her nightdress flapping. I swept her up in my arms, whirled her round and round, shook her playfully from side to side, her legs swinging, and buried my head in the long, warm hair on her shoulder.

The next morning I woke up with a slight pain in the small of my back. That day Carl and Kristina came to the residence, separately, to brief me on what had been happening in the embassy, and bring me papers to read. By the end of that day, the pain in my back was worsening. I asked Fiona to rub some linament into it, but she refused, so I got Emily to do it instead.

The following morning, Monday, I woke up and had difficulty getting out of bed. The pain in the small of my back was extreme. I struggled to dress, hobbled down to breakfast and ate my tea and toast lying on the settee. I just couldn't get back up again—my stomach muscles seemed paralyzed. I rolled onto the floor, put my hands on the coffee table and pushed myself up into a kneeling position. Fiona had come in, and was eyeing me contemptuously.

"I can hardly move," I gasped. "I think there's something seriously wrong with me."

"Good," she said, "I hope you die."

Apparently not forgiven, then.

I got myself upright, and a concerned Lena straightened my tie and handed me my cashmere coat. When I left Tashkent I was banned from the embassy. I did not recall having been formally unbanned, but I was going to reenter it now, having got back against all odds. I was going to do so with a straight back, a firm step and a smile on my face, even if it killed me.

I tried to get down from the Land Rover without any sign of trouble, but the pain made me sweat so that my clothes were drenched. I had great difficulty bending and unbending my midriff. As I got back into the embassy the staff overwhelmed me in a wave of affection, and I had to endure numerous hugs and slaps on the back. In fact, I too was so elated by the moment that the pain lost its edge. Most of my staff were in tears.

Some things had changed. The flag car was a new, top-of-the-line Discovery with leather seats. My office was now upstairs in the former dining room, large and luxurious. Kristina was in the ballroom, which was partitioned by curtains to make a conference room also. The defense section was in my old bedroom, and in the other former bedrooms were Daniel, Leonid and Victoria. Registry was now more spaciously housed in the former kitchens.

The downstairs staff had all followed me through the embassy to the foot of the old residence staircase. There they stopped and applauded as I walked up, and the upstairs staff had gathered on the landing and were applauding too. I almost didn't make it up the stairs. The pain was incredible. I was willing my body, with every last ounce of courage, to walk up those steps. The pain of keeping my back straight was indescribable. I couldn't breathe and my vision kept going. My smile must have looked like a rictus. Kristina later told me that everyone just thought I was overcome with emotion.

Finally I was alone in my office. Kristina brought me a cup of tea. I confided to her that I was sick, and asked her to phone Dr. Reimers to make an appointment for 1 P.M. Nadira lived close to the clinic, and I called on her en route. She was delighted to see me. She felt distressed because she had not understood what was happening to me in September, and had thought I was just making up a story. For the first few weeks I was in the hospital I had not contacted her, or indeed anyone. But finally messages started getting through to her. She really loved me, and in early summer had believed I was going to change her life and rescue her from what seemed an inevitable path to prostitution. She had believed those hopes dashed in September, then they came alive again.

Now she mopped my brow as I tried to gulp tea. I had a presentiment this illness might be serious and I might disappear again, so I gave her more money and told her to believe I loved her.

Ten minutes later I was lying on a bed in the international clinic. Dr. Reimers looked really worried, and called Dr. Ellen and their local staff. I was soon in an oxygen mask. My blood oxygen levels were down. Anything above 95 percent is normal, and anything below 90 percent is not sustainable. I was at 88 percent. Dr. Reimers thought it was pneumonia, while her colleague Dr. Ellen thought it was pulmonary embolism. An X-ray didn't establish which, but showed it was very serious and in both lungs. They decided to treat me for both. I was on a drip, and they injected antibiotics into the bag. They put blood-thinning injections straight into my midriff. I was in so much pain, I didn't feel needles. Dr. Reimers said they couldn't give me strong painkillers because I was going to need all my fight.

Then it happened for the first time. I couldn't breathe. Normal breathing happens without effort, and we don't notice the muscles that do it. But I seemed to have lost their use. I simply couldn't breathe. The pain in my chest was incredible, growing into an all-engulfing blackness. My body thrashed hopelessly and I half fell out of bed. Dr. Ellen screamed for help. Doctors came running and more injections went in. The oxygen supply was turned up until I could feel real force inside the mask. Suddenly, pain eased and I could breathe again. Dr. Reimers had been counting down the blood oxygen reading.

"Eighty-eight—eighty-five—seventy-eight falling quickly now— seventy-two—seventy-seven—seventy-two again—sixty-five! Christ! Sixty-five!"

That had been real panic. It was back up to the high eighties again. Surely I wasn't going to die now?

Dr. Reimers was talking to me.

"Ambassador Murray? Craig? Can you hear me?"

I nodded.

"Look, don't panic now. I know it feels bad, but Dr. Ellen was right. It's pulmonary embolism. Now we know what it is, we can treat it. Just a couple of months ago we had an American lady who had it, and she's fine now and back down in Samarkand. There's an air ambulance on the way here from Germany to take you back to London. So don't worry."

"I don't want to go back," I gasped.

Fiona came in. She looked worried, but seemed more angry than sorry.

"I am not staying this time," she said. "Emily and I are finished here. We're going back to London. There's no room on the ambulance. We'll go back British Airways. I gave the tenants notice to quit some time ago."

Suddenly she looked close to tears. I found I had nothing to say and no breath to say it with. She had kept up a tremendous, lonely vigil in Tashkent, but it was time to finish it now.

"Yes, I understand," I gasped.

Fiona melted away. Time passed, then it came again the second time. I gasped and tried to shout out, but couldn't. My back arched involuntarily until it was well clear of the bed. My head was banging against the bedstead. Dr. Ellen was holding my hand. I blacked out. A few hours later I came to. Dr. Reimers was opening my eyelids and looking into my pupils with a pencil torch.

"Don't worry," she said, "four more hours and the ambulance will be here."

Everything looked bright orange. I felt nauseous. I was not conscious of breathing at all, but could hear myself doing so in tiny, fast gasps. Then the pain came again, and this time it seemed to last and last, even after everything went black. Suddenly the pain took on a different quality, and my lungs seemed like blocks of ice. My feet were freezing, numb and hurting. Where was I? I opened my eyes. My chest didn't just feel pressed on; it was actually strapped with thick, luminous green belts. My back was uncomfortably resting on what felt like a plank, narrower than I. My eyes squinted. Consciousness was returning and I could see I was in a narrow tube, packed with equipment, plugged into me by a variety of tubes and cables. It was a plane! I was in an airplane, but a very small one. The door was open, and outside was a dark airfield apron, tiny crystals of snow swirling in the arc lights. That feeling of cold was real—it was incredibly cold. If I hadn't been strapped down, I could have reached an arm through the open door.

A man in a bright orange jumpsuit climbed a couple of steps into the plane, sliding the door closed behind him. It was so cramped he had to lean over me to stand beside my stretcher. He tucked the thin blanket delicately over my feet.

"Mr. Murray, good morning," he said jovially. He had a light voice with just a tinge of German accent. "It is four o'clock on a fine November morning. We are refueling in Murmansk, in the Arctic Circle. It is forty degrees below freezing. This is not good. But from now on, your life gets better. You are going to live. Just now, though, sleep."

He gave me an injection and I slipped away, thinking, Murmansk? Bloody Germans. No sense of direction.

I OPENED MY eyes again. Light was streaming through a large picture window. It was in St. Thomas Hospital.

"Are you awake, Mr. Murray?"

It was a pretty young Irish nurse I remembered from my stay here during my nervous breakdown.

"Would you like breakfast? Dr. Bateman says you can take your oxygen mask off to eat for a few minutes."

There were Rice Krispies and soggy toast. I was indeed back in St. Thomas's. It was three days since I had passed out in Tashkent. I was in the room next to my old one, a mirror image of it.

I was wheeled down for one of those scans where you go right inside a large machine while dyes are pumped into your bloodstream. An instruction kept coming through an earpiece for me to take a deep breath and hold it, but I could do neither, only breathe in shallow, quick gasps. That afternoon Dr. Bateman, a cheery, brusque character, came to see me, trailing a cloud of junior doctors and students. He looked at the scan results.

"Worse than I thought," he said breezily. "Multiple bilateral pulmonary emboli. That means, Mr. Murray, that both your lungs are full of blood clots. We can disperse them over the next few weeks with blood thinners. But you've had a close call. Wonder what caused it. Any history of embolus in your family?"

Not to my knowledge. Shortly afterward Professor Kopelman, my psychiatrist, came in and asked how I was feeling. I told him weak, and disappointed after that huge struggle to get back to Tashkent.

"Yes, we've all been wondering about that," he said. "Toxicology have run a whole range of tests, but not found anything yet."

An enigmatic comment, but now that the crisis had passed I was thinking along the same lines. It was an incredible coincidence that, returning against all the efforts of the government to keep me away, I had instantly succumbed to near-fatal illness—and without obvious cause.

Pulmonary emboli can be caused by deep vein thrombosis—DVT— and I developed this forty-eight hours after flying to Tashkent. But that convenient explanation has holes. DVT normally shows as a sharp pain in a leg or arm—you don't get DVT in the small of your back. I had no leg or arm pain. On top of which, it was only a six-hour flight, plus time on the ground in Yerevan, and I was in a comfortable business class where I could lie down. I had stayed hydrated, walked around a lot and even worn flight socks. Also, DVT was unlikely to result in both lungs being clogged with numerous clots.

Even had I developed a DVT, it would still be weird that after the hundreds of flights in my life, it was this disputed return that did it for me. But I don't buy the DVT theory. I simply don't know what really happened. I am intensely suspicious that, when powerful people had tried to get me out of Tashkent, I should immediately almost die on return there.

But it isn't too convincing to shout, "I have just been released from psychiatric care, and now they're trying to kill me."

So I kept my counsel.

All my friends now advised me not to go back again, but I was more determined than ever. It was a mixture of bloody-mindedness, of the belief I was doing an important job in Tashkent and of a desire to get back to Nadira. It was also professional pride—I wanted to prove that now, with better staff, I really could run a successful embassy.

My mum came and visited me in the hospital, which was very good. I had a happy childhood. I have two brothers and a sister, and we grew up poor, happy and extremely close. It's the sort of family where just remembering each other's existence makes you feel warm and supported. Fiona and Emily came, and Fiona and I took the first tentative steps toward building a new and different kind of relationship. I apologized for all the hurt I had caused.

Tony Crombie's investigation chuntered on, and I was preparing as best I could to defend myself. Kate Smith continued to be a help. The

Diplomatic Service Association (DSA) was affiliated with a real trades union, the FDA, and a real trades union official, Paul Whiteman, had been appointed to help me.[1] Paul was a chirpy fellow a bit younger than me, with thinning curly dark hair, an open face and spectacles. He had the weary air of someone who had seen it all before. I met him first with Kate Smith, and ran through the story, giving him a mound of papers to study.

On about our third meeting, Paul looked up at me, and said with an air of surprise, "You really are not guilty of any of this, are you? In fact, it's the most appalling attempt at a stitch-up I've ever heard of. And so badly done too."

He was now wholeheartedly with me, and a great support. I also met Gareth Peirce, the legendary human rights lawyer, then as now working for those detained for years in Belmarsh prison, held not only without charge but without even having been told why.[2] I was rather awed to meet her. She too was outraged at my treatment and anxious to help.

In December I had my interview with Tony Crombie. Most of the charges were easily answered. The accusation about girlfriends being given visas in return for sex came down to a single person—Kamola. I had rather suspected from the reference to buying air tickets that it was about her, but why the plural "girlfriends"? The evidence that we had sex was allegedly that I told someone so.

The only surprise came at the end of the interview when Crombie, an unimpressive, fumbling man, rather dramatically produced a sheaf of papers.

"There is an additional allegation," he said, "which, with the allegation of talking about the allegations, makes number twenty. Do you know this woman?"

The papers were a visa application. The photo was of a beautiful young woman named Albina Safarova, born in 1985.

"No," I replied, "never seen her before in my life."

"It says here on the application form," said Crombie, searching carefully, "HMA instructs issue. Now why would it say that?"

"Well," I said, "anyone can write that. It's plainly not my handwriting, and it's rather extraordinary there's no signature to that note."

"There is also," said Crombie, "a note from Lorraine Douglas, the visa officer. She says that you instructed issue."

The note read as follows:

From: Lorraine Douglas, Bogota
Sent: Tuesday November 18, 2003
To: Tony Crombie

Subject: CONFIDENTIAL—STAFF INVESTIGATION
    With regards to the points you raised:
    a) The visa issue to Albina Safarova, I did write on the back of the VAF
"HMA instructs issue."
    b) I was verbally told by Steve Brown and Angela Clarke that Dermot
Hassett was a contact of the ambassador. I have never seen them together,
however I think Dermot actually stated on the letter in question that he was
a good friend of the ambassador, or words to that effect.
    I hope that this clarifies the points you raised regarding the written
statement.

                                        Regards
                                        Lorraine Douglas

"Actually," I said to Tony Crombie, "she doesn't say I authorized issue. She says she was told I did. You know, I am one hundred percent certain that I have never even heard of Dermot Hassett. The expat community in Tashkent is very small. Now why would Steve Brown and Angela Clarke tell Lorraine Douglas he was a friend of mine?

"Another thought," I continued. "Have you ever run a visa section? No? I thought not. Well, I have. I have never known an entry clearance officer who would simply issue a visa to someone because they were a friend of a friend of the ambassador, even if the ambassador told them personally, let alone someone else saying so. They would at the very least insist on a signature from the ambassador. And I have known plenty who would still not accept that. To anyone who knows anything about immigration work, this doesn't add up at all."

Crombie looked crestfallen.

"Then how do you explain the letter from Dermot Hassett?" he demanded. A photocopy of this undated letter was also attached. Hassett's letter in support of the visa application of his fiancée was addressed to Steve Brown and included the line: "I can also confirm that the ambassador Mr. Craig Murray is also aware of these facts."

"Well, again, anyone can write that. I repeat to you," I said, "I have never, ever heard of Mr. Dermott Hassett. What does he say?"

"I am not talking to people outside the office. This is an internal investigation."

"Which is why it is useless."

The interview was over.

"What on earth was that about?" I asked Paul.

Paul looked at me intently. "Had you really never heard of him?"

"Honestly, not at all."

"In that case," said Paul, "what this is about, is that they know they can't put a finger on you on all the other stuff, so they've actually fabricated some evidence."

A YEAR LATER I gave the Safarova papers to Bob Graham, a highly seasoned investigative reporter of the old school. He tracked down Dermott Hassett, who confirmed to him that he had never met me. Astonishingly, he told Bob Graham that the British embassy had asked him to write in his letter that I knew all about it. He had thought it strange, but as he had been told that it would help the application, he had done it. I believe that this was indeed an attempt at the last moment to fabricate evidence against me, once it became clear the original charges wouldn't stick and I wouldn't resign.

Tony Crombie finalized his report, and he sent it to another senior diplomat, Edward Chaplin, later British ambassador in Baghdad. Chaplin agreed to Crombie's recommendations. The decision was that on seventeen of the now twenty charges, there was no case to answer.

But nonetheless, the whole affair was my fault. The recurrent phrases that dominated the report were "poor judgment" and "failed to show the judgment expected of a senior member of the diplomatic service."

My so-called involvement in the Safarova visa case was therefore "poor judgment," even though I had never even heard of the woman or her application. My remarks on the MCS review, which I had never made, were "poor judgment." The report refused to face the fact that the majority of the allegations had no evidence to support them, and were plainly both false and malicious. It was all covered in layers of fudge, and if there was any fault, it was mine. I was allowed one read of this report, which was then officially destroyed.

Three allegations went to a hearing:

Allegation 2, "that he regularly turns up at the office drunk or hungover and late before going home to 'sleep it off,' then returning to the office at 16.50 demanding people start work with him."

Allegation 12, "that he frequently takes the flag car out (with driver) until 02.00–04.30."

Allegation 19, "that, contrary to instructions, you discussed the allegations with your staff."

It was deemed that none of these potentially constituted gross misconduct, which was strange, because if true, Allegation 2 certainly was. There was therefore no tribunal, just a hearing before the director of corporate resources. Dickie Stagg had replaced Peter Collecott in this job, which was a major improvement. Dickie is bright, honorable and sensible. Goodness knows what he is doing in a senior position in the FCO. Had he been in post a year earlier, I doubt the administration could have done what it did to me without his trying to call a halt.

It turned out that the reason the charges were said not to constitute gross misconduct was that the evidence in both cases related to just a single incident. Staff in visa section had said that, on a single occasion, I had told them I was going home to sleep off a hangover. I can't remember it, but it was quite possibly a joke. The car misuse was similar. Paul Whiteman was at the hearing and simply said there was no case to answer. Dickie Stagg agreed.

I was found guilty, however, of talking about the allegations—again, an impeccably Kafkaesque result. I didn't do any of those things, but I talked about being accused of them.

I had to be found guilty of this, because I had already been judged. Sir Michael Jay had at the end of August banned me from my own embassy for talking to staff about the allegations, so to acquit me on this one would be to criticize the great Sir Michael. I had indeed told Kristina, but I felt personally that being in the middle of a nervous breakdown, brought on by these same false allegations, ought to be some defense. The office disagreed and I was given a written warning, stating that if I stepped out of line at all in the next twelve months, I would lose my job.

I had a right of appeal, which in a further Kafkaesque twist was to Sir Michael Jay. He listened with scarce politeness, and upheld the original decision. I made several written requests to Jay and Stagg requesting an investigation into how such a huge raft of untrue allegations came to be launched. I especially wanted a formal investigation into the Safarova visa case, which I believe revealed a potentially criminal conspiracy to frame me. I was turned down flat. The official investigation had concluded that my own poor judgment was the root of the whole problem.

For Christmas, I joined Fiona, Jamie and Emily at Gravesend, sleeping in the attic bedroom. We had a busy few days. When a household splits, you need an extra set of everything, and we spent several days shopping for everything—including car, computer and television—for Fiona. Shopping is fun, and these were surprisingly tension-free times.

I returned to Bryan's flat, from where I got medical clearance in mid-January to go back to Tashkent.

CHAPTER 17

Tashkent Again

I HAD INSISTED TO LONDON THAT CARL BE ALLOWED TO RUN THE embassy in my second absence, unlike the first when Adam Noble had been brought in above him. The staff were happy to see me on my second return, but it was more muted than the first. I was still not fully recovered, and tired easily. Most afternoons I slept on the sofa in my office. I was also worn down mentally by all these struggles. I was to discover that my experiment—I believe a successful one—in a more dynamic style of ambassadorship was at an end. I had achieved real influence through my approach, but only so long as the Uzbeks believed I had the British government behind me. It was now plain to all that this was not the case. There was real amazement among the diplomatic corps that an ambassador could survive such a determined attempt by his own government to get rid of him, and every bit of the media battle had been pored over in Tashkent. But whereas I had been a force, I was now more of a curiosity. My powers of analysis and depth of knowledge were still respected, and I was firmly a hero to the Uzbek opposition. But that could not disguise the grim fact that I had to struggle hard against becoming a lame duck. I was not sure I had the strength or the courage for that fight.

At least my private life had resolved itself and I was able to enter a new phase of happiness with Nadira. She was waiting for me in the residence when I arrived, and had sat up all night to be sure to be awake when I came in. It was a rapturous reunion. As the weeks went by I was to learn how truly devoted she was, and her support and kindness became essential to me. On her part, the love I had professed for her offered a dream in which she had never quite dared to believe. It now came true.

* * *

I HAD LOST A friend and ally. Richard Conroy, who ran the UN office in Tashkent, had been killed in an air crash shortly before my return.

An Uzbek came to see me on urgent business, having traveled from near Termez on the Afghan border. He refused to give Kristina or Leonid any details of what he wanted to discuss, and was most distressed when he discovered there would be an Uzbek interpreter at the meeting. He was, however, placated when I told him that I would trust Leonid with my life, and he sat down to tell his story.

He claimed that Conroy had come down to Termez to meet an important contact on counternarcotics business. This contact had formerly been an important player in heroin smuggling from Afghanistan, either direct or through the mountains of Tajikistan. He had subsequently fallen out with his erstwhile collaborators in the regime, and had written to Conroy offering full evidence of government involvement in the narcotics trade, and particularly the personal involvement of President Karimov and Minister of the Interior Almatov.

My visitor's story ran that Conroy had flown down to meet this man in Termez, and had been returning with him to Tashkent to formalize the evidence for the United Nations. An SNB agent had accordingly been placed on the plane by the government to shoot Conroy and the informer. The SNB man sat behind them and had killed both with a shot through the back of the head. What the SNB man did not know was that the government had also placed a bomb on the plane, just to make sure.

I thanked the visitor for his information. I told him that from my own sources I had no doubt that the Karimov regime was indeed involved in narcotics smuggling. But I had some difficulties with this version of events.

First, I had heard from many sources the rumor going round Tashkent that Richard Conroy had been shot through the back of the head before the crash, but given that everyone on board died, how did people know what had happened? Had it, for example, been radioed in to the control tower? I found that my visitor too could offer no satisfactory explanation of how he could know about the shootings from behind and who sat where.

The second doubt, which I kept to myself, was that this did not sound like Richard. A gentle man, deeply interested in economic development, he was a rather timid soul and the last person who would jet off to meet with an informant from the narcotics trade. He just wasn't that dynamic. The UN had multiple interests in the border at Termez, including the importance of the crossing for regional development and the flow of humanitarian aid, and indeed the UN, EU and the U.K. all had various counternarcotics programs involving this border. As titular head of the UN effort in Uzbekistan, Richard could visit the antinarcotics project. But to become operationally involved? It just didn't sound like Richard at all.

I thanked my visitor. After he had left, I asked Steve Brown to come see me. Steve had been heavily involved at the time of the air crash, and had helped Dr. Reimers to identify the corpse of Richard Conroy, and of one other person for whom we had consular responsibility.

This had been dreadful. The corpses had been badly charred, and were nearly all legless torsos, their lower halves having been scraped away as the bottom of the aircraft sheared off when it plowed along the ground. The bodies were laid on the floor in a hangar. The *hokkim* of Tashkent had tried to stop the identification effort. Looking at the grim and fragmented remains, he had instructed that each grieving family be given one corpse, or collection of bits; it did not matter which. Steve Brown had done a terrific job standing up to him and insisting that our protected nationals must be identified.

The *hokkim*'s callous instruction was a part of the usual Uzbek reaction of quickly clearing away any mess in order to return to the image of perfect harmony in Karimov's paradise. The aircraft wreck had been simply bulldozed away within a few hours of the crash, and new turf and paving put down immediately over the scars on the ground. Pilot error was blamed; there was never any attempt at proper investigation.

I had commended Steve to the FCO for his courage and perseverance in these dreadful circumstances—the charnel house smell had been overwhelming—and he had been awarded a £1,000 bonus for his efforts.

I now asked Steve if he had heard the various rumors about Richard Conroy's death. He had. I then asked him if there was anything about the corpses that might give credence to them.

He said there were two things that he did not understand. When he lifted the charred head of the first corpse for the doctor to cut into the cheeks, the brain had plopped out of the back of the skull, hitting his trousers and then landing on the floor. He had to pick it up and scoop it back into the skull. A human brain is a very slippery thing to hold, he said, like trying to pick up a handful of scrambled eggs.

Then the next corpse had done the same, and he made a strange discovery. The base and back of each skull had been cut away. A large rectangular chunk of every skull was missing, cut out by something like a circular saw. We both pondered but could think of no reason why an autopsy should have done this. I had seen many autopsy photos in Tashkent but had never come across this procedure. And here the cause of death was very straightforward—what could they hope to learn from cutting out the backs of the skulls? And why had the backs of the skulls not been replaced—indeed, where were they? Presumably the procedure had been carried out after the corpses had been moved to the makeshift morgue, or they would have had to be moved with their brains spilling out.

Steve and I thought about this for a while. Only one idea seemed to make any sense.

"Do you think," I asked, "that the backs of all the skulls could have been removed to hide the fact that two of the skulls had their back missing?"

We pondered some more. To put it at its weakest, if Richard Conroy's skull had been intact, it would have disproved my visitor's assertion that he had been shot through the back of the head. But with the mysterious absence of the back of the skull, you couldn't simply discount it.

"No obvious exit wound," said Steve. "But frankly, it was a bloody mess. There's one other thing, which Daniel first pointed out to me. There was one more body than the Uzbeks said there was, or than the passenger and crew lists showed."

"Are you sure? It wasn't just a case of a jumble of body parts?"

"No, I'm quite certain. There was one head more than there should have been."

In real life not everything gets neatly resolved, and I got no further with this. The extra person could, of course, most likely have been just an extra passenger let on by a friend of the crew without paying. But the mystery of the skulls remains open. Richard was such a nice man that I would somehow prefer it if his death had purpose. I like the idea of this quiet man leaving his desk for an adventure into some real counternarcotics investigation. But I don't quite believe it, and don't suppose I will ever really know.

ONE THING WAS PLAIN: nothing had caused the United States to waver one iota in its support of Karimov. John Herbst had left and been replaced by a new ambassador, Jon Purnell. A likeable and easygoing man, reputed not to be immune to the attractions of the opposite sex, the creased and homely Purnell came over as less of an ideologue than Herbst. At the end Herbst had left a bitter man. He had actually believed the U.S. propaganda about their ally Karimov, and only at the very end of his time in Tashkent did it seem to dawn on him that the Uzbek government had no intention of keeping any promises on democratization and liberalization.

I don't think Purnell ever believed it. But it was still his job to argue it. I first met him at another IMF lunch. He declared that he had every confidence in the Uzbek economic policy, for the simple reason that there were seventeen U.S. civil service advisers embedded in key positions in Uzbek economic ministries. I intervened to say that left us with two possibilities—either they were being ignored, or they were giving crap advice. Purnell looked shocked, but there was general merriment and an air of "Craig is back. Now things will be less boring again."

Donald Rumsfeld arrived in February 2004, and held talks with President Karimov on making the U.S. base permanent, and on support for Israel at the UN. The Americans had hit on the happy idea that it was a strong propaganda coup for a "Muslim" country like Uzbekistan to support Ariel Sharon's partition plans—as Karimov duly did. After his visit Rumsfeld gave a press conference in Tashkent and praised Karimov in these terms: "I am delighted to be back in Uzbekistan. I've just had a long and very interesting and helpful discussion with the president . . . Uzbekistan is a key member of the coalition's global War on Terror. And I brought the president the good wishes of President Bush and our appreciation for their stalwart support in the War on Terror . . . Our relationship is strong and has been growing stronger."[1]

I was able to use Rumsfeld's visit to achieve one thing. In my absence Mrs. Mukahadirova, the sixty-three-year-old woman who had taken the photos of the boiled body of her son Avazov and got them to the British embassy, had been tried for doing this. She was sentenced to six years hard labor for "dishonoring the good name of Uzbekistan." She would not have survived this sentence. I arrived back to find everyone tut-tutting but, as usual, no one doing anything effective. The U.K. had the local EU presidency, and I organized EU action with the Uzbek foreign minister. I also made plain both to the Uzbeks and to the Americans that I would kick up a major fuss during Rumsfeld's visit, including at his press conference. The pressure worked and, two days before Rumsfeld arrived, her sentence was commuted to a fine. Daniel, who had done much good work on this, came to tell me in delight, and I authorized the embassy to pay the fine for her. These small victories were very dear to us.

The German ambassador told me that the Open Society Institute, formerly known as the Soros Foundation, was being closed down by the Uzbek authorities. This was a definite sign that the Uzbek government was moving decisively away from the path toward democracy.[2]

In Uzbekistan the Soros Foundation did excellent work in education, including curriculum development, and provision of textbooks and other materials. They also worked on gender issues and in supporting the formation of local community groups to try to build up civil society. Following the "velvet revolution" that brought democracy to Georgia, the deposed Georgian president Edward Shevardnadze had flown immediately to Tashkent, and cautioned Karimov against the influence of international NGOs. Karimov therefore moved to act against them. A new registration process was introduced, which the Soros Foundation was deemed to have failed.[3]

I had decided to adopt a more clean-living style to reduce London's scope for criticism of me; in consequence I was taking care to get to work at 9 A.M. On Monday, March 29, 2003, I was up early, feeling in fine fettle. I gave Nadira a lingering kiss good-bye and set off from the residence in the flag car around 8.30 A.M.

We immediately ran into traffic jams. Something was plainly up—policemen were blocking the traffic everywhere, apparently at random, and the little knots of green-uniformed policemen who generally hung around on every corner, idly extracting bribes from passersby, were all swarming like a disturbed hive.

The traffic on my route got stopped every day at nine-thirty while Karimov passed; a sanitized corridor some four blocks wide was put in place every time he moved. This took an awful lot of manpower, but with forty thousand uniformed policemen in Tashkent, plus the same number of plainclothes security personnel, and slightly fewer Ministry of the Interior troops, this was not a problem. But Karimov seldom varied his timing, and this was not the calm, practiced morning routine.

Gafur worked his way to the embassy along a series of loops and back roads. When we arrived, the staff were gathered in a gaggle in Steve's office. Leonid explained that there had been a series of bombs in the city. As usual there was a complete media blackout of any bad news, but the telephone wires were buzzing and one youth radio station had reported a bomb in Chorzu market, before the station was taken off the air.

Giles Whittell of the *Times* had arrived to interview me, accompanied by a photographer he had hired locally. I told him I was going out to see what was happening, and invited him to join me. He jumped at the chance—this was the nearest thing to a scoop a journalist was likely to get in Uzbekistan. We piled into the Land Rover and headed for Chorzu market.

We didn't get far before we were stopped by a police checkpoint. Gafur tried another way, met another block, and then another way, another block. Sometimes we managed to get through a checkpoint; Gafur was good at bluffing, and while the union jack on the front and the diplomatic plate usually cut no ice with the police, in the pervasive air of chaos on this day we were having a little more luck. I told Gafur to tell the police that we were responding to a request from President Karimov for Scotland Yard to help with the investigation, a happy invention that may have had some effect. But every time we made a little progress there was a further layer of roadblock; we worked our way around, like getting through a puzzle maze. But at last, and rather to my amazement, we found ourselves in the heart of Chorzu, at the site of the bomb blast.

The location was just outside the market, in an enclosed triangular space between buildings, with something of the air of a courtyard. The buildings were of Russian colonial date. Two looked institutional, three stories high with large windows divided into small panes of glass. The third side looked like a squat, low warehouse building, perhaps disused, with plain windows heavily darkened by dust and cobwebs. The yard was cobbled, with a small railed area to one side containing a leafless tree surrounded by bare dirt; spring had not yet come to Tashkent.

The base of this triangular yard was perhaps thirty yards wide, with at most fifty yards from the base to the apex. So even at the center, you could never be much more than ten meters from a windowed wall. Yet I remarked that not a window was broken. Nor was there any other sign of an explosion. The tree was not damaged, there was no blood on the ground. I checked with the police, who confirmed it was indeed the site of the explosion. I found a policeman overladen with gold braid on his hat and shoulders. Adopting a conversational tone, I asked him if it was a large explosion. He just shrugged.

It was by now about 10 A.M. It was hard to make any sense of it all. Giles had found a stall holder who told him that there had been other bombs and that many policemen had been killed. I decided that the quickest way to discover what was happening would be to go and ask Zokirjon. Giles agreed to come too; I was a bit nervous about this, but I decided I could trust him not to expose my best source. This decision was based on my experience that, contrary to popular belief, British journalists are decent people with perhaps the strongest ethical code of conduct of any profession, a code within which the great majority of them work every day, in spite of constant temptation to break it.[4] So I decided I could trust Giles—but would Zokirjon take the same view? Anyway, we set off toward Syr Dar'ya.

Police were everywhere, with numerous checkpoints on every road, and drivers, passengers and luggage all being turfed out and checked again and again. Although not subject to search, we were continually delayed. As we came close to the president's residence at Durmen, security was particularly heavy. It seemed to take an age to get through all this. When finally we made it to Zokirjon's house, Giulia received us and insisted on making lemon tea. Zokirjon was not in, she explained, but we were welcome to wait until he came. As she said this, she motioned to us to remove our shoes, which she deftly collected and handed to a waiting man, who quickly moved to squat on the doorstep and start polishing them.

She would contact Zokirjon and tell him we were here. In the mean-time we could, if we wished, go somewhere cool to lie down. Perhaps we would stay for lunch? I caught her eye with what I hoped was a significant grimace, conveying "Do not offer them any girls." Just at that moment the details of hospitality at Zokirjon's house were not something I wanted plastered all over the *Times.* She gave me a secretive smile, which some-how conveyed without words that I shouldn't worry, she had thought of that already.

"We can't stop, Giulia," I explained, "it's a busy day. I was just hop-ing Zokirjon could tell me something about what's happening in town today."

"Oh, the bombs." She said it as though it were an everyday problem, hardly worth mentioning. "Would you like to speak to Zokirjon on his mobile? He is at SNB headquarters."

She picked up a phone, dialed the number, got a response and then handed it to me. Zokirjon's voice came through, loud and cheery as ever.

"Hello, my friend. Why you didn't call to say you were coming? I would prepare everything for you. Who are your friends?"

How did he know? Giulia hadn't told him.

"Journalists from England. But don't worry, they're OK. I trust them," I said, put on the defensive.

"If you trust, I trust."

"Giulia tells me you are at the SNB. What's going on?"

"A little trouble. When they have a problem, they call me in some-times to help."

"How big a problem?"

"Three, maybe four bombs. New style. Palestinian fashion. Is new style for us. They use girls."

"Many dead?"

"Not so many. Maybe six, maybe thirteen. We will recognize it later."

I relayed this to Giles. We wondered what "Palestinian fashion" meant, and both concluded that he meant suicide bombs, which at this time were at a peak in Israel.

One of Zokirjon's men indicated to us that there had been a further bomb—this time a car bomb—outside the president's Durmen resi-dence. On the way back we tried to get through to check, but could not get past the final checkpoint at the tractor factory. However, we had a clear view of the road running past the residence, and there was no sign of the kind of damage you might expect from a car bomb.

At Giles's request we stopped at this point to pose with the Land Rover and the flag, while the photographer took some shots for Giles's article. The photographer had said little all day and had become more and more nervous; he was now frankly terrified that he would get into trouble through his association with us (and that was, of course, a very real possibility). As we headed back to the embassy he started expressing his concerns volubly to Giles. It was past noon by the time I returned to my office, and Giles and the photographer left me to go do some interviews with dissidents.

Back in the embassy I sent a telegram to London reporting what I had seen so far and what Zokirjon told me. I also said that in the absence of any direct threat to the embassy, I did not intend that we should close. After speaking with Carl, I agreed to the temporary closure of the visa section in order to radically reduce public access to the building. The embassy was full of rumors about what had been happening.

The Chorzu bomb had allegedly gone off when the police were mustering in the square for a change of shift; it was said to be a woman suicide bomber and many police had been killed. Separately, a number of police had been killed in shooting incidents. A very large bomb had gone off near Bokhara. A car bomb had gone off at the Durmen residence, and a separate female suicide bomber had exploded outside Dietski Mir—the "Children's World" shop.

These were the main elements in a fairly consistent picture of what was happening, emerging from contacts across the city, from the international news agencies and from other embassies. But there was still no mention of it on Uzbek radio and television, and consequently the rumor mill was working overtime. The fact that you heard something from several places did not necessarily give corroboration—it could all just be repeating the same source. The absence of a free media not only prevents accurate reporting of information, it causes the wildest rumors to fly. At this stage I remained skeptical, largely because of the absence of any physical evidence of explosions.

The Children's World shop was close to the embassy, so I got in the car again to go there. This suicide bomb had allegedly gone off around nine-thirty—either just before or just after we had passed the spot in the morning on the way to Chorzu market.

At this site, and indeed on the way to it, there was a curious absence of policemen. We could park right outside the shop, and I got out and looked around. Again, no hole or crater or burn marks from the explosion. No blood. But the Plexiglas back of a bus stop was being refitted, and one of the large display windows of Children's World had evidently just been replaced—unlike the other windows, it had no signs transferred on, and there were puttied fingerprints around the edges. But none of the adjoining windows appeared damaged.

I called on a British engineer who had an office in the same building. There had been an explosion, he confirmed, a small one. Judging by the blood smeared on the road, there had been fatalities, or at least serious injury. But within minutes the police and fire department had arrived and simply sluiced everything down. Broken glass had been brushed up and glaziers appeared as though by magic. I asked whether there had been any attempt at all at forensic investigation.

"Not that I saw. Buggers just washed it all away and tidied it all up."

That evening I attended a couple of diplomatic functions, first at one of the Arab embassies and then at the German residence, where I arrived seriously late. Embassies had been exchanging information on what had happened. A consensus was developing that there had been one suicide bombing at Chorzu, at the site I had visited, which had hit a police muster parading for a change of shift. Six policemen had been killed. The second suicide bombing, at Children's World, had occurred when a female suicide bomber had been challenged by police; she had run, been shot at in the street and then detonated, presumably prematurely. At the Durmen residence a car bomb had detonated after being fired on at a police checkpoint. In Bokhara there had been a large explosion the evening before when police had raided a bomb-making factory. Finally, police had been shot at two checkpoints, and there was some sort of protracted shootout in process near the Durmen residence. Most estimated about twenty dead in all.

There was a German parliamentary delegation at their ambassador's residence, and he was on tenterhooks in case I infected them with any anti-Karimov sentiments. Like the U.S., the Germans had an airbase in Uzbekistan, the German one being at Termez. At least the U.S. diplomats had, by and large, the good grace to signal occasionally that they found canoodling with Karimov distasteful. The Germans seemed positively to relish it.[5] On this evening the German ambassador materialized at my elbow every time I spoke to one of his MPs. As it was late and had been a tiring day, I wasn't about to enter into controversy anyway. I found his attentions amusing rather than annoying. But I did make clear that I was skeptical about the official version of events.

I was worried about the lack of blast damage.[6] Enough of a bang to kill six people is going to leave some kind of damage on the ground, and certainly break windows that are fifteen yards away (and made of poor-quality glass). A car bomb worthy of the name will certainly leave a crater. I knew there had been at least one explosion, but from the damage it seemed more likely to be something like a hand grenade rather than a suicide bomb—people blowing themselves up generally go out with a bang, not a whimper.

Furthermore there was no history of bombing by Uzbek dissidents. There had been three bombs in Tashkent in 1999, but they had a different signature. They had been very large, very professional and very murderous, killing scores of people and doing a lot of damage to buildings. They had been tightly timed to go off in quick succession.

No serious analyst believed that these were really the work of the Uzbek opposition or the Islamic Movement of Uzbekistan. It was generally believed they were the work either of Karimov or of a faction in his regime. The regime certainly used them to outlaw the democratic opposition, and Mohammed Salikh, the leader of the Erk party who had stood against Karimov in the first post-independence election, was convicted of planning them and sentenced to death.[7]

The most popular theory in 1999 was that the man responsible was Ismail Jurabekov, who had controlled Uzbekistan's vast cotton industry. An immensely corrupt and wealthy man, he had been sacked and denounced by Karimov a month before the 1999 bombings, and came back into power immediately after them. It did not take long before people started to point out that this time too, he had been sacked a month before the bombings. But if it was him again, he must have in the meantime lost the use of professionals in the security services, because these bombs did not compare in professionalism to those of 1999.

This history wasn't the only thing that gave me pause. There had never been a suicide bomber in Central Asia. Why were they turning up now? And I got, from my own contacts, three more bits of information about the Chorzu bomb that changed the picture. The police normally did not muster in that yard. They usually mustered inside the fenced-off courtyard of the district police station. Only on that fatal morning had they received an order to muster in the nearby public yard instead. Second, a close friend's flat was in Chorzu, and she had counted thirty bodies laid out in plastic sheets, not six—yet there was no evidence of enough blast to kill even six. Third, and perhaps most significant, the evening before in Chorzu market the police had beaten a stall holder to death for not having the correct tax papers. This kind of brutality had become standard in the crackdown on the private trading sector, but a beating to death in public was unusual and a near riot by stall holders had ensued.

So we were left with conundrums. If there had been a planned operation involving suicide bombers across Tashkent, and in Bokhara, why had Chorzu market been the unlikely first target? Why not the procurator's office or the Ministry of the Interior? (It was a curious fact that, with Tashkent swarming now with police, there was no extra security at either of these two places and a suicide bomber could penetrate right to the lobby without challenge. It was, as I noted to London, as though the authorities knew where would and where wouldn't be a target.) How did the choice of Chorzu market police as first target relate to those police killing a stall holder there some twelve hours before? Why were those police told to muster outside, and not in their usual protected courtyard? How had so many died but no windows been broken? Why was there no forensic investigation? I knew there had been none at Children's World, and I had arrived at Chorzu less than three hours after the alleged explosion and found everything pristine there too.

There was further, and extremely strong, evidence that this was not the Islamic terrorist attack the authorities wished us to believe. It came from intelligence material. We had communications intercepts of the senior leadership of the Islamic Movement of Uzbekistan and of al-Qaida, based variously in Pakistan, Saudi Arabia and elsewhere. The airwaves were fairly humming with their traffic. They were all phoning each other up, and what they were saying precisely is: "Does anyone know what the hell is happening in Tashkent?"

None of them did know.

This was very inconvenient for the Americans, who desperately wanted it to be al-Qaida. The timing could not have been better—a fact that is worth bearing in mind. Two weeks later Colin Powell was due to certify to Congress that Uzbekistan was making progress on human rights and democracy, a certification necessary for certain aid payments.[8] Plainly Uzbekistan was in fact making no progress at all, and an attack by al-Qaida just at this time would divert attention from this. But here was concrete evidence from intelligence that neither al-Qaida, nor the IMU, had any part in the planning but were desperately trying to work out what was going on.

The U.S. response to this difficulty was to interpret it away. One record of a telephone call between two senior IMU figures had one asking if the other knew what was happening, and the other replying that he didn't know, but it seemed like some kind of "new group" was behind the Tashkent bombings.

There was an incredible footnote to this intelligence report from the U.S. National Security Agency. It explained that when the IMU said it appeared to be the work of a "new group," it did not actually mean a new group. Rather the new group was women, and this was the first deployment by the IMU of female bombers. There was some additional explanation about translation from Russian of the term "new group." The last struck me as particularly odd and I checked carefully—in fact the Russian words used were precisely analogous to "new group" in English.

I sent a sarcastic response to this report. It had, of course, no effect on Washington, who were now fully steamed up to attack this "al-Qaida" outrage and to pledge full support for their ally Karimov. Colin Powell rolled into action. As Giles Whittell reported: "Yesterday Colin Powell, the US Secretary of State, hinted broadly that American assistance would be forthcoming, particularly since the regime in Tashkent is under attack from Islamic militants linked to al-Qaeda. The US has thousands of troops based at the Khanabad airbase in southern Uzbekistan, which is used as a staging post for operations in neighbouring Afghanistan. Yesterday a State Department spokesman said that General Powell had telephoned Sadyk Safayev, the Uzbek foreign minister, and offered American help in containing the insurgency."[9]

Colin Powell must have known this had nothing to do with al-Qaida. But was there actually an insurgency, or was the whole thing cooked up by the Americans and the Uzbeks? Had they gone so far as to plant a few small bombs and kill off a few policemen themselves? If I am losing your sympathy and you don't believe such a thing is possible, I suggest you read Graham Greene's *The Quiet American,* and acquaint yourself with the historical truths behind it.

The Uzbek procurator general called a series of press conferences, to which the diplomatic corps were summoned along with journalists, where he gave a briefing on "facts." No questions were allowed. At the first he said the evidence was that these attacks were carried out by al-Qaida and Hizb-ut-Tehrir. At the second press conference he produced an alleged homemade suicide belt, and said that the bombers had each detonated explosives equivalent to about four pounds of TNT.

Having seen the sites of the explosions, I was certain that this last was totally untrue—the force of the explosions had been less than a tenth of that at most, something more akin to throwing a hand grenade. It could have been just bullets. It was also explained that eleven people had died near Bokhara, where police blew up an alleged bomb factory. After attending two of these so-called conferences, I declined to attend a third. Not only was no one allowed to ask questions, I felt the serried ranks of ambassadors were being used to give, for the benefit of the international journalists present, a spurious weight and credence to the rubbish the procurator general was spouting.

So what really happened in this "insurgency"? Well, the definite facts are as follows. On the evening of March 28, police attacked a home in a village outside Bokhara. There was a large explosion and eleven were killed. Uzbek authorities claim homemade bombs exploded. Local people claim the authorities shelled the house.

The same evening police beat to death, before a crowd in the marketplace, a stall holder at Chorzu market, after he refused to go to the police station to have his papers checked. He was a middle-aged man with a young family, with no particularly strong religious or political affiliation.

During the hours of darkness, two policemen were shot and killed in Tashkent in separate checkpoint incidents. The next morning, around first light, the police of Chorzu district were ordered to muster for a change of shift, not in their usual compound but in the triangular court-yard. Six policemen were alleged killed by an explosion at that muster, and one female, allegedly a suicide bomber. There was, however, no blast damage to windows, ground or vegetation. A reliable eyewitness I inter-viewed personally saw many more bodies taken away. Giles Whittell told me the hospital authorities were under strict orders not to give out any casualty figures.

About 9:30 A.M. a young woman was seen, dashing out from the pavement beside the Children's World store, running between two buses.[10] She was shot by two policemen with automatic weapons. She sank to her knees and then there was an explosion. Eyewitnesses could not say if she activated a suicide bomb, was carrying a bomb detonated perhaps by the bullets or was hit by a grenade or similar device.

Around the same time a small car—a Tico—failed to stop at a police checkpoint on the road going past the president's residence, at the adja-cent tractor factory. The car was fired on with automatic weapons and exploded. The procurator claimed this was a car bomb. Again I could find almost no evidence of blast damage.

In the course of the next forty-eight hours police raided a number of premises, chiefly in the Durmen area. Allegedly these were sieges, but I found eyewitnesses to two of the raids who said shots were fired only by the police. At least thirteen people were shot dead by police in these raids.

About a week after these events I was able to interview the parents of one of the alleged suicide bombers in my office. They had an interesting tale to tell.

They had two daughters, their only children. The younger was called Dildora; I am afraid I have forgotten the name of the other. The elder was a brilliant linguist; she spoke seven languages and had entered uni-versity. She was also a notably religious Muslim; she had asked her father if she could take the Muslim *hijab*, or head scarf. He had refused because it was banned at university. Both girls were in their late teens. They liked pop music, and were interested in boys, although neither had a steady boyfriend.

They showed me a picture of the girls, happy on holiday with their parents. They wore jeans and makeup; one had sunglasses perched on her hair; they had uncomplicated smiles and looked relaxed; they and their parents were standing with linked arms. They looked modern. It was a happy family photo.

Then one day in December, over three months previously, the girls had vanished. They just walked out the door one afternoon and never came back. They took nothing with them that you wouldn't take if you just nipped out to the shop. They did not say good-bye or leave a note.

Both parents were in floods of tears and I gently coaxed further details from them. There had been no argument; nothing had changed recently in their pattern of behavior; there were no boyfriends. I asked if they had given any impression of sharing a secret. The mother said on two occasions in the previous week the elder girl had received phone calls. They had been quite long, but the girl listened a lot and said very little. Afterward the girl had not volunteered who had called or what about. The mother had not asked, not wanting to seem to pry—she had, she said, been a teenager too, and as she gazed at her husband her rigid mask of misery dissolved for a second, but re-formed almost instantly. The phone call was perhaps nothing, but now she wondered . . .

Her voice trailed off. She was in an agony of self-reproach with which I could empathize—should she have said something? Could she have stopped it? Could she have saved her baby's life? I reminded her that the calls could well have been completely innocent, and unconnected to the disappearance. She gave me a half smile, grateful for my effort.

The parents had been frantic when the girls hadn't come home that evening. The next morning they had reported it to the police. The police told them to come back if the girls hadn't returned in three days. They had called every relative, every friend, every classmate. No one had seen them. No one had noticed anything wrong.

After three days they returned to the police. They were escorted from the police station to the headquarters of the secret police—the SNB. There they had given again the full details, and a great deal of information about the girls' habits and acquaintances. They were strongly questioned on their religious views. They had told the SNB about the two suspect phone calls, giving the approximate date and time. One desperate week later they had returned to the SNB for an update; they had been told the calls had been traced and were not significant. The SNB would not tell them who had made the calls. At the end of the interview the SNB officer told them they should best consider their daughters dead. A few days later two men in leather jackets who said they were SNB, but did not show any ID, arrived at the home and removed most of the girls' possessions.

About six weeks after the girls had vanished, they received a phone call from the elder. She had said they were OK and "in the north." She then quickly hung up. The bewildered parents conjectured she meant either the north of Tashkent, or Russia. They immediately reported the call, giving precise details of the time, to both the police and SNB. When they urged them to trace the call they were met with blank indifference.

About two weeks later they received a phone call late one evening from an unknown man; he asked if they wished to see their daughters. They were instructed to leave their home immediately and proceed to a location in Tashkent, where they should get into a white Daewoo Nexia.

They phoned a close relative and asked him immediately to phone both the police and SNB with the details of the rendezvous. Then, dawdling as much as they dared, they proceeded to the appointed spot, where they found a white Nexia parked. Two burly ethnic Uzbeks in leather jackets were seated in the front seats. They paid no attention to their gestures to them through the windscreen. Uncertainly, the husband opened the back door. Still no reaction. They slid into the backseat, and the car set off without a word being spoken.

The car headed north, threading its way through a maze of streets in old Tashkent, before eventually emerging onto the main road to Bilraz. To their amazement, it stopped at the roadside in Durmen, right beside the long wall of the president's compound. There one of the men got out, and said his first word to them: "Come!"

They got out and stood beside him on the sandy verge. He lit a cigarette, put it in his mouth and clapped his leather gloved hands together to keep warm on this frosty January night. They squinted into the headlights of oncoming vehicles; plainly their taciturn guide was expecting a car to arrive from the northeast, coming into Tashkent.

After about fifteen minutes a convoy of "five or six" vehicles passed them slowly, then drew up on the roadside some thirty yards behind them. I interrupted to ask what kind of vehicles. Saloons, not four-wheel drive, and mostly white, but it was dark with only orange sodium lighting.

They hurried toward the convoy, the mother stumbling and hurting her ankle. Their guide swore and barged ahead of them. The rear near-side door of a car in the middle of the convoy swung open. It was a white Lada Volga. They hastened to it, casting hurried glances into each car as they passed, looking for their daughters. The cars they passed each held three or four men similar to their own escorts. When they reached the open door, sitting in the back, dimly illuminated by the feeble interior light, was their oldest daughter.

She was resting back against the seat, on the far side from the curb. She looked happy to see her parents, but made no move toward the empty seat nearer them as they stooped to thrust their heads and shoulders inside the car. The mother moved to enter the vehicle, but was roughly hauled back by the shoulders, by their escort.

The daughter motioned to them not to try to come closer, but her smile appeared bright. She spoke to them briefly, assured them that both she and her sister were well and "being looked after," and told them not to worry. She then waved, and leaned over toward them—not to hug them, but to pull the door closed. The car hooted its horn, and the whole convoy headed off, including the vehicle that had brought them. A little farther up the road, still within sight, it turned off to the right. The next day the father visited the scene and decided this turning was just a way to get back onto the main road, heading whence they came.

They were left standing in the dark and cold. Relief that their daughters were alive mingled with despair at this brief meeting.

In Tashkent, as in the rest of the former Soviet Union, almost any vehicle will act as a taxi, and they quickly flagged one down. The driver grinned at them. "You're asking for trouble, standing outside the president's residence."

On return home they confirmed that their relative had contacted both the police and SNB as requested, and then they called them. Neither the police nor SNB had done anything about following them, or not anything they were prepared to admit to.

That was the last time they saw either of their daughters alive. Things fell into a settled routine after that. The hurt was slightly dulled by the knowledge that the girls were alive.

Until the morning of the Tashkent bombings.

That morning the SNB came to their house at two-thirty. They were taken down to SNB headquarters, where they were locked in a cell. They were not told why. At eleven-thirty an SNB officer entered and told them that their daughters were dead, and had been terrorists and suicide bombers. They had been allowed to return home.

Two days later the body of Dildora was returned to them. She showed, they insisted, no signs of injury other than a burned hand and a small burn mark on her stomach. I asked how small, and the father said about the diameter of a walnut. There was no puncture wound anywhere on the body. Nothing, her father said, that looked remotely like a cause of death. Her face was blue, but he anticipated my next question and said he could see no strangulation marks on the throat.

They had been told their second daughter was also dead, but no detail had been given, and no body returned.

Having told their story, they sat looking at me expectantly. I was once again uncomfortably aware that I had gained an inflated reputation in Tashkent as a righter of wrongs, and I felt inadequate. What I could do was listen, sympathize and assure them that there was a world opinion that cared about the truth, whatever the disregard of the authorities in Uzbekistan for that commodity. They thanked me and left.

So much didn't add up here. The Children's World bomb had gone off about 9:30 A.M. The SNB had apparently been unable to trace the girls for the preceding three months, but knew seven hours in advance that this was going to happen and took the parents in? And the evidence was clear that the dead girl at Children's World had suffered bullet wounds and an explosion, yet if the parents were to be believed, the body showed no such trauma. The burned hand and round burn mark were much more typical of torture cases, and the blue face? A favorite method of torture, used frequently all across Uzbekistan by the security services, was to place a gas mask on a victim's head and block up the filters. This had the advantage of suffocating without leaving telltale marks.

Even harder to understand was the late-night rendezvous. It was inconceivable that a convoy of vehicles had been able to pull up outside the president's residence without being challenged—and what terrorist group would run such a completely unnecessary risk?

To make matters more complex, I spoke the same day with Monica Whitlock of the BBC. She had been shown photographs by the authorities, said to be of Dildora's body, and it had been well and truly blown up. She had also seen photographs of the aftermath of one of the suicide bombings, featuring a severed head in a tree. I wondered if the blown-up body had been the other sister, and speculated that a photo of an exploded body doesn't necessarily say much about who exploded it, and a photo of a head in a tree not much about who put it there. She cautioned me about disbelieving things just because the government of Uzbekistan said them. I said that experience tended to point me that way.

I have skipped ahead from the date of the "insurgency" to complete the picture of why I was so dubious of the U.S./Uzbek version of a concerted al-Qaida attack. But from day one I had been sufficiently skeptical to question in detail the official version, both in diplomatic telegrams and in secret reports on intelligence channels sent to the JTAC—the Joint Terrorism Analysis Center. In my reports I made absolutely explicit that I was taking issue with the United States government's line that this was Islamic Movement of Uzbekistan and al-Qaida activity. I made plain that I believed the U.S. security services were ignoring or willfully misinterpreting the intelligence data. Rather to my amazement, JTAC agreed with me, and in two official analyses of the situation, drawing on all available sources, said that claims of involvement by IMU, al-Qaida or Hizb-ut-Tehrir could not be substantiated.

What do I now believe? Well, with all knowledge subsequently gathered, I think this was most probably an Uzbek government operation, possibly in agent provocateur mode. It is most likely that some form of attacks was carried out by young people who believed they were fighting for Islam, when in fact they were being kept, armed and targeted by the SNB. It is possible that the SNB themselves carried out some of the attacks, and then left a woman's body conveniently behind. They could certainly have arranged the police to muster outside, and I can't think of any other organization that could park a convoy outside the presidential compound. Did they take Dildora's parents in, seven hours in advance, and keep them locked up, in case the girls made a break for home or a phone call? Perhaps the missing one had already escaped. This is speculation. It is also worth noting that the only government figures killed were highly disposable junior policemen—why was no more important political target attacked?

I am absolutely certain that the State Department blamed al-Qaida, even though they knew this to be false. The U.S. had come under growing international attack for its support for Karimov's despicable regime. This "insurgency" was as politically useful and timely for Bush as for Karimov. Do I think the CIA had a hand, if the SNB organized it? Well, I bet they at least knew about it in advance.

One person who was distinctly put out by my refusal to believe the official version was that enthusiastic Warrior on Terror, Simon Butt. Six months later he was still furiously resentful, as he was writing a "staff appraisal" on me as he left his job (to become deputy high commissioner in Islamabad). He fumed in astonishment, "His first reaction to the terrorist bombings in Tashkent in March was to suggest the Government of Uzbekistan itself was responsible."

Plainly I am a deeply disreputable character.

CHAPTER 18

Once More unto the Breach

FOLLOWING THE TASHKENT DISTURBANCES THERE WAS, AS MIGHT be expected, a security crackdown. Thousands of actual or suspected dissidents were arrested in a huge sweep by the security services, and extra-judicial killings continued. One lady who was released came to tell me of the torture she had suffered while chained to a radiator in the basement of the SNB headquarters in Tashkent. She said that more than four hundred women were held in the basement, in eight small rooms and the corridor. There was nowhere to sit or lie on the floor that was not sticky with blood and urine.

At this time I first got to know well my neighbor, an aged professor who lived opposite the gates of the residence. He was blind and crippled; I was shocked to learn that both these were a result of beatings sustained in five years spent as one of Karimov's political prisoners. He had been a senior official of the now-banned Erk opposition party. His daughter had taken over that role, and she was for some time among the women in the SNB basement. One of her sons was now arrested, and the other on the run. Shortly after her release, she was assaulted by thugs on the lane where we lived and, while she was pinned down, paint was poured into her mouth and her legs broken with an iron bar. I gave the guards instruction that they were to admit any of the family to the residence at any hour of the day or night, and told the family to fight their way over to my gate if attacked in their home. The professor had a posse of great-grandchildren who played table tennis on an old trestle table in their front garden.[1]

A peculiar phenomenon soon became apparent in Tashkent. The police were arresting the wealthy. Anyone wearing Western clothes, or driving a Western car, was being stopped on the streets and, unless a senior government employee or family member, was taken in and held. It became apparent there were two strands to this. First, people were simply being shaken down for cash. Five thousand dollars was typically required as a bribe for release. To give an idea, that is substantially more than the cost of a Tashkent apartment. The police were cashing in big-time. Second, it also fit the general crackdown on any kind of independent private sector.

Our reception was filling up with people waiting to see me about such cases, when suddenly I had a desperate and brief phone call from Nadira. She had been arrested and taken to Jubilerski police station. Concern for her safety had precipitated us into the decision that she should abandon her apartment and move into the residence permanently. She had been arrested as she went to pick up her belongings.

I told Carl what was happening, and then dashed to the police station with Leonid and Gafur. As we pulled up outside, Nadira came rushing out and waved at me, then fell heavily down the station steps, injuring herself. She was bundled back inside by three leather-jacketed policemen. I had not seen it, but her legs had been kicked from under her when she had made a run for the door, on seeing the car. When I entered, she was sitting crying on a rough bench in the outer office of the station.

She was hysterical with fear, and it took me some five minutes to calm her down. Eventually she gasped out that they were trying to get her to sign a confession to being a prostitute and to trying to overthrow the government. That may sound a laughable combination, but this was no joke.

Leonid was explaining who I was to a leather-jacketed policeman behind a desk. Two others were standing in front of it. One repeatedly hit a large lump of wood off a concrete pillar, scattering large shards in all directions. The other had drawn his pistol and kept pointing it around, including at Nadira and at me, making firing noises with his tongue. Leonid was struggling with Uzbek police who, as usual, plainly had no idea what an ambassador was. But they seemed unimpressed. It should be recalled that they had for several days been given carte blanche to do what they wanted to the wealthier section of the population. Nadira, in her jeans and fashionable jacket, wearing the watch I had given her, must have looked an easy touch.

I called Leonid over and whispered to him, "This doesn't look good. Go outside and call Zokirjon. Tell him where we are and what is happening."

"But why?"

"Just do it."

Nadira pointed to the policeman with the pistol. "He said he would rape me."

The policeman looked at her furiously, stepped forward and screamed something at her in Uzbek. Nadira cowered, petrified.

"What did he say?" I asked.

Nadira just shook her head, crying. "What did he say? I can't help you if you don't tell me."

A female voice spoke behind me in English.

"He said that now he is going to kill her."

I looked round. A tall, elderly Russian lady stood by the wall, clutching her handbag tightly. She smiled at me encouragingly. She was Nadira's landlady, who had been meeting her to take back the keys of the flat, and who had extremely courageously come along to try to help when the police had pounced. She had an evil opposite number: on a bench sat a hunched old woman in a head scarf, kneading the bench with arthritic hands. Every street, every block of flats had its secret police informant, and this crone fulfilled this function in Nadira's block. She had already signed a statement to say that Nadira brought home men at all hours of the night, and had been seen carrying explosives.

The young policeman was waving the gun round again. I walked up to him, inside his gun arm, until our faces were touching. Mine was working with fury.

"You are not going to kill anyone, you fucking little cunt!" I spat in Russian. His eyes opened wide in surprise. "Now sit the fuck down and keep your stupid mouth shut."

Gafur came in and stood beside me. I walked to the desk and spoke to the senior policeman.

"Arrest that man," I shouted, pointing to the now-seated policeman. "He just threatened to kill that girl. There are witnesses. Arrest him immediately."

But he wasn't about to be bullied.

"But really, it is none of your business."

He turned to the third policeman, who had discarded his bit of wood. They spoke in Uzbek, and the policeman advanced toward Nadira. Gafur and I physically blocked him, and Leonid came back in and started speaking to the senior policeman in placating tones.

Just then the station phone rang, a white old-fashioned one with a dial. The policeman seemed inclined to ignore it. I rasped at him to answer it; something in my voice convinced him, and he did.

It was not Zokirjon, but someone senior in the police, whom Zokirjon had phoned. It had worked more instantly than I had dared to hope. The policeman straightened and adopted a respectful tone on the phone, and the whole room fell quiet. Then he put down the phone, apologized for the misunderstanding and started berating the old woman informant for false information. He said we were free to go. I asked for, and got, the witness statement against Nadira, which I tore up in small pieces and handed back to him. There was nothing to stop them from making another, but it seemed a wise end to tie. We had to carry Nadira back to the car, and we gave a lift home to the landlady, who declared she had finally made up her mind to leave Tashkent back to Russia. Nadira was on crutches for three weeks, but her mood recovered much quicker than her legs.

Now THAT MY relationship with Nadira was becoming regular, I met her parents more often. They had, in fact, moved to Tashkent for professional reasons. Nadira and I joined them for lunch one day, and I was given a bowl of soup containing the breastbone of the lamb, the bridegroom's portion. After lunch her father and I sat and discussed life over a bottle of vodka; he was a wry and interesting companion. In Uzbekistan, they have a dowry system where you pay for your bride. Eventually, with a bright twinkle in his eye, her father turned the conversation to this subject.

"Craig, you know our local customs regarding marriage?"

"Yes. Of course, I am happy to make an appropriate present for Nadira."

"You know, you should pay more if a girl is beautiful."

"Yes, I should jolly well think so."

"And Nadira is beautiful, is she not?"

"Yes, very beautiful."

"And you know, you should pay more if a girl is educated."

"I can see that."

"And Nadira has a university degree."

"Right."

"You know, you should pay more if a girl speaks foreign languages."

"Really?"

"And Nadira speaks five. Uzbek, Persian, Russian, Turkish and English."

"Hang on, Uzbek doesn't count."

"OK, she speaks four. Still, that's expensive. And she is the girlfriend of the British ambassador. That's valuable."

"But I'm the British ambassador."

"Yes, but think how much another man would pay for the former girlfriend of the British ambassador . . ."

We opened another bottle of vodka, and dissolved into giggles.

PARLIAMENTARY ELECTIONS were due in December 2004. The Uzbek government was instituting a new bicameral parliament with a second, upper house. This was a sham, as only President Karimov's supporters could stand for election, but nevertheless the EU had wasted millions of euros of aid funding on consultants who had helped draw up rules of procedure for Karimov's new puppet body.

The Uzbek opposition had historically wasted more energy attacking each other than they had spent on opposing Karimov. Nevertheless, after some excellent groundwork by a young man named Greg from the International Republican Institute, they had finally agreed to come together and consider forming a united opposition front. To this end, those of the party leaderships who remained within the country had agreed to hold a joint conference in the town of Kokand, to adopt a common platform with the aim of fighting the December elections together.

I was deeply skeptical that they would be allowed to participate in the elections.[2] But I thought the idea of uniting the opposition was highly desirable. I was invited to attend the conference, and set off one bright Saturday morning for the Ferghana Valley with Sasha, a new driver, and an old dissident poet named Mabit as my interpreter.

We had not long left Tashkent when Sasha pointed out that we were being followed by a Daewoo containing four leather-jacketed men. We stopped for tea at a *chaikhana* in the town of Angren, and the Daewoo stopped too, the men getting out and sitting at a table close to us. When we left, they again followed.

When we reached the control points at the tunnel into the Ferghana Valley, we were stopped for longer than usual. As we approached Kokand it was evident there were far more police checkpoints than usual. Several times they tried to stop us, and twice told us that Kokand was closed and tried to divert us down side roads. I ordered Sasha, who was very nervous indeed, just to keep on and ignore them, eventually instructing him not to stop at all at checkpoints, which resulted in several policemen diving into hedges to get out of the way. Sasha was sweating and his hands were visibly shaking on the wheel. All the time, that Daewoo was behind us. Otherwise the roads were empty except for police vehicles.

Finally we arrived at the main checkpoint before Kokand itself. At this point the road was a divided highway. One lane was blocked by red-and-white concrete-filled oil drums. Across the other was a trestle table. In front were two policemen, pointing their automatic weapons straight at us. At the table sat a fat policeman, his cap and uniform smothered in gold braid. Sasha stopped the car and looked at me inquiringly.

"Go and tell them it's the British ambassador, and I *am* coming through," I said.

I wasn't confident Sasha could deliver this with conviction. He got out and spoke to the decorative policeman, returning to get the car documents from the glove compartment. A great deal of conversation ensued, with documents being perused, and details of the documents read over police radios. After fifteen minutes of this, I ran out of patience. I got out of the vehicle, walked over and snatched the documents from the table. I picked up the police radio and threw it into the cotton fields. I ordered Sasha to get back in the car and drive through the roadblock, then I grabbed the front of the table and tipped it up, spilling the papers and pens into the fat policeman's lap. I had not realized it was on trestles, so the whole tabletop fell down smartly onto his lap; judging by his face, this hurt. The policemen behind me were panicking and waving their automatics in the air. Sasha gingerly edged the car past the collapsed policeman and his table, and we drove on into the town.

Little old Mabit the poet was jumping up and down on the front seat, hooting out of the window at the police, tears of laughter streaming down his old cheeks. He turned to me. "I have," he wheezed, "lived my life under Stalin, Brezhnev, Andropov, Karimov. I have waited so long to see someone do that!"

He roared again with helpless laughter. Just then, the Daewoo that had been following us for so long leaped out of a side street and drove, at speed, straight at the side of our car. It must have gone round a side way while we were stuck arguing at the checkpoint. I am not sure what happened next; Sasha spun the wheel and we slowed sideways, while still traveling on the same plane down the street. The Daewoo sped by, missing us by inches, and landed in the ditch as Sasha spun the wheel again and corrected us. He braked and halted, panting heavily, before driving determinedly on.

We reached the venue for the meeting, which proved to be the large, vine-covered courtyard of a private house. About sixty people sat on chairs facing a top table, at which sat the leading representatives of the parties. Represented were Erk, Birlik, the Free Farmers, the Peasants and Entrepreneurs' party, and numerous NGO and human rights groups. Together they were establishing a new force in Uzbek politics, the Democratic Forum. A row of journalists, including the BBC, sat at the back. Everyone appeared to be waiting for something to happen, and I was somewhat disconcerted when the chairman of the meeting, Ismail Dadjanov, told me it was me they were waiting for.

Ismail was a hearty-looking man with large spectacles who had a bluff manner and a natural air of authority. His hands were red and clawed. He was a vice chairman of the Birlik party, and some years previously a government mob had burned down his house with his wife and children inside. He had lost the use of his hands in his desperate but vain attempts to save them.[3]

I had come to observe the meeting, and I had not expected to be the main event—I had not even prepared a speech. But I stood when invited and addressed them, with Mabit interpreting in Uzbek. I said how much I admired their courage and bravery in working for freedom. I denounced Uzbekistan's state-dominated economic system and the lack of economic freedoms, the internal and external visa systems and the conscription of labor. I spoke of the need for freedom and democracy, and of my belief in the potential of the country and of the Uzbek people. It went down tremendously well, and I received a great ovation. After this, everyone signed a document founding the Democratic Forum, committing their organizations to work together until freedom and democracy were established.

Afterward I puzzled over the conundrum that this meeting had been allowed to go ahead. Many people who had tried to attend had been turned away, and particularly few delegates from outside the valley had got through, but the meeting had not been completely banned. I think part of the answer was that the government had good surveillance of the meeting and liked to have the opposition under easy observation. Afterward, we had the obligatory meal and much friendly talk. Several of those I met that day were to die in the Andijon massacre one year later.

BACK AT THE EMBASSY things were running well now. I had a good team, with Carl and Steve giving the management side the overhaul that was so badly needed, and relations between British and Uzbek staff rapidly improving. I was enjoying the opportunity to prove to London that, given half-decent staff, I could run a well-organized embassy. Everyone was very good about accepting Nadira, and Nick Ridout and his pleasant wife, Cathy, were the first to invite us, as a couple, to form part of a formal dinner party. This was kind of them, and went well, until after the meal when Nadira put on her Walkman. Plainly it was going to take some time for things to settle down.

Despite my efforts to avoid trouble, relationships with the Eastern Department were still poor, and once again a visit by Simon Butt was going to highlight these strains. This time I did not offer to put him up in the residence. He called at my office at the start of my visit, and rather took me aback by saying that I was not giving the Uzbeks enough credit for their reforms. I looked at him blankly, and asked what reforms he meant. He said that he was continually receiving letters from the Uzbek embassy in London outlining the steps being taken in economic and political reform; these seemed to him laudable. I was only reporting the negative.

I asked him for an example of a reform, and he said the Uzbeks had abolished two of the four counts liable to the death penalty. I explained that this was true. The death penalty had been abolished for genocide and for armed aggression against another state. But these counts had never been used. The other two counts, murder and attempting to overthrow the state or government, were frequently used and had not been abolished. Indeed, at the same time as the first two counts were abolished, the definition of attempting to overthrow the government had been widened, so that almost any opposition activity could now result in a death penalty. This was a move backward, not forward.

Simon left for a meeting, and I called in Daniel and asked if he knew anything about these letters from the Uzbek embassy in London. Daniel said that he had been receiving them regularly, but they were such obvious propaganda that he had done nothing with them. It had not occurred to him that anyone would take them seriously. I asked Daniel to find them and bring them to me, and he was right. Most of the claims on economic or political improvement were straightforward lies. I was astonished that London was paying any attention to this.

Simon Butt had a meeting that afternoon with Foreign Minister Safayev, and I received a phone call from Mr. Yusupov at the ministry to say that Safayev wanted to see Simon alone, without me. That was most irregular, so I sent a quick telegram back to London, requesting advice. When Simon returned for our lunch engagement, I told him about Yusupov's message, and I may have been mistaken, but I formed the impression it did not come as a surprise to him. Simon was, however, furious when I told him I had sent a telegram to request advice. Angela called me at lunch to say that a reply had come. We were to tell the Uzbeks that I was the ambassador, and Safayev could see Simon with me, or not at all. Simon was still more worked up, and said that he would send a telegram to get this overturned at a higher level. I was able to point out that the reply was from Sir Michael Jay. In fact, the Uzbeks quickly backed down and agreed to see me too.

In the car Simon again said that it was vital that we congratulate the Uzbeks on their reforms. I explained that these reforms were simply nonexistent. Simon referred again to the letters from the Uzbek embassy, and I said these claims were simply lies. Simon seemed horrified by this suggestion.

"Are you saying to me that these official letters from the embassy of Uzbekistan, from the ambassador himself, contain false information?"

"Yes, that's precisely what I am saying."

"But this is official government-to-government communication."

"I don't care. It's simply not true. If you don't trust me, ask Daniel."

"But how can you encourage reform without welcoming it when it happens?"

"Why aren't you listening to me? It's not happening."

Simon was not to be diverted from his line. On meeting Safayev, he immediately congratulated him on the reforms undertaken by the government of Uzbekistan, and said how much he appreciated his close relationship with the Uzbek embassy in London, and the useful information that they sent him. Safayev thanked him, and then turned toward me.

"I am afraid, Mr. Butt," he said, "that we have to make an official complaint against the British ambassador. He attended an illegal political gathering in Kokand. There he made a speech where he accused President Karimov of having a hundred thousand political prisoners, and of committing genocide."

"I said no such thing," I interposed truthfully. "I am happy to tell you what I did say."

"We know you said such things," said Safayev. "We have a tape of the meeting."

"Really, how?" I asked. "I should like to hear it."

"I assure you, Foreign Minister," said Simon, looking at me, "we take these accusations most seriously, most seriously."

In the car on the way back, Simon said to me, "I shall have to report this, of course."

"Report what you like," I said. "I didn't say those things. I essentially said the same as my Freedom House speech."

"Do you have a text?"

"No, I wasn't expecting to speak at all."

"That is very unwise. I never speak without a text."

"I can believe it."

"It means you can't prove your version of events."

"Except I have sixty witnesses. If you believe your mate Safayev, ask him for the tape. Look, I said nothing startling. The BBC was there, and other international broadcasters. Don't you think they would have reported it if I said Karimov had a hundred thousand political prisoners and was committing genocide?"

The Americans too were going into overdrive in their attempts to improve Karimov's image, and Freedom House was leading on this. Sikeena's replacement was a former minister from the Balkans, and they had a whole new agenda. The emphasis was on working with the Uzbek authorities. They brought out a Canadian pathologist to investigate, jointly with the Uzbek authorities, the case of an alleged torture victim. They held a major press conference to announce that he had died of strangulation with his belt and there were no other marks of violence. This was portrayed as vindicating the Uzbek authorities. In a second case, they announced that from photos of an alleged torture victim, the scars were healed and so could not have been the cause of death. It should be noted that these two cases were selected for investigation by the Uzbek authorities, but their findings were used by Freedom House and the U.S. embassy to argue that Amnesty International and Human Rights Watch were scare-mongering, and there was little torture in Uzbek jails.

THERE WERE TWO major highlights to our holding the local EU presidency. We hosted a visit by Chris Patten, external affairs commissioner, who was commendably robust with the Uzbek authorities and who took on board the unanimous view of the EU ambassadors that the EU's aid programs in the country were hopelessly misdirected.

On May 1, 2005, the EU expanded to admit the Eastern European states. This meant a lot to me personally as I had thrown myself into working heart and soul for this in Poland from 1994, when it seemed a distant dream, to 1998. On that day I held a party for all EU nationals in Uzbekistan, old and new, at the residence. This was a great success.

There was an amusing side to this EU expansion. Many more of the "new" EU member states had embassies in Uzbekistan than the "old" member states. Our new ambassadors included Poland, the Czech Republic, Slovakia, Slovenia, Latvia, Lithuania and Hungary. Uzbekistan had been a useful place for these countries to dump some of their old, communist-style, non-English-speaking diplomats. As a result many of the new EU ambassadors didn't speak English or French, and I found myself conducting EU meetings at which we had to keep switching into Russian as our only common language. Even more amazing, we were sometimes holding NATO meetings in Russian.

In May, I had to return to the U.K. for a six-month checkup on my heart and lungs. While there, I asked to call on Jack Straw, but was instead given an appointment with Bill Rammell, the FCO minister who had taken over responsibility for Uzbekistan. This was the only meeting or conversation I was to have with any FCO minister during my period as ambassador to Uzbekistan. This is a sad reflection on the fact that in the New Labour government, ministers' diaries were driven entirely by spin and the news agenda. If a crisis happened, and a country hit the news, it would get ministerial attention. The idea of quiet, unacknowl-edged work, to prevent a crisis, had no attraction to them. "Where's the headline?" was always the key question.

I was determined to persuade Rammell that we were making a funda-mental mistake in backing the Americans and Karimov. Rammell's heart was very much in the right place, but plainly he was a prisoner of his FCO briefing, which he held in front of him, and read to me. Simon Butt sat opposite me, next to Rammell's secretary, and he positively smirked as Rammell read out, "We believe it is essential that you encour-age reform by giving the Uzbeks full credit for reforms carried out."

He then recited a list of reforms, including the abolition of the death penalty counts. I explained patiently that this was all simple propaganda, and untrue. Rammell frowned, returned to his brief and said again that I must give the Uzbeks credit for steps forward. I replied that should I see any, I would.

As we left, I said good-bye to Simon on the staircase outside Ram-mell's office. Simon said that he wanted to see me back in his office about Safayev's comments on my speech in Kokand. I replied that I had to rush, but the comments were obviously nonsense.

"But I don't know that, Craig. You don't have any proof."

"Do me a favor. I don't need proof. Where's Safayev's proof? I told you before, the media were there."

"It really is difficult for me to know who to believe."

I was boiling with rage as I left. It seemed to me the general level of credence given to the Uzbek government was ludicrous, and to credit these completely daft allegations about what I had said . . .

Anyway, I had to run to an appointment just across Westminster Bridge in St. Thomas Hospital, for an ultrasound scan of my heart. The doctor undertaking the scan was chatty.

"You live in Uzbekistan, eh? Isn't that where the ambassador was accused of being naughty?"

But as the scan progressed he grew noticeably tense. At the end of the procedure, I was quite worried by his manner.

"Everything OK?" I asked cheerily.

"The consultant will be able to explain when he sees you," he said, hurrying quickly away. That appointment was not until I next returned to London.

Before returning to Tashkent, I called on Jon Benjamin in the Human Rights Policy Department. He said he had been surprised not to see me at the big meeting that had discussed my concerns over intelligence obtained by torture. There had been quite a heated debate, and while he had tried to argue the human rights case, in the current climate there had been no chance of reason prevailing. He wished I had been there. I said I wished I had too, but no one had told me about it. He said he was surprised, as the Eastern Department had been there.

I FLEW BACK TO Tashkent for what was to be the last time.

The story of Abu Ghraib had broken, and the U.S. torture and mistreatment of prisoners there. Jack Straw had made a public speech in response denouncing torture, which I considered in the circumstances to be monstrously hypocritical. Equally so was a circular to the diplomatic staff from Sir Michael Jay, which was issued while I was away, and I discovered on my return to the embassy. Jay's circular stated that we were unequivocally against torture, and should report any concerns we had about torture by our allies.

I was faced with a dilemma. I had been determined to keep my head down and do my job without further clashes with the FCO. But I could not abide such monstrous hypocrisy. After thinking it over, I decided to send another telegram, and to distribute it more widely and classify it less highly than my previous telegrams on torture and intelligence.

SUMMARY

We receive intelligence obtained under torture from the Uzbek intelligence services, via the US. We should stop. It is bad information anyway. Tortured dupes are forced to sign up to confessions showing what the Uzbek government wants the US and UK to believe, that they and we are fighting the same war against terror.

. . . This is morally, legally and practically wrong. It exposes as hypocritical our post Abu Ghraib pronouncements and fatally undermines our moral standing. It obviates my efforts to get the Uzbek government to stop torture . . .

DETAIL

In the period December 2002 to March 2003 I raised several times the issue of intelligence material from the Uzbek security services which was obtained under torture and passed to us via the CIA. I queried the legality, efficacy and morality of the practice . . .

I was therefore somewhat surprised to hear that without informing me of the meeting, or since informing me of the result of the meeting, a meeting was convened in the FCO at the level of Heads of Department and above, precisely to consider the question of the receipt of Uzbek intelligence material obtained under torture . . .

I understand that the meeting decided to continue to obtain the Uzbek torture material. I understand that the principal argument deployed was that the intelligence material disguises the precise source, i.e. it does not ordinarily reveal the name of the individual who is tortured. Indeed this is true—the material is marked with a euphemism such as "From detainee debriefing." The argument runs that if the individual is not named, we cannot prove that he was tortured.

I will not attempt to hide my utter contempt for such casuistry, nor my shame that I work in an organisation where colleagues would resort to it to justify torture. I have dealt with hundreds of individual cases of political or religious prisoners in Uzbekistan, and I have met with very few where torture, as defined in the UN convention, was not employed . . .

The torture record of the Uzbek security services could hardly be more widely known. Plainly there are, at the very least, reasonable grounds for believing the material is obtained under torture . . .

Nonetheless, I repeat that this material is useless—we are selling our souls for dross. It is in fact positively harmful. It is designed to give the message the Uzbeks want the West to hear. It exaggerates the role, size, organisation and activity of the IMU and its links with Al Qaida. The aim is to convince the West that the Uzbeks are a vital cog against a common foe, that they should keep the assistance, especially military assistance, coming, and that they should mute the international criticism on human rights and economic reform . . .

It seems to me that there are degrees of complicity and guilt, but being at one or two removes does not make us blameless . . .

MURRAY

I received a most tendentious reply, stating that there had been no such meeting "last week." I had not said it was in the last week, but "recently." This was typical of the tricky way the FCO nowadays responded to MPs and members of the public, but now they were applying the nonanswer technique to their own ambassador! The reply also referred me to a letter to Liberal Democrat MP Menzies Campbell. When this arrived by fax, I saw it did not address any of my key points. Plainly the FCO was not prepared to put in writing what I had been told back at my meeting with Kydd, Wood and Duffield.

CHAPTER 19

The Last Battle

I HAD BEEN UNDER THE STRICTEST INSTRUCTION NOT TO SPEAK TO the media in Tashkent, and was therefore surprised when the news department informed me that they had given permission to Nick Paton Walsh of the *Guardian* to do a feature article in May, along with a short documentary piece for Channel Four news. Nick came with his wife, Amy, and a camerawoman named Fiona. I let them follow me around with complete access for three days. The result was a four-page *Guardian* feature titled "The Envoy Who Said Too Much."[1] Here I spoke in public for the first time about my feelings of shock and betrayal when the false allegations had been brought against me.

A week later I was due to go on annual leave. I felt pleased indeed that we had managed to get the embassy working together so well after the traumatic events of the previous year. That summer the Eastern Department was due to have a complete change of all the relevant staff. Both Simon Butt and Dominic Schroeder were being replaced. I felt that we could achieve something worthwhile in the final two years of my posting, and that it would not be impossible to unite the international community to bring pressure for change in Uzbekistan. My health was the only major cloud on the horizon. I tired easily, and would have follow-up appointments in London about whatever had concerned the doctor in my heart scan.

Nadira had come with me to London when I had gone to see the doctors in May, and she was coming back with me on holiday now. She was really excited and loved London. The sense of freedom, the cultural mix, these are all things we take too readily for granted. The first time she had seen a policeman she had automatically moved to get out of his way, and the relief that you do not have to do that in London was a real joy to her. The fear in which people live in Tashkent is perhaps most fully appreciated when you see the joy of those released from it.

Just before I left Tashkent I received an e-mail from David Warren, the new head of personnel at the FCO. He instructed me to report to the FCO immediately on arrival.

Bloody hell, here we go again, I thought.

I replied that I was pretty tired out and had a lot of medical appointments. Could I not come later in the leave when I was rested? There was a curt response to this: No, I must report immediately.

An old friend, Bryan Harris, had kindly lent us his Docklands apartment for the summer. I left there on the morning of July 29 and went in by tube to the FCO, where I met David Warren, flanked by Howard Drake. I think it is fair to say that, from his initial appointment as my executioner, Howard had become ever more sympathetic to me as he saw what was unfolding, and we greeted each other in friendly fashion.

David Warren went straight to the point. He said that the breakdown in relationship between London and me was unsustainable, and that it was open to ministers to remove me as ambassador. I did not disagree, but said that I hoped that with the change of personalities at the London end, things might get better. I believed I had been treated very badly by the FCO. It would help if my concerns were taken seriously—for example, the FCO had simply not addressed the points I had raised in my recent telegram on torture and intelligence.

Warren countered that, in effect, the perceived breakdown was my fault. The FCO was not happy about comments I had made to the *Guardian*. I replied that I was suspicious of the news department's motives in setting up this interview, given the journalist's concentration on nightclubs and girlfriends. Warren then said, in effect, that the problems were my fault, and he warned me that the FCO did have the option to remove me from Tashkent and that was what would happen if the situation did not improve. This would not mean the end of my diplomatic career, as had been reported in the press; instead, I would be deployed elsewhere. I pointed out that while I did not want to get into the position of a standoff, it was unlikely that I would wish to continue in the service of the FCO if I was removed from my post in this manner. Warren said that this was certainly not what he wanted, as I was "a talented officer with a good record."

After this meeting I called round to the Eastern Department, where I met the new head of department, Simon Smith, an overweight man with a self-satisfied look, who regarded me with undisguised hostility. I supposed he had been briefed against me by Simon Butt. By contrast, the new deputy head, Andrew Page, appeared young, lively and genuinely interested. There is a minority of people who are in the FCO because they really care about trying to improve things in the world. There are a majority who like the power and the perks. On what was to be a brief acquaintance, I put Page with the minority and Smith with the majority.

Next stop was St. Thomas Hospital. There, a young female registrar looked at me far too gravely for my liking. She had the results of the scan, and said that the upper right valve of my heart was substantially enlarged, and the pressures in the heart chambers far too high. She was concerned it might be pulmonary hypertension, and was arranging an appointment at the national center at Hammersmith Hospital to check this out.

I didn't worry about this too much, and Nadira and I had great fun doing tourist stuff. We went to Hampton Court and the Cutty Sark, and to the theater. We went to Scotland with my uncle Tommy and stayed on Islay, visiting the distilleries that produce those wonderful, peat-flavored malts.

I came back for my first appointment at the Hammersmith Hospital, and came to earth with a bump. They carried out a number of tests, and again everyone spoke in hushed tones, with worried frowns. Then a nice lady came to my bed and asked if I had a bathroom on the ground floor, and someone to nurse me. They gave me leaflets. I couldn't read past the second line: "The mean survival period from diagnosis for patients with pulmonary hypertension is six months to three years."

Bloody hell. I was going to die, fast.

I was anxious to get back to Tashkent and work. I foresaw a repeat of the unpleasant wrangle over medical clearance of the previous summer, one of several ploys the FCO had tried to use to get me out of Tashkent.

I also had my five-yearly direct-vetting interview. Direct vetting, which used to be called positive vetting, is the security clearance system. A vetting officer had been assigned to my case, and had for some weeks been taking statements from people who had worked with me or knew me. This was the fifth time I had been vetted in my career, and it reached the same conclusion as before—I was unorthodox, but loyal and dedicated. The retired senior policeman who vetted me told me sympathetically that he had been set up with a false allegation early in his metropolitan police career. In my interview he was strictly and carefully neutral, but that opening comment established his sympathy. I was relieved; I had feared that the FCO would try to manipulate the vetting process to get rid of me.

It did. A couple of weeks after the interview, the policeman had called me in to see his report, which was fine. To my astonishment, I received a phone call from him a week later. He had, he said, been asked again to look at his conclusions. Could I answer a few more questions?

I should not reveal his name, but he was an honest and professional man and, without saying anything out of place, he made plain to me by his tone that he was furious at the pressure being put on him to find against me. At the end of the new process, he said that his conclusions remained unchanged.

In the meantime Dr. Thornton, a Foreign Office physician, had ascertained that, for a period, there was nothing to stop me from continuing to work. I would tire but not show many other symptoms, and then be liable to go out like a light. He put it to me that, when the heart attack came, I would have a greater chance of survival in London than in Tashkent. He said he would certify me fit to return to Tashkent, but personally recommended I stay in London. I said that I was not going to give satisfaction to those who had worked so hard to ruin my reputation and get me out of Tashkent. I had many faults, but not cowardice.

The medical clearance forms were signed. I was told that Dickie Stagg wanted to see me before I left, at four o'clock that afternoon.

I went round to the Eastern Department to tell them I was returning to Tashkent. They were in an internal meeting, and I opened Simon Smith's office door and poked my head round it to say good-bye. He looked annoyed at the interruption.

"Hi, everyone," I said breezily. "I just wanted to tell you I am on my way back. I got medical clearance and I'll fly tomorrow."

Andrew Page grinned and looked genuinely pleased. Simon Smith gave me a look that was undisguisedly hostile, mouth clenched, eyes steely behind his spectacles. That look conveyed to me not just dislike, but that he knew I would not be going back. I closed the door and leaned against it, wondering what could be happening. Presumably I would find out when I saw Dickie Stagg. Sweat rolled down my neck and my heart was fluttering wildly. As I walked down the stairs my vision turned orange. My legs felt heavy and my left arm seemed stuck out from my body. I stumbled along the wall, feeling my way into the ambassador's waiting room. There I flopped down on a couch and fell asleep, or passed out. About an hour later I came to, and walked gingerly out. The fresh air of St. James's Park revived me.

I called on Dickie Stagg at the appointed hour. He sat accompanied by the inevitable Howard Drake. There was, he told me, a problem with my direct-vetting status. I was not to return to Tashkent until it was resolved. I was incredulous.

"But there's no problem with my vetting," I said. "I have seen the report."

Dickie Stagg looked genuinely puzzled. He turned to Howard, who offered no help.

"Anyway, that will be resolved in due course," he said. "Until then, you are not to return to Tashkent."

I was not accepting that as the end of the interview. I asked if I might be able to see the vetting report again, accompanied by my trades union representative. Dickie Stagg agreed, and I went and found Paul White-man in the First Division Association offices. Paul was genuinely angry that the FCO was mucking me around yet again. He arranged to go with me early the next week and see the report.

The day before we went, I received an e-mail from a journalist called Stefan Wagstyl of the *Financial Times*. He introduced himself, and said that a telegram had come into his possession, allegedly written by me. It was my July blast against the receipt of intelligence obtained by torture.

The next morning Paul Whiteman and I looked at my positive vetting report in the basement of the Old Admiralty Building. I had wondered whether the FCO had in fact forced changes, but it was exactly as I had last seen it. Paul commented that there was nothing there to prevent my return to Tashkent, and plainly something else was going on.

It was. That same day the *Financial Times* had run an article about my telegram, with a few quotes from it. That evening, David Warren phoned me and said that I had been formally removed as ambassador to Tashkent. The Uzbek government had already been informed. I replied that I was sure that they were delighted.

It was the final insult to me from the FCO—they told the Uzbeks I was sacked before they told me. I was furious.

I contacted the BBC, and the next morning appeared on the *Today* program, a morning radio news program that is a national institution. As far as it is possible in five minutes, I gave a summary of the events related in this book. The result was a media storm. Unlike the year before, I had no longer any compunction about speaking to the media directly.

On October 15, 2004, I was formally suspended from duty. David Warren's letter read: "The comments you made in this morning's *Today* programme, and others that have been attributed to you in the media following your withdrawal from Tashkent, were potentially damaging to the FCO's standing and reputation. This may constitute gross misconduct."

I was again subject to disciplinary investigation, including an allegation that it was I who leaked the telegram to the *Financial Times*. That leak had finally enabled the FCO to defeat me, after a year of solid effort. A skeptic about the War on Terror, who opposed torture and the support of dictatorships, was finally done for.

I now had big problems, of which not the least was financial. As ambassador my monthly take-home pay was about £6,800. Over half of that was in tax-free allowances. The actual salary was moderate. Back on my salary, I was down to £3,200 net. I had a large mortgage and about £60,000 of personal loans and credit card debt. On £6,800 net that was quite manageable. On £3,200 it wasn't, especially as I was both giving a large monthly sum to Fiona and paying the mortgage on the Gravesend house. Debt and mortgage repayments and the money to the family exceeded my total income. Very quickly, the money ran out and the credit cards got canceled. Bryan had loaned us his flat, but the medical and other complications meant that we had already been there twice as long as expected. In a very few weeks, we were reduced to buying stale bread cheap from the local bakery and eating it toasted. Plainly the FCO was moving quickly to sack me, so the situation was desperate.

The other problem was Nadira. Three months earlier she had come on holiday. She had not expected to leave Uzbekistan forever, but now had featured extensively in newspaper reports about me, and could not go back without being slammed into jail at best. Nor had she signed up for what was becoming a life of squalid poverty. Furthermore her visitor's visa was running out. She did not want to claim asylum, because in such cases the Uzbek government has a reputation for taking reprisals against the family.

I signed Nadira up for an English-language course in London, paying out almost the last available cash for the large fees. She could now apply for a student visa, but the regulations forbade her from doing so in this country. She could not safely return to Uzbekistan, so the U.K. agreed she could apply in Dublin. We could not afford a hotel, so I got very cheap Ryanair tickets, flying at 6 A.M. and returning late the same night.

It was a cold, raw November day in Dublin. Driving sleet chafed our hands. We arrived at the British embassy and joined the visa queue that stood outside, fully exposed to the elements. We waited for almost three hours, and were the last to be admitted. Those behind us, who had waited for hours also, did not get in and had to return the next day. We hadn't eaten and I felt faint, standing there in the driving sleet. There were no toilet facilities available. Stuck outside an embassy like that, I deeply felt my fall from grace.

Worse was to come inside. The entry clearance officer refused to issue the visa. Everything was in order, and the college was approved by the Home Office, but he refused to accept the receipt for the fees from the college as evidence of acceptance on course, even though it had Nadira's name, the name of the course and "fees paid in full" all printed on it. He said that he needed a letter headed "Confirmation of Acceptance on Course." This was sheer unhelpful bloody-mindedness on the part of this surly, truculent man. I realized again how self-satisfied and unhelpful is the organization in which I had spent my working life. I also realized that people like to kick the fallen.

We trudged back into Dublin soaked through, cold and miserable. I had just enough money to buy a loaf of soda bread from a baker's. It was warm, nutty and delicious. We huddled together for warmth in a doorway, and Nadira looked up at me with a loving and trusting look.

"Don't worry, darling, you'll sort it out," she said.

I wasn't so sure I could.

I reached a real low when we returned to London. I seriously considered suicide. I was not depressed and ill, as I had been the year before. It just seemed to me the best intellectual solution. Soon the banks, credit card companies and building society would foreclose, and Fiona would lose the house. But I had over half a million pounds of life insurance. That seemed the obvious way to meet my responsibilities to Fiona, the children and, not least, Nadira.

Dr. Thornton saved my life. He told me that he believed it was right that suicide used to be a crime. Nowadays people dismissed that as ludicrous, but there was a real point. There was nothing more selfish and destructive than suicide. It left those behind with irredeemable feelings of guilt. Nothing could be more devastating for a child than the suicide of a parent. It was the ultimate desertion. He had seen families and people destroyed by suicide.

I was convinced.

In the end Nadira had to fly to Kiev to get her student visa. Uncle Tommy lent us a few hundred pounds to do this. Journalists were beating a track to my door by now, and I happily accepted their offers of lunch, insisting they invite Nadira too. I don't think they realized we wouldn't eat otherwise. Bryan's posh flat gave out an entirely false impression of affluence.

It was at this stage that Bob Graham, a freelance journalist, investigated the case of the Safarova visa, and determined that I really didn't have any connection with these people. He also pointed out to me the allegations made against James Cameron, first secretary at our embassy in Bucharest. Cameron had been involved in blowing the whistle on a visa scam there. This had led a government minister, Beverley Hughes, to resign after she falsely denied knowledge of the scandal.

As a result of blowing the whistle, Cameron had been accused of granting visas in return for sex. He had also been accused of having a flat in town that he used for entertaining women. As Bob Graham pointed out, these were identical to the allegations the FCO had thrown at me. The *Sunday Times* had reported that: "A senior Foreign Office diplomat and friend of Cameron's said staff at the Embassy in Bucharest are furious about his treatment. 'James is being set up with what appear to be completely unsubstantiated charges,' the diplomat said. 'These charges have been trumped up as a way of getting him back to London.'"[2]

All of which sounded very familiar.

From other journalists at this time, particularly Stephen Grey and Frederic Laurin, I learned the first details of the CIA's extraordinary rendition program. This is now well understood. The CIA was flying terrorist suspects, many of them completely innocent, around the world to destinations in which they could be tortured. They used apparently civilian aircraft, including Premier Executive, the company I had come across in Uzbekistan. Journalists had tracked their flight records, and Uzbekistan was a frequent destination for what have become infamous as "torture flights."

I now believe that, in protesting about intelligence obtained by torture in Uzbekistan, I had hit a still more sensitive point than I had realized. I had stumbled unwittingly across the extraordinary rendition program, and my objections were therefore threatening the legal and political basis of a major CIA strategy in the War on Terror. That would explain the ferocity of the attacks aimed to remove me, and to destroy my reputation as a respected and able diplomat.

I had also been hitting at the foundations of the U.K./U.S. intelligence-sharing agreement. This was put in place by Churchill and Roosevelt, and under it the CIA and MI6 exchange everything, as do the National Security Agency and Government Communications Headquarters. As the U.S. has four times the volume of intelligence that we do, our intelligence services view this agreement as of the highest importance, and are particularly anxious that there should be no derogation from the principle that everything should always be shared. On the other hand, important players in the U.S. intelligence community argue that it is an unequal bargain, and they shouldn't give everything to the U.K.

Therefore, if the CIA gets information from torture, we have to accept it in order to maintain the integrity of the agreement and the principle that everything is always shared. By arguing that we should not accept the Uzbek torture intelligence from the CIA, in the eyes of our security services I was attacking the great principle of this agreement, their most important asset.

* * *

ON THE PERSONAL SIDE, things began to look up. I had finally had enough, and Paul Whiteman was able to negotiate a leaving payment of £320,000 from the FCO, which was great news for Christmas. This was treated as income, so a huge cut went to the taxman, but I could pay the mortgage and debts, offer a divorce settlement to Fiona that went some way toward recognizing her tremendous contribution to my career, and feed Nadira and myself.

On May 13, 2005, Uzbekistan finally hit the front pages across the globe when Karimov's troops opened fire with heavy weapons on a crowd of twenty thousand democracy demonstrators in Andijon, killing over six hundred. Not all died immediately. The wounded were surrounded and left lying all night in Cholpan Square, with no water or medical treatment. The next morning troops moved through the crowd, shooting survivors in the head at point-blank range.

The unprincipled liaison between the West and Uzbekistan had already been under great strain. Karimov's increasingly closed economy was threatened by Western investors, who had more and more been driven out. Finally in November 2004, the major oil and gas development contract, the prize that the U.S. had been seeking since George W. Bush as governor of Texas met Safayev on behalf of Enron in June 1997, was awarded to Gazprom, the Russian state company.

This deal was negotiated between Gulnara Karimova and Alisher Usmanov, the Uzbek-born Russian oligarch, who bought a substantial number of shares in Corus, the British steel company. Usmanov was also a director of Gazprom responsible for their affairs in the former Soviet Union outside Russia.

Gulnara received a large cash payment—$88 million, according to my sources—on completion of the Gazprom deal, with further payments to come as gas was exported. Alisher Usmanov gave Putin a sweetener of 40 percent of the shares in Mapobank, an important Russian business bank with a close relationship to several blue-chip Western firms operating in Russia. The shares were made over to Piotr Jastrzebski, Putin's private secretary, who was a college friend of Alisher Usmanov and shared a flat with him.

This web was closely associated with Karimov's succession strategy. He was desperate for Gulnara to succeed him, and the cash and Russian support were building up her power base. Some sort of Alisher Usmanov/Gulnara Karimova alliance was Karimov's first choice to take over, in six or seven years' time. This was the background to the recent diplomatic revolution, with Karimov abandoning the U.S. and turning back to the embrace of Mother Russia.

It is worth recalling that the Karimov regime has been aggressively anti-Russian, in terms of propaganda, and of practical measures of linguistic discrimination. Approximately two million ethnic Russians have fled Uzbekistan since independence in 1991; about 400,000 are left.

This reorientation toward Russia went along with fierce antienterprise measures designed to stifle any entrepreneurial activity not under direct control of the Karimov family. This explained the physical closures of borders and bazaars, the crackdown on cash transactions and the channeling of all commercial activity through the state banks.

Relationships with the U.S. became increasingly rocky, as Karimov turned more and more to Russia, and to some extent, China. After Andijon, Karimov served the U.S. with six months' notice to quit their prized military base at Karshi Khanabad. The U.S./Uzbek alliance over, it suddenly became open season on Karimov. The U.S. and U.K. governments discovered that—Shock! Horror!—this guy Karimov had been an awful dictator! British ministers were at pains to claim that they had been in agreement with me about this all along. I started getting invitations to seminars in Washington.

WESTERN POLICY IN Central Asia is now in disarray. Afghanistan is touted as the great victory, but the fact is that Afghanistan now produces more opium than ever before. Life is so good for the drug lords that rather than smuggle opium, they are adding value and producing the heroin themselves, able quite openly to move great tankers of required chemicals into the country for industrial-scale production. Because Afghanistan produces more drugs than ever before, the heroin price in London and New York is at an all-time low in real terms. Ruined lives here are the lasting product of our policy in Afghanistan.

The General Dostum/President Karimov axis remains central to this drug traffic. Dostum is defense minister in Afghanistan and still America's leading hard man in the region. With Karimov also a U.S. protégé, the Karimov/Dostum drug link was tolerated for reasons of high policy. Karimov probably calculates that the U.S. still needs Dostum, so he will continue to face no interference in this lucrative enterprise. Meanwhile, ordinary people in Uzbekistan plunge further into despair. This story has no ending.

Nor is their any end to the use of torture as a weapon to further the Bush/Blair agenda and stoke the fires of Islamophobia with false intelligence. In October 2005 the British government, in a historic case before the House of Lords, argued for the right to use intelligence obtained under torture. They argued for a threefold use of this intelligence: to guide security operations, to detain without trial and as evidence in court of law. This was the first time in over two hundred years that a British government has sought to legalize the use of torture evidence. The law lords ruled that they could not use torture evidence in court, but could used intelligence from torture "operationally."

As FOR ME, I had the best possible news on the personal front. I was getting better! The right side of my heart was shrinking, and the pressure in the chambers of my heart was normalizing. My lungs were rewiring themselves. The pressure that my heart had been under as it struggled to force air through my clogged lungs had opened a hole there. But this was closed up for me by the Royal Brompton Hospital.

So here I am, reborn, reprieved and ready for battle. I will never forget those who still suffer needlessly in Uzbekistan, in Iraq and in so many other places on this spinning globe. I am not an especially good man, but I tried to stay true to basic values of human decency.

I am now a much wiser man than the brash, ambitious and hedonistic young ambassador who landed with his family in Tashkent. And the most important thing I have learned is this:

If you achieve a voice that will be heard, you should use it to speak up for the voiceless and oppressed. If you possess any power or authority, you must strive to use it to help and empower the powerless.

Sadly, public life in the United States and the United Kingdom has come to be dominated by those driven by arrogance and by corporate greed and personal acquisitiveness. We must strive to return some integrity to public life.

As you have seen, I am certainly fallible. I have never pretended otherwise. Yet, when I learned of men, women and children being tortured, I had no doubt that the only and overriding duty of a representative of Western values was to stop it.

Yet we see the Bush administration, which flaunts piety and family values, encouraging and subsidizing this torture. Vice President Cheney states that torture of "terrorist suspects" is a "no-brainer." The United States has so far retreated from civilized standards that senior politicians can torture and joke about it. The Military Commissions Act 2006 abolishes habeas corpus, legalizes torture and retrospectively exempts from prosecution those CIA and U.S. military who were delivering people up to torture in Uzbekistan and elsewhere.

It is a slippery slope toward brutal authoritarianism. Cheney and Bush are sliding down it yelling, "Wheeee! What a ride!" The rest of us had better start scrabbling back up fast.

NOTES

Chapter 1: Awakening
1. As he was the judge, and there was no jury, I suppose he had a point.
2. Most analysts believe these bombs were planted either by the Karimov regime, or by feuding factions within the regime.

Chapter 2: Instructions
1. A company called Ananov makes them in the original Fabergé Imperial workshops in St. Petersburg, with much of the original equipment.

Chapter 3: London to Tashkent
1. A British ambassador gets to travel first-class the first time he arrives at his new post, and the last time he leaves it. The reason for this is that there may be formal state greetings and farewells on these occasions. On other business trips he travels business class, and economy class on most leave journeys. Uzbek Air flies four times a week to London; two of these flights use a 747, which has first class. I had chosen my departure date specifically to make sure that we could fly first-class. It was not something I expected to do often with my family, so I was determined that we should take advantage of it.
2. This same outline holds broadly for all of Central Asia.
3. I had glanced at the Uzbek customs declaration, and I was rather glad that I did not have to fill it in—one advantage of diplomatic privilege. It asked you to itemize all hard currency but also all jewelry, watches and a lot of other stuff including "shoes over two pairs." More alarming, it asked you to list and present for inspection any videos, books, magazines, newspapers, documents or other printed material.
4. Prestige is a strange thing—there is, I suppose, no reason why an ambassador shouldn't go around town in a Mini. But your job is influence, and impressing on your hosts the power and the confidence of the country you represent is part of that. I find that props of pomp and circumstance help. That may be pathetic of me, but there you are. It is a difficult argument morally—I always despise to see ambassadors from dirt-poor countries swanning around in huge Mercedes and living a champagne lifestyle, while the people paying for this live in desperate poverty.

5. If this sounds palatial, that is because it was indeed a palace—and not just any old palace. It was the home of the Kerensky family, birthplace of Alexander Fyodorovich Kerensky, who led Russia from February to October 1917, in that brief dawn of hope when Russia might have entered mainstream European history and economic development. It was he who proclaimed Russia a republic in September 1917. I used to hold conversations with Uzbek dissidents in my office and wonder what other whispered words those bricks had heard. The Kerenskys were a Russian colonial family; lawyers, railway engineers and administrators. Their little palace was pretty, but obviously on nothing near the scale of the mighty mansions of St. Petersburg, so Kerensky's coming to power in St. Petersburg certainly showed that Russia was in the grip of truly revolutionary change before the Bolsheviks took a hand.

    According to embassy tradition, somewhere inside the building Kerensky's brother Nikolai was shot by the Bolsheviks in 1922. I have since been contacted by a descendant of Kerensky's who said he didn't have a brother, but it may have been a cousin.

6. In December 2005 the Uzbek government announced it was going to remove the barriers protecting the embassy "for beautification," as a part of the diplomatic row following the Andijon massacre.

7. I am giving away no secrets, as the embassy has since been internally rebuilt and reconfigured.

8. Stalin had deported trainloads of Koreans from the Russian border of Manchuria in the 1920s, dumping them in the Kara-Kum desert and leaving them to die. Somehow they struggled to oases at Nukus and Bokhara, and ultimately their community grew and added a new element to the region's already spectacular ethnic diversity.

9. The square is dominated by a huge golden globe. It encapsulates the vainglory of the regime because only Uzbekistan is marked on it. Uzbekistan starts around Dublin and ends around Beijing. Only a government with a serious humor deficit could erect such a monument. At night the globe and its massive Uzbekistan are picked out in numerous sparkling lights, and it rotates. It is incredibly tacky.

Chapter 4: Diplomacy

1. This is a striking illustration of just how much encouragement New Labour's abandonment of devotion to civil rights in the U.K. gives to dictators all around the globe.

2. In fact, far from combating the narcotics trade, Karimov and his friends are up to their necks in it. The destruction of the Taliban largely ended any threat from the IMU; only Karimov's persecution of Muslims now fuels the very small Islamic militant threat. There is no Islamic extremism in the Tajik government, and remaining Russian forces in the region are an important force for stability. The Uzbek economy produces very little because of mad centrist economic policies, and bans on Chinese goods were aimed to protect not domestic production, but import monopolies by the Karimov family and senior regime cronies.

Karimov's claim to be a reliable ally of the West was totally bogus; it was a short-term maneuver.

3. I still use it as a dressing gown.

4. A few months later his sister was to visit; she was the most tremendous person-age, and invitations started arriving to dinners with Countess X—I put X because she had at least eight titles and surnames, which I can't possibly remember. Like her brother she was in her early sixties, but she partied like a student, wore designer clothes and tons of jewelry and seemed to have fitted in Tashkent between endless parties with the glitterati at fashionable resorts. Her brother was shy and retiring by comparison, and never used a title or more than two surnames. I grew to like him immensely.

5. There was no formal monopoly, but all imports needed customs approval and no one else would get it.

6. The FCO described this to me as essential to the security of Western hydrocarbon supplies. I viewed it as essential to keeping oil prices down and ensuring the world's very limited hydrocarbon supplies were guzzled as soon as possible, largely by the U.S., with disastrous results in terms of carbon dioxide emissions and global warming. So you will gather I was a bit skeptical about all of this.

7. The Israeli ambassador told me, on the day we both presented our credentials, that Karimov had been a good personal friend of Ariel Sharon for over twenty years.

8. It lay a year in the future, but Sharipov, as a result of the critical articles John quoted, was framed and convicted on charges of underage sex, while his defense lawyer, Surat Ikramov, was kidnapped outside the courtroom, bound and gagged. He was then driven into the countryside, murderously beaten and left for dead in a ditch, but survived. By that time, the members of the security forces convicted of murdering the detainee in Ferghana had been released.

Chapter 5: The Ferghana Valley

1. By contrast, we maintain massive embassies in all Western European capitals, staffed by many senior diplomats. Yet, nowadays, if we want to discuss fish with Denmark or transport with France, it is no longer done by getting the embassy fish man to speak to the Danish Foreign Ministry fish man. Our London ministry of fish people will speak directly to the Copenhagen ministry of fish people, whom they probably meet twice a month anyway in Brussels. Two ministers from EU countries who want to talk bilaterally on any subject will do it directly, not through their ambassador. Yet there has been no significant reduction in the staffing of our EU bilateral embassies. Quite the opposite.

At the same time we are told that Africa is a priority, and the aid budget and political effort being spent on the continent is increasing. Has this been accompanied by an increase in senior diplomatic jobs based in Africa? No, again quite the opposite. Senior posts have been cut in Africa over a decade, and transferred to Western Europe and the United States.

The reason is that a self-serving FCO oligarchy quite likes to live in Copenhagen or Berlin, but the vast majority of top mandarins would not be seen dead in Kampala, or indeed Tashkent. Only one of the FCO's current fifteen directors has served in Africa, and that was Pretoria. They have eighty-seven Western Europe or U.S.-based tours between them.

To justify this predilection for serving in posts with access to Cannes or Aspen, there have been a number of "resource allocation" exercises, on one of which I was working at the time. This exercise had on a page a matrix of facets of an embassy's work—political, commercial, narcotics, immigration, terrorism, defense and others. Each embassy was given a score out of five for how important it was on each particular subject. The scores were determined centrally by the board. And, presto! It was discovered that our allocation of resources around the world was pretty well perfect.

To achieve this result required some farcical scoring. On narcotics, for instance, Tashkent scored two out of five and Copenhagen five out of five. Now, I am not saying customs cooperation with Denmark is not useful, but Uzbekistan is a massive transit route for heroin from neighboring Afghanistan. Berlin scored as highly as Lagos on immigration. In short it was decided that all the resources, and the vast majority of top jobs, had to be in really nice places to live. So that was a useful exercise.

2. The cutting of the tunnels gives a good example of the way that Karimov built his personality cult through the highly controlled media. The story was run on state media that a German company had offered to build the tunnels for no payment, provided they could keep the excavated spoils. Karimov had refused the offer, and declared that the Uzbeks would build the tunnels themselves. When the tunnels were dug, they excavated a huge quantity of gold and precious stones, which were used to benefit the nation.

This example of Karimov's wisdom and foresight is, of course, complete fabrication from start to finish. It says something not only about the Uzbek media, but about the level of education of the general population, that this story is still widely believed.

3. In Uzbekistan bread itself is treated as holy and must be respected. It certainly must never be thrown or dropped, and you must not swear or argue in the presence of bread.

4. Carpet-making had died out in Uzbekistan in the Soviet period. The Uzbeks had a carpet tradition, although not as strong as sometimes presumed. Bokhara carpets are the most famous Oriental rugs, but Bokhara was the market where they were sold. Most Bokhara carpets were Afghan or Turkmen in origin.

5. I was to visit several other breweries and wineries in Uzbekistan, and always found the same thing: brewing and wine-making are regarded solely as a science, not an art.

6. What he had told me very much squared with the briefing Chris Hirst had given me. Chris had told of a recent incident where the police had taken a dissident from bed in his underpants. When searched at the police station, he was discovered to have twelve bullets and a wodge of Hizb-ut-Tehrir

leaflets on his person—presumably the police claimed he had them down his undies.

Chapter 6: "A True British Gentleman"

1. There is a coda. About a year later I told this story to Nadira, just as I told you now. She burst out laughing, and asked if I didn't know that the men of Namangan were notoriously gay. I thought that she was having me on, but I checked with others and there is indeed a standing joke in Uzbekistan that the men of Namangan are gay. Whether this has some basis, or whether this is a misunderstanding of local culture, I don't know.

2. "Excuse me, Ambassador," asked the interpreter, "is the *sledge* important, or can I just interpret it as *hammer*?"

   "Try *fucking big* hammer," I suggested.

3. And indeed did so with the imported wool until June 2003. The textiles produced were exported. This was organized by the general manager in Tashkent. The factory never saw the revenue from these exports.

4. A year later the British government canceled this project, on the decision of ministers, on the grounds there was no conflict in the Ferghana Valley to resolve, so it was an inappropriate use of the Conflict Resolution Fund. Canceling this Andijon project further exacerbated economic distress and social tension, and contributed to the events that led up to the Andijon massacre in May 2005.

Chapter 7: Cry Freedom!

1. To Westerners, Tartars are an almost legendary people. When I served in Poland I was very interested in the raids of the great Tartar hordes. In Krakow every day a bugler still sounds the alarm from the City Church, cutting it off abruptly to mark the moment an arrow from a Tartar composite horn bow sliced into his predecessor's throat.

   I had always imagined the Tartars to be an Oriental people, rather Mongol in appearance, but in fact they are not at all. Their eyes have only the slightest trace of slant, many are blond, and to a stranger they are not easy to distinguish from Russians.

2. *Financial Times,* January 14, 2003.

3. *The Spectator,* May 26, 2005.

Chapter 8: The Embassy

1. It has gotten worse since; as of 2005 every educational institution must teach "National Education" for one day a week. This consists of Karimov's works mixed with a very tendentious version of history, and Uzbek folksinging.

2. One striking example was a brick factory in Tashkent, built by a British company with an ECGD loan. The project depended on a precontract committing the Uzbek government to purchase the bricks for many years. Once construction was complete, the Uzbek government immediately reneged on this contract. In consequence the company went bust. The Uzbek government then

confiscated the land and buildings, while the EBRD spinelessly sold the plant
and equipment—brand-new—to the Uzbek government at about a third of
cost.

Chapter 9: Merry Christmas, War Is Coming

1. At this point the pass is only some fifteen yards wide, so it is certainly possible. The historic fact does not seem to be disputed. But it makes little sense. The hills to either side are easily passable, even for an army. The main Tashkent/Samarkand road itself no longer runs through Jizzak or the gates, but some few miles south-west. This does not involve any major feat of engineering and, even if no road were there, there would have been nothing to stop an army taking that route. In fact, except in deep winter, you can walk pretty easily over the hills just a few hundred yards on either side of the famous iron gates. It would only make sense if there were gates in some kind of series of fortifications running along the hill-tops, but I have never seen this suggested. I was later able to spend a day search-ing, and I could find no physical or topographical evidence of such a system.
2. Even though Karimov is himself ethnically Tajik.

Chapter 10: Iron in the Soul

1. Uzbekistan has plenty of gas, but prefers to sell it to Russia, in contracts that chiefly benefit the president's daughter, rather than use it for the benefit of its own people.
2. Société Générale had agreed on a loan, but had then made stipulations about political risk insurance that Oxus had found impossible to fulfill.
3. The very existence of this town is a miracle of Soviet engineering. There was no oasis here—it was in the middle of hundreds of miles of featureless desert. It is one of the most remarkable places I have been, with a modern town starting into full swing at the clearly defined town boundary, and absolutely nothing beyond. The water comes in great pipes hundreds of miles across the desert.
4. It is also worth asking why the EBRD, which is supposed to promote private enterprise in former communist Europe, was lending money to Newmont, the world's largest mining company. Newmont has $165 million in loose change. Their executives probably spend that in restaurant tips. EBRD is supposed to bring "additionality" and fund stuff that wouldn't happen otherwise, not sub-massive corporations entering extremely low-cost, high-return operations.
5. Sir Richard Dearlove, head of MI6.
6. Under this agreement, made between Churchill and Roosevelt, the U.K. and U.S. share all of their secret intelligence with each other. The U.S. has much more to give, so the U.K. authorities are keen never to undermine the basic agreement that absolutely everything is shared. Many in MI6 were not happy with CIA methods in the War on Terror, but were of the view that we could not refuse to accept certain CIA material gotten through torture, or the whole agree-ment could collapse.
7. *The Point of Departure,* Simon & Schuster, 2003.

Chapter 11: Murder in Samarkand

1. She was also most put out that Simon Butt had left no note of thanks and no tip for the domestic staff, both of which are customary within the diplomatic service when staying with a colleague.

Chapter 12: *Pinafore,* Battlefield and Baseball Bat

1. I also had the chance to chat at dinner with old Mrs. Kalashnikova, another Tashkent resident. She told me her husband had been chief engineer in a Singer sewing machine factory, and it was the sewing machine action that gave him the inspiration for his firing mechanism.

2. I was able to initiate a tour that saw Ilios play his *dutar* in 2005 in venues including the Usher Hall in Edinburgh and the Purcell Room on the South Bank in London. The latter was completely sold out, and I sat in the audience swelling with pride at the ovation he received, and the fact I had brought about a degree of musical understanding in both directions.

3. The band has been going for almost thirty years. Like a football team, the line-up changes, but with the constants of Alan Reid's writing and the members' individual virtuosity, the style remains the same. Everyone should have at least one Battlefield Band album in their music collection—I recommend *Threads,* but there are plenty to choose from, and you can buy online.

Chapter 13: Love in a Hot Climate

1. Kristina is now the U.S. ambassador's social secretary.

2. Sadly, it didn't.

3. I suppose the blame must rest with the Soviets, who destroyed existing societal obligations, relationships and mechanisms, and replaced them with the *kolkhoz.*

4. Richard Conroy had told me that a UNDP study had established that the rural poor had sold off their household possessions to eat, and suffered a radical decline in living standards. I wondered who on earth a lady like this could find with money to buy.

5. I don't suppose it did much good, but when you encounter totalitarianism you have to keep chipping away at it. Lech Walesa once told me that it is the first crack in the marble that counts.

6. As part of its border closure program the Uzbek government was clearing the population of a high mountain village on the border with Tajikistan. This was allegedly for the villagers' own safety. They had been loaded into a bus at gunpoint. The bus had then allegedly fallen off the winding mountain road, killing everyone on board. Many believe the villagers, who were ethnic Tajiks, had in fact been shot. I don't think any independent observer ever got to the site, which was closed off by the military, so I simply don't know what happened.

7. Jurabekov was presidential counselor on agriculture, and the godfather of Uzbek cotton trading. He was one of the most feared men in the country. Our host was letting me know he had Jurabekov's support.

Chapter 14: Hammer to Fall

1. The Foreign and Commonwealth Office was to make much of this incident for propaganda against me.
2. Afghanistan is, of course, the great success of the War on Terror. Dostum is the minister of defense of the democratic Afghan government, and therefore a good guy. Karimov and Dostum were the linchpins of U.S. policy in Central Asia, so nothing is done about their heroin trafficking. As a result of the great allied success, Afghanistan now produces more opium and heroin than ever before. Now, that's not something much stressed in the Murdoch media.
3. I should make perfectly plain that, as far as I know, Andrew Mackinlay has never been in a strip club in Warsaw, or anywhere else, for that matter. Andrew was, of course, another of those antiwar MPs that Simon held in such contempt.
4. *The Spectator,* May 21, 2005.

Chapter 15: One Step Ahead of the Shoeshine

1. Locally engaged—in this case, the Uzbek staff.

Chapter 16: What Dreams May Come

1. They have since merged.
2. Played by Emma Thompson in the film *In the Name of the Father.*

Chapter 17: Tashkent Again

1. Donald Rumsfeld, press conference, Intercontinental Hotel, Tashkent, February 24, 2004.
2. George Soros had made billions of dollars out of currency speculation in the volatile markets of the late eighties, and poured a significant portion of this into promoting democracy and economic development in the former communist bloc from which he came.
3. For those organizations that did register, including Human Rights Watch, new limitations were placed on their activities, including that all meetings had to be reported in advance to the Ministry of the Interior and open to the Uzbek intelligence services, and all financial transactions had to go through Uzbek state banks.
4. It was also based on my having read *Extreme Continental,* Giles Whittell's excellent book on Central Asia.
5. Their aid agency was particularly appalling in this regard, and of all the Western ministers who visited Tashkent, the most frequent and the most obsequious to Karimov was Joschka Fischer, their trendy Green foreign minister.

    In November 2005, when the EU finally brought in sanctions against the Karimov regime, Germany immediately broke them by allowing Interior Minister Almatov into Germany. The next month Uzbekistan instituted an overflight ban on all NATO members—except Germany.
6. I had some knowledge of explosives from training courses. God knows why they teach us this stuff, but I had enjoyed several days mucking about with things that go bang at an establishment known simply as "the fort" in Gosport.

7. Salikh, a poet, had managed to get 15 percent of the vote against Karimov despite no media coverage other than vitriolic attacks on him, and in the face of every form of voter intimidation, electoral fraud and vote-rigging imaginable. Fortunately, he was safely in Germany by the time he was sentenced to death.
8. In 2003, Powell had signed off on such a certification, which must have been the most duplicitous document issued by the U.S. government since their treaties with the Native Americans.
9. *The Times,* April 1, 2004.
10. Eyewitnesses interviewed by the BBC World Service.

Chapter 18: Once More unto the Breach
1. I bequeathed them my proper table-tennis table when I left.
2. I was right in this, and in the event no opposition parties were allowed to register and take part.
3. In May 2005, Ismail fled the country following the Andijon massacre, and now lives in exile in the Ukraine.

Chapter 19: The Last Battle
1. *The Guardian,* July 15, 2004.
2. *Sunday Times,* June 13, 2004.

SELECT BIBLIOGRAPHY

Allworth, Edward. *The Modern Uzbeks.* Stanford: Hoover Press, 1990.

Aslan, Reza. *No God but God: The Origins, Evolution and Future of Islam.* London: William Heinemann, 2005.

Bailey, F. M. *Mission to Tashkent.* London: Jonathan Cape, 1946.

Burnaby, Fred. *A Ride to Khiva.* London: Century, 1983.

Burnes, Alexander. *Travels into Bokhara 1831–3: A Journey from India to Cabool, Tartary and Persia and a Voyage on the Indus.* New Delhi: Asian Educational Services, 1992.

Byron, Robert. *The Road to Oxiana.* London: Penguin Books, 1992.

Chomsky, Noam. *Failed States: The Abuse of Power and the Assault on Democracy.* New York: Holt Paperbacks, 2007.

———. *9/11.* New York: Seven Stories Press, 2001.

Dalrymple, William. *In Xanadu.* London: Flamingo, 1990.

Dickie, John. *Inside the Foreign Office.* London: Chapmans, 1992.

Forbes, Rosita. *Forbidden Road: Kabul to Samarkand.* The Long Riders' Guild Press, 2001.

Frye, Richard. *Bukhara: The Medieval Achievement.* Costa Mesa, CA: Mazda Publishers, 1996.

Gill, Alison, Ed. *Uzbekistan: Creating Enemies of the State.* New York: Human Rights Watch, 2004.

Grey, C. *European Adventurers of Northern India: 1785 to 1849.* New Delhi: Asian Educational Services, 1993.

Grey, Stephen. *Ghost Plane: The Inside Story of the CIA's Secret Rendition Programme.* London: Hurst & Co., 2006.

Hobson, J. A. *Imperialism: A Study.* London: James Nisbet, 1902.

Hopkirk, Kathleen. *Central Asia: A Traveller's Companion.* London: John Murray, 1993.

Hopkirk, Peter. *The Great Game: On Secret Service in High Asia.* Oxford University Press, 2001.

———. *On Secret Service East of Constantinople.* London: John Murray, 1994.

———. *Setting the East Ablaze: On Secret Service in Bolshevik Asia.* Oxford University Press, 1986.

———. *Foreign Devils on the Silk Road: The Search for the Lost Treasures of Central Asia.* Oxford University Press, 1984.

Johnson, Chalmers. *Nemesis: The Last Days of the American Republic.* New York: Metropolitan Books, 2007.

Jones, Ann. *Kabul in Winter.* New York: Metropolitan Books, 2006.

Khalid, Adeeb. *Islam after Communism: Religion and Politics in Central Asia.* Berkeley: University of California Press, 2007.

Kleveman, Lutz. *The New Great Game: Blood and Oil in Central Asia.* London: Atlantic Books, 2003.

Knight, E. F. *Where Three Empires Meet: A Narrative of Recent Travel in Kashmir, Western Tibet, Gilgit, and the Adjoining Countries.* New Delhi: Asian Educational Services, 1993.

Lubin, Nancy. *Calming the Ferghana Valley.* New York: Century Foundation Press, 1999.

Lunt, James. *Bokhara Burnes.* London: Faber and Faber, 1969.

McCoy, Alfred. *A Question of Torture.* New York: Metropolitan Books, 2006.

MacDonald Fraser, George. *Flashman in the Great Game.* London: William Collins, 1980.

Maclean, Fitzroy. *Eastern Approaches.* London: Penguin Books, 1991.

Macleod, Calum, and Bradley Mayhew. *Uzbekistan: The Golden Road to Samarkand.* Chicago: Passport Books, 1997.

Mardrus, J. C., and Powys Mathers, trans. *The Thousand Nights and One Night.* London: Routledge, 1986.

Markham, Clements, trans. *Narrative of the Embassy of Ruy Gonzalez de Clavijo to the Court of Timour at Samarcand A.D. 1403–6.* New Delhi: Asian Educational Services, 2001.

Marozzi, Justin. *Tamerlane: Sword of Islam, Conqueror of the World.* London: Harper Collins, 2004.

Marvin, Charles. *Reconnoitring Central Asia: Pioneering Adventures in the Region Lying Between Russia and India.* New Delhi: Asian Educational Services, 1996.

Mayer, Karl, and Shareen Brysac. *Tournament of Shadows.* London: Counterpoint Press, 1999.

Mayhew, Bradley, Richard Plunkett and Simon Richmond. *Central Asia.* Hawthorn, Australia: Lonely Planet, 2000.

Melvin, Neil. *Uzbekistan: Transition to Authoritarianism on the Silk Road.* Amsterdam: Harwood Academic Publishers, 2000.

Moorcroft, William, and George Trebeck. *Travels in the Himalayan Provinces of Hindustan and the Punjab, Ladakh and Kashmir; in Peshawar, Kabul, Kunduz and Bokhara from 1819 to 1825.* New Delhi: Asian Educational Services, 1989.

Newlands, George. *Christ and Human Rights.* London: Ashgate Publishing, 2006.

Patten, Chris. *Cousins and Strangers: America, Britain and Europe in a New Century.* New York: Owl Books, 2006.

Palmer, Mark. *Breaking the Real Axis of Evil.* Lanham, MD: Rowman and Littlefield, 2005.

Phillips, Peter. *Censored 2006: The Top 25 Censored Stories.* New York: Seven Stories Press, 2005.

Rand, Robert. *Tamerlane's Children: Dispatches from Contemporary Uzbekistan.* New York: Oneworld, 2006.

Rashid, Ahmed. *Jihad: The Rise of Militant Islam in Central Asia.* New Haven: Yale University Press, 2002.

———. *Taliban: Militant Islam, Oil and Fundamentalism in Central Asia.* London: I. B. Tauris, 2000.

Roy, Olivier. *The New Central Asia: The Creation of Nations.* London: I. B. Tauris, 2000.

Rumer, Boris, ed. *Central Asia: A Gathering Storm?* Armonk, NY: M. E. Sharpe, 2002.

Satter, David. *Darkness at Dawn.* New Haven: Yale University Press, 2003.

Short, Clare. *An Honourable Deception?* London: Simon & Schuster, 2005.

Soans, Robin. *Talking to Terrorists.* London: Oberon Books, 2005.

Soucek, Svat. *A History of Inner Asia.* Cambridge University Press, 2001.

Stern, Aurel. *On Alexander's Track to the Indus.* New Delhi: Asian Educational Services, 1996.

Taylor, Bayard. *Central Asia: Travels in Cashmere, Little Thibet and Central Asia.* New Delhi: Asian Educational Services, 1997.

Thackston, Wheeler, trans. *The Baburnama: Memoirs of Babur, Prince and Emperor.* New York: The Modern Library, 2002.

Thomas, Gordon. *Gideon's Spies: The Secret History of the Mossad.* New York: St. Martin's Griffin, Picador, 2007.

Thubron, Colin. *The Lost Heart of Asia.* London: Penguin Books, 2004.

Whittell, Giles. *Extreme Continental.* London: Indigo, 1996.

Wynn, Antony. *Persia in the Great Game: Sir Percy Sykes, Explorer, Consul, Soldier, Spy.* London: John Murray, 2004.

Younghusband, Francis. *The Heart of a Continent.* New Delhi: Asian Educational Services, 1993.

INDEX

ABOUT THE AUTHOR

Craig Murray was British ambassador at the embassy in Tashkent, Uzbekistan, from 2002 to 2005, having previously served as a diplomat in Africa and Eastern Europe. He is rector of the University of Dundee and an honorary research fellow in the University of Lancaster School of Law. He lives in London with his partner, Nadira.